THE OXFORD HISTORY OF THE BRITISH EMPIRE
COMPANION SERIES

THE OXFORD HISTORY OF THE BRITISH EMPIRE COMPANION SERIES

Volume I. *The Origins of Empire*
EDITED BY Nicholas Canny

Volume II. *The Eighteenth Century*
EDITED BY P. J. Marshall

Volume III. *The Nineteenth Century*
EDITED BY Andrew Porter

Volume IV. *The Twentieth Century*
EDITED BY Judith M. Brown and Wm. Roger Louis

Volume V. *Historiography*
EDITED BY Robin W. Winks

THE OXFORD HISTORY OF THE BRITISH EMPIRE COMPANION SERIES

Britain's Experience of Empire in the Twentieth Century
Andrew Thompson

Scotland and the British Empire
John M. MacKenzie and T. M. Devine

Black Experience and the Empire
Philip D. Morgan and Sean Hawkins

Gender and Empire
Philippa Levine

Ireland and the British Empire
Kevin Kenny

Missions and Empire
Norman Etherington

Environment and Empire
William Beinart and Lotte Hughes

Australia's Empire
Deryck Schreuder and Stuart Ward

Settlers and Expatriates: Britons over the Seas
Robert Bickers

Migration and Empire
Marjory Harper and Stephen Constantine

THE OXFORD HISTORY OF THE BRITISH EMPIRE

COMPANION SERIES

Wm. Roger Louis, CBE, D. Litt., FBA

*Kerr Professor of English History and Culture, University of Texas, Austin
and Honorary Fellow of St Antony's College, Oxford*

EDITOR-IN-CHIEF

India and the British Empire

EDITED BY

Douglas M. Peers and Nandini Gooptu

OXFORD
UNIVERSITY PRESS

Great Clarendon Street, Oxford, OX2 6DP,
United Kingdom

Oxford University Press is a department of the University of Oxford.
It furthers the University's objective of excellence in research, scholarship,
and education by publishing worldwide. Oxford is a registered trade mark of
Oxford University Press in the UK and in certain other countries

© Oxford University Press 2012

The moral rights of the authors have been asserted

First Edition published in 2012

Impression: 1

All rights reserved. No part of this publication may be reproduced, stored in
a retrieval system, or transmitted, in any form or by any means, without the
prior permission in writing of Oxford University Press, or as expressly permitted
by law, by licence or under terms agreed with the appropriate reprographics
rights organization. Enquiries concerning reproduction outside the scope of the
above should be sent to the Rights Department, Oxford University Press, at the
address above

You must not circulate this work in any other form
and you must impose this same condition on any acquirer

British Library Cataloguing in Publication Data

Data available

Library of Congress Cataloging in Publication Data

Data available

ISBN 978–0–19–925988–5

Printed in Great Britain by
MPG Books Group, Bodmin and King's Lynn

FOREWORD

The purpose of the five volumes of the Oxford History of the British Empire was to provide a comprehensive survey of the Empire from its beginning to end, to explore the meaning of British imperialism for the ruled as well as the rulers, and to study the significance of the British Empire as a theme in world history. The volumes in the Companion Series carry forward this purpose. They pursue themes that could not be covered adequately in the main series while incorporating recent research and providing fresh interpretations of significant topics.

Wm. Roger Louis

CONTENTS

List of Illustrations ix
Contributors xi

1. Introduction 1
   DOUGLAS M. PEERS AND NANDINI GOOPTU

2. State, Power, and Colonialism 16
   DOUGLAS M. PEERS

3. The Indian Economy and the British Empire 44
   DAVID WASHBROOK

4. Knowledge Formation in Colonial India 75
   NORBERT PEABODY

5. Colonialism and Social Identities in Flux: Class, Caste, and Religious Community 100
   ROSALIND O'HANLON

6. Nationalisms in India 135
   SUMIT SARKAR

7. Law, Authority, and Colonial Rule 168
   SANDRA DEN OTTER

8. Networks of Knowledge: Science and Medicine in Early Colonial India, c.1750–1820 191
   MARK HARRISON

9. Environment and Ecology Under British Rule 212
   MAHESH RANGARAJAN

10. The Material and Visual Culture of British India 231
    CHRISTOPHER PINNEY

11. Literary Modernity in South Asia 262
    JAVED MAJEED

12. Gendering of Public and Private Selves in Colonial Times Tanika Sarkar	284
13. The *Desi* Diaspora: Politics, Protest, and Nationalism Vijay Prashad	313
14. The Political Legacy of Colonialism in South Asia Nandini Gooptu	334
Index	357

LIST OF ILLUSTRATIONS

Map: India between the Wars (from Judith M. Brown and Wm. Roger Louis (eds.), *The Oxford History of the British Empire*, Volume IV. *The Twentieth Century*, p. 431) — xiv

1. Mihr Chand, Shuja ud-Daula, Nawab of Oudh. Goauche *c*.1772, after an oil painting by Tilly Kettle. Courtesy Victorian and Albert Museum. — 238
2. Nawab Walajah with Stringer Lawrence. Engraving from H. D. Love, *Descriptive List of Pictures in Government House and the Banqueting Hall, Madras*. Madras: Government Press, 1903. — 240
3. Government House, Calcutta, *c*.1870. Photographer unknown. Private Collection. — 244
4. Mayo College, Ajmer. Photograph by Lala Deen Dayal, *c*.1880s. — 245
5. *The Jackal Raja's Court*. Kalighat painting, *c*.1870. Courtesy Victoria and Albert Museum. 08144(b). — 249
6. *Kirat & Bhilli*, Ravi Varma. The god Shiva is disguised as a tribal hunter. Ravi Varma's images were first mass-produced as chromolithographs and subsequently circulated as postcards. Postcard *c*.1905. Private Collection. — 252
7. Reverse of a cabinet card photographic portrait created by S. Hormusji. Numerous photographic studios clustered around Kalbadevi Rd in Bombay. Many, like Hormusji, were Parsee-run and Parsees were enthusiastic commissioners of photography, *c*.1880s. Private Collection. — 255
8. *Evolution of Gandhi*, a chromolithograph by the artist 'Dinanath', tracing Gandhi's performance of an aesthetic of austerity. — 260

CONTRIBUTORS

SANDRA DEN OTTER teaches British, colonial, and postcolonial history at Queen's University, Canada. Her primary research interests are in nineteenth-century British and imperial political and legal thought and cultures. With a doctorate from Oxford, she has been a research fellow at the Center for European Studies, Harvard University and Clare Hall, University of Cambridge. She has written on the British idealists, the history of the social sciences, and on empire and law in colonial India.

NANDINI GOOPTU is Fellow of St Antony's College, Oxford, and she teaches history and politics at Oxford University. Educated in Calcutta and at Cambridge, she is the author of *The Politics of the Urban Poor in Early-Twentieth Century India* (Cambridge, 2001). She has published articles on a variety of subjects, including caste, religion, and spiritualism; urban development and politics; poverty, labour, and work. Her current research is concerned with social and political transformation in contemporary India.

MARK HARRISON is Professor of the History of Medicine and Director of the Wellcome Unit for the History of Medicine at the University of Oxford. He has written about many aspects of the history of science, medicine, and empire, particularly in relation to British India. His books include *Public Health in British India* (Cambridge, 1994); *Climates and Constitutions* (Delhi, 1999); and *British Medicine in an Age of Commerce and Empire* (Oxford, 2010).

JAVED MAJEED was Professor of Postcolonial Studies at Queen Mary, University of London from 1999 to 2011. He is currently Professor of English and Comparative Literature at King's College, London. His book publications include *Ungoverned Imaginings: James Mill's The History of British India and Orientalism* (1992); *Autobiography, Travel and Postnational Identity* (2007); and *Muhammad Iqbal: Islam, Aesthetics and Postcolonialism* (2009). He has also co-edited with Christopher Shackle *Hali's Musaddas: The Flow and Ebb of Islam* (1997) and has written a number of articles on the intellectual and cultural history of colonial India.

ROSALIND O'HANLON is Professor of Indian History and Culture in the Faculty of Oriental Studies, University of Oxford. Her publications include *A Comparison between Women and Men: Tarabai Shinde and the Critique of Gender Relations in Colonial India* (1994) and *Religious Cultures in Early Modern India* (2011), edited with David Washbrook. She is currently researching the history of Brahman communities in western India between the sixteenth and nineteenth centuries.

NORBERT PEABODY is a Senior Research Fellow of Wolfson College, Cambridge. He has also taught at the London School of Economics and Harvard University. His first book *Hindu Kingship and Polity in Precolonial India* won the 2003 Gladstone History Book Prize from the Royal Historical Society. He is currently writing another book exploring the links between traditional Indian wrestling (*kushti*), nationalism, and communal violence in India.

DOUGLAS M. PEERS is Professor of History and Dean of Arts at the University of Waterloo, having previously taught at York University and the University of Calgary. He is the author of *Between Mars and Mammon: Colonial Armies and the Garrison State in Early-Nineteenth Century India* (1995), and *India under Colonial Rule, 1700–1885* (2006). Edited works include: *Warfare and Empire* (1997) and *Negotiating India in the Nineteenth Century Media* (2000).

CHRISTOPHER PINNEY is Professor of Anthropology and Visual Culture at University College London. He has been conducting anthropological fieldwork in central India intermittently since 1982. Books include *The Coming of Photography in India* (British Library, 2008) and *Photography and Anthropology* (Reaktion, 2011). Recent articles include a study of Gandhi's intellectual debt to B. G. Tilak in *Public Culture* (2011). A book on Hindu images of punishment in hell (*Lessons from Hell*) is due from Tara Books (Chennai) in 2012.

VIJAY PRASHAD is the George and Martha Kellner Chair of South Asian History and Professor of International Studies at Trinity College in Hartford, Connecticut. His most recent book is *Uncle Swami: South Asian Americans After 9/11* (2012). His book, *The Darker Nations: A People's History of the Third World* (2007), was chosen as the Best Non-fiction book by the Asian American Writers' Workshop in 2008 and it won the Muzaffar Ahmed Book Award in 2009.

MAHESH RANGARAJAN is Professor of Modern Indian History at the University of Delhi, and currently Director, Nehru Memorial Museum and Library, New Delhi. He studied at Delhi and Oxford Universities. His works include *Fencing the Forest* (1996); *India's Wildlife History* (2001); and *Nature and Nation* (forthcoming). He has been Corresponding Editor of *Environment and History* and is co-editor of the two-volume *India's Environmental History*.

SUMIT SARKAR is retired Professor of History, University of Delhi. He also taught at Universities of Calcutta, Oxford, Witswatersrand, and Hawaii (Manoa). His books include: *The Swadeshi Movement in Bengal: 1903–1908* (1973, 2011); *Writing Social History* (1997); *Modern India* (1983); and *Beyond Nationalist Frames: Postmodernism, Hindu Fundamentalism, History* (2002); *Women and Social Reforms in India*, volumes i and ii (2008), edited with Tanika Sarkar. He received the Most Distinguished Scholar Award from the American Association of Asian Studies.

TANIKA SARKAR is Professor of Modern History at Jawaharlal Nehru University, Delhi, and has also taught at St Stephen's College, Delhi, University of Witswatersrand, and the University of Chicago. Her books include: *Bengal, 1928–1934: The Politics of Protest* (1987); *Words to Win: Amar Jiban, A Modern Autobiography* (1999); *Hindu Wife, Hindu Nation: Religion, Community and Nation* (2001); *Rebels, Wives and Saints: Designing Selves and Nations in Colonial Times* (2009); *Women of the Hindu Right* (1995), edited with Urvashi Butalia.

DAVID WASHBROOK is a Senior Research Fellow at Trinity College, Cambridge. Previously, he taught at Warwick, Harvard, and Oxford Universities. His major interests lie in South Asian and global history with a special emphasis on southern India on which he has published extensively.

Map. India between the Wars (from Judith M. Brown and Wm. Roger Louis (eds.), *The Oxford History of the British Empire*, Volume IV. *The Twentieth Century*, p. 431).

1

Introduction

Douglas M. Peers and Nandini Gooptu

A Flourishing Field of Studies

Historical studies of colonial India have enjoyed a remarkable efflorescence over the past generation. New perspectives and methodologies, coupled with the discovery and interrogation of new sources, and perhaps most importantly, a deepened appreciation of the politics of history, have generated a number of fundamental reassessments of the origins, consequences, and increasingly the meaning of imperial rule in colonial India and for its successor states. The debates which have been initiated have not only transformed our understanding of colonial India but have had an impact that stretches far beyond Indian history. They have not only made their mark upon the history and historiography of the British empire, but have informed historical studies in such diverse regions as Latin America, China, and the Middle East, as evidenced, for example, in the widespread adoption of the idea of the 'subaltern', first popularized by South Asian historians, when examining power relationships.[1] Most importantly, the cumulative effect of such works has been to prompt a reassessment of the relationship between imperialism and India, and how those relationships not only transformed India but had profound effects upon Britain and upon the wider British empire.

One fundamental consequence has been that we can no longer treat imperialism as simply a series of bilateral relationships: instead, it is best conceived of as a matrix of interconnections in which those that link the metropole with colonies such as India are certainly critical, but they are by no means the only ones in play. In addition to the bilateral links binding

---

[1] David Ludden (ed.), *Reading Subaltern Studies: Critical History, Contested Meaning, and the Globalization of South Asia* (London, 2002).

the centre to the periphery, we have become much more aware of the relationships that linked the various colonies with one another. Moreover, in our preoccupation with state-centred histories, those that privilege formal political structures, whether they pre-date, sustain, or succeed colonial rule, we have lost sight of the important cultural, economic, and political forces that operate either above or below the state. This focus on the state is in many ways an ironic testimony to the bureaucratic authoritarianism which characterized colonial rule in India and which has been carried over in modified form into its independent successor states. In the case of India, regional dynamics and differences have until recently been largely underestimated except insofar as they had an impact upon the local. This is most obvious in the tendency to treat Bengal and the northern Gangetic Plain as emblematic of India as a whole, ignoring much of India in the process as well as the shifting relationships between local polities, cultures, and economies.[2] These regions in turn were linked in with surrounding territories through long-standing maritime and overland communications. While imperialism often sought to impose its own structures and means on these regions, it is now clear that the direct remit of imperialism was never as complete or systematic as its proponents and critics have argued. This is not to deny the transformative, often disruptive, effect of colonialism upon its subjects. As the following essays demonstrate, colonialism's legacies were profound, multifaceted, and far-reaching. However, in mapping out the terrain, we must be mindful of the dangers of uncritically conflating colonialism with capitalism and globalization. While capitalism and globalization were certainly implicated in colonial rule, they are not synonymous.

We are thus faced with the challenge of examining the history of colonial India without reifying colonialism, either in terms of its contributions to progress and modernity (however defined), or in terms of an all-powerful colonial juggernaut that smashed through everything before it, politically, socially, economically, and culturally. In many instances, the changes observed by historians can be attributed to developments occurring either on the global plane or in some instances local initiatives. The essays in this collection are suggestive of the possibilities of thinking through and beyond the nation state and its precursors by juxtaposing the local with the global,

---

[2] For an example of a region-centred history, see Willem Van Schendel, *A History of Bangladesh* (Cambridge, 2009).

but in ways that do justice to the often contingent and frequently unstable relationship between the two.

Space precludes us from launching into an extensive review of the rich and varied historiography of colonial India. We will, however, delineate some of the major themes, while the contributors to this volume have each taken up aspects of that historiography in greater detail. In them readers can begin to explore a number of the major trends in Indian and imperial historiography. Nor do we propose to rehearse the major debates and controversies that have shaped that historiography. Readers interested in the origins and implications, as well as their permutations and transformations, of such so-called schools as the 'nationalists', the 'Cambridge School', or Subaltern Studies in either its early or later manifestations, can look to many recent surveys of Indian historiography.[3] Instead we intend to explore the positive outcomes and the analytical terrains opened up by the many variants of the critiques of nationalism and colonialism. Drawing upon the chapters in this volume as examples of historical analysis that exploit these opportunities, we will suggest ways forward for the writing of India's history.

Over the course of the last thirty years, the historiography of colonial India has been largely defined with reference to two dominant schools (usually referred to as the Cambridge School and Subaltern Studies), though neither of these was ever homogenous or static. Moreover, area studies programmes, as developed in the US, at times anticipated and at other times cut through the two, particularly because of their interdisciplinary orientation that enabled the application of anthropological and sociological methodologies and perspectives to the study of South Asia. All of these were responding to the limitations of early post-independence nationalist historiography, on the one hand, and the liberal imperial writings that stretch back to the pre-war period. While nationalist and imperial historiography fiercely disputed the objectives and consequences of colonial rule,

---

[3] Sugata Bose, 'Post-Colonial Histories of South Asia: Some Reflections', *Journal of Contemporary History*, 38 (2003), 133–46; Mushirul Hasan, *Making Sense of History: Society, Culture and Politics* (New Delhi, 2003); Michael Gottlob, *Historical Thinking in South Asia: A Handbook of Sources from Colonial Times to the Present* (New Delhi, 2003); Sanjay Subrahmanyam, 'Introduction: Making Sense of Indian Historiography', *Indian Economic and Social History Review*, 39 (2002), 121–30; Robert E. Frykenberg, 'India to 1858', in R. W. Winks (ed.), *The Oxford History of the British Empire: Historiography* (Oxford, 1999); Daud Ali (ed.), *Invoking the Past: The Uses of History in South Asia* (Delhi, 1999).

they shared a common preoccupation with political decision-making at the highest level and a fixation on British initiatives and Indian reactions.

What would become known as the Cambridge School emerged in the 1970s, though it was never confined to Cambridge nor to Cambridge-trained scholars. It was a type of historical writing, the hallmarks of which were intensive archival research in newly opened archives, with a consequent emphasis on the writings and actions of English-speaking elites whether they were in India or Britain.[4] Much criticism has been heaped on the Cambridge School, in part because some commentators have charged them with caricaturing nationalists as irredeemably venal, while others felt that actual imperial power (political, cultural, economic) was being masked by an exaggerated emphasis on collaboration between colonial and Indian elites. Yet this body of writing yielded a number of important insights. By shifting the emphasis in imperial historiography towards interaction between colonizer and colonized, albeit at an elite level, they restored a degree of agency to colonial subjects. In addition, they moved the focus from the national (or nation to be) towards the regional as they probed the complex political interplay at the local level. But it should be noted that the detailed regional studies associated with the Cambridge School privileged administrative or institutional understandings of the region, and their political analysis emphasized elite self-interest at the expense of the cultural, social, and ideological characteristics of these regions.

The Subaltern School offered a sustained critique of the elitism and overemphasis on material self-interest of the Cambridge School. It was also a reaction against the shortcomings of nationalist and Marxist historical writings in India; the former because of its reverential focus on nationalist icons and the latter because of its preoccupation with a very narrow definition of power grounded in class relations. It was this elitism and a lack of emphasis on culture that prompted a turn towards history from below which was most evident in the earliest writings of the Subaltern Studies Collective.[5] Peasants and labourers and other hitherto marginalized

---

[4] See the introductory chapter to Sumit Sarkar, *Modern India* (London, 1989); Anil Seal, *The Emergence of Indian Nationalism: Competition and Collaboration in the Later Nineteenth Century* (Cambridge, 1968); John Gallagher, Gordon Johnson, et al., *Locality, Province and Nation: Essays on Indian Politics 1870 to 1940*, reprinted from *Modern Asian Studies* (Cambridge, 1973).

[5] Two early works which exemplify the thrust of Subaltern Studies are Ranajit Guha, 'On Some Aspects of the Historiography of Colonial India', in R. Guha (ed.), *Subaltern Studies i:*

groups were given voice and recognized as agents in their own right, albeit in a very constrained way. In their early efforts to recover the histories of the overlooked, Subaltern Studies adopted a theoretical framework that drew inspiration from Gramsci's understanding of power (and from whom the term Subaltern was taken).[6] Methodologically, they introduced novel and creative ways of reading the archives against the grain and also turned to oral history.[7] They also opened up a wider terrain of historical analysis by going beyond narrow institutional and functionalist definitions of politics.

Meanwhile, perspectives from historical anthropologists, such as those of Bernard Cohn, suggested new ways of thinking about power, which, when coupled with insights gleaned from literary critics such as Edward Said and theorists such as Michel Foucault, opened up new and radically different ways of conceptualizing colonial relations.[8] This led to a shift within Subaltern Studies as culture, knowledge, and power came to be seen as not only inseparable, but mutually constitutive, and in adopting this position they were joined by other historians. An impassioned plea was made to re-examine not only what we knew about India, and how we knew it, but why we knew it. 'Knowledge is power' was the lesson lifted from Foucault, and many historians participated in what became a broad-based critique of post-Enlightenment epistemology, rationality, and modernity. In the words of Nicholas Dirks, 'Colonial knowledge both enabled colonial conquest and was produced by it; in certain ways, culture was what colonialism was all about.'[9] One collection of essays acknowledged its debt to Said by exclaiming: 'Orientalism, then, is not just a way of thinking. It is a way of conceptualizing the landscape of the colonial world that makes it susceptible to

---

Writings on South Asian History and Society (Delhi, 1982), 1–8, and David Hardiman, 'The Indian "Faction": A Political Theory Examined', in Guha (ed.), *Subaltern Studies*, i. 198–232.

[6] David Arnold, 'Gramsci and Peasant Subalternity in India', *Journal of Peasant Studies*, 11 (1984), 155–77; Ranajit Guha, *Elementary Aspects of Peasant Insurgency in Colonial India* (Delhi, 1983).

[7] Shahid Amin, 'Approver's Testimony, Judicial Discourse: The Case of Chauri Chaura', in R. Guha (ed.), *Subaltern Studies*, v. *Writings on South Asian History and Society* (Delhi, 1987). Shahid Amin developed this article into a book: Shahid Amin, *Event, Metaphor, Memory: Chauri Chaura, 1922–1992* (Berkeley, 1995).

[8] See e.g. Bernard S. Cohn, 'The Command of Language and the Language of Command', *Subaltern Studies*, iv (1985), 276–329.

[9] Nicholas Dirks (ed.), *Colonialism and Culture* (Ann Arbor, 1992), 3.

certain kinds of management.'[10] Yet ironically, because of its focus on texts, even critics sympathetic to many of the positions taken by Subaltern Studies have pointed to a seeming retreat back to an elite-centred history. Critics also charged Subaltern Studies with producing an exaggerated sense of imperial power and omnipotence, one which was at odds with the limited empire view of the Cambridge School.

The net impact of this efflorescence can, however, be measured in the significant gains made in our understanding of colonial India. New areas of research have been opened up, such as gender, science, the environment, and material culture. Moreover, as we have come to appreciate the complexities of colonialism in India, so too have we begun to reassess the impact of colonialism upon metropolitan British history. And finally the dynamism of modern South Asian historiography has fostered opportunities for dialogue between Indian history and other histories.[11]

Beyond Enduring Binaries

Somewhat paradoxically, despite the flourishing state of Indian historiography, we reached somewhat of an impasse due to the proliferation of a number of seemingly intractable binary positions. Historians, including authors in this volume, are now seeking to forge analytical frameworks and engaging in empirical enquiry to help transcend these binaries. One binary, that has been a constant in Indian historiography, is that of the colonizer/colonized, typically understood in a unidirectional way, and framed in terms of political, economic, or cultural domination whether individually or in some combination. The challenge in thinking through this binary is complicated by an underlying paradox that faces all historians of India: namely how to square the putative liberal values and principles embedded within imperial ideology, including liberal economics, with the frequent recourse to authoritarian forms of rule and conservative instincts which were such a signal feature of colonial policy-making. Chapters by Peers, Washbrook, and Den Otter engage with these issues. Each of them has

---

[10] Carol A. Breckenridge and Peter van der Veer (eds), *Orientalism and the Post-Colonial Predicament: Perspectives on South Asia* (Philadelphia, 1993), 6.

[11] Two examples of this are the essays in Gyan Prakash, Florencia E. Mallon, et al., 'AHA Forum: Subaltern Studies', *American Historical Review*, 99 (1994), 1475–1545, and the publication of and subsequent response to Dipesh Chakrabarty, *Provincializing Europe: Postcolonial Thought and Historical Difference* (Princeton, 2000).

moved beyond simply cynically attributing this paradox to a conflict between rhetoric and reality. Washbrook demonstrates that the imperatives of colonialism, as conceived in extant historiography, do not adequately explain economic changes in British India. He sees colonialism at work in the economy, but not in the narrow sense of exploitation, nor necessarily in the interest of capitalist globalization and British industrialization. Indeed, colonial economic policy in India often acted to the detriment of some sections of British capitalists and entrepreneurs. Instead, it functioned to support colonial political ends as much as a liberal economy. Rather than bilateral relations, its logic was tied to wider imperial developments, Britain's global concerns and strategic interests in the region east of the Mediterranean, including the expansion of overseas commerce, control over Asian markets, and the need to build military strength to complement naval power. 'The militarily inflected process of state formation', security concerns, and military fiscalism of the colonial state are emphasized by Peers to account for regressive forms of revenue collection as well as attenuated liberalism, the entrenchment of conservatism, and the attendant stiffening of hierarchical social institutions. Den Otter, in her analysis of colonial law, discusses how liberal jurisprudence was subjected to the contradictory pulls of the 'requirements of a despotic state' as well as being modified by the compulsions of legal practice and the interface with custom. O'Hanlon's essay goes one step further and delineates a number of contradictions, including the extent to which colonial rule was intrusive or inclined towards benign neglect, all-knowing or ignorant, and makes a persuasive case for the need to move beyond such juxtapositions.

Increasingly historians have sought ways out of this impasse in conceptualizing the relationship between colonizer and the colonized by exploring a range of other possibilities beyond resistance or collaboration, such as dialogue, appropriation, exchange, negotiation, contestation, and hybridization. There is, at the same time, an overt recognition of the multiple locations of power within colonial Indian society, where relations are not directly shaped or determined by either the colonial state and its policies, or its implicit counterparts within Indian nationalism. The analysis of the colonial encounter has thus been extended to encompass relations among Indians themselves, with the perspective that divisions among Indians and among Europeans are as important as the obvious divide between Europeans and Indians.

In this volume, Peabody has eschewed the European/native, agent/patient dichotomies, and illuminated the critical role played by Indians in the formation of colonial knowledge, and not simply as providers or translators of raw information, as suggested by Bayly.[12] Further, he stresses historicity, and draws attention to the fact that Western knowledge was not static, nor was Indian knowledge, and the two were shifting and intertwined. Similarly, Den Otter, following on the work of Radhika Singha[13] and others, has explored the dialectical nature of law in colonial India. Den Otter approaches law as negotiated and contested space. As law penetrated more deeply, and affected the daily lives of colonial subjects, it encountered more opposition and engagement, much beyond intellectual and elite circles, that in turn helped to refocus and reshape the law. Mark Harrison shows the dialogic nature of colonial science and medicine, as interactions took place between and among Europeans and Indians, often beyond the ambit of the colonial state and its scientific and medical establishment. In so doing, he exposes the considerable trade in ideas and therapies between Indian and European practitioners. The old model of colonial science is criticized for treating the colonies as a kind of neutral space, neglecting the ways in which the development of science and technology may have been simultaneously enabled and distorted by colonial power relations. Empire, despite the often conservative and constraining nature of its political systems, was at times liberating and enabling for scientists and others, though less so as time progressed.

One of the principle analytical characteristics of the study of modern Indian history has been the extent to which it has been framed in terms of nationalism and colonialism, creating yet another binary within Indian historiography. Empirically too, the focus has been on phenomena and processes that have to do with the colonial encounter and the history of nationalism, usually cast in terms of challenge-response; domination-resistance/collaboration. This has happened despite, or indeed because, of strong critiques of both colonialism and nationalism, and the burgeoning literature which seeks to expose and probe their limits. The emphasis in

---

[12] C. A. Bayly, *Empire and Information: Intelligence Gathering and Social Communication, 1780–1870* (Cambridge, 1996). See also Michael Dodson, *Orientalism, Empire, and National Culture: India 1770–1880* (Houndsmill and New York, 2007).

[13] Radhika Singha, *A Despotism of Law: Crime and Justice in Early Colonial India* (Delhi, 2000).

postcolonial studies on colonialism and its effects has to a degree served to accentuate the fixation on the colonialism/nationalism duality. While critiques of nationalism and colonialism did open up new areas of study, they often remained analytically mired in the colonialism/nationalism binary. Historians involved in Subaltern Studies began to tackle this, but they too failed to escape the constraints of the nationalist optic, intent, as they were, to offer a critique of nationalism. Most authors in this volume advocate a need to surmount this obstacle and they seek to conceptualize their problems through alternative analytical frameworks. This is not to say that the analytical significance of colonialism and nationalism are denied, but they are often seen as framing the context rather than invariably exerting a determining influence.

Sumit Sarkar, for example, offers a perspective that stresses the presence of multiple nationalisms as well as the contested and fragmented nature of nationalism. He also notes the irony that there has been both too much focus on nationalism and not enough—too much because it has been too quickly juxtaposed against colonialism and not enough because of the difficulties of thinking beyond that binary. He urges us to focus instead on 'a simultaneous crystallization of many collectivities': 'Indian', religious, caste, linguistic, ethnic, class, and gender. Tanika Sarkar similarly points to multiple identities whose histories transcend the constraints of nationalism. Prashad, in his discussion of the Indian diaspora, narrows the definition of diaspora by claiming that it only makes sense if it can be set alongside nationalism and the notion of a parent nation. In this way, he extends the purview of nationalism as an imagined community beyond the territorial borders of the subcontinent. Pinney and Majeed look beyond the colonial state and consider the various non-state actors, organizations, and institutions that comprise what is commonly known as civil society, and how they negotiated the competing claims made upon them. Gooptu contends that postcolonial political developments cannot be interpreted simply as the product of the encounter between colonialism and nationalism and the teleology of the independent state-nation. Instead, she draws attention to multiple histories of political engagement, including those devoid of a nationalist referent, that have come to shape India's much-celebrated democratic polity.

A further binary with which historians of India have had to grapple is tradition/modernity, which in its simplest or crudest guise aligns Britain and the empire with modernity and India with tradition. The essays which follow do not assume that modernity is a particular evolutionary stage. Nor do they conceive of modernity as Western post-Enlightenment rationality, nor as a fixed, monistic, normative concept. Instead, modernity is thought of as a process of becoming (and one in which the end point is itself constantly under revision) rather than a state of being. That way, the possibilities of plural and overlapping modernities can be explored, not privileging, or in Majeed's words, 'endlessly engaging with European colonialism as their only possible referent'.

In this context, Sumit Sarkar critiques the analytical tendency to judge the legitimacy or authenticity of nationalism, even if done so implicitly, on whether such expressions managed to stand outside the framework of colonial modernity, seen as a fixed yardstick against which other expressions can be compared. The consequent tendency to celebrate supposedly untainted indigenous modernities stands the risk of lapsing into romanticism. Although coming from different directions, Tanika Sarkar, Den Otter, and Peers stress the importance of political and financial expediency, rather than Western cultural imperialism driven by post-Enlightenment epistemology, in shaping government policy. Nevertheless, Tanika Sarkar emphasizes how colonialism brought with it a new public sphere in which identities could be promulgated and she brings out the role that Indians played in forcing through social reforms. Yet, at the same time, her work reveals the compromises which arose from a shared commitment to patriarchy-bolstered conservatism on the part of the government and Indian reformers, notwithstanding their common use of a rhetoric of reform that is often assumed to be synonymous with modernity. Gooptu considers colonial modernity as a limited analytical frame to account for the nature of the independent Indian state, and emphasizes instead the imperatives of power and hegemony in postcolonial politics.

Pinney, on the visual arts, and Majeed, on literary cultures, most directly address the question of modernity, but instead of labouring to define the analytical space of modernity, they examine how practitioners, writers, and artists struggled towards their own engagement with modernity, thus focusing on the process of becoming. Majeed provides a detailed study of modernity as a dynamic process, which took place within a context framed in part by the impact of colonial rule, but yet was never completely derivative of colonialism. Critical to his study is how indigenous writers and texts positioned themselves with respect to modernity. Modernity in this instance is not the globalized form, nor an all-encompassing episteme, but malleable and multifaceted. Individuals embraced specific aspects of the modern and introduced their own expectations and understandings, thus becoming modern on their own terms. Colonialism was but one of a constellation of reference points, as South Asian writers engaged with and experimented with self-definitions, grounded within a shifting concept of modernity. Moreover, he goes further to argue that in its self-aware break with tradition, modern poetics in South Asia required the ongoing presence of tradition as a backdrop against which their modernity could be signalled. In this way, he takes issue with the idea that hybridity is uniquely colonial and therefore simply a product of the encounter between tradition and modernity. In his chapter, Pinney elaborates on the idea that visual, material, and performative cultures are constitutive of imperial power as well as a site of contestation against it. In so doing, he employs the analytic categories of 'transculturation' and 'purification' to consider forms of engagement and resistance. He adds a further category, that of 'autonomy', to draw attention to a domain of cultural activity wherein there is limited traceable colonial impact or influence. In this way, Pinney presses us to dispense with the tradition/modernity prism. By moving our focus away from tradition versus modernity in this way, we can, as Peers has implied in his chapter, rethink the equation of liberal with modern, and illiberal with tradition, as has all too often been the case.

Regional and Transnational Histories

Conceptualizing Indian history in terms of its regional dynamics has started to offer a promising escape from the deeply entrenched binary positions noted above.[14] Historians have, of course, focused on regions in the past, but mainly from a political perspective. The Cambridge School, for example, examined locality and province as constituted by colonial administration and politics, and regions so defined were static, politically defined formations. Moreover, some of what were largely politically defined regions have dominated the historiography in such a way as to lead historians to infer broader patterns, often based on the Indo-Gangetic plain. Ironically, the nationalist response often reinforced that predilection to define regions

---

[14] David Washbrook. 'Towards a History of the Present: Southern Perspectives on the Nineteenth and Twentieth Centuries', in D. Chakrabarty and R. Majumdar (eds), *From the Colonial to the Postcolonial: India and Pakistan in Transition* (New Delhi, 2007), 323–57.

narrowly in political terms and was equally prone to generalizations in their efforts to construct a nationalist narrative. Consequently, little attention had been paid to other ways in which regions could be understood, for example, culturally, ecologically, or economically. Equally problematic has been the failure to challenge the conventional political geographies of India, for example, by considering intra-regional dynamics. In reintroducing regions into Indian historiography, we must be mindful that regions can be defined in multiple ways, and that their boundaries are not static but instead emerge out of discrete historical processes and change over time.

Several essays in this volume offer examples of how regions can be fruitfully reworked into Indian history, and how the interplay of caste, language, and local ecologies were framed within regional dynamics. Washbrook stresses that imperialism played an important role in reversing the eighteenth-century trend towards the development of stronger, more regionally grounded economies in South Asia. Positing counterfactual trajectories of economic transformation in India, he postulates that if colonialism did not intervene, India's economic development would not have followed the classical model of capitalist change, but rather achieved its own equilibrium, one which was more grounded in regional dynamics. Rangarajan and O'Hanlon discuss the sedentarization of agriculture as the most profound socio-economic change in colonial India, but both emphasize not only pre-colonial, but regional antecedents. Rangarajan shows how regional practices of resource use, cultivation, and livestock rearing forced colonial designs to be modified, and gave rise to a variegated pattern of ecological change in the subcontinent, that thwarts generalizations and grand theories about the environmental history of South Asia.

O'Hanlon notes that regional differences frustrate simple narratives and explanations of social change. On the one hand, there was an overarching rhetoric of modernization and universal values, yet, on the other hand, in their day-to-day operations, the British adjusted their principles to regional needs and demands, real or perceived. Here the British were often dependent upon, or derivative of, pre-colonial political formations, particularly the various regional successor states that had begun to emerge in the turbulent eighteenth century. Both O'Hanlon and Majeed note that technology, particularly communications, and print culture helped buttress regional languages and identities, and shaped regional histories, while also creating links that transcended the local. Majeed, at the same time, draws attention to the interaction and cross-fertilization between various regional vernacular traditions in shaping the history of vernacular literary production, the emergence of new genres or the transformation of already existing ones. With reference to the visual arts, Pinney argues that often the rediscovery of tradition reinvigorated regional forms—even if there was considerable reinvention—as a means of counterbalancing larger trans-regional forces, including those derived from colonialism.

It is important, however, when invoking regional dynamics not to lose sight of the supranational context in which India was placed and the transnational connections that often came into play. As historians have started to show, colonial expansion often relied on pre-existing global economic and cultural links, while Indians themselves forged global connections, independently of British colonialism.[15] Den Otter brings out the transnational flow of ideas of the law and jurisprudence that transcended the empire/colony dichotomy. So too does Harrison in his study of colonial science, by fracturing the image of a monolithic colonial state and demonstrating the complex interplay and tensions between the metropole and the periphery. In particular, he shows how Indians participated in the flow of scientific ideas that brought in other Europeans besides the English. He drives home the importance of less formal networks of exchange, as these reveal that the flow of ideas and information was much more open and unstructured, and less agenda-driven than histories of imperialism have hitherto suggested, and that these flows take place within a wider transnational perspective. The two-way flow of ideas is also apparent in the ways in which Indian aesthetics had an influence on European romanticism, as noted by Pinney. Prashad analyses the Indian diaspora as simultaneously global—because of its spatial scope and integration in the operations of a global economy, but also regional in that the *desis* (people of Indian origin) came from specific regions such as the Punjab, Tamil Nadu, Bihar, and Gujarat, and the particular histories of those regions of peasant struggles or tribal uprisings shaped the nature of migrations and subsequent diasporic experience. In Prashad's account of the diaspora and transnational analysis, we also see the importance of taking into account the peculiarities of the power relationships of colonialism, rather than simply tracing the lineaments of global networks and unraveling entangled histories.

---

[15] Robert Travers, 'Imperial Revolutions and Global Repercussions: South Asia and the World, c.1750–1850', in D. Armitage and S. Subrahmanyam (eds), *The Age of Revolutions in Global Context, c.1760–1840* (London, 2009), 161.

As the essays in this volume demonstrate, there is much to be gained if we can think through and beyond the binaries that are so deeply entrenched in Indian historiography. We can come to appreciate better the vitality of regional dynamics as well as the transnational flows of capital, people, and ideas, and with respect to the latter, we see how these flows occurred below and above the level of the state.

Select Bibliography

JANE BURBANK and FREDERICK COOPER, *Empires in World History: Power and the Politics of Difference* (Princeton, 2010).

ANTOINETTE BURTON (ed.), *After the Imperial Turn: Thinking With and through the Nation* (New York, 2003).

DIPESH CHAKRABARTY, *Provincializing Europe: Postcolonial Thought and Historical Difference* (Princeton, 2000).

—— *Habitations of Modernity: Essays in the Wake of Subaltern Studies* (Chicago, 2002).

RAJNARAYAN CHANDAVARKAR, 'Historians and the Nation', in Chandavarkar (ed.), *History, Culture and the Indian City* (Cambridge, 2009), 191–205.

BERNARD S. COHN, *Colonialism and its Forms of Knowledge: The British in India* (Princeton, 1996).

FREDERICK COOPER, *Colonialism in Question: Theory, Knowledge, History* (Berkeley, 2005).

RICHARD M. EATON, '(Re)imag(in)ing Otherness: A Postmortem for the Postmodern in India', *Journal of World History*, 11 (2000), 57–80.

RANAJIT GUHA and GAYATRI CHAKRAVORTY SPIVAK (eds), *Selected Subaltern Studies* (Oxford, 1988).

SUDIPTA KAVIRAJ, 'Modernity and Politics in India', *Daedalus*, 129 (2000), 137–62.

DANE KENNEDY, 'Imperial History and Post-Colonial Theory', *Journal of Imperial and Commonwealth History*, 24 (1996), 345–63.

DAVID LUDDEN (ed.), *Reading Subaltern Studies: Critical History, Contested Meaning, and the Globalization of South Asia* (London, 2002).

ROSALIND O'HANLON and DAVID WASHBROOK, 'After Orientalism: Culture, Criticism, and Politics in the Third World', *Comparative Studies in Society and History*, 34 (1992), 141–67.

GYAN PRAKASH, 'Writing Post-Orientalist Histories of the Third World: Perspectives from Indian Historiography', *Comparative Studies of Society and History*, 32 (1990), 383–408.

—— 'Can the Subaltern Ride? A Reply to O'Hanlon and Washbrook', *Comparative Studies in Society and History*, 34 (1992), 168–84.

SUMIT SARKAR, *Writing Social History* (Delhi, 1997).
SANJAY SUBRAHMANYAM, 'Introduction: Making Sense of Indian Historiography', *Indian Economic and Social History Review*, 39 (2002), 121–30.
DAVID WASHBROOK, 'Orients and Occidents: Colonial Discourse Theory and the Historiography of the British Empire', in J. Brown and Wm. R. Louis (eds), *Oxford History of the British Empire* (Oxford, 1999).

2

State, Power, and Colonialism

Douglas M. Peers

How can the same nation pursue two lines of policy so radically different without bewilderment, be despotic in Asia and democratic in Australia, be in the East at once the greatest Mussulman Power in the world...and at the same time in the West be the foremost champion of free thought and spiritual religions, stand out as a great military Imperialism to resist the march of Russia in Central Asia at the same that it fills Queensland and Manitoba with free settlers.[1]

The British Raj, despite its claims to reform and liberalism (frequently but not always or simply an *ex post facto* rationalization), was fundamentally a cautious and conservative regime. It was one wherein the imperatives of security and stability which stemmed from the anxieties and ambivalences over ruling such a complex and variegated land dictated the form and function of the state and produced the kinds of paradoxes noted above. India, as many believed, was acquired by the sword and ultimately could only be maintained by the sword—a belief that was further reinforced by the Rebellion of 1857–8. The ensuing ideologies and the way these became manifested in both the structures and the actions of the state reflected a hybrid polity, one that did not simply arise from the importation of British structures, ideologies, and practices into Indian society, nor was it one that drew seamlessly from indigenous antecedents. Instead, it was a melding of diverse influences, ones that were frequently in a state of tension yet held together however precariously by overarching apprehensions about security and informed by constant reminders of just how isolated the British were

---

[1] J. R. Seeley, *The Expansion of England* (Chicago, 1971), 141.

from their subjects.[2] As Sir George Clerk, a key administrator in the nineteenth century, observed: 'There are two modes of governing India—with the people, or without the people. Our predecessors adopted the former—the Mahomedans in their Indian dominions, for six centuries; the Hindoos in their kingdoms for much longer.'[3] The British leaned towards the latter, and even when they made gestures towards political or economic inclusion, the social and cultural gap remained wide and consequently undermined many of the principles to which they appealed: economic improvement, social reform, and political development, to name but a few.

The situation in which the British found themselves prompted the famed legal scholar Sir Henry Maine to declare that 'the British rulers of India are like men bound to keep time in two longitudes at once... the paradoxical position must be accepted in the extraordinary experiment, the British government of India, [of] the virtually despotic government of a dependency by a free people.'[4] Any attempt to come to grips with the nature of the colonial state in India is confronted by this paradox of a liberal regime employing markedly illiberal means to perpetuate its rule. As Uday Singh Mehta has observed, 'It is tempting to see the triumph of liberalism and the concurrent extension of empire as either discontinuous facts that do not relate to each other or as plainly contradicting each other, and therefore casting doubt on the authenticity of the former.'[5] Not only were the means of colonial rule decidedly out of step with prevailing liberal ideologies, so too the consequences for the end result of colonial rule was often the ossification and retardation of social and political institutions and the frustration of indigenous development, aspects of colonial rule that are further developed in David Washbrook's contribution to this collection.

---

[2] Two recent works which help illuminate the origins of these tensions, and particularly the extent to which the British in forging their state were conscious of the challenges of applying British ideas to an alien environment are Robert Travers, *Ideology and Empire in Eighteenth Century India: The British in Bengal* (Cambridge, 2007) and Jon Wilson, *The Domination of Strangers: Modern Governance in Eastern India, 1780–1835* (London, 2008).

[3] Memo by George Clerk on the Government of India under the Company, 1857, L/PS/20/MEMO33, Oriental and India Office Collections, British Library (hereafter OIOC).

[4] Sir Henry Maine, *The Effects of Observations of India on Modern European Thought* (Cambridge, 1875).

[5] Uday Singh Mehta, *Liberalism and Empire: A Study in Nineteenth Century British Liberal Thought* (Chicago, 2000), 194.

There is, furthermore, a second paradox at work: the roots of the state are traceable back to a commercial body, the English East India Company, for whom profit, not territory, was ostensibly the priority. Recently, Philip Stern has questioned the prevailing wisdom that the Company only came to think of itself as a political entity following their victory at Plassey in 1757. His work shows that prior to 1757 not only were persons associated with the Company aware of and encouraging claims of political sovereignty, but these understandings had begun to inform its actions and positioning.[6] And by the early nineteenth century, contemporaries had come however reluctantly to view expansion as inevitable if not always desirable. The economist and critic R. D. Mangles in 1840 quoted one official who declared: 'Our largest and most frequent acquisitions have been made since the declaration of the legislature, in 1784, that to pursue schemes of conquest and extension of dominion are measures repugnant to the wish, the honour and the policy of the nation.'[7] But officials in India, civilian as well as military, did not necessarily agree. In 1844, subscribers to the *Mofussilite*, a newspaper popular amongst Britons resident in India, were told of a report in *The Times* of London that lamented the failure of Anglo-Indian society to take adequate notice of recent financial and commercial reverses in Britain. According to *The Times* this was not due to apathy or oversight: it instead signalled that the Raj was trapped in a 'politico-military phase'.[8] *The Times*'s juxtaposition of a modern commercial society against a military empire was and is a familiar one for it draws attention to the question of how a commercial operation like the East India Company, so closely bound up with precocious capitalism, could become so deeply and apparently perpetually embroiled in costly warfare and continued to do so despite—or perhaps because of—the growth of modern industrial society in Britain. According to other commentators, the situation was not likely to change and it was expected that the frequency of wars would likely remain high for the foreseeable future.

The end result was that Indian budgets were powerfully constrained by military spending, leading to what can best be described as military fiscalism, for not only were military charges for the whole of the colonial era

---

[6] Philip Stern, '"A Politie of Civill & Military Power": Political Thought and the Late Seventeenth-Century Foundations of the East India Company State', *Journal of British Studies*, 47 (2008), 253–82.

[7] R. D. Mangles, 'Present State and Prospects of British India', *Edinburgh Review*, 71 (1840), 361.

[8] 'An Essay on the Present State of Things', *Mofussilite*, 10 Mar. 1848, p. 156.

the single largest drain on government revenues, depriving other areas of government operation of much-needed investment, but when efforts were made to curb military spending, they rarely enjoyed long-term success. During the early period of colonial rule, military spending amounted to more than half of the government's revenues: by the 1920s it continued to hover around 40 per cent, and as officials ruefully noted, this was much higher than most other countries, including Britain at around 17 per cent, Canada barely registering at 2 per cent, France at just over 11 per cent, and Italy topping the list at 22 per cent.[9]

There is a third paradox: the successor regimes to the colonial state have experienced quite remarkably different historical trajectories, with one, India, having experienced a relatively smooth political transition to become what commentators have commonly labelled the world's largest democracy. In contrast, the military in Pakistan has not only frequently intervened politically but it has sunk its roots deeply into the economic and agricultural life of the state. Debt servicing and defence spending, such familiar traits of the colonial state, consume two-thirds of public spending in Pakistan.[10] Ayesha Siddiqa has detailed in her book the characteristics of what she has termed 'Milbus' (combining the words military and business) and shows just how effectively military interests have come to dominate Pakistan's economy.[11] Any explanation for how the army came to exert such a profound influence must begin with the colonial state. Nowhere was the privileged position enjoyed by the military more obvious than in the Punjab, Baluchistan, and the North-West Frontier Province where not only were the military continuously engaged in patrolling an ever-volatile border, but following the mutinies of 1857–8 the Punjab became the principal recruiting ground for the army, thereby further militarizing local societies.[12] Moreover, the administrative machinery introduced by the British into the Punjab and extended, albeit in modified forms, to the frontier regions was highly paternalistic and personalized. The challenges facing Pakistan's leadership in 1947 were further

---

[9] Secretary of State for India, Some Financial Considerations Arising from the Esher Report, 1920, L/MIL/15/5/1905 (OIOC). See also Course of Military Expenditure, 1898/99–1912/13, L/MIL/17/5/1903 (OIOC).

[10] Tariq Ali, 'The Colour Khaki,' *New Left Review*, 19 (2003), 11.

[11] Ayesha Siddiqa, *Military Inc.: Inside Pakistan's Military Economy* (London, 2007).

[12] See Rajit K. Mazumder, *The Indian Army and the Making of the Punjab* (New Delhi, 2003), and Tan Tai Yong, *The Garrison State: The Military, Government and Society in Colonial Punjab, 1849–1947* (New Delhi, 2005).

compounded by their having inherited little of the civilian infrastructure which had been built up by the British, for much of that passed after partition to India. Yet the dominant role played by the Punjab in supplying the army with recruits meant that what was then West Pakistan acquired a large army, one that proved to be all too willing to fill the administrative and economic vacuums which followed independence. Moreover, the bloody experiences of partition encouraged the military to stand forth as the defender of national honour and survival. This militarization of post-1947 Pakistan was, however, largely confined to West Pakistan, and contributed to the strains within Pakistan that culminated in the traumatic fissure in 1971 of that state into Pakistan and Bangladesh.

****

It is therefore not surprising that the colonial state was characterized by a number of contradictions. This chapter will take these paradoxes as its point of departure, and examine some of the institutional, material, and discursive processes and structures that account for them by concentrating on two particularly important and entwined imperatives of colonial rule—stability and security—with particular emphasis on the nineteenth century as it was during that period that many of the key characteristics of the colonial state were consolidated. While such imperatives are common to all states, the circumstances of colonial rule in India, and how the British interpreted their relationships with their subjects, enabled the military to gain considerable purchase on the structures, ideologies, and practices of colonial rule, and in so doing left an unmistakable footprint on the making of the colonial state in India, turning it into a garrison state.

The degree to which the military was embedded within the colonial state is well illustrated by John Malcolm's oft-quoted axiom that, 'Our government of that country is essentially military, and our means of preserving and improving our possessions through the operation of our civil institutions depend on our wise and politic exercise of that military power on which the whole fabric rests.'[13] More than a century later, as the British prepared for their imminent departure from India with the spectre of a civil war before them, officials once again declared, 'Long experience has shown that, at the last resort, the loyalty and impartial obedience of the Armed Forces is

---

[13] John Malcolm, *The Political History of India from 1784 to 1823* (London, 1823), ii. 245.

the bedrock of government.'[14] Tellingly, when in 1946 the Cabinet Mission met with Muhammad Ali Jinnah, leader of the Muslim League, one of the most forceful arguments the British delegation made in favour of a federation, at least in their eyes, was that it would provide greater security as it would enable defence in depth against any threat from Afghanistan.[15] And it is no coincidence that in August 1947, as the British prepared for their departure from India, detailed instructions were issued to British troops at Lucknow to take special care that they take with them the flag that had continuously flown at the Residency since the famous siege of 1857–8, lest this iconic symbol of colonial authority fall into Indian hands. The colonial preoccupation with security was not lost on their subjects, prompting one nationalist writer to complain, 'War, oppression and exaction may be said to have been the normal political condition of India.'[16] Later, when General Wavell was announced in 1943 as the penultimate Viceroy, intelligence reports indicated that this had aroused fears within the country that the British were intent on imposing a military regime to forestall nationalist activities.[17]

Regional dynamics played an important role in determining the shape of the garrison state and we must be mindful of the dangers of treating colonial India as an unvariegated landscape. While the idea of a garrison state can be said to typify colonial rule in India, the historical context in which it emerged was firmly rooted in the Bengal Presidency and it was further shaped by British experiences in asserting and later consolidating their authority in north-western India, particularly the Punjab. The Bengal Presidency, and later the Punjab, possessed the most contested frontiers, both provided what would become at different points in time idealized recruits, so-called martial races (first Brahmans and Rajputs from Awadh and later Sikhs and Muslims from the Punjab), and they were both believed to promise the most reliable land revenues which were needed to sustain the army. The militarization of the institutions, practices, and customs of colonial rule did not penetrate as deeply into the Bombay and Madras

---

[14] Note on the Possibility and Extent of Troubles in India (marked top secret), July 1946, L/WS/1/1008, 29 (OIOC).

[15] Record of an Interview between the Cabinet Delegation, the Viceroy, and Jinnah, 4 Apr. 1946, L/PO/12/2 (OIOC).

[16] Dadabhai Naoroji, *Essays, Speeches, Addresses and Writings (on Indian Politics) of the Hon'ble Dadabhai Naoroji* (Bombay, 1887), 26.

[17] Intelligence Summaries, 2 July 1943 (marked top secret), L/WS/1/1433, p. 225 (OIOC).

presidencies though security imperatives were never absent. Consequently, the colonial state that came to dominate India was largely configured by the historical experiences of colonial rule in northern India, a feature of South Asian historiography that is sometimes lost sight of.[18]

The origins of this garrison state can be tracked back to the mid-eighteenth century. In its simplest formulation the garrison state is characterized by the all-pervasive presence of the military within the decision-making process, the priority given to the military in terms of resource allocation ('military fiscalism'), and the emphasis placed on using the threat (usually in a very public way) of military force as a means of securing political and strategic objectives. Officials in India had by 1766 concluded that their position in India could only be secured by the application of military force. Directors of the East India Company were warned that,

To us it evidently appears, there remained but the alternative to advance as we have done and grasp at the whole power, or shrink back into our primitive condition of simple merchants; to abandon our possessions, disband our forces, and rest our future hopes on the clemency of Princes who will not easily forget or forgive the superiority we have maintained[19]

Secure frontiers were not the only strategic imperatives that informed military policy in India. Equally important was the widely shared belief that the best means of heading off any combination of internal and external threats was to ensure that the willingness and capacity of the British to use force was never questioned. In the words of one army officer, 'The common and conventional phrase, "that we hold India by the force of opinion," is mere idle talk, unless we translate the word opinion into the knowledge that the natives possess of our superior military skill and power—allow the sources on which this conviction is founded to fall into decay or perish, and then see how many years' purchase this empire would be worth.'[20] Hence, while there might not have been a widely shared public commitment

---

[18] David Washbrook. 'Towards a History of the Present: Southern Perspectives on the Nineteenth and Twentieth Centuries', in D. Chakrabarty, R. Majumdar, and A. Sartori (eds), *From the Colonial to the Postcolonial: India and Pakistan in Transition* (New Delhi, 2007).

[19] Bengal to Court of Directors, 31 Jan. 1766, Rt. Hon. Charles F. Greville, *British India Analyzed: The Provincial and Revenue Establishments of Tippoo Sultaun and of Mahomedan and British Conquerors in Hindostan, stated and considered in three parts*, 2 vols. (London, 1793), Appendix number 46.

[20] Colonel Firebrace, 'A Chapter in the History of John Company', *United Service Journal*, 3 (1844), 34.

to expansion for much of the period up to 1858, institutionally, culturally, and ideologically there was a predilection for the use of force, and when this was coupled to the financial appetites of the resulting military forces as an ever-growing army required increasing amounts of revenue to sustain it, there was often little alternative to expansion. This is not to say that conquest was inevitable. But as one commentator reflected, 'During these sixty years India has had Governors-general of all qualifications and temperaments, yet very few of them have avoided war.'[21] John Malcolm elaborated upon this and reminded his readers that 'Those to whom the local government of our Eastern Empire was entrusted have had every motive to preserve peace and to avoid war. Nevertheless, they have almost all engaged in war, and those who have avoided doing so have confessedly left it as an inheritance to their successors.'[22]

Officially the government and the East India Company were opposed to expansion, and frequently urged their officials to eschew conquest. But the Company never seriously urged their officials to relinquish gains, and they also provided the forces with which to protect their trade against the French and other real or imagined threats. Moreover, their officials in India took advantage of communication lag and vague instructions as to their responsibility to protect the Company's territories to maintain their forces in sufficient strength to head off any combination of threats. As Sir Bartle Frere later reminisced, 'We never stopped in conquering India for considerations of home policy, or in obedience to any orders from London. Some of our greatest acquisitions were made, in our own generation, by men who came out sincerely determined to avoid extension of boundary, but the course of conquest was never stayed till we got to the barriers of the mountain regions which surround India on the land side.'[23]

The extent to which policy was conditioned by local circumstances is also evident in that suspicions of unchecked military authority, which were such a prominent feature in British political discourse since the era of the English Civil Wars, were much more muted in India, if observable at all. Consequently, there were fewer checks and balances in India against rising military influence for the European population there, who with a few exceptions, accepted their very tenuous grip on India, a belief that was most dramati-

---

[21] John Chapman, 'India and Its Finances', *Westminster Review*, NS 4 (1853), 177–99.
[22] 'Lord Ellenborough and the Affairs of India', *Fraser's Magazine*, 29 (1844), 472.
[23] Sir Bartle Frere, *Letter to Sir John Kaye* (London, 1874), 28.

cally confirmed by the Rebellion of 1857–8. Whatever chances that the military's grip on the political and financial structures of British India was loosening in the mid-nineteenth century were quickly dashed by the events of 1857–58. The mammoth uprising of Indian troops in the Bengal army, coupled to widespread revolt in north-central India, was taken as a vivid reminder of just how precarious British rule was.

While there were a number of theories in circulation as to the extent of unrest as well as to the origins of the Rebellion, few doubted that British rule would, for the foreseeable future, continue to depend on military force, and that the need for order took precedence over social and political reform. The reasons for this was that it was increasingly assumed, in the much more racialized atmosphere of post-1858 India, that the differences between Indians and Europeans were deeper and much less tractable than had been hitherto assumed. In his criticisms of the Ilbert Bill, which was intended to give Indian and European magistrates equal authority over Europeans and which had triggered massive protests in India and in Britain, Stephen insisted that 'there can be no dispute as to the fact, whatever we may think of it, that Europeans in India are essentially and always must be neither more nor less than a handful of foreigners, divided from the general population of the country by every line of demarcation which can estrange one man from another.'[24] The basis for such arguments, while sharpened by recent events in India, drew much of its strength from the militarized reading of Indian society that had been in circulation for some time.

The granting of greater political freedoms in India was therefore constrained by this focus on difference. It was also accompanied by fears that if political rights were extended to the Europeans domiciled in India, the alleged incompatibility between Indians and Europeans would be exacerbated by European settlers, not subject to military or administrative discipline, once they gained power.[25] Fears of what Europeans would do should they gain greater political clout was a recurring theme in political discussions in India. Wellington was especially suspicious of the trouble that European settlers could unleash, as was Charles Woods, the long-serving Secretary of State for India in the mid-nineteenth century. Episodes such as

---

[24] Sir James Fitzjames Stephen, *Letters on the Ilbert Bill reprinted from The Times* (London, 1883), pp. vi–vii.
[25] Charles Wood to Charles Canning, 10 Aug. 1860, MS Eur F78/L.B.4 (OIOC), and Wood to Elgin, 28 Aug. 1862, MS Eur F78/L.B.11 (OIOC).

the indigo rebellions in mid-nineteenth-century Bengal that were sparked by the brutal nature of plantation life as well as the difficulties in securing convictions on Europeans charged with assaulting and even murdering Indians confirmed such fears. Consequently, for many there appeared to be no alternative to the kind of benign despotism that Stephen and others advocated.

Many argued that it was in fact a zeal for reform—which had not taken into account the fundamentally conservative nature of Indian society—which triggered the revolt in the first place. The Age of Reform—always stronger in rhetoric than in practice—had come to an end. Liberalism, as Stephen had noted, had its boundaries—in this case it was the English Channel. In its place came a much more restricted view of the role of the state: maintenance of order took priority, and progress was increasingly narrowed to material and technological development. Relations with traditional elites were reinforced in an effort by the British to co-opt those they deemed the natural representatives of Indian society. Disraeli was convinced that 'respect for the military power controlled by social conservative territorial aristocrats was fundamental to India's peaceful governance'.[26] This is where Dalhousie and others had erred in their over-enthusiasm for reforms that would undermine such authority figures. Liberals on the other hand argued that in fact the reverse was true: the Mutiny came about because reform had been so haphazard and incomplete. The Indian economy needed to be rapidly overhauled and modernized. These views were forcefully articulated by officials like John Strachey and Richard Temple and publicized by *The Economist* and the *Guardian*. But they were the minority—the consensus was that Indians should be ruled as far as possible through institutions and with the assistance of individuals with whom they could identify. This led Lord Lytton to declare that 'Politically speaking the Indian peasantry is an inert mass. If it ever moves at all, it will move in obedience, not to its British benefactors, but to its Native Chiefs and Princes, however tyrannical they may be.'[27]

Fears for the security of colonial rule were not easily calmed, and as later events demonstrate, the state still largely understood its survival as relying ultimately on its capacity for decisive military intervention. Memories of the

---

[26] Ira Klein, 'Materialism, Mutiny and Modernization in British India', *Modern Asian Studies*, 34 (2000), 562.
[27] Lytton to Strachey, 11 May 1876, MS Eur E218/18 (OIOC).

events of 1857–8 were intricately woven into the fabric of the colonial state, as witnessed in 1888 when the Viceroy, Lord Dufferin, reminded his council of the Mutiny, and insisted that 'we should always remember the lessons which were learnt with such terrible experience thirty years ago, and never allow ourselves to slumber under the soothing influences of peace and comparative prosperity'.[28] The ways in which the British had come to understand themselves and their position in India, coupled to their reading of Indian society, played a crucial role in the origins and evolution of the garrison state as did many of the more tangible and obvious reasons for this emphasis on the military. So too did careerism. At the height of Anglo-Russian rivalry for Central Asia, sceptics charged that 'KCB mania' (eagerness for knighthoods) was a major impetus behind many of the attempts of officers to convince decision-makers as well as the wider public in Britain of the imminent dangers of a Russian attack.[29]

The fact that the military and concerns over security enjoyed such widespread currency did not mean that their grip on decision-making went unchallenged or that alternative approaches did not enter circulation. Critics of the military were numerous, starting with Philip Francis in the eighteenth century, continuing through the nineteenth century and into the twentieth century as diverse groups sought to shape the emerging colonial state, including missionaries, free traders, nationalists, and domestic politicians from across the political spectrum. Pointed accusations were made of the impact that the demands of the army had upon governance and finances, the crippling consequences the military had on the growth of representative and responsible institutions, the obstacles they threw up to the emergence of civil society, as well as the questions that were raised about their accountability. Such criticisms did not pass unnoticed, and while the fundamental preoccupations with security and stability were ever present (and in fact were often conceded by critics of the colonial state), the ensuing debates and the compromises that arose in turn are fundamental to any understanding of the often contingent and ambivalent actions of the colonial state.

Even the army's most outspoken champions acknowledged that force had its limits, especially when it might not overcome local resistance which

---

[28] Minute by Lord Dufferin, 8 Dec. 1888, MS Eur E240/3 (OIOC).
[29] Major General Sir C. M. MacGregor, 'The Defence of India: A Strategical Study', L/PS/20/G1, p. 104 (OIOC).

would then reflect badly on the omnipotence of the colonial state. For example, the army was often reluctant to engage in what we would now term low-level counter-insurgency operations where not only were the enemy's forces hard to pin down but there were few if any assets to capture.[30] And as events in the twentieth century would demonstrate, the indiscriminate use of force increasingly provoked political criticism at home and in India. Nowhere was this better exemplified than in the outcry which followed General Dyer's orders for troops under his command at Jallianwalla Bagh to open fire on an unarmed crowd.[31] Somewhere between four hundred and a thousand civilians died. Dyer was exonerated in the subsequent enquiry (and in fact was feted by some for having shown the decisiveness that was associated with vigorous rule), yet senior officials in India concluded that his actions had strengthened nationalist support.

By 1945 few colonial officials laboured under the delusion that they could rely on force to maintain their authority. They could no longer assume the loyalty of their Indian troops (as well as some British units posted to India as evidenced by protests mounted by RAF units eager to return to Britain), and there was growing recognition that public opinion at home and in India was becoming increasingly critical of the use of force to bolster imperial rule. The limits to what military force could achieve in India had become apparent in 1942–3 when not only was the army being pushed back by Japanese thrusts through Burma into north-eastern India, but colonial authority within India was being undermined by the 'Quit India' movement that left large tracts of northern India, especially in Bihar, effectively beyond British rule. So complete had been the breakdown of British authority that many of the troops needed on the eastern frontier had to be redeployed to try and prop up civil administration. In their assessment of the situation in 1946, the chiefs of staff concluded that 'we consider that a plan which visualizes the reconquest of India against the opposition of the Indian Armed Forces is unrealistic, since, quite apart from the difficulty of providing the necessary forces, it seems extremely doubtful whether in face of world opinion such a campaign could in fact be undertaken'.[32]

****

[30] Political Letter from India, 13 Nov. 1841, Operations against the Hill Tribes, F/4/1874 (OIOC).
[31] Viceroy to Secretary of State, 12 July 1919, L/PO/6/4 (OIOC).
[32] Chiefs of Staff Committee Joint Planning Staff, Internal Situation in India, 6 Jan. 1946, L/WS/1/1008 (OIOC).

This recurring emphasis on the military as the ultimate bulwark of colonial rule was bolstered by contemporary understandings of Indian society and history, especially when such assessments reinforced prejudices imported from Britain. Not surprisingly given their numbers and influence and the fact that they were often seconded to civil and political duties, military officers played a crucial role in shaping British understandings of Indian society and their place within it. Collective anxieties over possible reactions to British rule led many officials to champion a cautious approach to Indian society, and they urged the necessity of drawing upon pre-colonial practices, though their comprehension of these was often warped by colonial needs and/or colonial misreadings of local practices. This led to the widespread custom of casting India in largely military terms. John Lawrence reminded Lord Dalhousie that 'Public opinion is essentially military in India. Military views, feelings and interests are therefore paramount. If matters go well, the credit rests with the military, if they go wrong, the blame is thrown on the civil power. The views of the Commander in Chief are essentially those of his cloth, perhaps a good deal exaggerated, but still their views.'[33] Such impressions drew strength from particular readings of Indian society, ones that played up orientalist differences as well as ones that sought analogies with pre-modern feudal social organizations. As a recent study of legal culture in mid-nineteenth-century Britain has argued, 'the English political class of the late 1860s were Hobbesian pessimists about human nature. In this view, human beings, when left to their own devices, were naturally inclined to egotism, aggression, and violence.'[34]

Not surprisingly, then, there was ready acceptance of the view that India's natural political order was that of an 'oriental despotism'.[35] This can be glimpsed, for example, in Robert Cust's defence of the practice in which he argues that while 'It is true, that in a free country, such a degree of centralization is not desirable, and the evil effects of such a system are shewn in France, where liberties are periodically lost by the over-weening power of the Executive Government... it is a melancholy fact, which it may be as well to admit, that a really efficient and responsible form of absolute

---

[33] John Lawrence to Lord Dalhousie, 20 Sept. 1850, MS Eur F90/3, (OIOC).
[34] R. W. Kostal, *A Jurisprudence of Power: Victorian Empire and the Rule of Law* (Oxford, 2005), 20.
[35] P. J. Marshall, *The Making and Unmaking of Empires: Britain, India, and America c.1750–1783* (Oxford, 2005), 201.

government, is the best system for the rule of an Asiatic country.'[36] If oriental despotism was considered the natural state in India, late Victorian defenders of British rule stressed that what they offered was 'fettered oriental despotism' as contrasted with previous regimes with their 'unfettered oriental despotism'.[37] 'Fettered oriental despotism' would manifest itself in many ways, for example it underpinned the widespread practice of uniting the responsibilities of the collector and the magistrate in one person.

Such readings of Indian society had a long pedigree: in the eighteenth century Robert Clive had insisted that 'Hindostan is accustomed to a military government; an army may be kept in discipline and protect the rights of the natives without exciting their jealousy; a judicious use of our resources ought to render the British arms paramount in India; but luxury and abuses have pervaded both the military and civil service.'[38] Even critics of the East India Company and its policies subscribed to such views. One reviewer in the *Westminster Review* noted with regret, 'Let it be remembered that, both within and without the general confines of India, there are kingdoms and clans whose people habitually resort to force and deadly strife on what we deem light occasions.'[39] Another author reminded his readers that 'In the East, aggrandizement is justified as a manly, honourable and legitimate course of policy: in the West this principle is restrained and modified by laws and manners, and disguised under a variety of pretexts, which deceive the vulgar, and very often those who make use of them.'[40] Military values were thus seen as deeply ingrained in north Indian society and were manifested in codes of conduct, dress, and even domestic architecture. This was less apparent in the south, and when it came to identifying the so-called martial races, it is significant that the British were convinced that few southern Indian communities possessed these qualities.

---

[36] Robert Needham Cust, 'Collector of Revenues in the North West Provinces', *Calcutta Review*, 23 (1854), 138–9.

[37] Charles Lewis Tupper, 'Our Indian Protectorate', London, 1892, L/PS/20/H43, p. 319 (OIOC).

[38] Clive to Court of Directors, Apr. 1765, in Rt. Hon. Charles F. Greville, *British India Analyzed: The Provincial and Revenue Establishments of Tippoo Sultaun and of Mahomedan and British Conquerors in Hindostan, stated and considered in three parts* (London, 1793), 812.

[39] John Chapman, 'India and Its Finances', *Westminster Review*, 4 (1853), 180.

[40] A. White, *Considerations on the State of British India* (Edinburgh, 1822), 128.

The deification of the soldier-administrator, with its attendant preoccupation with clearly defined hierarchies of rule and preference for vigorous and direct action, reached its apogee in the so-called Punjab school of administrators. Tellingly, Robert Montgomery, for many the quintessential Punjab official, was praised for being a 'man of action rather than deliberation'.[41] Ellenborough drew similar lessons from the experience of the Indian Rebellion, claiming that 'the best education for every civil servant in India is service in the native army'.[42] While not all of the officials who comprised this school were from the army (John Lawrence being but one example), their values and practices were saturated with a military ethos, frequently captured in romanticized views of the differences between Indians and Europeans and of the value of colonial rule in counteracting many of the less desirable traits of modern industrial society. Curzon claimed in 1907 that 'outside of the English universities no school of character exists to compare with the frontier' and that 'on the outskirts of empire [will] be found an ennobling and invigorating stimulus for our youth saving them alike from the corroding ease and morbid excitements of western civilization'.[43]

The British Raj was therefore a garrison state in terms of both its form and its content, for it was not only structurally geared towards conquest but was, moreover, culturally and ideologically grounded in conquest. The fact that there was such a broad degree of consensus over the centrality of the military to the maintenance of colonial authority did not mean that the army had totally usurped the authority of their political masters. Nor should it be inferred that civilian officials unquestioningly surrendered to the imperatives of the army. There were certainly those who questioned the army's pre-eminent position in Anglo-Indian society just as there were many officials who believed that British rule, if it were to survive in the long run, must establish a more substantial and persuasive claim to legitimacy. The history of British India was littered with examples of civil–military conflict, most famously in the epic clash at the beginning of the twentieth century when the Viceroy, Lord Curzon, attempted to strengthen his authority over Lord Kitchener, the commander-in-chief, by arguing that

---

[41] Tim Allender, 'Robert Montgomery and the Daughter Slayers: A Punjabi Education Imperative, 1855–1865', *South Asia*, 25 (2002), 100.

[42] Meredith Townsend, *Annals of Indian Administration*, vol. iii (Serampore, 1859), 258.

[43] George Nathaniel Curzon, *The Romanes Lecture* (Oxford, 1907), 56–7.

Kitchener 'came out to India in order to destroy the Military Dept [a civilian body that oversaw military finances] and to set himself up as military dictator in its place'.[44] Curzon miscalculated how much support he enjoyed in London and in the end he was backed into a corner from which he had no option but to resign.

Not even celebrated reformers like William Bentinck, Thomas Babington Macaulay, or the Marquis of Ripon could make much headway against such beliefs, for they too yielded to the strategic imperative that British India was always under threat, if not from without, then most certainly from within. Like other liberal intellectuals, Sir James Fitzjames Stephens made an exception of India when dealing with the liberals' belief that moral force was separate from and not determined by physical force. Memories of the Rebellion, plus a long history of viewing Indian rule as dependent upon a show of force, led him to argue in 1883 that British rule was 'essentially an absolute government, founded not on consent but on conquest'.[45] This in turn led to a prioritizing of military needs in policy-making and financial transactions that created an increasingly efficient financial mechanism but at the cost of economic development. Yet war was sufficiently profitable to enough groups that they would continue to cooperate and in so doing helped to bolster the fiscal military state.

Hence, the colonial state was marked by anxiety as well as hybridity, not only in its melding of European and Indian forms and practices, but hybrid in its retention of pre-modern characteristics alongside those normally associated with the advent of modernity. This complicates ideas that colonialism helped usher in a transition from pre-modernity to modernity. Some have suggested that colonial India was the 'laboratory for the creation of a liberal administrative state'.[46] The Raj might in some of its militarily and economic ambitions be characterized as modern, but it was decidedly pre-modern and perhaps even anti-modern in many of its social, cultural, and political aspirations. There has been a tendency to conflate colonialism and modernity (a characteristic of many early writings which has ironically and problematically been reinvigorated by some—but not

---

[44] Curzon to Balfour, 30 Mar. 1905, MS Eur F111/412 (OIOC).
[45] James Fitzjames Stephen, 'Foundations of the Government of India,' *Nineteenth Century*, 80 (Oct. 1883).
[46] Thomas R. Metcalf, *Ideologies of the Raj* (The New Cambridge History of India, iii/4; Cambridge, 1994), 29.

all—scholars in postcolonial studies). By placing questions of security and stability at the centre of this analysis (and with them the military attitudes and institutions which played such an important role in interpreting and promoting such concerns), we are better placed to reconcile the paradox noted at the outset which is also at the heart of the debate over modernization and colonialism—one which sought in India relief from the pressures of modernity as evidenced in the following declaration by Francis Yeats-Brown: 'Western civilization bullied and bored me...Here in India I was finding myself.' Even those regimes which have customarily been singled out as signalling periods of reform, periods when liberalism reasserted itself, could not escape the imperatives of security and stability, and while they might chaff at some of the more reactionary aspects of military priorities, they could not but be informed by some of the underlying logic. Witness, for example, the recurring themes of medievalism and belief in social hierarchies that underscored the forms of benevolent despotism espoused by liberal reformers. Yet it was never a static structure, and as the colonial state grew to maturity in the years after the Indian Rebellion of 1857–8, its more overtly militarized characteristics softened.

****

With such weight attached to the military, it is not surprising that the army was given first demand on the revenues of the colonial state. But its influence did not end there for the kinds of fiscal strategies that were employed, and their attendant revenue policies, were also shaped by military imperatives and values. As one important commentator on Indian affairs (and one-time senior employee of the East India Company) declared, 'The military expenditure of the East India Company furnishes the key to its general policy. In India, it can be safely said that the history of war was synonymous with the history of its finances.'[47] Its ability to maintain an army in peace as well as in the field, properly equipped and regularly paid, was what distinguished it from its Indian rivals.

Before the rise of the modern welfare state, modernity—at least in political terms—can be understood as a combination of ideological and institutional developments that facilitated the efficient prosecution of war for that was the principal preoccupation of the state. In eighteenth-century

---

[47] John William Kaye, *The Administration of the East India Company: A History of Indian Progress* (London, 1853), 421.

Britain, between 60 and 70 per cent of total income was going to the army and navy during time of war, falling to 40 per cent in peacetime.[48] And debt servicing, itself a legacy of warfare, took up much of the remainder as taxes were insufficiently flexible to meet the rapidly growing costs of war; but they were elastic enough to enable the government to meet its debts. Britain's capacity to mobilize increasing amounts of human and financial resources has led some to conclude that the British regime had by the late eighteenth century become a 'fiscal-military state'. Pre-modern states also demonstrated an affinity for war, but in such cases the state was the natural extension of the sovereign, and was conducted by a range of intermediaries whose links to the sovereign were all too often defined in personal rather than fiscal terms.

Military fiscalism did not simply reflect a government's capacity to wage war; the powers it took upon itself to mobilize resources meant that it penetrated more deeply into society than had its forebears. It had to create offices and committees to oversee its expanded authority. Hence, the bureaucracy of the modern state, which was one of its more obvious characteristics, was largely a response to the increasingly depersonalized nature of rule, the growing economic complexity of contemporary societies, and the technical and organizational demands initiated by military developments. Consequently, ledgers and logistics often took precedence over lances and longbows. Wellesley's victories in southern and central India were inconceivable had he not been able to raise the necessary monies for his campaigns and had he not tapped so effectively into indigenous logistical practices. By way of contrast, contemporary observers highlighted the logistical weaknesses of their Indian opponents.

Yet the domestic British state was never as militarized as was its Indian counterpart. In Britain, while the state became more expert at meeting military requirements, it was also quick to wind down its wartime establishment during those brief periods of peace. In India, while armies were reduced following periods of war, they were never reduced by the same degree that was common in Europe. The principal reason for this was that in India possible external threats could always be found at hand and even were this not the case then the potential for internal revolt was ever present. Military charges remained high. Just prior to the outbreak of the Indian Rebellion, Henry Lawrence reckoned that the 'the expense of the army,

---

[48] Lawrence Stone (ed.), *An Imperial State at War: Britain from 1689–1815* (London, 1994), 9.

including the dead-weight, is eleven millions a year, or nearly one-half the revenue of India'.[49] Military charges had grown by 44 per cent over the previous twenty years yet revenues had only grown by 35 per cent.[50] And while over the next century there were years in which economies were introduced, military costs remained the largest single item of government expenditure, and generally hovered around 40 per cent, spiking upwards to well over half government expenditure during wartime.[51] The Welby Commission on military expenditure looked at the period between 1858 and 1896/7. Expenditure rose from 1858 until 1863, then levelled off until 1885 and then grew again. A further measure of the significance attached to military budgets was that section 67A of the Government of India Act of 1919 explicitly excluded military costs from the consideration of the Legislative Assembly, even though the British acknowledged that there were risks attendant on this as it provided Indian nationalists with a ready grievance against colonial rule.

Another characteristic of military fiscalism in India that needs to be borne in mind is that it was not a purely colonial invention and here again we find evidence of the hybrid nature of colonial rule. As recent scholarship has forcefully and helpfully reminded us, pre-colonial states in India were never as stagnant as much scholarship would have us believe. An earlier tradition of historical narratives depicted colonial rule as a massive and sudden rupture, suggesting that Plassey was engineered by the British who were eager to supplant quickly Indian rulers, and then use the resulting land revenues to bolster their commercial domination over Asian trade. This then sent shock waves into the Indian economy that worsened as the British cranked up their demands.

With the benefit of hindsight, it is clear that the British did usher in a transformation. But changes were also being initiated by Indian states that were adjusting their political and military systems so as to try and gain the upper hand over their rivals which included, but were not restricted to, the British. Such regimes, while careful to retain at least the outward forms of Mughal rule, were also developing much more efficient means of revenue

---

[49] Henry Lawrence, 'The Indian Army', *Calcutta Review*, 26 (1856), 185.

[50] 'Appendix to Report from the Select Committee on Indian Territories', *Parliamentary Papers*, 10 (1852), 276–9.

[51] Secretary of State, Some Financial Considerations arising from the Esher Report, 1920, L/MIL/15/5/1905 (OIOC).

extraction, replacing earlier systems by which an aristocracy was given land grants in return for military service with methods of revenue farming which directed revenues directly back to the ruler from which he could then pay for military services.[52] Indian rulers had also engaged in the allegedly 'modern' practice of counting and classifying their subjects. This also allowed rulers to mortgage anticipated revenues in deals struck with large Indian capitalists like Jagat Seth. The increased certainty of funding then enabled them to equip and discipline standing armies that were akin to those that we normally associate with European forms of military organization.[53] In Mysore, Haider Ali introduced major military reforms, some of which were borrowed from the preceding Wodeyar state.[54] Ranjit Singh's Punjab also exhibited characteristics similar to those we normally associate with the fiscal-military state. Indigenous developments such as these ironically helped facilitate the consolidation of colonial rule for they created crucial footholds for the British. The British were better able to access Indian resources largely because their competitors' political, administrative, and financial structures were already set up and functioning in ways that the British could comprehend and eventually co-opt. These included standing armies, cash-based revenue systems, sophisticated banking networks, and a legal infrastructure. In the case of the Punjab, the British were able to exploit pre-existing foundations, further militarizing its administration, which in turn would have consequences for present-day Pakistan.

But a word of caution is in order: the British did not simply assimilate such systems wholesale. C. A. Bayly's warning that 'The Company's regime was evidently something more than a white Mughal Empire' must be borne in mind.[55] Nor should we try and squeeze political culture and organization in India into a rigidly Western model, for as Sudipta Kaviraj has noted, the nature of the Indian state, while changing, was still sufficiently different from that of Europe to caution us against drawing simple parallels. In India, for example, the state had customarily not been so involved in regulating

---

[52] David Washbrook, 'India, 1818–1860: The Two Faces of Colonialism', in Andrew Porter (ed.), *The Oxford History of the British Empire: The Nineteenth Century* (Oxford, 1999).

[53] Seema Alavi, *The Sepoys and the Company: Tradition and Transition in Northern India, 1770–1830* (Delhi, 1995).

[54] Sanjay Subrahmanyam, *Penumbral Visions: Making Politics in Early Modern South India* (Ann Arbor, 2002).

[55] C. A. Bayly, 'The British Military-Fiscal State and Indigenous Resistance, India, 1750–1820', in Lawrence Stone (ed.), *An Imperial State at War: Britain from 1689–1815* (London, 1994), 324.

social relationships—the caste system had largely seen to that.[56] Hence, the transition from Indian rule to colonial rule cannot be said to be seamless, despite the considerable overlaps.

What the garrison state in India did share with its Indian opponents was a very restricted revenue base. As one observer noted, 'If in England we become involved in war, we immediately lay on additional taxes to meet the additional expense. In India, with vastly greater liability to war, we can do no such thing; however urgent the occasion, the income for at least the two-thirds which arise from the land tax and, indeed, for much more, must remain very nearly as it is.'[57] Taxes in India were even more inelastic than those in Britain, with the added challenge that the British had only the most imperfect understanding of the economy that they were coming to dominate. And their ability to tap into Indian revenues was further frustrated by their own limited resources as well as their apprehensions about what might happen should they misstep. Unlike Britain where indirect taxation proved to be a successful financial strategy, the British in India were largely dependent upon land revenues. In the words of one official, 'There are fifty different ways in which the English tax-gatherer may get at the poor man. But in India the approaches to the mud hut of the labourer are few; and the tax-gatherer must advance by them or keep away altogether; he has been going a long time along the same beaten roads.'[58] The annual revenue of the Mughal empire has been estimated at £30 million per year. The East India Company initially acquired through conquests in the eighteenth century the rights to about £6 million of revenue-producing lands. Their principal opponents, the Marathas and Mysore, had secured the rights to approximately £5.7 million and £2.4 million respectively.[59]

Yet these figures do not reveal the full story, and here Bayly's caveat cited above is borne out—the British were generally more successful in realizing such revenues for they were able to employ more efficient mechanisms for securing their intended share of the revenues. An earlier emphasis on excessive taxation demand as a consequence of colonial rule and the

---

[56] Sudipta Kaviraj, 'Modernity and Politics in India', *Daedalus*, 129/1 (2000), 137–62.
[57] Chapman, 'India and Its Finances', 195.
[58] Kaye, *The Administration of the East India Company*, 421.
[59] Rajat Kanta Ray, 'Indian Society and the Establishment of British Supremacy, 1765–1818', in P. J. Marshall (ed.), *The Oxford History of the British Empire: The Eighteenth Century* (Oxford, 1998), 517.

concomitant rural impoverishment has been revised. But according to P. J. Marshall, Rajat Datta, and others, the difference was not so much in appetite but rather in the efficacy of tax extraction. Marshall has estimated that tax demands grew by 20 per cent in Bengal between 1757 and 1793. Such demands did take place in the midst of profound transformations, a crippling famine of 1769–70, as well as fluctuating prices including a prolonged depression in the 1790s that increased the real burden on cultivators. Rajat Datta has taken this argument further, suggesting that the impact should be seen more in terms of increased commercialization rather than a simple increase in tax demands.

The financial demands of the army, when coupled with the Company's commercial imperatives, encouraged the Company to develop and refine instruments of financial management. The accounting procedures of the Company were, until the mid-nineteenth century, far in advance of those used by the British government. And in choosing between predictability and reliability, the revenue systems introduced into Bengal by the Permanent Settlement of 1793 (usually referred to as the zamindari system in which settlements were made with large revenue farmers) was intended to ensure reliability in such a way as to allow for better forecasting, but more importantly ensure a steady revenue stream which would prove attractive to potential investors in the Company's loans. Quicker and more reliable access to revenue sources enabled the British to tap into indigenous credit networks more effectively. The British were also determining their revenue demands with security in mind for they wished to co-opt or at least placate potential sites of resistance by trying to win over key sectors of rural society, and in Bengal this took the form of settling with the closest approximation of a landed gentry. Elsewhere it was most obviously manifested in the importance that the British attached to the surviving Indian aristocracy who were given limited political authority within their princely states. Their most zealous champion, Lord Lytton, opined, 'It is undoubtedly true that, for all practical purposes, the people of India is political dumb. But it is not politically insentient; and, as a body politic, the seat of its motive power is in its head; that is to say, in its hereditary aristocracy. As the head wills, the body will move.'[60]

---

[60] Memo by Lytton on the Declaration of Victoria as Empress of India, 11 May 1876, L/PS/20/MEMO33 (OIOC).

The key to military fiscalism in India, however, lay in the Company's ability to fund its liabilities through loans that were issued at very favourable rates of interest which covered periods of deficits that not surprisingly arose because of increased military expenditure during years of military campaigning. Between 1814 and 1828, 70 per cent of the government's deficit was underwritten by loans; the remainder was covered by internal indebtedness or advances from the Company's commercial operations. By 1814 the prevailing interest rate was 6 per cent—despite a series of expensive wars in Nepal, central India, and Burma, the rate fifteen years later was still ranging between 5 and 6 per cent.[61] Across the same period, debt serving charges dropped from around 15 per cent in 1815 to 11 per cent in 1825, spiking over the next three years because of the extraordinary costs of the Burma War, then declining to around 10 per cent.[62] The Indian debt in 1834 stood at £35 million, carrying an annual charge of £1,778,000 a year. But because the rate of interest in 1834 was just over 5 per cent, the cost of the debt had risen more slowly than the total amount of debt. The total debt had grown by 60 per cent, but debt servicing charges had only increased by 42 per cent.[63] Put another way, the Indian debt was little more than two years' income which one contemporary estimated was less than most other national debts.[64] Prevailing interest rates would remain at these levels up until the Indian Rebellion, and even the catastrophic shocks of that event did not seriously imperil the Company's credit rating. In 1856, the biggest slice of the Bengal debt (which was £44 million of the total Indian debt of £50 million) enjoyed an interest rate of 4 per cent, or £2,140,577 a year.[65] The crisis of 1857/8 not surprisingly pressed hard on Indian capital. The Company had to raise their rates, but not by much—a 5 per cent loan opened in 1857 realized nearly £4 million in India by early 1858 which when combined with another offering at 4 per cent raised the India debt from £50 million to £56 million.[66]

By taking advantage of favourable rates of interests as well as its more centralized revenue collection and distribution, not only were the British

---

[61] Memo on the Indian Debt, 1828, PRO 30/12/32/1 (Law Papers).

[62] Statistics compiled from SC on EIC, PP, 1831/32, X, Pt 1, Appendix 4 and Memo on Indian Finances, n.d., PRO 30/12/32/1 (Law Papers).

[63] Frederick Hendriks, 'On the Statistics of Indian Revenue and Taxation', *Journal of the Statistical Society of London*, 21 (1858), 255.

[64] Chapman, 'India and Its Finances', 179.

[65] Hendriks, 'On the Statistics of Indian Revenue and Taxation', 249.

[66] Ibid. 253.

able to raise the money to keep a large army in being during peace as well as war, but they also strengthened their links with indigenous capital. It was estimated that by 1830 about 25.5 per cent of the Indian debt was owned by Indians and over the course of a series of loan issues of the 1820s, Indian subscribers contributed about 25 per cent of the paid-up capital.[67] This practice of turning to Indian investors led one writer to describe the British with some justice as 'agents of native capital'.[68] But Indians did not necessarily give willingly to such loans. An element of coercion was used, especially on Indian princes who were told that subscription to Company loans would be taken as proof of their commitment to their alliance. By extracting loans from Indians the British not only tried to draw them more closely into their orbit but also tried with mixed success to avoid pressing too hard on the limited supply of British capital.

Another example of how well integrated strategic and financial affairs had become under the British can be seen in their alliances with surviving Indian rulers. Subsidiary alliances, which were a crucial component of the practice of indirect rule, were another key component of military fiscalism for they enhanced the Company's military position while deflecting the costs onto their allies. These alliances normally entailed a British promise to provide military protection in the form of a subsidiary force in return for which they were to be guaranteed a cut of the ruler's revenues.

While many contemporaries were quick to praise the Company for its ability to finance its military operations with considerable sophistication, there were also a good number who were quick to appreciate that these came at a considerable cost. Military fiscalism enabled the British to mobilize and maintain an impressive military force but it proved to be a considerable drag on the Indian economy, frustrating economic development at key junctures by limiting the government's financial options and by absorbing capital and resources which might have been put to more productive use. Unlike white settler colonies where economic development was not hindered by having to bear much by way of military costs, colonies of conquest—especially India—found much of their wealth siphoned off to supporting the military forces. While some Indian groups stood to benefit—suppliers, financiers, and the sepoys who, at least until the mid-nineteenth century enjoyed wages that compared favourably with those

---

[67] Select Committee on the East India Company, *Parliamentary Papers* (1831/2), X, Pt 1, p. xx.
[68] George Campbell, *Modern India* (London, 1852).

within rural society in India—the overall gains were limited. Critics charged that military expenditure came at the cost of investment in infrastructure, thereby doing little to benefit Indian society or prospective British investors. For observers like J. W. Kaye, the frequency with which the governments of India resorted to war was largely the reason why so few reforms had taken hold. Wars cost money, and many wars cost a lot of money which in the case of India meant that rural society had to bear the brunt. He reminded his readers that 'a few fertile provinces are drained of their wealth, that an expensive war beyond the frontier may be prosecuted'.[69] Writing in 1857, another charged that 'the debt already incurred by the Company was solely occasioned by territorial aggrandizement, and it is impossible that the cost of a gigantic war in India can be borne by the Indian revenue of the East India Company'.[70] Similarly, the burden of military costs following the Rebellion of 1857–8 frustrated efforts to increase spending on public works.

For such critics, India had to be liberated from the fiscal-military grip of the East India Company—capital must be encouraged and British entrepreneurs invited into India. Writing in 1840, R. D. Mangles claimed that 'the direct drain of money occasioned by the late war, and by our present political relations, is an evil scarcely worth notice, when compared with the mischief inflicted upon the general wealth and prosperity of the country, by the unavoidable concomitant neglect or postponement of the many important matters requiring legislative measures or administrative regulation'.[71] Furthermore, military spending on supplies had little trickle-down effect on the Indian economy for much of the army's material needs were met by British suppliers (and this would remain the case into the twentieth century).

This tension between the military imperatives and economic development can also be glimpsed in the Punjab, where the government intervened to prevent a capitalist transformation of its economy by passage of legislation intended to preserve the agricultural holdings of those communities from whom they recruited from moneylenders and outsiders. The 1900 Land Alienation Act dictated that land could not be transferred

---

[69] John William Kaye, 'The War on the Sutlej', *North British Review*, 5 (1846), 259.

[70] 'The East India Company', *Bentley's Miscellany*, 42 (1857), 419. The classic mid-century statement remains Richard Cobden, *How Wars are Got Up in India: The Origin of the Burmese War* (London, 1853).

[71] R. D. Mangles, 'Present State and Prospects of British India', *Edinburgh Review*, 71 (1840), 368.

to non-agricultural classes. Widows were condemned, often against their will, to remarriage with brothers-in-law, so as to preserve family fortunes and ensure the reproduction of army recruits. Such measures were clearly intended to preserve a critical recruiting grounds for 60 per cent of the nearly 700,000 recruits who joined the Indian army in the First World War came from the Punjab. From that perspective, it is clear that military fiscalism was instrumental in perpetuating what Bayly has aptly termed 'archaic globalization'.[72] Military fiscalism helped to ossify social and economic relations and worked to frustrate indigenous economic developments on several levels.

****

By bringing the military into discussions about the nature of colonial rule, we not only appreciate better the imperatives that informed the actions and institutions of the colonial state, but come closer to reconciling the long-standing debate between historians as to the state's footprint upon Indian society. For some time, historians have been divided between those for whom the colonial state was omnipotent, single-minded, and intrusive, and those who have championed the notion of a 'Limited Raj'. For the former, colonial rule—whether it is measured materially or discursively—effected a sweeping transformation of Indian society, not only transforming its economic, political, and social structures, but inscribing upon India its own constructions of Indian cultural identities. The latter have instead posited a state that trod warily upon Indian society, not out of respect or admiration for India, but because they lacked the resources to enforce their will, and were apprehensive about the consequences of more forceful actions. The truth lies somewhere in between, and is predicated upon the kinds of paradoxes noted above, paradoxes that arose in large part because of the militarily inflected process of state formation in India. Few officials, even as late as 1947, would have quibbled with James Fitzjames Stephens's declaration in 1883 that British rule was 'essentially an absolute government, founded not on consent but on conquest'.[73]

---

[72] C. A. Bayly, '"Archaic" and "Modern" Globalization in the Eurasian and African Arena, c.1750–1850', in A. G. Hopkins (ed.), *Globalization in World History* (London, 2002).

[73] Rebuttal to the Ilbert Bill, published in *The Times* on 1 Mar. 1883.

It is within this world of Anglo-Indian militarism, and its manifestation in military fiscalism, that we can see most clearly that fundamental paradox of imperial rule—its ability to look simultaneously forwards and backwards. Military victories were signal proof of European superiority, confirmation that the British were destined to rule, yet explanations of such victories blended together the modern and anti-modern for success was frequently accounted for by invoking character traits that were rooted more in the past than in the present. And in their efforts to meet the financial demands of their army in India, the British yoked together modern instruments of financial management with regressive forms of revenue collection.

But in employing such concepts as military fiscalism and militarism, as well as the ideologies, institutions, and processes that defined each of them and the relationships that lay between them, we need to take care not to repeat—or even worse—reify some of the conventional juxtapositions that are invoked in efforts to map out their consequences for India as well as in drawing comparisons with other kinds of state formation. Some of the more common of these dualities include Indian versus British, colonial versus pre-colonial, and Western versus Eastern. Such oppositions ultimately contribute to the drawing of boundaries that in practice never existed or at least never in as stark a form as some historians have assumed. In particular, there is an implicit fascination with an alleged disjunction between the modern and the pre-modern, which is all too often simply a shorthand for the West versus the rest. Liberal historiography has always been distinctly uncomfortable with the military, believing that force was a last resort, only employed when other options had failed, and then only under strict civilian control. Societies deemed inferior or stalled along some universal evolutionary scale were the ones in which the military had not been brought under civilian control. A close reading of colonial rule explodes this simple juxtaposition, for in consolidating their grip on India, strategic imperatives entailed adjustments to local circumstances, at least insofar as they were understood by the British. The Marquis of Hastings, identified as a Whig prior to his departure for India, captured such sentiments when he reflected that 'the subjection of the military to the civil power is a most just principle, but in its application advertence must be made to local peculiarities'.[74]

---

[74] Hastings to William Elphinstone, 20 Mar. 1820, MSS Eur F89/2/A/1/4 (OIOC).

Select Bibliography

C. A. Bayly, *Empire and Information: Intelligence Gathering and Social Communication in India, 1780–1870* (Cambridge, 1996).

H. V. Bowen, *The Business of Empire: The East India Company and Imperial Britain, 1756–1833* (Cambridge, 2005).

Dipesh Chakrabarty, Rochona Majumdar, et al. (eds), *From the Colonial to the Postcolonial: India and Pakistan in Transition* (Delhi, 2007).

Frederick Cooper, *Colonialism in Question: Theory, Knowledge, History* (Berkeley, 2005).

Ayesha Jalal, *Democracy and Authoritarianism in South Asia* (Cambridge, 1995).

Sunil Khilnani, *The Idea of India* (London, 1997).

Uday Singh Mehta, *Liberalism and Empire: A Study in Nineteenth Century British Liberal Thought* (Chicago, 2000).

Thomas R. Metcalf, *Ideologies of the Raj* (The New Cambridge History of India, iii/4; Cambridge, 1994).

Barbara N. Ramusack, *The Indian Princes and Their States* (The New Cambridge History of India, iii/6; Cambridge, 2004).

Sudipta Sen, *Distant Sovereignty: National Imperialism and the Origins of British India* (London, 2002).

Burton Stein, *Thomas Munro: The Origins of the Colonial State and His Vision of Empire* (Delhi, 1989).

Eric Stokes, *The English Utilitarians and India* (Oxford, 1959).

Robert Travers, *Ideology and Empire in Eighteenth Century India: The British in Bengal* (Cambridge, 2007).

Jon Wilson, *The Domination of Strangers: Modern Governance in Eastern India, 1780–1835* (London, 2008).

3

The Indian Economy and the British Empire

David Washbrook

Very few historical debates have been as long term, as bitter, and quite as inconclusive as that concerning the fate of the Indian economy under British rule. Issues were first joined in the last third of the eighteenth century, at the very moment when the English East India Company was raising its flag over India. In virtually the first English-language history of the country, his *History of Hindostan* published in 1768, Alexander Dow launched a savage attack on the Company for ruining the economy of Bengal.[1] And, just eight years later, Adam Smith in his *Wealth and Poverty of Nations* portrayed the Company as a leading threat not only to the prosperity of India, but to that of Britain and the future of 'commercial society' in general.[2] Nor have the controversies died down very much since. The idea that Britain 'drained' India's wealth and despoiled its economy was basic to the Indian nationalist movement, which arose from the later nineteenth century, and subsequently informed both the economic policies which India's post-independence governments followed and the tenor of its national historiography.[3] In the present age of 'global history', colonial policies in relation to the devastating famines, which swept India in the later nineteenth century, have been subsumed into the comparative history of 'genocide'.[4]

---

[1] Alexander Dow, 'An Enquiry into the State of Bengal', prefixed to A. Dow (ed.), *A History of Hindostan . . . to the . . . Settlement of the Empire under Aurungzebe*, translated from the Persian of Muhammad Kasim Hindu Shah Frishta (London, 1768).

[2] Adam Smith, *An Inquiry into the Nature and Causes of the Wealth of Nations*, vol. ii of *The Glasgow Edition of the Works and Correspondence of Adam Smith*, gen. eds R. H. Campbell and A. S. Skinner (Indianapolis, 1981).

[3] G. Balachandran, *India and the World Economy 1850–1950* (Delhi, 2003).

[4] Mike Davis, *Late Victorian Holocausts: El Nino Famines and the Making of the Third World* (London, 2001).

Yet, while it has rarely been easy to generate enthusiasm about its successes, British rule has also never wanted for those prepared to defend its economic record and to look elsewhere for the sources of India's poverty. Early Company officials, from Philip Francis to Thomas Munro, claimed to be struggling to restore a Golden Age of prosperity and plenty, which had been brought to ruin *previously* by civil war and 'Islamic tyranny'. Later, social theorists as diverse as John Stuart Mill and Karl Marx could at least credit Britain with having laid the institutional foundations for modern economic growth—even if very little seemed to come of them. And their views would find echo, down the years, in the interpretations of liberal economic historians, such as Morris David Morris and Tirthankar Roy.[5] In these days of 'neo-conservative' global agendas and a new imperialism, some historians, such as Niall Ferguson, have even begun to offer the British empire's guardianship of the Indian economy as a model for the present.[6]

The battle has been relentless and shows no signs of calming down. But, as perhaps in all historiographical battles so clearly involving strong political sensitivities, it may also have generated more heat than light. Even the most basic issues of empirical fact—population levels, GDP growth, per capita incomes—remain subject to frenzied dispute, especially for the first century of British rule when, it might be thought, the available data are too fragile to withstand the grandiose theoretical constructions often put upon them.[7] From the second half of the nineteenth century, at least, the sources of evidence become firmer—although still very inadequate by modern standards. But the potential gulfs in interpretation between proponents of competing economic theories become all the wider. Indeed, this last feature is particularly striking and a crucial reason, perhaps, why the debate has proved so intractable. The 'perverse' economic history of India over the last two hundred years—which, from some angles, moved from prosperity to poverty—stands as a direct challenge to most of the classical theories of the development of capitalism and the progress of modernity. This marks out the debate as exceptionally important. But it also indicates that there has always been much more than 'history' at stake in it. After two hundred years, it is still very difficult to offer even a basic narrative of what might

---

[5] Morris D. Morris (ed.), *The Indian Economy in the Nineteenth Century: A Symposium* (Delhi, 1969); Tirthankar Roy, *The Economic History of India 1857–1947* (Delhi, 2000).

[6] Niall Ferguson, *Empire: How Britain Made the Modern World* (London, 2003).

[7] Morris (ed.), *Indian Economy*.

have happened to the Indian economy across this period, which is not immediately at risk of being shot down by one or other side—and, sometimes, by both at the same time although for different reasons.

To begin at the beginning: plainly, the nature of the Indian economy (or, perhaps, of the several regional economies comprising South Asia) at the point of the colonial conquest is crucial to understanding subsequent change. It is indisputable that parts of it had been heavily involved in international trade for centuries, were highly monetized and constituted centres of textile manufacture of world significance. But, as generations of historians as diverse as Marx, W. H. Moreland, and Irfan Habib have queried, was it nonetheless groaning under the political weight of a rapacious 'Oriental Despotism' and with few 'potentialities' for future development?[8] Or was India, as Adam Smith had it, almost at the same stage in the development of 'universal civilization' (capitalism) as Britain itself?[9] And, as many 'revisionist' historians of early modern Eurasia writing in the last twenty years would argue, still expansive, showing signs of innovation and accumulation and proving remarkably resistant to whatever forces of oppression were thrown against it?[10]

What happened to this economy over the first half of the nineteenth century, before the impact of the new technologies of railways and steam-shipping became visible, also is represented between the widest parameters of interpretation. Plainly, India's manufacturing industry was squeezed by the loss of overseas, and some elite domestic, markets to the products of Britain's Industrial Revolution. Manufactured exports dwindled: leaving, by the 1830s and 1840s, opium as one of the country's few internationally saleable products, responsible for upwards of 40 per cent of foreign earnings.[11] But, given the inevitable preponderance of agriculture, did this reflect a minor contraction and redeployment of manufacturing skills to service non-elite domestic markets unreachable (by the available means of

---

[8] Irfan Habib, 'Potentialities of Capitalist Development in the Economy of Mughal India', *Enquiry* (Winter, 1971); W. H. Moreland, *From Akbar to Aurangzeb: A Study in Indian Economic History* (London, 1923).

[9] Smith, *Wealth of Nations*, esp. bk II.

[10] D. A.Washbrook, 'Progress and Problems: South Asian Social and Economic History, c.1720–1860', *Modern Asian Studies*, 22 (1988), 57–96.

[11] K. N. Chaudhuri, *The Economic Development of India under the East India Company, 1814–1858: A Selection of Contemporary Documents* (Cambridge, 1971), introd.

transport) to Britain's new industrial products? Or did it represent huge forces of 'de-urbanization' and 'de-industrialization', driving a far larger proportion of India's workforce onto the land and into petty commodity production than ever before? Certainly, the fragments of evidence that we have suggest that the frontier of land cultivation moved ahead very rapidly in these years. However, other evidence (albeit no less fragmentary) also suggests that it was accompanied by a substantial increase in population.[12] But how could such a population increase be sustained in the context of what looks, in every other respect, to have been a period of acute economic crisis? And should the contraction of India's 'traditional' artisanal industries, rendered obsolete by the rise of superior technologies elsewhere, be greeted as an unequivocal 'loss'? Or should it be seen as the occasion for the Indian economy to 'restructure' itself in order better to fit into an expanding world economy: where investment in agriculture, in which India had competitive advantages, would bring greater means to consume manufactures brought from abroad, which were cheaper and of higher quality than any its 'old' industry could have produced?

The questions—and paradoxes—remain as complex for the economic history of the next one hundred years. From the middle of the nineteenth century, the new transport technologies made their impact and a period of steady 'expansion' set in, encouraged by the free trade policies of the British empire, which lasted up to the First World War. Cash cropping for overseas markets—in wheat, cotton, and oil-seeds—now took off. But so too did the reciprocal opening-up of India as a major market for 'foreign' industrial manufactures.[13] A frontier for the expansion of Indian capital and labour abroad, especially around the Indian Ocean littoral, also developed, helping to offset signs of environmental constraint which were beginning to appear within the country itself. Towards the end of the nineteenth century, 'modern' forms of industry arrived albeit slowly and in a few limited areas. Better sources of data have allowed economic historians at least to

---

[12] Dharma Kumar, *Land and Caste in South India: Agricultural Labour in the Madras Presidency in the Nineteenth Century* (Cambridge, 1965); Sumit Guha, *Health and Population in South Asia: From the Earliest Times to the Present* (London, 2001).

[13] B. R. Tomlinson, *The Economy of Modern India, 1860–1970* (Cambridge, 1993); Tirthankar Roy, *Economic History*.

hazard guesses at rates of increase in per capita income at this time: where growth of between 0.75 per cent and 1.25 per cent a year would seem the most accepted (or least disputed) figure.[14]

But even this may have been achieved only at a considerable cost to some Indians. Per capita income growth was sustained by a downturn in India's rate of population increase in the later nineteenth century, caused by rampant epidemic disease and a series of devastating famines.[15] The 'positive' number, which it purports to represent, was achieved in part at the 'negative' price of human catastrophe. Moreover, why should devastating famines have punctuated India's development in the one era of British rule marked by relative economic prosperity? And why should high value-added forms of modern industrialization have taken so long to emerge and have been so small in scale?

But, at least, there is evidence of growth in this period. In the interwar years, per capita incomes may have fallen by up to 15 per cent as the world economy contracted and India lost many of its overseas markets for agricultural products. Also, ecological constraints began to produce a general downturn in food crop yields.[16] To add to the problems, the population surged upwards once more—at least recovering, and probably surpassing, its rates of growth in the early nineteenth century. But, ironically, Indian industry prospered and advanced at an ever more rapid rate—although nowhere near fast enough to compensate, in the short term, for the crisis of the agrarian economy. During the Second World War, of course, all sectors of the economy enjoyed considerable expansion, urged on by the war effort. But the strains attendant upon faster growth also showed themselves in the Bengal Famine of 1943 and in a general crisis of food supply, which necessitated state intervention in the food market on a regular basis for the first time since the early nineteenth century.[17]

When the British finally 'quit' India in 1947, they left behind a society in which life expectancy was 26.6 years, 90 per cent of the population was rural,

---

[14] Alan Heston, 'National Income', in Dharma Kumar (ed.), *Cambridge Economic History of India*, ii (Cambridge, 1983).

[15] Leela Vasaria and Praveen Vasaria, 'Population', in Kumar (ed.), *Cambridge History*, ii.

[16] George Blyn, *Agricultural Trends in India 1891–1947: Output, Availability and Productivity* (Philadelphia, 1966).

[17] Amartya Sen, *Poverty and Famines: An Essay on Entitlement and Deprivation* (Oxford, 1981); Christopher Baker, *An Indian Rural Economy 1880–1955: The Tamilnad Countryside* (Oxford, 1984).

and 55 per cent of it lived below the international poverty line.[18] But, also, three times more human beings subsisted in South Asia than when they had first taken power; the basic technologies of modernity, including the second largest railway network in the world, had been established; and, not least, a series of disparate regional economies—once sprawled across an area larger than Western Europe—had been integrated into a single national market with significant opportunities for future development in the modern world. Do these represent achievements to be deprecated or applauded?

More particularly, what explains the peculiar twists and turns, paradoxes and contradictions, which we have seen in trying to provide even a basic narrative of events? Perhaps the most celebrated formula of critics of 'British' India over the last one hundred years has been the idea of a 'drain' of wealth, which enriched Britain while removing from India resources which might have been used to drive forward its own 'modernization'. And it is beyond question that Britain, at all times, drew a surplus from India, which played a crucial strategic role in its own economic growth: during the Napoleonic Wars, following the deterioration of its trading position between the 1870s and the First World War, and during the crisis of the interwar Depression, this surplus was important in preserving Britain's own economic stability.[19] But while the 'drain' undoubtedly helps to explain Britain's own remarkable economic 'development', there have always remained questions about how far it really explains India's 'underdevelopment'. It would take a pre-Smithian understanding of economics to suppose that, because one party in a bilateral transaction makes a profit, the other must necessarily be making a loss. A difficult issue long haunting the 'drain' debate has been how much of Britain's surplus represented 'legitimate' payments for services provided to India, which promoted the latter's growth and could not have been obtained elsewhere as cheaply. A second issue has been posed by the question of whether, had more surplus been retained in India, it would have been used to realize a greater investment 'potential' rather than being 'wasted' on luxury consumption, as was so much of the country's residual wealth. But a third, and perhaps more fundamental, question has come up in recent years as means of econometric measurement have improved: was the 'drain' ever large enough

---

[18] R. Gopalaswami, *Census of India 1951*, i. *Demographic Tables* (Delhi, 1954).
[19] Balachandran, *World Economy*.

to represent a significant agent of transformation in the trajectory of the Indian economy at all?

In the most careful of recent considerations, G. Balachandran has estimated that it cannot be calculated at more than the equivalent of 1–1.5 per cent of India's GDP—a substantial amount but hardly the difference between a transition from 'tradition' to 'modernity'.[20] Even more strikingly, Angus Maddison has shown that, relative to their GDP(s), the direct flow of resources from India to Britain was extremely low by the comparative standards of other contemporary colonial empires: for example, representing only one-tenth the flow between Java and the Netherlands.[21] And, while his statistics may no doubt be disputed, their point gains force from the views of hosts of economically active Britons during the Age of Empire itself. Consistently throughout the history of British India, heavy criticism was launched by British economists and businessmen at the constraints posed to possibilities of British trade, investment, and settlement in India, especially by the policies of the colonial state itself.[22] As it were, large sections of British economic enterprise felt themselves unable to create the relations necessary to 'drain' enough profit out of India, whose economic performance under colonial rule was widely held a disappointment in the metropolis.

But if a large section of British economic society was consistently frustrated at its inability to 'exploit' India, it seems hard to account for the latter's economic history largely in terms of the effects of that 'exploitation'. And no less difficult to conceive it as providing the principal reason why Britain conquered—or, at least, held—India in the first place. The final paradox thrown up by the 'economic' history of 'British India' must be doubts that British imperial purposes were ever principally—or, at least, in a direct bilateral sense—economic in intent. Yet, if not, then the underlying research agendas informing two hundred years of colonial economic history may rest upon false premises; and it may be necessary to look to other areas to explain the economic outcomes which flowed from the British conquest of India.

---

[20] Balachandran, *World Economy*, introd.
[21] Angus Maddison, 'Dutch Income from Indonesia, 1700–1939', *Modern Asian Studies*, 23/4 (1989), 645–70.
[22] Chaudhuri, *Economic Development*.

Economic Implications of Company Rule

The first of these other areas must be the character of the colonial state itself, whose policies—at least from the early nineteenth century—can sometimes appear optimally designed to suppress economic activity whether undertaken by Indians or the great majority of Britons. After the abandonment of early experiments with a Permanent Settlement, aimed specifically at restricting taxation and stimulating capital accumulation, the East India Company government from the 1810s opted for policies of revenue maximization in most of its territories outside Greater Bengal. These policies were pursued relentlessly and, between the 1820s and 1850s, in the face of a withering price depression, which increased their burden since they were collected in cash.[23] They marked the second half-century of British rule in India with a 'revenue offensive' which, in the Permanently Settled areas, was matched by a 'rental offensive' conducted by the new Indian landlord class and having much the same effect.[24]

This was not least because these policies were accompanied by an investment strategy, whose regressive implications were no less palpable. While, as we shall see, state-directed investment in public resources in India may never have been high, it can hardly ever have been lower than in the years leading up to the 1840s. The government of Madras, for example, spent less than 0.5 per cent of its revenues on the maintenance of irrigation works. Moreover, it even attacked principles of 'private' investment on the land—disallowing large numbers of *inams* (tax immunities), which had been granted under previous regimes for constructing irrigation works.[25] To queries about the apparently regressive nature of its revenue policies, it also formulated a remarkable (and, as we shall see, fallacious) economic sociology of India: supposing it to consist of a society of static and self-reproducing 'village communities', which could yield—and, so it was claimed, always had yielded—the bulk of their surplus to their rulers without serious consequence to their internal mechanisms of reproduction.[26]

---

[23] C. A. Bayly, *Indian Society and the Making of the British Empire* (Cambridge, 1988).
[24] Sugata Bose, *Agrarian Bengal: Economy, Social Structure and Politics 1919–1947* (Cambridge, 1986).
[25] Nilmani Mukherjee, *The Ryotwari System in Madras, 1792–1827* (Calcutta, 1962).
[26] Eric Stokes, *The English Utilitarians and India* (Oxford, 1959).

Nor were the Company's trade policies of a much different stripe. It was a ruthless monopolist, laying claim to 'sovereign' rights over many of the valuable commercial trades in India—opium, salt, betel, alcohol—and, until 1830, using its state powers to enforce quasi-monopolies in other areas, such as textile manufacture. Moreover, then—facing dwindling returns, risky overseas markets and pressures from home—it precipitously abandoned these market positions, causing chaos in the monetary system where the products involved had been crucial to general processes of cash exchange.[27] But concern for the condition of the monetary economy was never very high on the Company's list of priorities: in spite of declining inflows of specie, occasioned by the contraction of India's overseas trade, it continued to export Indian silver to meet its trading needs in China, greatly contributing to the Indian price depression.[28]

Equally, it showed scant regard for the general economic interests of any wider British community. It early set itself against large-scale British settlement and, after parliament removed its rights to exclude British subjects at will, still retained strong prerogatives to deport any deemed to be acting against 'British' interests as judged by itself. It also heavily restricted the ability of Britons to acquire land rights—outside the towns or the remote hill-stations—and progressively disinterred the rights which they previously had enjoyed to gain liens on the revenues or to farm monopolies. Its elaboration of an ideology sharply distinguishing between 'public' and 'private' rights hit against the private rights of Britons as much as Indians. Further, it resisted attempts by parliament to reduce its wider monopolies over bi- and multilateral trade (especially with China) and, although formally losing these rights in 1813 and 1833 respectively, clung onto their substance for very much longer. Control over the land revenues and over 'sovereign' monopolies on key products left the greater part of India's commercial and financial systems in its hands, deep into the supposed age of 'free trade'; and the principal item of trade taken to China by 'private' British traders was opium, produced under Company licence.

The hopes that many in Britain had expressed at the time that the Company's frontier of conquest was moving forward, that an era of enlarged trade and prosperity was about to dawn, were thoroughly dashed by the

---

[27] Kumar, *Land and Caste.*
[28] Asiya Siddiqi, *Agrarian Change in a North Indian State: Uttar Pradesh, 1819–1833* (Oxford, 1973).

second quarter of the nineteenth century. After initial growth to 1820, British exports to India stagnated until the 1840s[29] and opportunities to make direct investments, other than in the hills, even diminished in a context of swingeing depression. Restlessness in parliament with the Company's management of the Indian economy increased apace: its twenty-year Charter renewals becoming the occasion for bitter recriminations and demands for reform. Some reforms were, indeed, implemented: with pressures on the Company to increase its levels of capital investment, especially in irrigation, as the price for renewing the Charter in 1833. But unease continued to grow, necessitating significant, if belated, changes in several of its policies—less regressive landlord/tenant laws in Bengal, a 'new' *ryotwari* system and *inam* settlement in Madras—as the Charter renewal of 1853 approached. But, finally, even these reforms failed to satisfy parliament, which actually refused to renew the Charter: leaving the Company an incongruous and illegal organization for the last five years of its life before it was displaced by direct Crown rule in 1858.

Several key questions are raised by the economic policies of the Company: why should it have followed such regressive strategies; and why, given that so many British (not to mention Indian) business interests failed to benefit from it, should British parliaments have let it do so for so long? Familiarly, in critiques of imperialism from Adam Smith to J. H. Hobson, it has been held that monopolies, while denying benefits to the majority, provide super-profits to a few who sustain their position by political 'corruption'. And, certainly in Smith's day, this cannot be disputed in India's case. The early years of the Company's expansion saw huge fortunes laid up by the few Britons who were involved in the process and who exercised a strong influence in an 'unreformed' parliament.[30] But, from the turn of the nineteenth century, the number of direct beneficiaries from a Company India, now turning towards stagnation and depression, becomes harder to assess. Of course, at its highest levels, the Company was dependent on British banks and merchant houses to sustain its fiscal system and these gained enhanced opportunities for profit as its early relationships with Indian banking houses were progressively discarded. But association with the Company also became more hazardous as India's foreign trade declined:

---

[29] Chaudhuri, *Economic Development*.

[30] P. J. Marshall, *East India Fortunes: The British in Bengal in the Eighteenth Century* (Oxford, 1976).

witness the financial devastation caused by the 'indigo crisis' of the late 1820s and the Calcutta banking collapse of the 1840s. Further, it was clearly becoming more difficult to sustain 'private' influence over 'public' affairs as attacks were launched on 'old corruption', both in India, under Cornwallis's reforms, and in Britain, as parliament lurched—albeit uncertainly— towards reform. No doubt the 'new', more professional Company bureaucracy did well out of the transition, paying itself salaries on a previously Indian royal scale.[31] But, much though the reverse often seems the case, bureaucracies are rarely permitted to run governments entirely for their own benefit. The logic of the Company's economic policies in this era—and, no less, the willingness of 'political Britain' to put up with them—remains mysterious.

But the mystery may start to clear if attention is turned to what the Company was spending its heavy revenues on and to the implications of its policies outside India. The highly aggressive revenue strategies of the period reflected efforts to maintain the huge military machine, which the Company had built up in the course of its conquests, long after it had consolidated its position as the dominant power within India.[32] This machine was used continuously to expand the frontiers of 'British India' towards the northwest (Sindh, Punjab, and Afghanistan); and also to advance overseas, supporting Nelson's fleet in Egypt as early as 1799 and then shifting towards South East Asia (Sri Lanka in 1796, Java in 1811, Singapore in 1819, Burma in 1824) and onto Canton in 1839. Indian military power became the quintessential complement to British naval power in building the British empire east of the Mediterranean, creating opportunities for British trade, investment, and profit which would collectively outweigh anything to be obtained bilaterally from India itself.[33]

In effect, India became the crucial pivot in a multilateral system of imperial economy and force: supplying not only soldiers but also key items of commodity trade (opium, cotton) and labour to support an empire which, otherwise, Britain—from its tiny island base off north-west Europe—would scarcely have been able to maintain. Indian revenues paid

---

[31] C. A. Bayly, *Imperial Meridian: The British Empire and the World 1780–1830* (London, 1989).

[32] Douglas M. Peers, *Between Mars and Mammon: Colonial Armies and the Garrison State in India, 1819–1835* (London, 1995).

[33] A. K. Bagchi, 'The Other Side of Foreign Investment by Imperial Powers: Transfer of Surplus from Colonies', *Economic and Political Weekly*, 37/28 (2002), 2229–38.

for the army; Indian monopolies supplied the trade goods; and, ultimately, Indian personnel and expertise (in commerce and administration) compensated for the difficulties and costs of keeping 'white men' in the tropics. The Company's economic strategies were very much geared to the development of this wider system. Aggressive and regressive taxation systems in India might deny resources for productive investment and, where the bulk of revenues was spent on the military, sap other forms of consumption. But they supplied the means to keep the external frontier rolling forward and to guarantee social order and 'business as usual' behind it. If problems arose within India, they, too, were to be met by looking overseas: the Company's principal response to 'de-industrialization' was to promote emigration abroad; and, in the depression of the 1820s to 1850s, to seek new means of 'vent' in foreign markets. The Indian economy was progressively less valued for any potential of its own and was governed in ways which would make that potential ever more difficult to realize. But it serviced valuable 'global' interests and, as these grew more considerable, it cannot be held surprising that—whatever the economic disappointments inside India—British parliaments should have been reluctant to dispose of the Company's government entirely for all that they criticized and resented its Indian performance. Nor, in many senses, did they ever do so. For, even after the abolition of the Company and the transition to Crown rule, the basic orientation of British Indian economic policy remained much the same albeit subject to new imperatives as the century advanced.

Contradictions of Colonial Development

From the 1850s, in the wake of the transport revolution, the long depression over the Indian economy lifted and new opportunities for export cash-cropping burgeoned in many areas. The recovery also lifted prices, which rose steadily until the First World War. In turn, this reduced the real weight of the land revenue demand and restored opportunities for capital investment. The colonial state increased its own levels of investment (especially in irrigation) and also encouraged greater private participation in the Indian capital market, especially via railway construction. Eventually, the more buoyant economic conditions began to stimulate industrialization.

Nonetheless, the colonial state's principal interests continued to lie in meeting the needs of the military and the expansion of overseas commerce; and its domestic Indian policies were, in many ways, inflected towards these goals to the detriment of opportunities for capital in India, not just indigenous but British too. The military budget (especially if increasing government debt incurred for military reasons is included) still absorbed the great bulk of revenues, and attempts were made to compensate for the loss of the real value of land revenues by imposing increasing imposts on the sources of reviving trade. Military (and debt) expenditures left very few resources for anything else and irrigation policy was placed in a tight straitjacket: with the exception of Punjab which—as the main recruiting ground of the post-Mutiny army—enjoyed a lavish patronage. Otherwise only schemes which would bring an instant increase in revenue yields were supported. Even the railways—by far the largest capital investment project undertaken in British India—were designed to serve the ends of defence and foreign trade: their main routes were laid out, after the Mutiny, to improve military security and to move goods to and from the ports. Industry, when it first began to arise, shared the latter orientation.[34] The first spinning mills served the China trade and Calcutta's jute factories manufactured sacking for global markets. Also, the colonial state began ever more actively to promote the export of Indian labour skills and even that of rare resources of indigenous capital. Between the 1850s and 1914, more than 2 million people left the shores of India to work not only as labourers, but as clerks, policemen, and market sellers in British imperial economies as far distant as the Caribbean; and Indian capital, especially via the Nattukkottai Chetty bankers of the south, became heavily involved in the opening of Burma.[35]

By contrast, in India, the colonial state appears at times to have set its face against a faster pace of transformation wrought by the expansion of the world economy. Where cash-crop markets and mechanisms of credit and debt began to threaten social transitions, it was quick to try and stop them—widely passing tenancy and indebtedness Acts to keep the peasantry on the land. After the Indian Mutiny, it became haunted by fears of agrarian revolt, which would tie down its international army in India and render the maintenance of its rule more difficult.[36] Equally, it gave precious little encouragement to the growth of any industry aimed at serving domestic

---

[34] Daniel Thorner (ed.), *Investment in Empire: British Railway and Steamshipping Enterprise in India, 1825–1849* (Philadelphia, 1950).

[35] Hugh Tinker, *The Banyan Tree: Overseas Emigrants from India, Pakistan and Bangladesh* (Oxford, 1977).

[36] D. A. Washbrook, 'Law, State and Agrarian Society in Colonial India', *Modern Asian Studies*, 15 (1981), 649–721.

markets: either by redirecting its purchasing policies or by setting up tariff protections or by deepening the modern banking system (which was entirely export-oriented). If domestic industry did develop in colonial India, it would be the result of anything but inducement by the colonial state.

This last feature, of course, has conventionally been understood in terms of the colonial state maximally helping British manufacturers exporting to India. The transport revolution had finally opened up India as a mass market for British industrial goods and the attenuation of India's own industrialization would serve to keep it so. Also, as Amiya Bagchi has argued, British 'free trade' could easily be overestimated even in this era: via various forms of racial and national prejudice, as well as residual corruption, the local agencies of the colonial state continued to favour certain British businessmen at the expense of potential Indian rivals. This created unofficial forms of monopoly, limiting the general development of resources: in terms of potential factor allocation, India might easily have had steel, coal, and other major industries much earlier than it eventually did and producing at lower costs than Britain's own.[37]

That British economic policy in India should have been influenced by the likes of the Lancashire textile lobby and should have involved collusive practices between public and private agencies cannot, of course, be denied. But, importantly, these policies and practices did not only discriminate against rival Indian entrepreneurs. They also effectively cut out large sections of British business and capital from 'exploiting' India. India may have become a vital market for certain sections of British industry, especially those associated with the first phases of industrialization such as (ironically) cotton textiles. But it very much did not for many others, such as machine tools or other more sophisticated products generated out of the secondary phases of industrialization. Such products required markets based on higher incomes and rates of growth than could be found in India. From the 1880s, these sectors of industry (famously from Birmingham, the home of the British machine tool industry and of Joseph Chamberlain) launched an increasingly vehement attack on Britain's empire of 'free trade', with India at its pivot, and demanded policies of imperial protection, which would boost industrial investment throughout the empire. 'Birmingham' strongly vied with 'Lancashire' to be the dominant voice over British

---

[37] A. K. Bagchi, *Private Investment in India 1900–1939* (Cambridge, 1972).

imperial policy, offering visions of a very different kind of empire for the industrial age.[38]

Of course, the 'Birmingham' lobby did not win the political debate at the time and imperial protectionism was delayed until after the First World War. But the general point that it was seeking to make might be held exemplified by Britain's economic relationship with India over the twenty-five years leading up to that cataclysm. India might have been Britain's most important market for textile exports but, as the axis of the world economy shifted from trade to investment, its overall importance to Britain's external economy declined. Apart from the railways, very little private British capital was ever invested there. The 'potential' of India's iron, steel, and other industries went a-begging and, between 1890 (when the main stage of railway construction was completed) and 1914, the proportion of total British overseas capital invested in India fell sharply from 19 per cent to 10 per cent.[39] Perversely, while few imperial Britons in 1914 would have denied that India was the jewel in their crown, this was very much not because of the profits earned directly from it. India's relative economic stagnation in the 'golden age' of the world economy before 1914 marked out how far its own development was being sacrificed to providing military power and promoting economic growth in other parts of Britain's empire.

After the First World War, this necessarily changed—with the contraction of the global economy, which India had been serving, and of British military power. In the 1920s and 1930s, the colonial state made desperate efforts to alter its historic orientation: conceiving a discourse of Indian development; introducing tariff protections for imperial industries; and even proclaiming itself to have an 'Industrial Policy'. The nature of Britain's economic relationship with India showed signs of changing as the (albeit small) amounts of British capital locked up in the old colonial trades began to disperse (or to be taken over by Indians) and new inflows of industrial investment (most famously, by Lever Brothers) started to arrive.[40] But the adverse economic circumstances of the times, as well as the rise of an increasingly vociferous

---

[38] E. H. H. Green, *The Crisis of Conservatism: The Politics, Economics and Ideology of the Conservative Party 1880–1914; Trade and Empire* (London, 1995).

[39] S. B. Saul, *British Overseas Trade, 1870–1914* (Liverpool, 1960).

[40] B. R. Tomlinson, *The Political Economy of the Raj 1914–1947: The Economics of Decolonization in India* (London, 1979).

Indian national movement, brought out new contradictions. As the global economy crashed around their ears, 'India' and 'Britain' turned in on themselves, becoming more truly 'national' economies, whose complementarities were increasingly limited and whose rivalries became more pronounced. The colonial state experienced growing difficulties in holding them together and in hiding its ultimate metropolitan biases. In particular, the protracted negotiations to set a tariff regime capable of serving the interests of both British and Indian industry revealed how far those interests were becoming divergent. With the demise of Britain's once multilateral free trading empire, the colonial 'game' was up in India (at least economically) even before the Second World War made decolonization inevitable.

Crisis of the Indian Economy in the Early Nineteenth Century

But if, from the time of the conquest, the British colonial state had abandoned more than a peripheral interest in the domestic development of the Indian economy—and had looked outwards and towards international military power for its purposes—why should this have been so? And, given that state policies do not entirely determine the course of economic histories, what difference might this have made to India's possible history, to its alternative trajectory of development? Looking back to the circumstances of the Company's rise to power, answers to the first question are not self-evident. Long-standing tendencies in 'Western' history and social science to depreciate the pre-colonial economies of South Asia have usually been rooted in attempts to assess their 'futures' and 'potentialities' for further capitalist development. But very few comparisons of them with other economies in their own times have found them so wanting. Paul Bairoch, for example, has estimated that, as late as 1750, South Asia still possessed 28 per cent of the world's total manufacturing capacity.[41] In addition to a world-dominant position in the manufacture of textiles, it also sustained a wide range of other, high-quality artisanal industries. The occasional glimpses which we have of its agricultural systems suggest that they were capable of generating crop yields equivalent to the best in the world and living standards (at least for skilled workers) as high than those in, say,

---

[41] Paul Bairoch, 'International Industrialization Levels from 1750 to 1980', *Journal of European Economic History*, 11 (Fall 1982), 269–325.

contemporary Britain.[42] What led the emergent Company state to throw away the advantages which might have come from closer cultivation of its valuable new Indian assets? The question is even more teasing because there were signs of an alternative. Had the path to future development laid out in Cornwallis's Bengal Permanent Settlement of the early 1790s been followed, the colonial state might have had a very different economic orientation: military authority would then have been definitively subordinated to civil politics; taxation rates would have been restrained to promote capital investment; a strict barrier would have been set to territorial expansion.

That this did not happen can, perhaps, be put down to the eventual intertwining of two different strands of historical logic. One of these arose out of the circumstances of the Company's conquest. In the first place, it was by origin a maritime agency whose first claims to political hegemony were established at sea. South Asian economies critically depended on inflows of specie metal (of which they produced little) deriving from overseas trade. Aggressive naval strategies, which were little contested by South Asia land-based powers, gave Europeans preponderant influence over the Indian Ocean from as early as the seventeenth century, which eventually turned into British naval dominance by the late eighteenth. The Company was able to exert a stranglehold over many of the regional economies of South Asia by controlling their access to markets and money overseas.

And, second, economic power became converted to political power as it connected with new processes of state formation then taking place inland. There is much to suggest that the Mughal empire itself generated forms of 'military fiscalism' as it sought to tap economic expansion in order to build an overbearing military machine. But such tendencies were developed to new heights under the successor regional states, which contested power after the beginnings of its demise at the turn of the eighteenth century. As Christopher Bayly has argued, these states elaborated new systems of taxation and monopoly—bringing them into closer relationship with long-established networks of commerce—to pay for new and more expensive technologies of warfare.[43] The Company supplied them with both military

---

[42] Prasannan Parthasarathi, *The Transition to a Colonial Economy: Weaving, Merchants and Kings in South India 1720–1800* (Cambridge, 2001).

[43] C. A. Bayly, *Rulers, Townsmen and Bazaars: North Indian Society in the Age of British Expansion, 1770–1870* (Cambridge, 1983).

and commercial services, giving it a growing position of influence, which it eventually used to subvert and conquer them.

The Company rose to power in India, then, as an organization designed to look overseas and absorptive of the military fiscalist capacities of the indigenous states which it swallowed. Moreover, it also rose in a world political context which could hardly have been better guaranteed to strengthen these tendencies. From 1792, Britain's century-long struggle with France reached its apogee in the Revolutionary and Napoleonic Wars, which lasted for twenty-five years and, as their implications stretched from Java to the New World, became the first truly 'global' wars. Whatever hopes Cornwallis might have had, as he reached Calcutta in 1789, that he could set the Company's Bengal colony on a path to peace, prosperity, and progress modelled on an (albeit very narrow) vision of English domestic experience, were soon thereafter to be dashed. India emerged in 1815 at the fulcrum of an expanding global system of military and commercial power, which would secure British world supremacy for the next half-century. The Indian colonial state would service these wider imperial military and commercial needs, which became more important to Britain than anything which bilateral connections to the Indian economy might yield.

This course can be seen to have been further assured by the cross-cutting of another strand of historical logic. From the turn of the nineteenth century, many of the regional economies of South Asia began to decline and to start their own precipitous journey towards 'de-industrialization'. The most common cause of this has been seen in the impact of Britain's own Industrial Revolution, which began to take markets away from South Asia's textile industries. But it is possible to think that there must have been much more to the problem. On the one hand, while export markets were certainly lost, poor transport conditions made it very difficult for British manufactures to reach more than a few elite markets within India. Why should this promote what, by most accounts, was a very severe shift in economic orientation onto the land and away from industry? Moreover, why should it not have elicited a more obvious response from within the Indian textile industry itself? Faced now with competition from a new and superior technology, the most obvious response of South Asian textile manufacturers might seem to be that of adopting this technology for themselves. And, looking at the circumstances of their industry in the eighteenth century, it is not clear why they should not have done so. Mercantile capital and entrepreneurial expertise abounded; there was already a highly skilled workforce; most importantly, cotton actually grew in India, which it did not in Britain. From many angles, it appears absurd that Britain's Industrial Revolution should have been based so much on the manufacture of a fibre which it could not produce and in whose handling it was previously known to be inept.

But, in fact, there seems precious little evidence of any such attempted response by Indians or the 'new' imperial Britons. As early as the 1770s, the Company had tried to introduce then-modern methods of silk manufacture into Bengal (albeit that they failed). However, now, even the attempt appears lacking and India let a crucial opportunity to enter the 'new' world economy at a much higher level in the value-added chain than agriculture go a-begging for half a century. If the exact circumstances of the period are examined, however, they do suggest an explanation—if only one which then needs further explaining. As noted earlier, from the 1820s the economy began to spiral into a price depression, which lasted for nearly thirty years. Very few entrepreneurs have ever been known to risk heavy investments, not least in a new technology, in the middle of a depression. But what caused the Indian depression and why did it last so long? Again, the impact of the British Industrial Revolution on the world economy may provide part of the answer: it reduced price levels in a wide range of commodities across the globe. Yet very few depressions in the rest of the world were as deep or as long lasting as that in India.

The problem may partly be resolved by looking at the domestic economic consequences of the political settlement following the colonial conquest, which had a crushing impact on Indian sources of demand. Although we have no way of measuring it, consumer demand within India must always have been many times greater than that provided by external trade (for all the latter's strategic importance in attracting specie).[44] During the eighteenth century, such demand substantially increased: swelled by the proliferating regional courts and armies of the period and articulated by an expansion of commercial networks as military fiscalism brought more closely together the functions of trade and government, generating a series of great banking houses. But the consequences of the Company's rise to power largely reversed these trends. On the one hand, as it bureaucratized the state, it separated government and commercial functions—at least for

---

[44] Sushil Chaudhury, *From Prosperity to Decline: Eighteenth-Century Bengal* (Delhi, 1995).

Indian bankers—and disorganized indigenous institutions of capital. On the other, as it consolidated its political hegemony, it dismantled many of the regional courts and armies: commanding, literally, soldiers and courtiers to beat their swords into plough-shares, and confiscating their means of consumption. While it spent a lavish patronage of its own, this was never likely to compensate for the lost sources of demand. An important part of its revenues was spent abroad; and, while British officers and officials might pay themselves on a Mughal scale, they did not have the same tastes in indigenous fashions and goods.[45]

The deep depression of the 1820s to 1850s, then, was created not only by changes in the world economy outside India, but also by the economic consequences of the Company's seizure of power within it. Industrial investment, again, is never likely to flourish in economies with weak financial mechanisms and an absence of local markets to serve. India's chance to occupy a higher place in the modern world economy's value-added hierarchy disappeared with the reduction of its indigenous banking systems and the dwindling of its consuming classes. In the context of domestic economic collapse, the Company's decision to utilize it as the base for outward military and commercial expansion was now more or less made for it.

Indeed, India's low profile of domestic consumption can be seen to provide important clues not only to why it struggled (except as a drugs-supplier) in the world economy of the second quarter of the nineteenth century, but also to why it failed to rise above any but the lowliest position over the next hundred years. The prodigious increase in cultivation in the first half of the nineteenth century was driven much more by subsistence need than the pursuit of commercial profit: where the prices of agricultural commodities (with a few exceptions like opium) were falling. Agriculture provided the only alternative (other than emigration) to the sources of employment being lost not only in industry, but in a vast array of 'services' once consumed by India's political elites and disparaged by their British successors. 'Peasantization' became the social theme of the day as an increasing proportion of the workforce moved out onto the land and into petty commodity production. Surveys from the eighteenth century suggest that no more than 60–65 per cent of the workforce may have been directly engaged in agriculture at the time. But by the end of the nineteenth century,

[45] Bayly, *Indian Society*.

it was closer to 80 per cent.[46] 'Traditional village India', as seen even by the Victorians, was not the India that might have been seen by their predecessors a century earlier.

Moreover, the deepening of India's peasant economy in these years presented major problems to the logic of capitalist development, once the new transport technologies made their impact from the 1850s. Peasants are not only poor, but produce many of their own subsistence needs outside the market. Problems of demand can be seen to have dragged back the potential of economic growth in the period 1860–1914 to promote stronger domestic industrialization. The volume of British cotton textiles 'forced' on Indian consumers, for example, has often been seen to mark out a potential modern cotton industry, which India might have developed in this period had the colonial authorities not 'suppressed' it. But, in the early 1900s (when British cotton exports to India were reaching their greatest extent), the volume of those exports represented just 25–30 per cent of total British cotton production—which itself, by then, was responsible for only 2.5 per cent of Britain's GNP.[47] India had the scope for a modern cotton industry little more than a quarter the size of that in Britain, which would represent the equivalent of 0.6 per cent of Britain's GNP. Once more, this hardly seems the 'lost' basis of a far-reaching transition. Moreover, even to achieve this size of market, tariffs would have had to be imposed: raising prices and further constricting demand. After peasant petty commodity production became the driving force of the economy, from the 1820s, it is possible to wonder whether anything short of a fundamental restructuring of demand—of the kind associated with a social revolution—could have moved the Indian economy significantly into the modern industrial age. And a thin, alien, and increasingly uncertain British colonial state, with more important economic interests elsewhere, was never going to be the agent of such a revolution.

Although, momentarily, the second great crisis of the world economy—in the 1920s and 1930s—did hint at it. Then, as agricultural prices fell faster than those of industrial products (for the first time since the mid-nineteenth century), new pockets of consumer demand appeared among the small salaried and urban classes created from the 1850s by the revival of

---

[46] Dharma Kumar, 'The Forgotten Sector: Services in the Madras Presidency in the First Half of the Nineteenth Century', in Kumar (ed.), *Colonialism, Property and the State* (Delhi, 1998).

[47] Francois Crouzet, *The Victorian Economy* (London, 1982), ch. 7.

the economy. Industrialization proceeded at a faster pace (helped also by the final arrival of tariff protection) and, in its last days, colonial capitalism, as we have seen, did begin to find new priorities in India.[48] A new colonial economy, marked by the state abandoning its military and external orientations to foster domestic production and consumption, appeared on the point of forming. But, by this time, the political contradictions of colonialism were too glaring for it to go very far and it dissolved in the context of the Second World War. Nonetheless, even its brief emergence demonstrates that colonialism had possibilities of economic development other than those pursued in India before 1914: Indian poverty and agrarian stagnation were never its necessary corollaries and, under different conditions and guided by different sets of interests, it might have promoted more significant economic growth.

Situating the Colonial Intervention

However, that point opens a further and final series of questions about the layers of meaning to be taken from India's economic experience under colonialism. How far did South Asia possess the possibilities of an alternative—and better—economic history during the nineteenth and twentieth centuries had it never fallen under British rule at all? This question has, implicitly and explicitly, haunted the economic history of colonial India almost from the beginning and is extremely difficult to avoid. Any attempt to assess South Asia's economic performance under the British must take part of its evaluation from a 'counterfactual' model of what would/could/should have happened otherwise. But, obviously, answering any such question is also extremely problematic. The reasons why events may *not* happen are theoretically infinite and, in some ways, counterfactuals are constrained only by qualities of historical imagination.

Also, in India's case, there are a number of special problems. A first is whether there would have been *an* Indian economy at all without British rule. The political trends of the eighteenth century strongly suggest that South Asia was moving away from a loose Mughal imperial political system and towards a series of tighter, more compact regional states—based on the dynamics of military fiscalism and practising their own competitive forms of mercantilism. It was the British conquest which both resurrected the

[48] Baker, *Rural Economy*.

imperial political level and imbued it 'nationally' with the centrist state qualities arising out of the regional military fiscalist transformation. And it can be doubted that any other power in South Asia without access to the overseas trade connections and military technologies of the Europeans (if not necessarily the British) could have done so. A unitary (and proto-national) 'Indian' state/economy—as opposed to a series of regional states/economies—was more a consequence of colonial rule than an alternative to it.

The same, too, may be true of any context of world economy in which a hypothetical 'modern' India might have developed. As we have suggested, Britain's conquest of India played a key strategic role in the building of a British empire east of the Mediterranean. Without the men, money, and material gained from India, Britain's own resources were too sparse to have accomplished this end. But many historians would also argue that this empire was crucial to providing the institutional framework within which the modern world economy developed in the nineteenth century.[49] Without such a framework, there might not have been any such economy—or, at least, only one of a very different kind—and 'modern' India itself would have had no wider context of 'modernity'—or only a very different one inconceivable in form—in which to grow.

In the last twenty years, too, a number of other issues have made the specification of appropriate counterfactual models yet more difficult. In particular, most of the classical theories of economic development conceived in 'the West' over the last two hundred years have collapsed: undermined both by the latter-day and very different growth of 'the East' and, even more, by wholly unanticipated forms of 'post-industrial' economy in 'the West' itself. Those theories—Smithian, Marxist, Weberian—presupposed full industrialization to represent completion of a historical process, which was expected to follow universally the path taken first in 'the West'. Differentials of 'development', and explanations for them, could be read off simply against a scale replicating Western experience. But, if the West has fallen off the end and the East has proceeded to prosperity by other means, the scale's calibrations no longer have much credibility. One further consequence of this has been to undermine understandings of how 'the West' came to achieve its own precocious modernity in the first place; and

---

[49] Ferguson, *Empire*.

even of what that modernity might consist. Currently, there are a large number of different theories of the 'rise of the West', and of the first Industrial Revolution, competing for intellectual space. But, if we no longer know with any certainty why 'the West' rose, or how its modernity was achieved (if it ever was), it seems especially futile to inquire how India might, or might not, have followed the same mysterious course had it not been colonized.

Nonetheless, some comparisons with recent theories of Western development may be useful to mark sets of differences in South Asia's case, which can help to establish not failed quasi-Western trajectories, but the logic of the region's own patterns of economic growth and reproduction before the colonial era. These may then make stronger bases from which to launch hypothetical projections into 'non-colonial' futures and to clarify more precisely what the colonial conquest did and did not change. Ken Pomeranz, for example, has hypothesized the 'Great Divergence' represented by the super-growth of the Western economies to have resulted from acute ecological strains, which found responses in the adoption of fossil fuels and in the capture of the natural resources of the Americas.[50] But, in South Asia before the nineteenth century, there are few signs of any such constraints: land and forest resources were plentiful in most areas and there was little pressure to pursue substitutes or imports. Whatever else, colonialism did not 'deny' India an ecologically directed path to industrialization.

W.W. Rostow, by contrast, saw Western exceptionalism in long-term patterns of accumulation and investment which promoted successive 'stages of growth'[51] But, in South Asia, accumulation was very difficult to sustain. As Ashin Das Gupta has argued, although merchant fortunes might grow very large, they rarely lasted for more than a generation or two.[52] And, while Prasannan Parthasarathi has found skilled workers capable of earning very high wages in comparative terms, Ravi Ahuja has also shown that they cannot have been able to keep them for very long: famine hit precisely the area of Parthasarathi's study in 1718–19, 1728–36, 1747, 1769, 1781–3, 1789, 1792, and 1798. Indeed, the instabilities caused by famine appear a recurrent

---

[50] Kenneth Pomeranz, *The Great Divergence: China, Europe and the Making of the Modern World Economy* (Princeton, 2000).

[51] W. W. Rostow, *The Stages of Economic Growth: A Non-Communist Manifesto* (Cambridge, 1960).

[52] A. Das Gupta, 'Indian Merchants and the Trade in the Indian Ocean', in T. Raychaudhuri and I. Habib (eds), *Cambridge Economic History of India*, vol. i (Cambridge, 1982).

feature of pre-colonial South Asian economies.[53] They were partly the product of wars generated by the state system. But, perhaps even more, they were the product of a highly precarious monsoon agriculture: dependent either on the vagaries of the winds or else on mountainous snow-melts, which brought annual floods of terrifying power. These were offset by very little fixed investment, gained by cumulative or other means. The Mughal empire's efforts at canal-building, for example, scarcely bear comparison with those of its contemporary Chinese empire. And, while tax concessions certainly encouraged some 'private' investment on the land, it was never on the scale to be seen in the great land-drainage schemes of the Netherlands or eastern Britain from the seventeenth century. But, then, it is not clear that any early modern technologies existed which could cope with the extraordinary forces of nature to be found in South Asia, whose economy was always a heavy gamble on the monsoon.

Or again, Neil McKendrick has made Britain's 'Commercial Revolution' of the eighteenth century the key to 'Industrial Revolution' later in the nineteenth.[54] A national market came to develop in imported items of consumption (including, ironically, Indian textiles), which lent themselves to mass-production methods. But it is difficult to detect similar processes of national 'homogenization' in Indian fashion and taste. A disproportionate amount of consumption was enjoyed by aristocracies who, by definition, pursue distinction not homogeneity. Elsewhere, the caste system—within which differences were expressed, above all, in styles of dress—promoted innumerable, separate 'niche' markets. Indeed, rather than towards goods and commodities, Indian consumption preferences appear to have been oriented much more towards services. As Dharma Kumar especially has noted, South Asia at the time of the conquest possessed a strikingly large 'service' sector for any pre-modern economy.[55] But 'human' services cannot be mass-reproduced and give rise to few linkages with the rest of the economy.

Or again, many historians from Karl Marx have seen the subordination of labour to capital—expressed in the destruction of guild-craft and the

[53] Parthasarathi, *Transition*; Ravi Ahuja, 'Labour Relations in the Early Colonial Context: Madras 1750–1800', *Modern Asian Studies*, 36 (2002), 793–826.

[54] Neil McKendrick, John Brewer, and J. H. Plumb (eds), *The Birth of a Consumer Society: The Commercialization of Eighteenth-Century England* (London, 1982).

[55] Kumar, 'Forgotten Sector'.

dominance of the merchant over the artisan—as crucial to change. But in South Asia, as Parthasarathi has argued, caste-organized artisans were able to mount effective resistance to merchant power, which was often weakened by its own contradictory relationship to state power.[56] The warrior-ruler and the merchant-prince were inclined to inhabit very different social worlds. While the circumstances of the eighteenth century, and the rise of military fiscalism, brought them closer together, it by no means resolved their tensions. Merchant fortunes were no less at risk of confiscation under Tipu Sultan of Mysore, or the Nawabs of Bengal, than they had been under the Great Mughals.

However South Asia is viewed, it is hard to see it set on a path to replicate the kinds of growth experience followed by the 'Western' economies. But this does not—necessarily and inevitably—mean that it was therefore undergoing no growth experience at all and was 'static'. Rather, and in the first place, it points to a number of distinctive features, which South Asian economies possessed and which are not immediately reconcilable with 'Western' anticipations of growth. High degrees of skill specialization, elaborate service economies, and potentials to garner great short-term wealth are not usually associated with conditions of chronic subsistence instability, low levels of fixed capital formation, and an open land frontier. But here they plainly were: setting up a very distinctive logic of economic expansion and social reproduction.[57]

Three mechanisms can be seen as crucial to this logic. The first was highly extended relations of exchange, which ameliorated the instabilities encountered in any one area by bringing in goods and services from others. India's long sea-coast facilitated the movement of bulk trades: for example, in grain and salt. But the remarkable Banjara (itinerant communities) caravans of pack bullocks, which traversed the interior from the late medieval period, even opened up this facility overland. Bengal's textile industry could be supplied with raw cotton from Gujarat on the other side of the subcontinent. Exchange was further facilitated by cash, and a growing cash economy was evident in parts of South Asia from the eleventh century. It drew in the new supplies of specie metal, from the Americas and Japan, available from

---

[56] Parthasarathi, *Transition*.

[57] David Washbrook, 'India in the Early Modern World Economy: Modes of Production, Reproduction and Exchange', *Journal of Global History*, 2/1 (July 2007).

the sixteenth century and reached new heights of sophistication with the minting of the Mughal emperor Akbar's celebrated silver rupee.[58]

The second set of mechanisms concerned elaborate forms of risk-sharing, whose imperatives stamped a wide range of institutions. For example, as C. A. Bayly and Sanjay Subrahmanyam have seen, mercantile houses pursued complex risk-averting strategies: splitting their activities between many different trades and building up diverse 'portfolios' of assets.[59] This meant, of course, that they were always likely to keep the bulk of their investments liquid—rather than risking the added hazards which came from 'fixing' them down. But it was not only enterprises of proto-capitalism, which betrayed such strategies. As anthropologists have long seen, the *jajmani* system of intra-local, non-market exchange can be seen to function to a logic anticipating adversity and maximizing the means to recover from it.[60]

And a third set of mechanisms related to mobility. In bizarre contrast to the idea of a society of static 'village communities', elaborated by the colonial authorities, early modern South Asia was extraordinarily mobile. The vast Banjara caravans criss-crossing the interior represented but one of many forms of 'flexible' labour market, featuring artisans, soldiers, and even peasants, whose movements are traceable down to the modern age through their habits of preserving their own caste-styles and languages.[61] In agriculture, labour and capital pursued not land, but water and silt—creating seasonal patterns of movement of surprising scale. Village tenure systems also universally anticipated the attraction of large numbers of 'temporary cultivators', who would come and go as hydraulic opportunities shifted.

These mechanisms appear to have been extremely effective in coping with the problems of instability, which the economy faced. The recuperative powers of South Asian economies were remarkable: as Bayly has seen, even the devastation caused by the invasions and wars of the early eighteenth century could gain rapid compensation as labour and capital moved

---

[58] Frank Perlin, *The Invisible City: Monetary, Administrative and Popular Infrastructures in Asia and Europe, 1500–1900* (Aldershot, 1993).

[59] Sanjay Subrahmanyam and C. A. Bayly, 'Portfolio Capitalists and the Economy of Early Modern India', *Indian Economic and Social History Review*, 24/4 (1988), 401–24.

[60] T. Scarlett Epstein, *Yesterday, Today and Tomorrow: Mysore Villages Re-visited* (London, 1973).

[61] D. H. A. Kolff, *Naukar, Rajput and Sepoy: The Ethnohistory of the Military Labour Market in Hindustan, 1450–1850* (Cambridge, 1990).

to other 'high zones' of production and consumption.[62] Moreover, there would seem evidence of fairly consistent expansion in territory and population over a long period. Several historians have seen secular growth trends in many parts of South Asia, rising in the eleventh and twelfth centuries and continuing into the eighteenth. Irfan Habib's argument, that the population reached its limit (of 160 million) in 1600 and stagnated thereafter until 1800—under Mughal oppression and the 'chaos' of the eighteenth-century civil wars—is now widely contested. Ashok Desai and Sumit Guha estimate a population nearer 115–20 million in 1600, which may have grown (if at a chequered pace) towards 140–60 million by the onset of the colonial era.[63]

Further, there is also evidence of a distinctive 'development' dynamic with the potential to raise the 'quality' of production and consumption. Specialist skills and services were inclined to proliferate with growing wealth, manifested in ever more dense and elaborate systems of caste in the richer river valleys; new technologies were designed to meet demands from particular niche markets (sword steels that were harder than any that can be made today; new fabrics to meet distinctive tastes); investments in irrigation were made to maximize the production of exchangeable crops, if not to secure local supplies of food against the vagaries of the climate (which were unmanageable).

South Asian economies possessed their own logics of development and may, no doubt, have gone on successfully pursuing them, and generating ever more services, manufactures, and extended relations of exchange for a considerable period longer had changes in technology, overseas markets, and the distribution of world power not brought the external forces of British imperialism to intrude. Admittedly, some of these forces were already anticipated in the rise of the military fiscalist regional states of the eighteenth century—and increasing dependence on overseas markets and foreign supplies of specie did make South Asian economies peculiarly vulnerable to external influence. But, expressed through the political form of the regional state, these forces appear much less threatening to the established mechanisms of economic growth and reproduction. Eighteenth-century South Asian states could never control the movement of

---

[62] Bayly, *Rulers*.
[63] Irfan Habib, 'Population', in Raychaudhuri and Habib (eds), *Cambridge Economic History*, i; Guha, *Health*; Ashok V. Desai, 'Population and Standards of Living in Akbar's Time: A Second Look', *Indian Economic and Social History Review*, 15/1 (1978), 53–79.

populations; their competitive needs for cash restrained their predatory habits towards merchants and bankers; and their desire for strong economies to underpin their war machines drew them towards risk-sharing forms of investment (for example, via production-sensitive revenue systems). Many South Asian regional economies remained dynamic to the dawn of the colonial era, 'developing' in their own distinctive ways.

But that dawn did come and, thereafter, they developed as parts of the wider transformations taking place in an imperial system of global economy. However, what this view of these pre-colonial systems may also highlight is why some of the interventions brought by colonialism proved to be particularly cruel and, eventually, to convert the economic reputation, which India enjoyed in the world, from a repository of great wealth and manufacturing skills to a charnel-house more associated with famine and early death. At several key points, the nature of the colonial intervention directly disrupted the three key mechanisms of economic reproduction, but failed to replace them with anything as effective.

Reflecting both European cultural norms and fears at the thinness of its social power, for example, the Company state early set itself against the physical mobility of South Asian populations—at least within India. It set out to dismantle many of the broader labour markets, which previously had existed but which it now saw as a threat to 'order', not least treating the Banjaras as incipient criminals. It also sought to tie peasants to land, lest they evade taxation, and thus inhibited the movement of labour and capital in pursuit of water. 'Sedentarization' was a key theme of the first half of the nineteenth century, no less than 'peasantization': which, itself, drove more artisans, soldiers, and service personnel into subsistence agriculture—bringing forward the day when land and natural resources would run out.[64] But the Company also struck heavily against a wide range of other risk-averting strategies: its refusal to lift or moderate cash revenue demands in the face of crop failure or price depression transferred commercial risks onto producers and away from itself. And it seriously affected the functioning of extended relations of exchange within the economy (if very much not outside it) by presiding over the decline of domestic consumption and excluding from the revenue system indigenous banking capital, which was reduced to peddling and petty moneylending functions.

[64] Bayly, *Indian Society*.

Of course, the displacement of these mechanisms was meant to open the way to new technologies and exchange systems brought by 'modernity'. Roads and railways would replace the transport functions of the Banjaras; fixed investment in irrigation would ease the problems of climatic instability; Western-style banks would allocate capital to production. But, in the context of a state constantly looking outwards and obsessed, above all, with the costs of its military power, somehow these new systems and technologies never quite consolidated themselves—or, at least, consolidated themselves sufficiently to meet growing needs, as population expanded and natural resources finally became pressed.

The Great Famines of the 1870s and 1890s shocked the late Victorian British public, which until then, appears to have believed the reports on 'the moral and material progress' of India issued annually by its Secretary of State. But they arose out of the strict logic of colonial development. Population pressure had intensified farming in areas of the highest climatic precariousness, many of which had never been intensively cultivated before. It was sustained by the promise of returns on cash crops, particularly cotton, which could be carried via the new transport system to railheads and ports—whence grain from other areas was supposed to be brought in return. However, in the face of crisis, a transport system biased towards moving goods 'outwards' proved inadequate to bringing back and distributing sufficient food 'inwards'. And with the limits of available land now being reached, there was nowhere to which the peasantry could move.[65] In the Ceded Districts of Madras, between 1876 and 1878, about a third of the population died and the area took more than a generation to recover. Famines, no doubt, had happened often enough under the logic of the 'old' economy. But it can be doubted that one so 'Great' would ever have happened here—in a part of the Deccan previously used more for grazing Banjara cattle herds than for cultivation—nor that its depth and the time taken to recover from it would have been so considerable. Colonial development involved increased risks to peasants and labourers and, whenever it failed, the human costs were always likely to be high. Whatever 'moral and material progress' the Indian economy may have achieved under British rule, it had an inbuilt tendency to disintegrate in ways which rapidly became highly immoral and revealed a distressing lack of material.

[65] David Arnold, *Famine: Social Crisis and Historical Change* (Oxford, 1986).

Select Bibliography

A. K. BAGCHI, *Private Investment in India 1900–1939* (Cambridge, 1972).

CHRISTOPHER BAKER, *An Indian Rural Economy, 1880–1955: The Tamilnad Countryside* (Oxford, 1984).

C. A. BAYLY, *Rulers, Townsmen and Bazaars: North Indian Society in the Age of British Expansion, 1770–1870* (Cambridge, 1982).

—— *Indian Society and the Making of the British Empire* (Cambridge, 1988).

RAJNARAYAN CHANDAVARKAR, *The Origins of Industrial Capitalism in India: Business Strategies and the Working Classes in Bombay, 1900–1940* (Cambridge, 1994).

SUMIT GUHA, *The Agrarian Economy of the Bombay Deccan, 1818–1941* (Delhi, 1985).

DHARMA KUMAR (ed.), *The Cambridge Economic History of India*, ii. *c.1757–1970* (Cambridge, 1983).

MORRIS D. MORRISS (ed.), *Indian Economy in the Nineteenth Century: A Symposium* (Delhi, 1969).

OM PRAKASH, *European Commercial Enterprise in Pre-Colonial India* (Cambridge, 1998).

TIRTHANKAR ROY, *The Economic History of India, 1857–1947* (Delhi, 2002).

ASSIYA SIDDIQI, *Agrarian Change in a Northern Indian State: Uttar Pradesh, 1819–1833* (Oxford, 1973).

B. R. TOMLINSON, *The Economy of Modern India, 1860–1970* (Cambridge, 1993).

DAVID WASHBROOK, 'India in the Early Modern World Economy: Modes of Production, Reproduction and Exchange', *Journal of Global History*, 2/1 (July, 2007).

4

Knowledge Formation in Colonial India

Norbert Peabody

Over the last twenty-five years, the historiography of South Asia has witnessed a growing appreciation that empire was not forged solely on the anvil of superior Western military technology and/or economic organization. Perhaps with the crucial exception of naval dominance, there is now good cause to doubt that the British enjoyed clear military advantages over their Indian rivals until relatively late in the colonial encounter, say, around the turn of the nineteenth century.[1] Similarly, there is also growing evidence that the British industrial economy did not fuel the growth of empire but was one of its by-products that owed much to competition from sophisticated, indigenous Indian forms of agricultural production and manufacturing that the British encountered and eventually (at least with regard to industry) suppressed.[2] Instead analysis of colonial domination of India has increasingly focused on the, often, cryptic connections between knowledge and power.[3] Building upon the idea that no form of knowledge is objective,

---

[1] Jos J. L. Gommans, 'Indian Warfare and Afghan Innovation during the Eighteenth Century', *Studies in History*, 11 (1995), 261–80; Douglas M. Peers (eds), *Warfare and Empires: Contact and Conflict between European and Non-European Military and Maritime Forces and Cultures* (Aldershot, 1997); and Randolph G. S. Cooper, *The Anglo-Maratha Campaigns and the Contest for India: The Struggle for Control of the South Asian Military Economy* (Cambridge, 2003).

[2] Prasannan Parthasarathi, 'Rethinking Wages and Competitiveness in the Eighteenth Century: Britain and South India', *Past and Present*, 158 (1998), 79–109.

[3] This general insight, of course, derives from the well-known writings of Michel Foucault, who first made the power/knowledge connection visible through his analysis of several institutions (such as the prison, asylum, and clinic) associated with the modern European state, and Edward Said, who explored the links between orientalist scholarship and colonial rule in the Arab world. However, in the specific context of South Asian colonial history, Bernard S. Cohn was surely the first to systematically explore various aspects of the power/knowledge proposition. Initially at least, Cohn developed his line of thought independently of (and in some instances in anticipation of) Foucault and Said. See esp. two compilations of Cohn's essays, *An*

impartial, or unimplicated—but rather harbours within it naturalized biases, agendas, and predispositions—it is now clear that the new discursive formations that developed under British rule had the effect of producing among the subject population an asymmetrically constituted, uncritical consent for many aspects of the colonial project. This capacity did not entirely dispense with the need to exercise overt, coercive force, but certainly it limited the requirement of its application to more predictable arenas.

An important dimension of this understanding has been a concern for how colonial ways of 'knowing the country' were instantiated on the ground through the creation of seemingly benign institutions and administrative structures. The census, the geographic and archaeological surveys, public health regimes, and colonial architecture and town planning all helped turn colonial ideas about India into lived realities for ordinary Indians.[4] Moreover, the effectiveness of these technologies of rule rested on their capacity to fashion novel forms of individual subjectivity, one of whose principal characteristics was self-regulation in conformity with colonial power in what several authors, developing on Foucault, have termed 'colonial governmentality'.[5]

The aim of this chapter is not to question the analytic usefulness of these insights, which remain foundational and undiminished. Rather it will question the ontological status of the new forms of colonial knowledge and attendant institutions that emerged during British rule. Until relatively

---

Anthropologist among the Historians and Other Essays (Delhi, 1986) and *Colonialism and Its Forms of Knowledge: The British in India* (Princeton, 1996).

[4] Bernard Cohn, 'The Census, Social Structure and Objectification in South Asia', in *An Anthropologist Among the Historians and Other Essays* (Delhi, 1987), 224–54; Arjun Appadurai, 'Number in the Colonial Imagination', in Carol A. Breckenridge and Peter van der Veer (eds), *Orientalism and the Post-Colonial Predicament* (Philadelphia, 1993), 314–39; Matthew H. Edney, *Mapping Empire: The Geographic Construction of British India* (Chicago, 1990); David Arnold, *The Tropics and the Traveling Gaze: India, Landscape and Science, 1800–1856* (Seattle, 2006); Veena Talwar Oldenberg, *The Making of Colonial Lucknow, 1756–1877* (Princeton, 1984); Marriam Dossal, *Imperial Designs and Indian Realities: The Planning of Bombay City, 1845–1875* (Delhi, 1991).

[5] Michel Foucault, 'Governmentality', in Graham Burchell, Colin Gordon, and Peter Miller (eds), *The Foucault Effect: Studies in Governmentality* (Hemel Hempstead, 1991), 87–104; David Scott, 'Colonial Governmentality', *Social Text*, 43 (1995), 191–200; Ann Laura Stoler, *Race and the Education of Desire: Foucault's History of Sexuality and the Colonial Order of Things* (Durham, 1995) and *Carnal Knowledge and Imperial Power: Race and the Intimate in Colonial Rule* (Berkeley, 2002); Gyan Prakash, *Another Reason: Science and the Imagination of Modern India* (Princeton, 1999).

recently, there has been a tendency within the field of colonial studies to situate the genesis of colonial ways of knowing entirely within a European episteme (however much that episteme may have been transposed geographically to the extra-European world). The role of indigenous actors, agendas, and ways of knowing in the construction of these discourses has been downplayed.[6] The implication has been that European colonizers were solely responsible for introducing new knowledges and practices that radically transformed indigenous societies.[7]

Instead, I shall suggest here that it is no longer tenable to insist that the forms of knowledge through which colonial rule was established were fully European in origin and development but, rather, were created out of conditions that entailed considerable collaboration—intended and unintended, conscious and unconscious, wanted and unwanted—between the British and, at least, certain key indigenous groups. These Indian groups were often able to harness, redirect, and indeed shape aspects of the emergent forms of knowledge that were being created during the colonial encounter in order to establish and/or deepen a privileged position in local society that itself was divided along various lines including class, status, party, and, of course, gender. By working through and, in some cases, beyond conditions of possibility raised by the colonial encounter, they often had a profound, but unacknowledged, impact on the formation of colonial knowledge.

This suggestion is not to downplay the transformations that took place during colonial rule; nor is it to advocate a simple 'continuity thesis' as an alternative to arguments about 'colonial rupture'. Rather it is to suggest that one must locate the trajectories of social and political change as much in ongoing, indigenously constituted political struggles and social divisions as in colonially constituted ones. Moreover, in uncovering the heterogeneous origins and objectives of colonial knowledge, this essay stresses the often

---

[6] e.g., Edward Said, *Orientalism* (New York, 1978); Gauri Viswanathan, *Masks of Conquest: Literary Study and British Rule in India* (New York, 1989); Ronald Inden, *Imagining India* (Oxford, 1990); Gyan Prakash, 'Writing Post-Orientalist Histories of the Third World: Perspectives from Indian Historiography', *Comparative Studies in Society and History*, 32 (1990), 383–408; Thomas R. Metcalf, *Ideologies of the Raj* (Cambridge, 1994); and Nicholas B. Dirks, *Castes of Mind: Colonialism and the Making of Modern India* (Princeton, 2001).

[7] Part of the truth effect of this prevailing view rests on the problematic assumption that indigenous society prior to European colonization was internally integrated and largely consensual. Against this backdrop of cultural harmony and political equilibrium, any form of social change becomes rooted solely in external (that is, European) causes.

unstable, ad hoc, and contradictory aspects of its formation and historical unfolding. In the process, it will cause us to question a number of prevailing analytic dichotomies—including such well-entrenched binary oppositions as European/native, colonizer/colonized, and agent/patient—that typically inform the analysis of colonial rule.

Historicity

One of the features of the European encounter with India that distinguishes it from the colonial encounters with, say, large swathes of sub-Saharan Africa or Oceania is that it developed over such a long period of time during which the nature of the engagement between Europeans and Indians varied considerably as did the balance of power. One tends to forget that, from the time of Queen Elizabeth I's initial granting of a charter to the East India Company on the last day of 1600 until the British secured the *diwani* of Bengal in the 1760s, the British presence in India was restricted to a limited number of trading outposts (or factories) situated mostly along the coast. And although the economic activities at these factories certainly had profound knock-on effects on the indigenous polities of the subcontinent,[8] this did not constitute 'colonial mastery' in the usual sense of the term. During most of this early period, English military power in India was still dwarfed by, at least, the larger indigenous polities—especially the Mughal and Maratha empires in north India as well as the kingdom of Mysore in the south. The still marginal position of the British in India was compounded by the fact that until the later eighteenth century the British also had several European rivals on the subcontinent, including the Portuguese, Dutch, and French, and indigenous polities availed themselves of these rivalries when defining their relations with the British.

The absence of substantive territorial power on the subcontinent does not mean that this was a golden age of open-minded, empathetic understanding of India. One can certainly discern, what Sanjay Subrahmanyam has called, a proto-orientalist 'will to power' dating from at least as early as the beginning of the seventeenth century in many European representations

---

[8] C. A. Bayly, *Rulers, Tradesmen and Bazaars: North Indian Society in the Age of British Expansion, 1770–1870* (Cambridge, 1983); David Washbrook, 'Progress and Problems: South Asian Economic and Social History', *Modern Asian Studies*, 22 (1988), 57–96.

of India—particularly those relating to her political and religious traditions.[9] Nevertheless these representations were not immediately connected to institutions and technologies of rule in India and indeed appear to have had little impact there for a surprisingly long time. More often than not, these representations were intended to account for uncertain conditions of trade or diplomacy to a European audience back home rather than to establish preconditions for rule among a native audience in India. Sir Thomas Roe, who was ambassador of King James I at the Mughal court from 1616 to 1618, may have devoted considerable space in his diaries to describing Jahangir's authority in terms of oriental despotism, but this was of little concern to the 'world seizer' who did not even find Roe's embassy of sufficient interest or importance for mention in his own memoirs. The fact that representations associated with the European will to power circulated for so long before there was a noticeable British territorial expansion in India indicates that these representations, while surely a necessary component of the growth of the British empire, in and of themselves, are not a sufficient explanation.

Even during the ensuing period of aggressive military conquest, from about 1760 to about 1830, when the Company was first laying down the foundations of a more recognizable state, the Company remained heavily dependent upon Indian capital and lines of credit (to say nothing of the indigenously organized military labour markets) to sustain its power.[10] These pragmatic requirements greatly shaped how the British understood and ultimately dealt with many aspects of India that had not been considered previously. It perhaps was only from the second quarter of the nineteenth century, when the British were consolidating their rule on the subcontinent, that they developed anything like the sort of unfettered imperium that one so commonly associates with the empire. Thus in considering the entire course of the colonial encounter, it becomes clear that most of the political conditions and material needs that defined the British engagement with India changed dramatically over time as did the bureaucratic arrangements they developed in order to cope with these

---

[9] See esp. two recent compilations of essays by Sanjay Subrahmanyam: *Mughals and Franks: Explorations in Connected History* (Delhi, 2005) and *From the Tagus to the Ganges: Explorations in Connected History* (Delhi, 2005). However, as we shall see below, not all aspects of indigenous society were equally and uniformly denigrated.

[10] Bayly, *Rulers, Tradesmen and Bazaars*, esp. chs. 5 and 6; Washbrook, 'Progress and Problems'.

circumstances. It should be unsurprising, therefore, to find that the forms of knowledge that emerged under these shifting conditions also varied in their scope, audiences, institutional linkages, and modes of deployment, even where some individual representational motifs—such as oriental despotism—remained persistent.[11]

And yet there has been an abiding tendency among many analysts to retrospectively interpret the literary representations of the early colonial encounter through the institutions and sensibilities of 'high' colonialism of the later nineteenth century. This backwards reading of colonial history, in which the past is seen purely and solely as a prologue to the present, has been particularly prevalent in the fields of literary criticism and cultural studies. In part, this predisposition rests on their overly narrow understanding of discourse insofar as they locate its power almost exclusively in textual representations without an adequate consideration of how these representations relate to and are informed by wider administrative structures of the state and technologies of rule. Ironically, this connection was the major insight of Foucault and, even if Said was erratic in applying it to his own interpretive practice (especially in his later work), his more programmatic statements often affirmed it as well.

Gauri Viswanathan's well-known essay on Elihu Yale's late seventeenth-century cabals to acquire Fort St David near Madras (and his subsequent trial for insubordination) is a blatant, but nonetheless representative, example of this predisposition to read early colonial history anachronistically.[12] Here Viswanathan interprets Yale's territorial desires as a product of an 'imperial ambition' for 'national aggrandizement' that was only held in check by a jealous East India Company Court of Directors in London.[13] Yet in describing the confidently acquisitive environment of conquest that supposedly fostered Yale's ambition, Viswanathan is surely jumping the gun by a good century in suggesting that the Company's 'maneuverings and expansionist designs of the mid-1600s...vastly increase[d] the sphere of

---

[11] Of course, other discursive themes were constantly being added to the orientalist canon. Caste, for example, did not become centrally important to colonial understandings of India until the 19th century. Significantly, these emergent themes often substantially resituated earlier themes, even where they were not replaced entirely.

[12] Gauri Viswanathan, 'Yale College and the Culture of British Imperialism', *Yale Journal of Criticism*, 7 (1994), 1–30.

[13] Ibid. 13.

English influence over both its Portuguese, Dutch, and French competitors and the many princely rulers who comprised their trading partners'.[14] During Yale's governorship of Madras the British territorial possessions in India were minuscule, the prospects for further expansion remained highly uncertain, and there is little evidence in contemporary Company records to indicate that, in this regard, it could hope for anything more. A more convincing explanation for Yale's rancorous disputes with the Company's directors lies as much in his adaptation of Indian notions of shared sovereignty and decentralized territory as in an inebriating 'culture of British imperialism'. There is much evidence to support this thesis, including Yale's complaints that the Company treated him 'as if I were a cipher and *had no shair in the government*' and Viswanathan's own characterization of Yale's desire to establish 'his own little empire within an empire'.[15] Yet Viswanathan characteristically resorts to anachronism to forestall any inquiry into this type of influence by claiming that the British settlement in Madras was a 'world as far removed from the town surrounding it . . . as England was from India'.[16] Of course, this sort of apartheid mentality did not develop in Madras until much later.[17]

The propensity for retrospective historical projection has led to several interrelated distortions and lacunae in our understandings of colonial discursive formations. First, it tends to render discourses as unduly monolithic, integrated, and stable over time, obscuring any meaningful history of contradiction, contestation, and transformation. Too often they have been portrayed as emerging fully formed at some, rarely specified, point in the seventeenth or eighteenth centuries (or earlier) and then as remaining, more or less, unitary, internally consistent, and static thereafter. The classic example of this is surely provided by Ronald Inden who claims that virtually all European-trained scholars of India from James Mill to Romila Thapar have defined indigenous society in terms of just a few interrelated, mutually reinforcing 'essences'—sacred kingship, caste, village India, and Hinduism—whose content and articulation have remained remarkably constant

---

[14] Ibid. 14. Viswanathan thus remarkably credits the East India Company with *both* fostering and thwarting imperial expansion.

[15] Ibid. 26 (emphasis added) and 10.

[16] Ibid. 14.

[17] David Washbrook, 'South India 1770–1840: The Colonial Transition', *Modern Asian Studies*, 38 (2004), 479–516, esp. 484–7.

over time.[18] The huge irony here is that if earlier generations of orientalist scholars were guilty of denying a history to India, then many engaged in the self-proclaimed post-orientalist critique have largely transposed that timeless fixity onto Western intellectual history.[19] Although it would be distorting to label these characterizations of the West as 'occidentalism' or 'orientalism in reverse' (for these representations of the West were never imbricated with wider institutions and technologies of rule as was the case with 'orientalism'), these characterizations nevertheless unduly homogenize both the synchronic multiplicity and diachronic mutability of Western thought about India.

This fractiousness has been charted along several different fault lines. Tensions, for example, crept up between the aims and practices of officials at different levels and locations in the colonial bureaucracy. The discrepant orientations of officials in London and in each of the Presidency capitals are well documented,[20] but we are also beginning to see how this permeated down all the way to the lowly British officer in the Indian *moffusil* as colonial officials occupying different positions in the bureaucratic hierarchy had to contend with different political pressures and diverse practical tasks. This fact has led Arjun Appadurai to make the important suggestion that the intended disciplinary effect of such colonial institutions as the all-India census and land surveys was directed as much towards the colonial bureaucracy itself as towards the native population.[21] Even among the rarefied elite group of policy framers, articulations of British policy towards India were beleaguered with controversy and dissension. The iconic status in cultural studies of Macaulay's famous Minute on Indian Education of 1835, which called for the creation of a class of natives that was 'Indian in blood and colour, but English in tastes, in opinions, in morals and in intellect', has obscured the fact that the 'great Indian education debate' between orien-

---

[18] Inden, *Imagining India*.

[19] In this regard, a notable exception among those drawing direct inspiration from Said is Nicholas Dirks, whose *Castes of Mind* charts several significant historical transformations within orientalist discourse from the late 18th to 20th centuries particularly in the change from 'historical' to 'ethnographic' modes of thought as the empire shifted its modus operandi from conquest to cementing native loyalty.

[20] For differences and tensions between Calcutta and Madras, for example, see Phillip B. Wagoner, 'Precolonial Intellectuals and the Production of Colonial Knowledge', *Comparative Studies in Society and History*, 25 (2003), 783–814 and Washbrook, 'South India'.

[21] Arjun Appadurai, 'Number in the Colonial Imagination', in Breckenridge and van der Veer (eds), *Orientalism and the Post-Colonial Predicament*, 314–39.

talists and anglicists raged for over half a century within (and beyond) official administrative circles before the anglicists finally achieved the upper hand (and even then never definitively so).[22] Finally, there was also considerable disagreement between those within Company service and those critics on the outside who wanted to see it reformed (or abolished). The British did not speak with one voice on the empire in India, even among those who were part of its official apparatus.

Secondly, the purely teleological reading of colonial discourse not only accords its early articulators with an uncanny prescience but it also simultaneously denies any formative significance to their own contemporary, situationally determined agendas. This denial serves to decontextualize discourses from the specific circumstances in which they were written and against which their authors intended them to be read. Elsewhere, I have shown how recent post-orientalist attempts to read the early nineteenth-century writings of James Tod about Rajput kinship through the later nineteenth-century lens of caste has blinded us to Tod's own reflections on nationalism.[23] Rather than positing an unbridgeable ontological dichotomy between Europe and India, Tod constructed a more segmentary relationship between the two that was deployed precisely because it established useful links between Europe and India.[24] Tod's motivation for positing durable bonds with select Indian groups (such as the Rajputs) was informed by the ongoing global rivalries between the British, French, and Russians that were being played out simultaneously in European and extra-European contexts.[25] This broad imperial outlook (as opposed to a more narrowly defined colonial one) made it imperative for the British to ally key Indian groups with their struggle against their European rivals, which Tod

---

[22] Lynn Zastoupil and Martin Moir, *The Great Indian Education Debate: Documents Relating to the Orientalist-Anglicist Controversy, 1781–1843* (Richmond, Surrey, 1999).

[23] Norbert Peabody, 'Tod's *Rajast'han* and the Boundaries of Imperial Rule in Nineteenth-Century India', *Modern Asian Studies*, 30 (1996), 185–220.

[24] For a related (but independently formulated) argument about the use of segmentary classification in colonial India, see Thomas R. Trautmann, *Aryans and British India* (Berkeley, 1997), 6–12. See also Susan Bayly, 'Caste and Race in Colonial Ethnography', in Peter Robb (ed.), *The Concept of Race in South Asia* (Delhi, 1995), 165–218.

[25] For an important precursor of this argument, see C. A. Bayly, *Imperial Meridian: The British Empire and the World, 1780–1830* (London, 1989).

attempted to accomplish by appealing to the emerging discourse on nationalism.

Thirdly, the retrospective reading of colonial history does not take adequate account of the precise conditions under which colonial knowledges were initially formulated. Nor does it assess the impact of the specific processes, sequences, and temporalities by which component elements were combined, ordered, extended, and systematized over time. Colonial discourses were not cut from whole cloth in a day. Their introduction to the colonial field was rarely uniform, coordinated, or, initially, all-encompassing. As a result, they did not induce among Indians a complete amnesia of alternative ways of knowing and being, which were derived from indigenous knowledge systems. Moreover, even where they were methodically implemented, colonial ways of knowing never completely effaced indigenously inspired ones owing to the ways in which the two, while often overlapping, were never completely coterminous, and the degree of incommensurability between colonial and indigenous ways of knowing meant that native knowledges never became completely obsolete. The inattention of much discourse theory to these processes and temporalities has had the distorting effect of blinding us precisely to the contexts through which much native agency manifest itself during the colonial encounter and thus has systematically negated the presence of Indians in its history except as objects of that history. It is to the recuperation of this native presence in recent historiography that I turn my attention in the following section.

Agency

A desire to explore the agency of the native and to restore her negated presence to history, of course, is not an entirely new project. Several commentators have noted that this goal, after all, was the *raison d'être* behind the founding of the Subaltern Studies Collective when, in the early 1980s, a number of Indian and British scholars became increasingly dissatisfied with how the elite biases of earlier historiographies—whether colonialist, nationalist, or (somewhat ironically) Marxist—had effaced the distinctive historical experiences, practices, and legacies of subaltern groups.[26] Initially, members of the collective set about this restoration by

---

[26] e.g. Rosalind O'Hanlon, 'Recovering the Subject: *Subaltern Studies* and Histories of Resistance in Colonial South Asia', *Modern Asian Studies*, 22 (1988), 189–224; Ramachandra

attempting to endow the subaltern with a self-constituting, inherent, and autonomous presence, which allowed for the subaltern to remain as a fully conscious subject, even if her agency was ultimately blunted by the dull, material compulsions of coercive power—a position which informs the title of Ranajit Guha's famous essay 'Dominance Without Hegemony'.[27]

By the end of the decade, however, with the growing influence of discourse theory, the Subaltern Studies project had largely morphed from 'recovering the subject' to explaining why the subject was ultimately unrecoverable. Subaltern passivity was no longer simply a historiographical bias that needed to be corrected; it now was historical fact that needed to be explained. And once again Indians disappeared from readings of colonial history, albeit for slightly different reasons. Once the British arrived on the scene Indians apparently became passive onlookers to the colonial encounter, leaving little discernable impact on the forms of knowledge or social institutions that developed during British rule. Or if they did occasionally take to action, they did so in ways that were so overdetermined by the terms of the colonial discourse that subaltern efforts at resistance served only to reinscribe the dominant discourse's authority. Thus, as Ashis Nandy has suggested,

the *ultimate* violence which colonialism does to its victims [is] that it creates a culture in which the ruled are constantly tempted to fight their rulers within the psychological [here I might add, the epistemological] limits set by the latter. It is not an accident that the specific variants of the concepts with which many anti-colonial movements in our time have worked have often been the product of the imperial culture itself and, even in opposition, these movements have paid homage to their respective cultural origins.[28]

Guha, 'Subaltern and Bhadralok Studies', *Economic and Political Weekly* (19 Aug. 1995), 2056–8; Sumit Sarkar, *Writing Social History* (Delhi, 1997), esp. ch. 3; Richard M. Eaton, '(Re)imag(in)ing Other²ness: A Postmortem for the Postmodern in India', *Journal of World History*, 11 (2000), 57–78.

[27] Ranajit Guha, 'Dominance Without Hegemony and Its Historiography', *Subaltern Studies*, vi (Delhi, 1989), 210–309. See also Veena Talwar Oldenberg, 'Lifestyle as Resistance: The Case of the Courtesans of Lucknow', in Doug Haynes and Gyan Prakash (eds), *Contesting Power and Everyday Social Relations in South Asia* (Berkeley, 1992), 23–61.

[28] Ashis Nandy, *The Intimate Enemy: Loss and Recovery of Self under Colonialism* (Delhi, 1983), 3. See also Partha Chatterjee, *Nationalist Thought and the Third World: A Derivative Discourse?* (London, 1986), and Gayatri Chakravorty Spivak, 'Can the Subaltern Speak?', in C. Nelson and L. Grossberg (eds), *Marxism and the Interpretation of Culture* (Urbana, 1988), 271–313.

This view then conceives indigenous action as resistance which is ultimately isomorphic with, and reactive towards, a 'totalizing' colonial discourse insofar as resistance is only able to exploit internal contradictions within the terms and conditions initially posited by the dominant discourse rather than ever being able to shift debate to new terrains. In ways that are somewhat reminiscent of Max Gluckman's use of the Aristotelian distinction between rebellion and revolution in his study of the Swazi *ncwala*, this view presents resistance as ultimately reinforcing the structure of subaltern subordination rather than ever fundamentally transforming it.

However, Rosalind O'Hanlon has noted that this position generally assumes 'that discourses have an existence which is prior to, and hence unsullied by, the interventions of those over whom they have jurisdiction'.[29] Colonial discourses are viewed as having their genesis entirely in Western epistemologies and institutional constructs before the issue of native resistance to them or agency through them (for not all forms of native social action can be classified as 'resistance') is ever considered. But as O'Hanlon further remarks, historically this is not the case owing to the ways in which the very creation and elaboration of much orientalist scholarship depended upon the authority and expertise of native informants who manipulated (whether deliberately or subconsciously) the knowledges that they passed on to orientalists. As a result:

the seemingly omnipotent classifications of the Orientalist were vulnerable to purposeful misconstruction and appropriation to uses which he never intended, precisely because they had incorporated into them the readings and political concerns of his native informants.[30]

Thus in recent years there have been a number of studies that have focused on the formative period of the eighteenth and early nineteenth centuries for it is here, at its very beginnings, that one can see that a multiplicity of voices and agendas, not all of them of European origin, have been inserted into orientalist discourse. Moreover, in remaining alive to the significant intercourse that took place across the colonial divide, these studies have suggested that orientalism was a more multifarious and open-ended set of practices than the unilinear, reductionist, and teleological picture that once prevailed.

---

[29] O'Hanlon, 'Recovering the Subject', 216.
[30] Ibid. 216–17.

Several dimensions and aspects of this interchange have now come under scrutiny. First, it is important to remember that Europeans (especially early on) did not regard all forms of indigenous knowledge as grotesque, flawed, and needing European reform. Indeed in many areas—including botany, medicine, metallurgy, astronomy, and even textile production—it was just the opposite; Indian forms of knowledge were actively sought precisely because they were held to be superior. Admittedly many of these appropriations were restricted to technical matters, but not always. Some borrowings were far more broadly classificatory in (re)orientation. Richard Grove, for instance, has shown how European botanical science was radically transformed in the wake of the writings of Garcia da Orta and H. A. van Reede tot Drakenstein whose respective *Coloquios dos simples e drogas he cousas medicinais India* (first published in 1563) and *Hortus Indicus Malabaricus* (first published in twelve volumes from 1678 to 1693) were largely based on Indian (Ayurvedic and Ezhava) systems of botanical knowledge and were explicitly acknowledged as such.[31] Grove even shows that the Ezhava basis of van Reede's *Hortus Malabaricus* had an impact beyond South Asian botany for it ultimately influenced a significant portion of Linnaeus's classification scheme.[32] No doubt, the wholesale adoption by Europeans of indigenous Indian systems of knowledge as described by Grove was exceptional. Moreover, Grove's claim that this constituted 'an Ayurvedic and Ezhava epistemological hegemony' in the botanical sciences is surely overstated as the institutional structures through which this knowledge was disseminated—through botanical gardens, professional societies, and global networks of information and materia medica transfer—were largely European in constitution and articulation.[33] Nevertheless he does remind us of a time, now largely forgotten, when *some* aspects of European intellectual attitudes towards India were characterized by what Thomas Trautmann has called 'Indomania', rather than 'Indophobia'.[34]

---

[31] Richard Grove, 'Indigenous Knowledge and the Significance of South-West India for Portuguese and Dutch Constructions of Tropical Nature', *Modern Asian Studies*, 30 (1996), 121–43. See also Kapil Raj, *Relocating Modern Science: Circulation and the Construction of Knowledge in South Asia and Europe, 1650–1900* (Basingstoke, 2007).

[32] Ibid. 139.

[33] Ibid. 127.

[34] Trautmann, *Aryans and British India*, ch. 3. For another notable study highlighting the role of early British affect(ion) towards India in fostering the hybridity of colonial knowledge, see

For Trautmann, however, European regard for Indian forms of knowledge did not lead to the comprehensive *replacement* of one by the other but rather to the *fusion* of the two.[35] His studies of nineteenth-century orientalist philology, for example, show how the discipline blended from two intellectual frameworks—the European (and Middle Eastern) philological tradition and the Brahmanical tradition of *Vyakarana* (the science of grammar and linguistics). This synthesis developed directly in response to (erroneous) claims by European philologists that all Indian languages derived from Sanskrit and counter-arguments initially proposed by Brahman specialists in *Vyakarana* that the Dravidian languages had an independent origin. Significantly, as Trautmann shows, the proof that Dravidian languages did not derive from Sanskrit could not have been deduced from either intellectual tradition standing alone. The European tradition contributed the segmentary, organizational system, based on the branches of a 'family tree', which governed how the differences and interrelationships between languages were ultimately conceived. But importantly, orientalist philology was not only receptive to authoritative statements by local pandits concerning the distinctiveness of the Dravidian group of languages (which previously had not been appreciated within the European tradition) but also accepted indigenous methods of analysis and standards of proof deriving from *Vyakarana* in order to do so. Remarkably, these classical Indian methods—such as identifying the roots of words and applying rules governing their systematic transformation—came to inform philological practice more generally thereafter.[36]

If Grove and Trautmann have provided rich, in-depth case studies of how specific Indian forms of knowledge contributed to the refashioning of European forms, then Christopher Bayly has shown us how broadly systemic this intercourse became during early colonial rule. Through his analysis of how British rule at least initially relied upon many of the same information sources and networks—newswriters, spies, *dak* runners (postal courier), and learned members of local society—that pre-colonial polities

Lynn Zastoupil, 'Intimacy and Colonial Knowledge', *Journal of Colonialism and Colonial History*, 3 (2002).

[35] Thomas R. Trautmann, 'Inventing the History of South India', in Daud Ali (ed.), *Invoking the Past: The Uses of History in South Asia* (Delhi, 1999), 36–54 as well as his 'Hullabaloo about Telugu', *South Asia Research*, 19 (1999), 53–70.

[36] For a superbly documented study of the collaborative dimensions of the related academic discipline of epigraphy, see Wagoner, 'Precolonial Intellectuals'.

had utilized, Bayly argues that much of the content of colonial knowledge of India derived from an ongoing engagement with Indian knowledge systems. It was only from the early nineteenth century that colonial government began to reject these indigenous institutions, which tended to be highly localized and densely multifarious, in favour of their own, more panoptic but attenuated 'knowledge institutions', such as the army, the political department, and the revenue, medical, legal, and educational services.[37] By showing how colonial knowledge was cobbled together from a plethora of diverse sources, Bayly provides one of the most convincing explanations of why orientalist knowledge never formed 'a coherent system of thought... [but] remained self-contradictory, fractured and contested'.[38] Moreover, unlike Trautmann's 'Indomania', Bayly has also shown that this collaboration need not necessarily be founded on any great affection for India. Instead, he has documented the conditions of uncertainty and paranoia among the British, created by gaps in their knowledge that in some sense drove colonial officials to seek out more and better information about local society, even where they despised it.[39]

Although Bayly must be commended for drawing attention to the specific informational networks that sustained the British intellectual engagement with their native subjects, his understanding of the stimuli animating this engagement has nevertheless remained somewhat one-dimensional insofar as they have focused almost exclusively on British fears and anxieties. Bayly offers much less about the engagement from an Indian point of view. In Bayly's analysis Indians remain ciphers: simple providers of raw information, intelligence, and data. He does not explore their specific agendas or how they actively attempted to realize those agendas through a self-interested fashioning of orientalist discourse itself. In other words, because Bayly treats knowledge as neutral and disinterested information, rather than as the larger structuring logics that order, orient, and ultimately give meaning to that data,[40] we do not see exactly how indigenous information

---

[37] C. A. Bayly, *Empire and Information: Intelligence Gathering and Social Communication in India, 1780–1870* (Cambridge, 1996), 143.

[38] Ibid. 370.

[39] See also Nigel Leask, *British Romantic Writers and the East: Anxieties of Empire* (Cambridge, 1992).

[40] This criticism of Bayly follows from Dirks, *Castes of Mind*, 309 and 355 n. 24. Despite my favourable citation of Dirks on this matter, readers should be wary of his egregious misrepresentations in the same book of many other aspects of Bayly's writings.

networks had a formative capacity. As a result, the indigenous agency that Bayly claims to have uncovered may only be of the limited, reactive sort outlined by Nandy (restricted to filling in the gaps in colonial knowledge), and his findings in and of themselves may not undermine the most far-reaching claims of discourse theory.

Eugene Irschick, on the other hand, has given more positive shape to this formative capacity with his notion of 'dialogue', by which he shows that colonial discourse was truly heteroglossic insofar as it betrays the agenda, influences, and effects of both indigenous peoples and colonial power.[41] Irschick's study of British agrarian land revenue policy in late eighteenth- and nineteenth-century Chingleput District (Madras) shows how the emergence of sedentary agricultural society in the Tamil country must be traced back to impulses emanating from both the British and, at least, certain key local groups, especially the *mirasidars*, a type of local landlord. In tracing the multiple origins of this social construct, Irschick provides a clear picture of what local Indian actors actually hoped to accomplish through their engagement with the British. He shows, for instance, how *mirasidars* acted to deepen their control over local agrarian society by shaping British understandings of 'traditional' agricultural relations in an idealized past in order to curb the mobility of agricultural labour, thereby fixing it to the specific lands over which the *mirasidars* alleged exclusive proprietary rights. *Mirasidars* were then able to use their increased dominance over local society in turn to exert leverage over the colonial state in order to keep the rate of tax they owed to the British at historically low levels. Significantly, the *mirasidars* accomplished all this in direct opposition to the colonial state's stated goal of maximizing its agrarian revenue.

Irschick's programme of highlighting the multi-authored dimensions of colonial knowledge has been broadly salutary. However, his characterization of the process by which this occurs as 'dialogue', with its connotations of an open-ended, uninhibited, and above-board exchange of ideas, may not be entirely apt for much of the later colonial encounter. Several commentators have remarked that it does not take adequate account of how the growing

---

[41] See Eugene F. Irschick, *Dialogue and History: Constructing South India, 1795–1895* (Berkeley, 1994). Thomas Trautmann has also developed a closely related idea of 'conversation' and these two authors now appear to use these terms interchangeably. See Trautmann, 'Inventing the History of South India' as well as his 'Hullaballoo about Telugu'. However, Irschick gives greater shape and specificity to the underlying agendas (colonial and native) motivating the dialogue.

asymmetries of power that were developing on the subcontinent, especially towards the end of the eighteenth century, deadened the free exchange of ideas and knowledges between Indians and the British.[42] As these asymmetries became more firmly established, it is clear that the British increasingly defined the sites around which discussion took place and canvassed local opinion or consulted native 'intellectuals' only when and where it suited them.[43] Moreover, as time wore on the prospects for meaningful dialogue became ever more restricted as British officials ceased to develop the requisite linguistic skills or forms of cultural 'literacy' in Indian life-ways, and many stereotypes by which they understood at least certain established topics—such as the nature of the state in India—became increasingly crystallized within a canon.[44]

However, the foreclosure of open dialogue does not mean that the agency of Indians was fully suppressed during the later nineteenth century. Rather it manifested itself in other ways. First, it is becoming increasingly apparent that fully conscious, above-board dialogue was not the only way in which Indian ideas and practices filtered into and ultimately helped shape colonial discourses. Much of this Indian influence came through more oblique or veiled channels. This important realization builds upon the fact that most data, utterances, and representations are richly polysemic or heteroglossic and are, therefore, capable of addressing more than one agenda simultaneously. As a result we are beginning to appreciate that while native informants were collaborating in doing the work of colonialism, they often inserted aims and ambitions into the information they passed onto their colonial masters about which the British initially were only dimly, if at all, aware. Recently, this recognition has been illustrated with respect to the all-India census, which for many years now has been the *locus classicus* for studies on the colonial construction of 'traditional' Indian society.

Ever since Bernard Cohn's famous essay on the topic, social historians have appreciated how the British collection of numerical data on caste in

---

[42] e.g. Washbrook, 'South India', 482 and Dirks, *Castes of Mind*, 310–11.

[43] In this respect, Irschick's representation of the open-ended exchange of knowledges between Europeans and Indians may be more appropriate in his recent study of the early 18th-century German missionary Bartholomaus Ziegenbalg. See Eugene F. Irschick, 'Conversations in Tarangambadi: Caring for the Self in Early Eighteenth Century South India', *Comparative Studies of South Asia, Africa and the Middle East*, 23 (2003), 3–20.

[44] See esp. Sanjay Subrahmanyam, 'Profiles in Transition: Of Adventurers and Administrators in South India, 1750–1810', *Indian Economic and Social History Review*, 39 (2002), 197–231.

India was not simply referential but was, in fact, generative.[45] The census's use of caste as a way of streaming undifferentiated data, he argued, helped create many fundamental characteristics of this form of social organization that many previous scholars uncritically accepted to be an ancient and unchanging bedrock of Indian society. In other words, the caste-based colonial censuses of the later nineteenth and early twentieth centuries did not objectively describe some already/always extant reality that was independent of and external to the gaze of the colonial state. Instead, the censuses actively created many of the social forms that they purported to describe. Not only did they institute 'a process of classifying and making objective' that gave rise to new ways of representing group identities,[46] but they also gave practical form to those representations by establishing new institutional 'arenas' of political struggle and contestation though which those representations could become a lived reality for ordinary Indians.[47]

Cohn's essay gave rise to a large number of studies that have examined various aspects of this enterprise. Rashmi Pant, for instance, showed how specific bureaucratic routines associated with the actual administration of the census during the later half of the nineteenth century set in motion various discursive practices that resulted in caste identities becoming standardized, their numbers simplified, the boundaries between them solidified, and the hierarchical relationships among them codified.[48] Richard Saumarez Smith explored how, as the census changed from 'an instrument of tax to an instrument of knowledge' during the course of the nineteenth century, caste identities were increasingly abstracted from the multivalent local contexts in which they had been embedded and inserted into a more 'synthetic vision of the whole of Indian society'.[49] Building upon these earlier insights, Arjun Appadurai suggested that the classificatory schemes

---

[45] Cohn, 'The Census'.

[46] Ibid. 250.

[47] For this latter insight Cohn was building on the earlier observations of G. S. Ghuyre, *Caste and Race in India* (Bombay, 1969) and M. N. Srinivas, *Social Change in Modern India* (Berkeley, 1960).

[48] Rashmi Pant, 'The Cognitive Status of Caste in Colonial Ethnography: A Review of Some Literature on the North West Provinces and Oudh', *Indian Economic and Social History Review*, 24 (1987), 145–62.

[49] Richard Saumarez Smith, 'Rule-by-Records and Rule-by-Reports: Complementary Aspects of the British Imperial Rule of Law', *Contributions to Indian Sociology*, NS 19 (1985), 153–76. See also his 'Between Local Tax and Global Statistic: The Census as Local Record', *Contributions to Indian Sociology*, NS 34 (2000), 1–35.

associated with the colonial census were part of larger universalizing forms of knowledge rooted in Western, numerate technologies and has proposed that their application was much more regulatory, rather than referential, in nature. They were intended to discipline both natives as well as members of the fractious colonial bureaucracy.[50]

But by looking at debates within the administrative correspondence that surrounded the earliest colonial censuses that were taken at the turn of the nineteenth century, I have shown that early British administrators were not generally interested in collecting population statistics that were differentiated according to caste identities.[51] Indeed a good many British officials expressed outright hostility towards caste-centred enumerations of populations as they were difficult to administer and cumbersome to use. They preferred much simpler schemes based on gender, age sets, and/or broad occupational or sociological categories (such as, agricultural v. manufacturing or rural v. urban). However, data on caste nevertheless crept into the colonial census largely because the British employed local Indian officials to collect census data for them, and these local officials based their censuses on late pre-colonial household lists (known as *khanasumari*s) that were caste-sensitive.[52] As a result, many native officials, even when unprompted by British superiors, returned early colonial census data that was differentiated on the basis of caste.

There are at least two interrelated reasons why data on caste was important to the indigenous polities of the late pre-colonial era. First, caste difference was one of the principal ways through which differential tax obligations were assessed and local hierarchies of privilege were established. Different castes were not only taxed in different ways but also at different rates with privileged castes typically enjoying significant tax concessions.[53] The enumeration of caste identities thus became important in administering the structure of privilege and status within many pre-colonial polities. Secondly, data on caste was also crucial for the state's ability to assess its revenue situation. Despite recent portrayals of the pre-colonial polity as

---

[50] Appadurai, 'Number in the Colonial Imagination'.

[51] Norbert Peabody, 'Cents, Sense, Census: Human Inventories in Late Precolonial and Early Colonial India', *Comparative Studies in Society and History*, 43 (2001), 819–50.

[52] See also Sumit Guha, 'The Politics of Identity and Enumeration in India c. 1600–1990', *Comparative Studies in Society and History*, 45 (2003), 148–67.

[53] Ibid. 153.

existing in a condition of fiscal innocence,[54] a mounting wealth of evidence shows that many of the larger and more centrally located polities, at least, were acutely interested in maximizing their revenue streams and controlling the flows of cash through their treasuries because the military was increasingly paid in cash, rather than by land-revenue assignments. As it became important to amass, account for, and shift funds, many pre-colonial polities developed highly complex administrative bureaucracies that were staffed and run by Brahmans and other literate/numerate 'scribal' castes who had the requisite skill sets to undertake these tasks.[55] The status and influence of these groups thus rose dramatically during the late pre-colonial era, often at the expense of the older landed aristocracy, and this constituted one of the major points of tension and conflict within many indigenous polities on the eve of colonial expansion.

During the colonial transition, many of these literate officials worked their way into the colonial bureaucracy where they actively shaped how the British viewed Indian society precisely in order to perpetuate and deepen their locally privileged positions.[56] Making knowledge about caste central to understandings of the financial underpinnings of the state was one such way that they made their skills essential. That the British did not initially understand what these local informants were up to is beside the point. They accepted the divisions of data on the basis of caste because the data was still useful to their purposes, albeit for different reasons. With time, of course, the British began to use this caste data in the disciplinary way described by Smith, Appadurai, and others, but by that time the scribal castes had cemented their position both within the colonial bureaucracy—where they became indispensable arbiters of caste custom and privilege—as well as within local society.

Secondly, it has been noted that, even where Indians adopted European forms of knowledge, the uses to which they put them did not always conform to the desires and intentions of their European framers. Michael Dodson, for example, has explored how James Ballantyne, the superintendent of Benaras College in the mid-nineteenth century, introduced new forms of 'useful knowledge' based on Western science to the curriculum to

---

[54] e.g. Dirks, *Hollow Crown*, ch. 4.
[55] Susan Bayly, *Caste, Society and Politics in India from the Eighteenth Century to the Modern Age* (The New Cambridge History of India, iv/3; (Cambridge, 1999), esp. ch. 2.
[56] Ibid. ch. 4.

undermine the faith of the college pandits in the authority of Vedas.[57] And indeed many pandits willingly helped facilitate Ballantyne's project by translating European scientific systems of thinking into Sanskrit and more than a few adopted the new techniques of analysis to which they were introduced. Yet surprisingly, the pandits were well able to apply this new knowledge to their own ends by showing that it was 'a reflection of that which could already be accounted for in the shastra'.[58] Thus although it is clear that the introduction of Western science caused the pandits to look at the shastra in a different light, the foundational premise of Brahmanical learning—as an activity of recovery rather than discovery—remained intact. Moreover, in arguing that European techniques of analysis already existed within Indian texts, they questioned the claims to authority over it that were enunciated by the British.

Sumit Sarkar has similarly shown that colonial discourses were never 'totalizing', in the sense that they did not completely erase the traces of older indigenous ways of knowing, on account of the specific processes and temporalities of their introduction. Sarkar, for example, has called attention to how some forms of disciplinary knowledge, such as Western, linear clock-time associated with factory and office work, were imposed on Bengal in a highly compressed time period in comparison to similar developments in Britain, where these regimes emerged more organically—and less visibly—over a much longer epoch.[59] This sudden introduction of clock time did not completely blind Bengalis to colonial power; in some respects, just the opposite. It heightened awareness of it precisely because of the ways that Bengalis still had memory—however fragmentary—of alternative Indian forms of recurring time associated with the cycle of the yugas. Significantly, this memory did not manifest itself in the reassertion of a heroic, but doomed, indigenous authenticity in which traditional values held over from an earlier era were uncritically plied in the face of colonial

---

[57] Michael S. Dodson, 'Re-Presented for the Pandits: James Ballantyne, "Useful Knowledge," and Sanskrit Scholarship in Benaras College during the Mid-Nineteenth Century', *Modern Asian Studies*, 36 (2002), 257–98. See also Michael S. Dodson, *Orientalism, Empire, and National Culture: India 1770–1880* (Basingstoke, 2007).

[58] Ibid. 298. For a similar example of how subaltern groups were able to resist/reinterpret the master-narratives of elites, see also Shahid Amin, 'Gandhi as Mahatma: Gorakhpur District, Eastern UP, 1921–1922', in Ranajit Guha (ed.), *Subaltern Studies*, iii (Delhi, 1984), 1–61.

[59] Sumit Sarkar, 'Renaissance and Kaliyuga: Time, Myth and History in Colonial Bengal', in *Writing Social History* (Delhi, 1997), 186–215.

dislocations.[60] Instead Sarkar shows how Bengalis engaged in a much more complicated bricolage of knowledge systems and world views as they creatively, if at times inchoately, disarticulated and recombined elements of *both* discourses to formulate critiques of colonial power as well as of more locally constituted social hierarchies articulated along the lines of caste and gender.

Sarkar's findings are significant insofar as they help us reconfigure and refine our understandings of exactly what sort of power a particular discourse is able to exert. Sarkar shows that the formative capacity of colonial discourse does not lie so much in its ability to set boundaries or parameters within which people's thought and action are contained or limited. Rather its power rests more on its ability to establish a site or centre from which thought and action is launched.[61] It defines a point of departure, but not the extent of a universe. In showing how a discourse establishes an initial point of reference, this view remains alive to the important ways in which the definition of the site may shape any future engagement with it. But by remaining sensitive to how a colonial discourse interacts with other ways of knowing and being which overlap but are not congruent to the colonial discourse, Sarkar shows how the limits of a discourse are always provisional and contingent. Ultimately, limits are determined much more conjuncturally by how the discourse combines with other forms of knowledge and social forces, some of which lie beyond its own terms and which bring to it unanticipated and unexpected content in a way that meaningfully contributes to its overall formation.

Dis/continuities and Dichotomies

The position advocated in this chapter thus diverges from much previous discourse theory. In charting the 'radical ruptures' that colonialism has wrought on India, discourse theory has assumed that all socio-political change is colonially induced. Part of the truth effect of this prevailing view rests on a dubious romanticism about indigenous society prior to

---

[60] For a classic example of this sort of Geertzean 'two systems' approach to social change, see Nicholas B. Dirks's analysis of the Don Quixote-like actions of Venkannan Cervaikarar during Pudukkottai's Agrarian Rebellion of 1853–4 in *The Hollow Crown: Ethnohistory of an Indian Kingdom* (Ann Arbor, 1993), ch. 10.

[61] For a related argument in the postcolonial context, see Norbert Peabody, 'Inchoate in Kota: Contesting Authority Through a North Indian Pageant-Play', *American Ethnologist*, 24 (1997), 559–84.

European colonization that problematically assumes that it was internally consistent, thoroughly integrated, and largely consensual. Against this backdrop of social harmony and political equilibrium, any form of social change becomes, by default, foreign (that is, colonial) in origin.[62] But once one appreciates that indigenous society on the eve of colonialism was both internally divided and dynamic, one can begin to see how some aspects of the social transformations under colonial rule were linked to processes of change that were at least partially rooted in indigenously constituted political tensions and social disjunctions. As a result, one begins to realize that colonial transformations often had a more hybridized ontological status than generally recognized. From this vantage point, 'the colonial' becomes somewhat less fully European in constitution and more the product of an encounter (however asymmetrical) between British and Indian societies.

Several significant implications for the course of further research on colonialism follow from this appreciation. First, to be able to assess precisely what effects the British had on India, one must develop much more sophisticated understandings of the socio-political transformations that were already underway there during the late pre-colonial era precisely because these processes had a discernable impact on the texture and unfolding of colonialism itself. This means that any exploration of the impact of colonialism on India must include some assessment of the *status quo ante*, something that a number of studies neglect.[63] Moreover, the *status quo ante* must not be seen as an idyllic era of social integration and political harmony. Rather analysts must remain sensitive to the social heterogeneity, political contestations, and historical variability that characterized indigenous Indian society prior to the arrival of Europeans. Europeans were not the only vectors of socio-political change in India, and the refusal of many scholars to address this basic fact may represent one of orientalist scholarship's most persistent legacies. An important corollary of this awareness is that one must also pay greater attention to indigenous social divisions along the lines of caste and gender so as to be able to assess exactly which Indian groups were able to realize their aims and ambitions and at whose expense,

---

[62] Thus is this regard, discourse theory curiously shares much with the acculturation theories of Melville Herskovits and others that were popular in the 1950s and 1960s.

[63] See e.g. Clare Anderson's otherwise laudable *Legible Bodies: Race, Criminality and Colonialism in South Asia* (Oxford, 2004).

both under the old regimes of the late pre-colonial era as well as under colonialism.

Secondly, from a comparative perspective, one must also be aware that the blanket term colonialism (as applied in the singular) to diverse cases of European domination over non-Europeans across geographic space and historical time may, in some circumstances, obscure more than it reveals. Because the texture of colonialism owed much to local conditions, colonialisms' institutions, logics, and experiences also varied widely. As Jorge Klor de Alva has recently suggested with respect to racial categorizations across (and beyond) the Spanish colonial world, the nature of colonialism was remarkably fluid and variable.[64] Much more comparative analysis of colonialism(s) is still needed to bring out the qualities and effects of these differences.

Finally, it is now clear that the colonial landscape was inhabited by a great multiplicity of groups whose constitution was neither discrete nor stable from context to context, and each of these groups had different agendas as well as different capacities to realize them. The existence and persistence of indigenously constituted social, political, and gendered hierarchies has meant that Indian engagement with the British was never uniform. The same can be said about the British and their engagement with Indians. As a result, divisions among Indians and among the British could be as significant as the divisions between Indians and the British. This position, of course, means that many of the stark analytic dichotomies around which most discourse theory has been organized must be re-examined and re-thought. Such neat two-column entries of binary oppositions—such as European and Indian, colonizer and colonized, agent and patient, perpetrator and victim—no longer hold in the way that they once did. One of the great challenges before us is to develop more sophisticated descriptive techniques, analytic tools, and theoretical frameworks for dealing with the multiple constituted, overlapping, and hierarchically graded forms of agency to which the historical and ethnographic records now increasingly bear witness.

---

[64] J. Jorge Klor de Alva, 'The Postcolonization of the (Latin) American Experience: A Reconsideration of "Colonialism", "Postcolonialism", and "Mestizaje"', in Gyan Prakash (ed.), *After Colonialism: Imperial Histories and Postcolonial Displacements* (Princeton 1995), 241–75.

Select Bibliography

C. A. BAYLY, *Empire and Information: Intelligence Gathering and Social Communication in India, 1780–1870* (Cambridge, 1996).

SUSAN BAYLY, *Caste, Society and Politics in India from the Eighteenth Century to the Modern Age* (The New Cambridge History of India, iv/3; Cambridge, 1999).

BERNARD S. COHN, *An Anthropologist among the Historians and Other Essays* (Delhi, 1986).

——*Colonialism and Its Forms of Knowledge: The British in India* (Princeton, 1996).

NICHOLAS B. DIRKS, *Castes of Mind: Colonialism and the Making of Modern India* (Princeton, 2001).

MICHAEL S. DODSON, 'Re-Presented for the Pandits: James Ballantyne, "Useful Knowledge," and Sanskrit Scholarship in Benaras College during the Mid-Nineteenth Century', *Modern Asian Studies*, 36 (2002), 257–98.

EUGENE F. IRSCHICK, *Dialogue and History: Constructing South India, 1795–1895* (Berkeley, 1994).

ROSALIND O'HANLON, 'Recovering the Subject: *Subaltern Studies* and Histories of Resistance in Colonial South Asia', *Modern Asian Studies*, 22 (1988), 189–224.

NORBERT PEABODY, 'Tod's *Rajast'han* and the Boundaries of Imperial Rule in Nineteenth-Century India', *Modern Asian Studies*, 30 (1996), 185–220.

——'Cents, Sense, Census: Human Inventories in Late Precolonial and Early Colonial India', *Comparative Studies in Society and History*, 43 (2001), 819–50.

SUMIT SARKAR, *Writing Social History* (Delhi, 1997).

SANJAY SUBRAHMANYAM, *Mughals and Franks: Explorations in Connected History* (Delhi, 2005).

THOMAS R. TRAUTMANN, 'Inventing the History of South India', in Daud Ali (ed.), *Invoking the Past: The Uses of History in South Asia* (Delhi, 1999), 36–54.

PHILLIP B. WAGONER, 'Precolonial Intellectuals and the Production of Colonial Knowledge', *Comparative Studies in Society and History*, 25 (2003), 783–814.

DAVID WASHBROOK, 'Orients and Occidents: Theories of Colonial Discourse and the Historiography of the British Empire', in Robin Winks (ed.), *The Oxford History of the British Empire*, v. *Historiography* (Oxford, 1999), 596–611.

——'South India 1770–1840: The Colonial Transition', *Modern Asian Studies*, 38 (2004), 479–516.

5
Colonialism and Social Identities in Flux
Class, Caste, and Religious Community

Rosalind O'Hanlon

The study of India's major social institutions and their changing forms under colonialism has a long and complex intellectual history. From the closing decades of the eighteenth century, British scholars and Indian intellectuals alike sought to understand the nature of Indian social and political change as the East India Company began to assume the role of a regional political power with authority deriving directly from the old Mughal imperial centre in Delhi. For much of the high colonial period many British and some Indian observers saw this relationship as a process of modernization. On this understanding, India's most important social institutions were its caste system and its archaic and dominating forms of religious community. These hampered the development of stable states, impeded efficient forms of economic organization, and blocked the emergence of the forms of personal liberty that were the hallmark of a modern civil society. Although itself founded in war and conquest, Britain's imperial mission was to foster the institutions and values of a modern civil society and so enable India to shake off these paralysing inheritances from the past.[1]

This liberal paradigm of modernization was profoundly affected by the Indian Rebellion of 1857, and further shaken by the increasingly astringent and penetrating critiques made by Indian intellectuals. By the closing decades of the nineteenth century, these critiques of 'British India' covered a wide field, from the effects of a heavy land revenue burden and the

---

[1] For a survey of British attitudes, see Thomas R. Metcalf, *Ideologies of the Raj* (Cambridge, 1995), 28–65.

destruction of India's handicraft industry to the deficiencies of Indian provincial governments in their responses to periodic crises of famine and plague. They also exposed the disparities between Britain's liberal ideals and the reality of its authoritarian and racially based governing institutions in India: disparities given a sharper edge by the mobilization of Indian manpower and resources on the huge scale demanded by the First World War. Underlying these critiques, and articulated most clearly by Gandhi, was an increasingly confident public exposition of India's own traditions of good government.[2] Writing from a range of different political perspectives, some British observers also argued that a government founded on conquest could not in the end act as an instrument of modernization, however fervent its public rhetoric about the civilizing mission of empire.[3] The popular violence that accompanied India's passage to independence in 1947, which to many contemporary observers appeared to emerge from deeply ingrained religious antagonisms, lent further weight to these critiques.

As simple models of Indian modernization lost ground, more nuanced approaches sought to replace them. For much scholarly analysis in the postwar decades, the postcolonial world was made up of distinctive cultural regions. Historians and anthropologists working from this 'area studies' perspective often took the view that India represented an 'exceptional' society, its dominant forms of social hierarchy and religious community rooted in a unique cultural history not susceptible to explanation through familiar historical models. These approaches, many of them indebted to Louis Dumont's representation of caste as India's distinctive and defining social institution, raised important wider questions.[4] Yet they were vulnerable to the argument, articulated most clearly in the work of Edward Said and developed in the later work of the Subaltern Studies Collective, that colonial knowledge-gathering itself constituted an exercise of power, to which historians and anthropologists had been insufficiently attentive when they turned to colonial archives for their source material.[5]

---

[2] C. A. Bayly, *Origins of Nationality in South Asia: Patriotism and Ethical Government in the Making of Modern India* (Delhi, 1998), 62–132.

[3] See e.g. the journalist William Digby's *Famine Campaign in Southern India 1876–1878* (London, 1878).

[4] Louis Dumont, *Homo Hierarchicus* (London, 1970).

[5] For an introduction to these debates, see Vinayak Chaturvedi (ed.), *Mapping Subaltern Studies and the Postcolonial* (London, 2000).

It is understandable that these questions about the particularities of India's social development have continued to provide a significant framework for debate. Perhaps most obviously, India's deep regional differences seem to challenge any straightforward narrative of social change. From the late eighteenth century, the East India Company set about imposing a new imperial order on an India then moving in strongly regional directions, as many post-Mughal successor states deepened their penetration of local revenue networks and strengthened their appeal to local loyalties.[6] This shift back to a new form of imperial centre made the combination of regional and all-India dynamics particularly complex. The encouragement of vernacular languages, the rapid growth of print technologies and audiences, and the establishment of regional political institutions helped to develop and deepen these regional identities and attachments. But at another level, the colonial state provided from the early nineteenth century a framework within which colonial subjects began to discover themselves as Indians too.

Again, the nature of some Indian social institutions has presented particular challenges. Colonial India possessed in caste a long-established, pervasive, and multilayered social institution. With its contested role in Hindu religious culture and its great regional diversity, caste has presented a peculiar challenge to historians and anthropologists. Its study has been deeply affected by successive intellectual trends, from the structuralist approaches of the 1970s emerging out of the influential work of Louis Dumont, to the focus on texts and colonial knowledges that dominated much of the scholarly work on colonial caste in subsequent decades.[7] More recently, the focus has moved to the historicity of caste. Susan Bayly and others have argued that while the principles of *varna* and *jati* were themselves of ancient origin, these only came to be extended comprehensively throughout Indian society from the eighteenth century, initially as a

---

[6] C. A. Bayly, *Indian Society and the Making of the British Empire* (Cambridge, 1988), 1–106; Stuart Gordon, *Marathas, Marauders and State Formation in Eighteenth-Century India* (Delhi, 1994); Kate Brittlebank, *Islam and Kingship in a Hindu Domain: Tipu Sultan's Search for Legitimacy* (Delhi, 1997); Muzaffar Alam, *The Crisis of Empire in Mughal North India: Awadh and the Punjab 1707–1748* (Delhi, 1986); Richard B. Barnett, *North India between Empire: Awadh, the Mughals and the British 1720–1801* (New Delhi, 1987); Kumkum Chatterjee, *Merchants, Politics and Society in Early Modern India. Bihar: 1733–1820* (Leiden, 1996).

[7] For connections between caste and colonial knowledges, see esp. Bernard S. Cohn, *Colonialism and Its Forms of Knowledge: The British in India* (Princeton 1996) and Nicholas B. Dirks, *Castes of Mind: Colonialism and the Making of Modern India* (Princeton, 2001).

consequence of the strengthening power of scribal and ritual elites in the post-Mughal successor states, and then over the course of the nineteenth century as these movements of upward mobility were reinforced by the legal, religious and administrative strategies of the British colonial state. Caste from this perspective is essentially diverse and historically mutable, but also a continuing and recognizable characteristic of Indian social life, standing alone as a distinctive mode of thought and action.[8]

The study of class in colonial India has also posed significant challenges, given the strongly agrarian character of colonial society and the apparent dominance within India's colonial economy of forms of capitalism that apparently failed to initiate wider social transformation, depending more for profits on the exploitation of a very large pool of labour working at low levels of productivity.[9] The search therefore for elements of class formation took the form of sometimes mechanistic and determinist debates about 'modes of production' in agrarian society.[10] These approaches proved difficult to apply too rigidly in the Indian rural setting, in which there were seldom sharp distinctions in ownership of capital and land. For historians concerned more with questions of consciousness and identity, class emerged rather as an expression of a peculiar primordial rural consciousness, which survived the shift into the environment of factory and mill.[11] Recent work has challenged these assumptions, but tracing the interplay of class and caste, the rural and the urban, has undoubtedly remained very complex.[12]

The same difficulties have attended the study of religious community in colonial India. Many historians have detected the emergence in some

---

[8] Susan Bayly, *Caste, Society and Politics in India from the Eighteenth Century to the Modern Age* (Cambridge, 1999). For the development of caste identities in early modern India, see Rosalind O'Hanlon and Christopher Minkowski, 'What Makes People Who They Are? Pandit Networks and the Problem of Livelihoods in Early Modern Western India', *Indian Economic and Social History Review*, 45/3 (2008), 381–416 and Rosalind O'Hanlon, 'The Social Worth of Scribes: Brahmins, Kayasthas and the Social Order in Early Modern India', *Economic and Social History Review*, 47/4 (2010), 563–95.

[9] B. R. Tomlinson, *The Economy of Modern India 1860–1970* (Cambridge, 1993), 30–91.

[10] Utsa Patnaik (ed.), *Agrarian Relations and Accumulation: The 'Mode of Production' Debate in India* (Bombay, 1990).

[11] See e.g. Dipesh Chakrabarty, *Rethinking Working Class History: Bengal 1890–1940* (Princeton, 1989).

[12] See in particular the critique in Rajnarayan Chandavarkar, *The Origins of Industrial Capitalism in India: Business Strategies and the Working Classes in Bombay, 1900–1940* (Cambridge, 1994), 1–20.

settings of more composite and self-consciously bounded forms of religious community identity. This was particularly in urban milieus, where new media for communication and new arenas for public debate gave older symbols a wider mobilizing potential. Here also, local British officials seemed to deepen and prolong conflict by their efforts to identify and work through 'natural' community leaders, by their attempts to find a 'balance' between Hindu and Muslim interests, and by their insistence that all questions of religious rights should be determined by appeal to legal precedent through the colonial courts.[13] At the same time, as Nandini Gooptu has argued, some of these arguments come dangerously close to a teleology, in which a monolithic all-India Hinduism emerged inexorably out of older and more diverse religious identities, and in which all forms of popular affiliation were ultimately overwhelmed by religious consciousness.[14]

The roles and forms of Indian agency in the colonial social setting have also been characterized in sharply divergent ways, reflecting wider disagreements about the transforming power of the colonial state.[15] This was a state of considerable longevity, thinly peopled with British personnel, adept at searching out Indian partners and able to transfer intact many of its instruments of rule to Indian successors. This combination of circumstances has seemed to pose the question of Indian 'agency' in a particularly sharp form. Depending on the context in which its institutions are studied, characterizations of the colonial state seems to fluctuate between hyperactive concern and wilful neglect, compendious knowledge and staggering ignorance, pervasive power and crippling impotence, extraordinary sensitivity to opposition and crude repression. These contradictions have made it difficult to arrive at a coherent understanding, particularly in the present intellectual climate in which study of 'the state' tends to be seen as an aspect

---

[13] For some regional examples, see Sandria B. Freitag, *Collective Action and Community: Public Arenas and the Emergence of Communalism in North India* (Berkeley, 1989); Peter van der Veer, *Religious Nationalism: Hindus and Muslims in India*, (Berkeley, 1994); Katherine Prior, 'Making History: The State's Intervention in Urban Religious Disputes in the North-West Provinces in the Early Nineteenth Century', *Modern Asian Studies*, 27 (1993), 179–204 and Gyanendra Pandey, *The Construction of Communalism in Colonial North India* (Delhi, 1990).

[14] Nandini Gooptu, *The Politics of the Urban Poor in Early Twentieth Century India* (Cambridge, 2001), 5.

[15] Partha Chatterjee, *The Nation and Its Fragments: Colonial and Postcolonial Histories* (Delhi, 1995), 35–75 and Ranajit Guha, *Dominance Without Hegemony: History and Power in Colonial India* (Cambridge, Mass., 1997).

of 'elite' history, attracting less scholarly attention than was the case a generation ago.

Yet if the social history of colonial India has seemed sometimes to present acute intellectual difficulties, scholars in the field have also enjoyed some incomparable advantages. For many parts of Britain's formal empire, the study of social history is made difficult by the paucity of written materials that pre-date the coming of colonialism, making it difficult to trace key processes of colonial social change. With its particular linguistic, literary, and political history, India offers extraordinary richness in this respect, and our understanding of what is distinctive about colonial social change has been significantly enhanced by research into the subcontinent's late precolonial history. The colonial state itself, in turn, amassed extraordinary quantities of information about its subjects, even though this information emerged refracted through the state's political purposes and its acquisition uneven across many areas of Indian politics and society.

If sources have proved one area of significant advantage, methodologies have proved another. In part because of the challenges set out above, Indian historians have often been able to make a substantial intellectual contribution within wider fields of social and cultural history. In studies of class and material social relations, for example, the work of the Subaltern Studies Collective has been widely influential in its construction of a colonial 'history from below' and its search for connections between class-consciousness and older forms of rural solidarity.[16] Other historians have developed substantial critiques of the monolithic understanding of class found in Western scholarship, and explored the multilayered and fluid nature of working-class 'consciousness' in colonial India, set in the context not just of the workplace but also of the neighbourhood and in urban public arenas where community identities were expressed and contested.[17] Another area in which new approaches have been developed for the study of what were effectively relations of class has been the emergence of new public spheres in colonial India. Various forms of cultural capital determined access to these new arenas, from literate skills and bilingualism to mastery of the cultural vocabularies of regional and community identity. From this perspective too, class identities look more fluid and contextual

---

[16] See e.g. the debates in Chaturvedi, *Subaltern Studies and the Postcolonial.*

[17] Chandavarkar, *Origins of Industrial Capitalism* and Gooptu, *Politics of the Urban Poor.*

than monolithic, and inseparable from the cultures of India's linguistic regions.[18]

In many Indian settings, class identities were often couched in the language of caste solidarity and assertion, and drew on a caste-based language of purity, piety, and social worth. Caste is, of course, at one level a distinctively Indian form of hierarchy, without simple parallels in other colonial settings. Nevertheless, historians exploring its changing colonial forms have developed a much larger appreciation of the ways in which the colonial environment gave new shape and impetus to caste organization: in urban settings where it could offer great social advantage, and in an agrarian order characterized by sharper class differences often expressed in the language of caste hierarchy. Other historians again have explored the interplay between caste, agrarian social change, and the emergence of new regional and ethnic identities.[19] In recent years, too, historians have increasingly understood the interface between the settled agrarian order and the internal frontiers of hill and forest to be fluid and shifting rather than immutable, and have traced the implications of its movement for caste, class, and regional identity.[20] In a similar way, more integrated approaches to intellectual history have amplified our understanding of the history of nationalism in India. Kum Kum Chatterjee has explored the discourse of political critique developed by eighteenth-century Indian state administrators and servants.[21] Christopher Bayly traces these themes into the nineteenth century and beyond, to demonstrate the origins of many of the intellectual themes of later Indian nationalism in these discourses, often inflected through regional histories and more local forms of patriotic attachment.[22] This and other studies have made it clear that India's political culture had before the coming of colonialism developed many of the characteristics once thought to be uniquely Western in origin.

---

[18] See e.g. Veena Naregal, *Language Politics, Elites and the Public Sphere: Western India Under Colonialism* (Delhi, 2001).

[19] See e.g. Eugene Irschick, *Dialogue and History: Constructing South India 1795–1895* (Berkeley, 1994).

[20] Sumit Guha, *Environment and Ethnicity in India 1200–1991* (Cambridge, 1999) and Ajay Skaria, *Hybrid Histories: Forests, Frontiers and Wildness in Western India* (Delhi, 1999).

[21] Kum Kum Chatterjee, 'History as Self-Representation: The Recasting of a Political Tradition in Late Eighteenth-Century Eastern India', *Modern Asian Studies*, 32 (1998), 913–48.

[22] C. A. Bayly, *Origins of Nationality in South Asia: Patriotism and Ethical Government in the Making of Modern India* (Delhi, 1998), 63–132.

The success of these more integrated approaches suggests that it is most productive to explore structures of caste, class, and religious community as elements in a wider social history, rather than expressions of a unique or exceptional colonial past. This essay seeks to identify some of the most important of them, and to trace out the changes that link them, with a broad focus on the nineteenth century. In the argument offered below, the creation of a predominantly sedentary and agrarian society, and the growing separation between landed, commercial, military, and scribal forms of power are taken to be the most far-reaching consequences of the coming of colonialism in India, and to mark the sharpest reverse of pre-existing historical trends. The essay begins therefore by exploring this process of sedentarization in its many dimensions.

'Sedentarization', Demilitarization, and the Making of Agrarian Societies

Many regional studies have emphasized the mobility of late pre-colonial India's regional societies. This derived in part from the close relationships that developed between royal, scribal, commercial, and military power. To compete in the fluid political world that emerged as Mughal authority shrank from the early eighteenth century, developing regional states needed the services of a wide range of skilled and specialist communities: corporations of Hindu and Jain bankers to finance their operations, new classes of revenue farmers to maximize the flow of revenue from agrarian production, specialist communities of accountants and administrators to oversee state finances, military entrepreneurs to recruit armies during the campaigning season, merchants and artisan producers to supply luxury commodities.[23]

These opportunities for mobility extended more widely into agrarian society. Relatively low levels of population in relation to land, even in the more densely settled riverine tracts of the subcontinent, meant that local power-holders frequently needed to work hard to attract communities of cultivators with offers of secure forms of tenure and reduced revenue demands. The structures of agrarian society themselves facilitated this high degree of mobility. Regional military labour markets in many parts of India offered seasonal employment to farmers and pastoralists during the dry season, the associations with military service providing important local

---

[23] See n. 6 above.

signifiers of honour and status.[24] Pastoralists and hill people moved between the forest margin and settled agriculture, valued for their skills as bowmen, crop watchers, or garrison soldiers.[25] In the unsettled conditions of the eighteenth century, north India's great corporations of military monks were able to develop their skills and their commercial interests as protectors of shrines, pilgrims and monastic wealth, and increasingly to offer their regiments for service to regional power-holders.[26] Communities such as the Banjaras, specialist carriers and wandering dealers in grain and other commodities, flourished along with their caravans of pack bullocks. They bore arms for assault and plunder as well as for defensive use, and whenever their herds had suffered particular damage through warfare, they would obtain permission to settle in forest tracts where they would find resources enough to live while their herds recovered.[27] These forms of mobility both underpinned the commercial and political dynamism of many regional societies in the eighteenth century, and reflected the circumstances of periodic warfare, political disruption, and famine in others.

Ironically, of course, it was this very combination of a wide range of valuable commodity trades flourishing within an open and still fluid political system, multiple opportunities for entrepreneurs and investors able to benefit from the commercialization of state power, and a plentiful supply of local military labour, that offered to the East India Company its early opportunities for expansion. But if mobility created the environment for British expansion from the early conquest of Bengal in 1757, it quickly became a focus for anxiety, as the Company emerged out of the wars of the late eighteenth and early nineteenth century that left its major Indian rivals defeated and reduced in authority. The main thrust of its social and economic policy after 1820 lay in the drive to tie peasant communities more closely to the land, to restrict opportunities for formerly mobile populations of military men, pastoralists, hill people, and hunters, and to bring into

---

[24] Seema Alavi, *The Sepoys and the Company: Tradition and Transition in North India 1770–1830* (Delhi, 1995) and Dirk Kolff, *Naukar, Rajput and Sepoy: The Ethnohistory of the Military Labour Market in Hindustan 1450–1750* (Cambridge, 1990).

[25] Guha, *Environment and Ethnicity*, 30–82.

[26] William Pinch, *Peasants and Monks in British India* (Berkeley and Los Angeles, 1996), 23–47.

[27] See e.g. the account by Colonel Mark Wilkes of the grain-carriers who supplied Cornwallis's army during the campaign against Tipu Sultan: Colonel Mark Wilkes, *Historical Sketches of the South of India* (London, 1817), iii. 208–11.

being peaceable communities of settled and productive cultivators who would be easy to police and easy to tax.

'Sedentarization', as historians have called it, was a complex process.[28] From its move in 1765 to secure from the Mughal emperor rights to collect land revenues in Bengal, the logic of the Company's position in India pointed to an ever deeper engagement with agrarian societies and their revenues. Internal tax revenues substituted for imported bullion in the purchase of Indian commodities for export and quickly became a vital means of paying for the Company's rapidly expanding armies. From the Permanent Settlement in Bengal in 1793, which identified Bengal's large landlords as exclusive title-holders to the land at a fixed revenue demand, to the settlements with peasant farmers that came to dominate agrarian policy in the Madras and Bombay presidencies, colonial officials engaged in a continuous and intricate set of debates about Indian agriculture. Economists and political observers back in Britain as well as the local 'collectors' of revenue found themselves absorbed in lengthy public debate about the true nature of the state's interest in its revenues, the role of the state in regulating relations between landlord and tenant, what forms of land tenure were appropriate in the different Indian settings, and what levels of revenue demand were most likely to maximize productivity, particularly in the cash crops that from the second decade of the nineteenth century were beginning to displace craft manufactures as India's principle export.[29] Abstruse debate gave way in many cases to pragmatism on the ground, as local officials and revenue collectors struggled to reconcile theory with local realities.

Following the shock of the Mutiny-Rebellion of 1857, British policy moved gradually but decisively to reduce the burden of revenue demand on Indian agriculture. In many parts of India, smallholders, sharecroppers, and tenant farmers still struggled to surmount drought, famine, debt, and epidemic disease. In the more ecologically favoured regions of Madras and Bombay, Gangetic India, and the Punjab, however, the second half of the century saw the gradual emergence of those large and powerful 'dominant peasant' castes that were to become the defining feature of Indian agrarian society in these regions by the time of the First World War. Vellalas, Patidars,

---

[28] Many historians have discussed this process. See esp. C. A. Bayly, *Indian Society*, 136–68; Irschick, *Dialogue and History*, 14–66; and Radhika Singha, 'Settle, Mobilise, Verify: Identification Practices in Colonial India', *Studies in History*, 16/2 (2000), 151–98.

[29] Burton Stein (ed.), *The Making of Agrarian Policy in British India 1770–1900* (Delhi, 1992).

Kurmis, Marathas, Jats, and others benefited not only from this progressive lightening of the tax burden, but also from new irrigation schemes, improving transport infrastructure, and expanding markets for agricultural commodities. Other artisan and service communities in herding, dairy farming, and market gardening also gained from this development in settled agriculture and the growth of demand in expanding colonial cities. This fundamental reshaping of the contours of Indian agrarian society in favour of wealthier and settled farming communities, which produced what Eugene Irschick has called 'the rise in esteem of sedentary agriculture as a form of culture', was to have profound consequences for a wide range of social, cultural, and political processes in Indian society.[30]

'Sedentarization' meant more than attaching rural people more firmly to the land. It also meant bringing more marginal land under the plough, and the progressive extension of state control over the forests and thick scrublands that still constituted formidable internal frontiers in many hill areas. Here, concern with the productivity of agriculture ran closely alongside the struggle for security. After the defeat of the Maratha power in 1818, it was from communities of independent hill chiefs, pastoralists, swidden-farmers, nomad herdsmen, and hunters that the early Company state faced its most intractable resistances. Forest people such as the Bhils, Kolis, Ramoshis, and Gavlis of western India, or herdsmen such as Gujars and Bhattis of the north had often been able to strike hard bargains with the regional power-holders of the eighteenth century, and their pacification posed a continuing challenge. Some hill chiefs were offered pensions and allowances providing they refrained from raiding and helped with local policing duties. Other forest people, former guardians of frontiers and forts, were given employment as watchmen and guardians of passes.[31] Their opportunities as military auxiliaries disappearing and their access to wasteland for grazing progressively restricted, many carriers and nomadic herdsmen took to cultivation or to developing more settled herds. In western India by the 1880s, for example, Banjaras were reported to have become cultivators and market gardeners and petty dealers in grain, fodder, wood, and milk. Progressively excluded from their older forest livelihoods, many other hill communities found themselves pushed towards the cash cropping areas of Gujarat, central India, and the southern deltas, providing a larger pool of dependent

---

[30] Irschick, *Dialogue and History*, 191.
[31] Guha, *Environment and Ethnicity*, 130–49.

migrant labour as seasonal demand fluctuated.[32] Ironically, the pressures and resentments created here found explosive outlet in the Rebellion of 1857, as pastoralists and forest people everywhere saw in the collapse of Company authority the opportunity to avenge themselves on the settled farmer.[33]

There were other formidable challenges to these attempts to take the mobility out of rural society. Many occupational groups possessed long traditions of seasonal military service. Farmers offered themselves as troopers through the local military labour markets. Successor states increasingly developed their own standing regiments, officered by European mercenaries. Many larger landowners possessed their own armed retainers, supported by land grants or military pensions, while hill people guarded passes or garrisoned forts. Monks and carrier herdsmen developed military skills as a necessary part of their specialist skills in guarding shrines or transporting grain or livestock over long distances. The unsettled conditions of the later eighteenth century drew larger numbers of rural people into these forms of livelihood. The East India Company found itself drawn progressively into the 'pacification' of these groups. The armies of defeated regional states were disbanded, although as Seema Alavi has described, the Company at first found roles for many different categories of Indian military people in its expanding armies.[34] Large groups of mercenaries and 'freebooters', the armed retainers of the southern warrior chiefs or the Pindaris of western India continued to offer resistance into the 1820s, but had been 'settled' or repressed by the end of the decade. Hill people, hunters and pastoralists found themselves identified in the Company's emerging classifications of population as 'criminal tribes'.[35]

Demilitarization proceeded in subtler ways too, as the Company moved to concentrate the instruments of force into its own hands. This represented a profound change in an agrarian society where the collection of revenue at

---

[32] See e.g. Jan Breman, *Of Peasants, Paupers and Migrants: Rural Labour Circulation and Capitalist Production in Western India* (Delhi, 1985).

[33] For the agrarian dimension of the Indian Rebellion of 1857, see esp. the older works of Eric Stokes, *The Peasant Armed: The Indian Rebellion of 1857* (Oxford, 1986), and Ranajit Guha, *Elementary Aspects of Peasant Insurgency* (New Delhi, 1983).

[34] Alavi, *The Sepoys and the Company*, 227–63.

[35] Meera Radhakrishnan, *Dishonoured by History: 'Criminal Tribes' in British Colonial Policy* (Hyderabad, 2001); Radhika Singha, *A Despotism of Law: Crime and Justice in Early Colonial India* (Delhi, 1998); and Anand A. Yang (ed.), *Crime and Criminality in British India* (Tucson, 1985).

local level had so often been backed up by the threat of armed force. As Peter Marshall has described, the permanent settlement in Bengal failed to produce better revenue returns in large part because its major landholders had been seriously weakened by the loss of their independent coercive powers, with the abolition of their pensions and land grants made for the maintenance of soldiers, guards and police.[36] Demilitarization and sedentarization came together in other ways. The Company early identified corporations of warrior monks as threats to its authority and campaigned hard to expel them from its territories, offering some of them pensions and estates to settle down.[37] From the first decade of the nineteenth century the Company's army contractors pressed for areas of indigenous horse-breeding in Gujarat to be brought under its control, and in Haryana offered pastoralists secure land tenure if they turned to settled horsebreeding.[38] The Rebellion of 1857, which saw a large-scale revival of older military labour markets in the Gangetic heartlands of the revolt, provided a further large stimulus to demilitarization. Military recruitment shifted to the sturdy 'martial races' of the Punjab, taking a major avenue for non-agrarian service out of Gangetic India.[39]

Other changes in Indian society and economy also pushed more people into direct forms of dependence on the agrarian economy. The defeat of regional political rivals meant not only the dissolution and partial assimilation of their armies, but also the end of service for large numbers of specialist artisans and skilled people: petty office-holders, contractors, household servants and entertainers, animal keepers, attendants in female quarters. Some of these found employment readily elsewhere, but many others were thrown back into agriculture. Owing to the progressive weakening of Indian handicraft production from the 1820s, there had been greater dependence on smallholdings brought about by disruption to elite consumption and disturbances to the links between producers, middlemen, and trading firms in the unsettled political conditions of these decades, as

---

[36] Peter Marshall, *Bengal, the British Bridgehead: Eastern India 1740–1828* (Cambridge, 1987), 139.

[37] Pinch, *Peasants and Monks*, 25; see also his *Warrior Ascetics and Indian Empires* (Cambridge, 2006).

[38] Alavi, *The Sepoys and the Company*, 255–9.

[39] For the aftermath of the Mutiny-Rebellion, see Thomas R. Metcalf, *The Aftermath of Revolt: India 1857–1870* (Princeton, 1964).

well as by competition from Lancashire.[40] Uneven and modest as they were in many areas, upward movements in population growth from the 1840s also contributed to this greater pressure on the land for livelihood.[41]

At very many levels, then, Indian agrarian society lost many of its older range of occupational possibilities and much of the accompanying elaboration of different forms of status and honour. The weakening or disappearance of indigenous states, the decline of opportunities for military service, the conversion of local systems for watch and ward into paid employers of the state, the contraction of their forest base for pastoralists, forest people, petty rajas, and warrior chiefs, all transformed opportunities for service and employment as well as avenues to dignity and honour. As agrarian society in many areas came to be dominated by settled communities of peasant producers, distinctions based on wealth and landholding were coming to replace these older hierarchies of honour and status. Rights to land were becoming much more central as the means to livelihood and the possession of land started to be defined in new and exclusive ways. For tenant farmers, sharecroppers, pastoralists, and displaced forest people that constituted new classes of labouring poor in many parts of rural India, their non-possession of land now defined them as dependent menials. All of these processes meant that the older mobility of labour was restricted and its bargaining power weakened, as non-agrarian economic opportunities declined, and pressure on the land grew. Of all the social changes associated with the coming of colonialism in India, this multilayered process of sedentarization went most strongly against the grain of pre-colonial social and political development, and emerged most directly out of the colonial state's need for a productive and secure agrarian order.

Sedentarization and the Making of Colonial Caste

These same processes also had far-reaching implications in many other areas of social organization. For some historians, caste hierarchies in their 'modern' colonial form—the emergence of the new 'dominant peasant' castes, a greater pervasiveness in the language of *jati* and *varna*, the development of new forms of 'clean' caste respectability and piety, and the construction and

---

[40] Tomlinson, *The Economy of Modern India*, 104–5.
[41] Leela Visaria and Pravin Visaria, 'Population 1757–1947', in Dharma Kumar (ed.), *The Cambridge Economic History of India*, ii. *c.1757–1970* (Cambridge, 1983), 463–532.

wider application of more rigid forms of untouchability—emerged primarily from Indian responses to the knowledge gathering and the political strategies of the colonial state. Revenue systems, population surveys and census reports increasingly required Indians to identify themselves in caste terms. Colonial legal codes law enshrined distinctions between the practices of different castes. Developing constitutional reforms were based around representation by caste and religious community, and came to incorporate special forms of provision for 'backward' and 'depressed' castes.[42]

As Susan Bayly has argued, however, changes in caste may be better understood in the context of Indian engagement within the broader changes of sedentarization. Older seigneurial groups, especially in ecologically unfavoured areas, came under increasing pressure in the first half of the nineteenth century, as military employment and status was closed off to them, and their older landed position came under challenge by new communities of successful peasant farmers not demeaned by direct contact with the plough. These groups sought in turn new means of consolidating their authority over menial rural communities, extending to them an unclean status previously limited to a narrow range of occupational specialists. At the same time, 'clean' agrarian castes who were the beneficiaries of colonial agrarian policy responded with their own increasingly caste-based assertions of respectability, piety, and virtue, which found expression in new kinds of devotionalism. Marking off clear boundaries of rank and honour for such communities offered a very useful social strategy in a competitive agrarian social order. Caste associations and conferences offered a wide range of social advantages in urban settings, too, as a means of enhancing community solidarity and extending social networks.[43] 'Modern' untouchability was in a real sense the creation of the important roles taken by these communities in the construction of railways and docks, in factories and mills, and in the armies of sweepers required in expanding colonial cities.[44] The language of caste could also offer great political advantage. The non-Brahman movements of western and southern India were both a means of building alliances across a broad range of class and caste communities, and

---

[42] Dirks, *Castes of Mind*, 125–228. For a critique, see S. Bayly, *Caste, Society and Politics*, 97–143.

[43] S. Bayly, *Caste, Society and Politics*, 187–232.

[44] Oliver Mendelsohn and Marika Vicziany, *The Untouchables: Subordination, Poverty and the State in Modern India* (Cambridge, 1998), 88–92. Vijay Prashad, *Untouchable Freedom: A Social History of a Dalit Community* (Oxford, 2000).

of asserting the centrality of agrarian castes to the regional vernacular tradition and its culture.[45]

This perspective offers us a more historically informed understanding of the interplay between sedentarization and the development of caste in its particular colonial forms. However, sedentarization rarely produced claims that were constructed only in caste terms. Rather, the new community histories and claims to new forms of status and identity that proliferated in so many agrarian settings during the nineteenth century were constructed out of a complex interplay between caste, local forms of patriotism and piety and the vernacular literary forms in which they were expressed, and narratives about the mythological as well as the historical past. These new regional, community, and caste identities also contained a striking new consciousness of class, expressed in a search to find new ways of dignifying the labour of the farmer. These arguments drew on older discourses about the roles of the warrior and the farmer in protecting the land and making it fruitful, attempting to establish an equivalence between them. Colonial caste was thus only one element within these new assemblages of history and community identity, and from this perspective a particularly mobile and mutable one.

This interplay emerges in a range of recent regional studies. William Pinch has explored the history and culture of the newly formed peasant and artisanal elites of Gangetic India, who had prospered with the economic expansion of the late nineteenth and early twentieth centuries. From the 1880s, Kurmi, Yadava, and Kushvaha peasants drew on their proximity to the important centres of Vaishnavite belief and practice in the region to claim the status of Kshatriya protectors of these sacred sites, accompanying their assertions with new forms of Vaishnavite devotionalism, a purification of social practices to avoiding meat and intoxicants, and a strong historical narrative presenting themselves as descendants of India's ancient Aryans, entitled to recognition as part of the wider Aryan Hindu community. A consciousness of changing class relations in the countryside accompanied this drive to purify religious practice, in a strongly argued assertion of the nobility and value of labour on the land. Intellectuals and spokesmen for these newly prosperous agrarian communities argued that tilling the earth

---

[45] Eugene Irschick, *Politics and Social Conflict in South India: The Non-Brahman Movement and Tamil Separatism 1916–1929* (Berkeley, 1969) and Rosalind O'Hanlon, *Caste, Conflict and Ideology: Low Caste Protest in Nineteenth Century Western India* (Cambridge, 1985).

was a noble vocation, carried out by men of status and respectability in ancient times, and dignified by its associations with the earth, the wellspring of all prosperity.[46]

A new consciousness of the worth of settled agriculture also emerged among the Vellala communities of the Tamil country who had prospered as settled farmers by the end of the nineteenth century.[47] Here, however, the interplay between caste, class, and regional culture took a very different form, and arguments about *varna* status assumed nothing like the central importance that they did in the north. For the Vellala intellectuals who put forward new understandings of Vellala history and identity, Vellalas were like clouds: they fertilized the soil and made it prosperous for other communities. Their values of generosity, honesty, compassion, and purity had provided the basis for the region's ancient Tamil civilization, in which local farmers had given food, clothing, and shelter to the incoming Aryans, who were wandering shepherds and hunters. Arguments about *varna* status were less important in this construction than the quality of kingliness itself, diffused through the sacral landscape that was home to Tamil culture to include a much wider putative community of farming people intimately connected by their history and the worth of their labour to the land.[48] Here, then, arguments about *varna* were subsumed into a wider discourse linking sedentariness, culture, and local ethnicity. These associations were to provide the ideological framework for the non-Brahman movement from the early decades of the twentieth century.

The interplay between caste, class, and regional cultures took a different form again in the Maratha country. By the later nineteenth century, the seventeenth-century Maratha warrior Shivaji and his tough *mavali* soldiers drawn from the mountains of the western Deccan had become icons of Indian and sometimes explicitly Hindu resistance to external invasion.[49] For wealthy Maratha cash crop farmers, smaller commercial cultivators, and upwardly mobile artisans, these associations between warriorship, agriculture, and local patriotic virtue offered both an ideological alternative to the dharmic values of the region's influential commercial and scribal elites, and

---

[46] Pinch, *Peasants and Monks*, 81–138.
[47] Irschick, *Dialogue and History*, 195–9.
[48] Ibid. 200.
[49] Bayly, *Origins of Indian Nationality*, 108–10; O'Hanlon, *Caste, Conflict and Ideology*, 164–86.

a framework with which to build wider political solidarities in the countryside. For the non-Brahman intellectuals in western India who articulated these new associations, the claim to Kshatriya status for all these cultivating communities was important, but this was a Kshatriya status whose meaning was also deeply inflected by regional tradition. Warriorship here simply represented the other side of the coin from agriculture, both of them honourable activities essential to the protection and prosperity of the country, and both equally well represented in the family histories of many Marathas themselves. As they had in the time of Shivaji, local farming communities large and small had always turned their hand alternately to farming and military service as season and local political circumstances demanded, and knew its forts and strong places as well as they knew its stretches of black fertile soil.[50]

In each of these regional settings, therefore, the process of sedentarization needs to be understood as an interplay between caste, class, and regional tradition. Indeed, what is clear from these examples is that regional tradition so powerfully inflected the meaning of particular *varna* categories so as to make them difficult to understand in any meaningful way abstracted from their regional settings. In the Gangetic regions, with their proximity to powerful centres of Vaishnavite devotionalism, Kshatriya status was now acquiring the much more strongly dharmic characteristics of devotional piety, running alongside warriorship as its main characteristic. In western India, Kshatriya status took its meaning from Maratha history, construed not as warriorship in the abstract, but as the natural identity of farming communities who had always turned their hands as readily to tilling the soil of the Deccan as to defending it against invasion. In the discourses of the south, *varna* categories were simply much less important in making these arguments about the dignity of agriculture, since the sacral qualities of the land pervaded its communities in such a way that all regarded themselves as kings of the countryside. In each of these examples, too, what we see is a resistance to the construction of farming merely as an agricultural pursuit: farming is seen as an activity deeply bound up with the defence as well as the prosperity of the land. If the colonial state sought a more comprehensive monopoly of formal military employment after 1857, it was

---

[50] O'Hanlon, *Caste, Conflict and Ideology*, 152–64.

much less easy to efface the cultural role that military service had always occupied in agrarian society.

Scribal and Commercial Elites in the Colonial Political Economy

Closely allied with this first process of sedentarization was a second that marked the high colonial period of the nineteenth century, the consolidation of the social authority and political power of new scribal and commercial elites and the forms of dharmic Hinduism with which they were associated. As suggested above, this process also had important origins in the late pre-colonial period, in the new opportunities for skilled ritual, service, and commercial people of different kinds that opened up in India's pre-colonial regional states. While these states often depended on the close interrelation of royal, commercial, and scribal power, for these communities the dharmic values of purity and piety were more important than those of lordly or warrior status. Yet these values were held in balance in the late pre–colonial period by other imperatives, as rulers continued to seek support from other sources of sacral power in the deities of hills and forests, or turned for more immediate military support to the hill chiefs, pastoralists, and warrior nomad peoples who lived on their borders.

The emergence of a more settled agrarian order, with its military dimensions increasingly a dependent arm of the Company's own military machine, had the effect of removing these countervailing imperatives. As the Company transformed itself from trader to revenue collector, an earlier generation of individual translators, secretaries, revenue assistants, and interpreters were gradually fused together into a colonial bureaucracy and associated professional classes. The process was a gradual and uneven one, shaped by regional differences in the Company's political and economic development, and by the differing Indian service communities that peopled its major administrative centres. By the 1860s, India's colonial bureaucracy was large, complex, regionally varied, and above all multilayered, and was supported by attendant legal, commercial, and educational institutions. Its personnel ranged from petty clerks and struggling graduates in commercial offices, to successful professionals, doctors, lawyers, and writers. Not all of these were drawn from older scribal specialists. Many were Brahmans, Kayasthas, or Muslim service gentry, but colonial administration also drew in traditional artisan and commercial communities, whose skills as printers, accountants, or revenue administrators enabled them to prosper.

For all their internal differentiation and regional variety, however, these older scribal elites and the skills of literacy and bilingualism they commanded were drawn into a distinct colonial social formation. They were uniquely well placed to dominate the new bureaucratic structures and the new kinds of public sphere that were emerging in India's regions from the 1820s, as not only English but vernacular languages began to develop their own print cultures and their own audiences of readers, intellectuals, religious commentators, political observers, and social critics. From the 1840s, when the rate of publication of vernacular periodicals quickened, these new communities of readers, commentators, and critics were in a position to shape public debate right across the field of social and political issues: debate about the value of old and new forms of learning, about aspects of Hindu belief and practice, about the moral, intellectual, and social significance of caste, about the education, marriage, and social status of women, about Indian political institutions and forms of British civic responsibility, about India's history and languages, and above all its identity and structure as a nation.[51] Vernacular print opened new areas for potential cultural assertion, both in setting standards for pure or correct speech, and in defining the proper forms of print language. This was particularly the case in north India, where the decline of Persian as the language of a composite literary-administrative elite opened up a space for intense contestation between proponents of Hindi and Urdu.[52] Vernacular print could also threaten the cultural marginalization of lower languages, mixed languages, and languages of the street.[53] Particularly from the 1880s, when regionally based political and civic organizing acquired new all-India dimensions, literate skills, bilingualism, and supra-local social networks conferred additional advantages on these older scribal elites.

India's older commercial communities—Khatri, Marwari, Agarwal, Oswal, Chettiar, and others—likewise found significant new opportunities

---

[51] C. A. Bayly, *Empire and Information: Intelligence Gathering and Social Communication in India, 1780–1870* (Cambridge, 1996), 180–246. For regional examples, see Douglas E. Haynes, *Rhetoric and Ritual in Colonial India: The Shaping of a Public Culture in Surat City 1852–1928* (Berkeley, 1991); Francesca Orsini, *The Hindi Public Sphere, 1920–1949: Language and Literature in the Age of Nationalism* (New Delhi, 2002) and Naregal, *Language Politics*, 145–264.

[52] Christopher R. King, *One Language, Two Scripts: The Hindi Movement in Nineteenth Century North India* (Delhi 1994).

[53] See e.g. Sumanta Bannerjee, *The Parlour and the Street: Elite and Popular Culture in Nineteenth Century Calcutta* (Calcutta 1989).

as India's colonial economy expanded. Colonial India was, as B. R. Tomlinson has put it, a 'private enterprise economy', in that decisions about resource allocation now came to be concentrated in the private sector.[54] The rapid expansion in India's new colonial cities after 1860, the demand for services of many kinds created by the Indian army, developments in transport infrastructures and in new industrial enterprises offered attractive rewards for communities with the capital to invest and the social networks to protect themselves against risk. The growing value of land as sedentary agriculture expanded, together with opportunities for moneylending, also made the colonial agrarian environment a very favourable one for banking, commercial, and trading communities looking for safe forms of investment. The growing prosperity of many commercial communities was reflected in cultural shifts, as they turned away from older patrician models of social worth to emphasize the virtues of the pious Vaishya—thrift, restraint, and dharmic purity.[55]

In addition to new opportunities for settled farming, therefore, the colonial order that emerged from the early nineteenth century also offered important new forms of power to established scribal and commercial elites. It was not only the power of these new elites that gave Indian society in the nineteenth century its distinctive colonial character, but the equally significant feature of their growing separation. If the early colonial state sought to separate out military from agrarian functions, it was also a fundamental and distinctive feature of India's colonial economy and society that landed, commercial, and scribal power were to become more disengaged from one another. Commercial communities developed their own specialist economic operations in the colonial environment, and distanced themselves from patrician and warrior elites. New classes of wealthy farmers prospered as the setting for commercial agriculture grew more favourable. Scribal power also became more separate, as the colonial bureaucracy expanded and developed often into peculiar forms of dependence on the administrative structures of the colonial state, education, and public employment.

---

[54] Tomlinson, *The Economy of Modern India*, 95. Tomlinson estimates that in no decade between 1872 and 1947 did the state's share of Gross National Product rise above 10 per cent. For the strategies of commercial elites within the colonial economy, see esp. Ritu Birla, *Stages of Capital: Law, Culture and Market Governance in Late Colonial India* (Durham, NC, 2009).

[55] C. A. Bayly, *Rulers, Townsmen and Bazaars: North Indian Society in the Age of British Expansion, 1770–1870* (Cambridge, 1983), 246–369, and for a regional example, David West Rudner, *Caste and Capitalism in Colonial India: The Natukottai Chettiars* (New Delhi, 1995).

In this setting, political power and social worth became much more tightly linked to the possession of land, capital, and scribal skills than had been the case for much of the eighteenth century, and the social consequences of their absence incomparably harsher.

From the 1860s, the consequences of these changes were felt at every level of Indian society. Above all, what these new and more separated forms of commercial and scribal power did was to set the stage for new and distinctively colonial forms of conflict. One of the most striking features of this setting lay in the ambivalent political position of regionally based scribal elites. Their skills of literacy and bilingualism enabled them to take a commanding position in new arenas for public debate over a wide range of social and political issues. However, this sat very ill with their status as an urban or small-town professional class acutely aware of their dependence on clerical employment in mills, firms, offices, and educational institutions controlled by the British or by successful Indian entrepreneurs, and conscious of its insecurity and small returns. This classic ambivalence of a colonial bourgeoisie is best exemplified in the culture of Bengal's *bhadralok* middle class, which emerged from the late eighteenth century as older communities of service people, traditional Brahman literati and smaller rent-receivers found they needed to supplement their incomes with professional or clerical jobs in the emerging bureaucratic and educational institutions of Calcutta and other towns.[56] Many people in this stratified middle class possessed some means of livelihood in commerce or land. Most, however, were heavily dependent on clerical employment and deeply protective of their hegemonic position as arbiters of Calcutta's rich literary and political culture. Over the longer term, these relationships were to shape the growth not only of Bengal's regional nationalist tradition, but also of its emerging movement of militant Hinduism.[57]

In other regional settings, the power of new scribal elites and their relation to commercial and landed wealth took rather different forms. Colonial Bombay from the early nineteenth century continued to be dominated by older merchant elites, Gujarati Bania, Bhatia, Khoja, Marwari, and

---

[56] Bengal's *bhadralok* culture has been the subject of extensive discussion. For a recent exploration, see Tithi Bhattacharya, *The Sentinels of Culture: Class, Education and the Colonial Intellectual in Bengal 1848–1885* (New Delhi, 2005).

[57] See in particular here, Andrew Sartori, *Bengal in Global Concept History: Culturalism in the Age of Capital* (Chicago, 2008), and Joya Chatterjee, *Bengal Divided: Hindu Communalism and Partition, 1932–1947* (Cambridge, 1994).

others.[58] Some older scribal elites, Saraswat and Chitpavan Brahmans and Prabhus, entered the administration of the East India Company and a number went on to work in educational administration in Bombay and Poona.[59] However, these did not come to constitute anything like the same dominating urban literary and professional elite at the centre of a regional culture. In western India as in the south, therefore, the real ground of cultural and political contest lay not in the commanding position of an urban culture pitted against a predominantly Muslim rural one, but in a struggle to define the history and cultural meanings of a predominantly agrarian regional tradition. This struggle lay at the core of non-Brahman political agendas in these regions. These relations were different again in the Gangetic regions, where new Hindu commercial and agrarian elites competed with an older Muslim service gentry. Here, the distinction between cultures of the city and the countryside was less clear-cut, and the struggle to define the meaning of regional vernacular tradition even more difficult to resolve.

This sharper differentiation between forms of commercial, scribal, and landed wealth, and the narrowing of the range of social opportunity that accompanied it, was felt with particular intensity amongst India's expanding new populations of urban poor. Increasingly sharp distinctions of class emerged in India's expanding colonial cities as wealthy commercial communities and professional middle classes developed their own prosperous residential areas. These differences also emerged more subtly and perhaps more importantly in the sharp awareness of social exclusion evident amongst many communities of the labouring poor. In these settings, as Nandini Gooptu has argued, consciousness of class often emerged most sharply not in direct economic action, but in religious and cultural assertion. Here, the older martial culture of north India's mobile armed peasantry re-emerged in new forms, as the urban poor asserted themselves as the armed defenders of Hinduism, descended from powerful Kshatriya warriors. For young men, in particular, this new martial role opened up powerful new roles, sometimes aggressively physical, in public arenas that seemed hitherto dominated by scribal and commercial elites. In their attacks on the Muslim communities who stood as their most immediate

---

[58] Christine Dobbin, *Urban Leadership in Western India: Politics and Communities in Bombay City 1840–1885* (Oxford, 1972).

[59] Naregal, *Language Politics*, 100–44.

rivals for market and living space and for urban employment, they drew on the rhetoric of the Arya Samaj and the Hindu Sabha to articulate a wider theory about the downfall of India's warrior classes at the hands of 'Muslim outsiders'.[60] Here, colonial India's distinctive forms of class and social exclusion found expression in religious assertion, and in the drive to find other means to activate an older independent martial physical culture squeezed to the margins of colonial society.

Language, History and Identity: The Consolidation of Regional Vernacular Communities

The essential setting for the consolidation of the power of scribal and commercial elites lay in the emergence of new kinds of vernacular language communities in India's regions. Again, there were important pre-colonial antecedents. Many historians have noted the growth from the early modern period of increasingly distinct vernacular language communities. As Cynthia Talbot has argued in the case of Andhra, regionally based state elites in some parts of early modern India promoted the development of vernacular literary communities as they became increasingly aware of the need to express and document their own martial prowess and religious gifting in more local terms. At the same time, local forms of popular devotionalism expressed in oral traditions stimulated the development of vernacular language communities.[61] Overlapping these emerging communities of vernacular speakers and readers were the pan-Indian language communities of Persian and Sanskrit, with their very different communicative roles and worlds of reference.[62] This was a multilayered world of linguistic practice, containing not only the more local arenas of emerging vernacular communication, but also, as Christopher Bayly has argued, a wider regional form of 'public' debate and discourse at the level of the Hindustani

---

[60] Gooptu, *The Politics of the Urban Poor*, 185–243. See also Rosalind O'Hanlon, 'Military Sports and the History of the Martial Body in India', *Journal of the Economic and Social History of the Orient*, 50/4 (2007), 490–523.

[61] Cynthia Talbot, *Precolonial India in Practice: Society, Region and Identity in Medieval Andhra* (Delhi, 2001).

[62] Muzaffar Alam, 'The Pursuit of the Persian Language in Mughal Politics', *Modern Asian Studies*, 32 (1998), 317–49 and Sheldon Pollock, 'The Sanskrit Cosmopolis: Transculturation, Vernaculatization and the Question of Ideology', in Jan Houben (ed.), *Ideology and the Status of Sanskrit* (Leiden, 1996).

'ecumene'.[63] The interest of early orientalists in India's classical languages, the continuing administrative need for Persian, and the interest of medical, military, and revenue departments in regional vernaculars meant that the Company continued its engagement with these different linguistic levels until well into the 1830s and the decade of anglicizing reform under Bentinck.

Far-reaching changes took place over the next century. It is not possible here to trace the interplay between the developing language and educational policies of the East India Company, the strategies of missionary societies in developing print vernaculars and Indian social and intellectual engagement with the opportunities for new kinds of communication that vernacular print brought with it.[64] This interplay was a complex process, and some of these themes have been touched on above. What is important to appreciate is the transformation in the social position and political significance of India's regional vernacular communities in the century after 1820. From the multilayered and overlapping linguistic world of the early nineteenth century, there had emerged by 1920 a widely held conception of India as home to a fixed number of discrete and standardized regional languages. Linguistic, cultural, and political changes here moved in parallel. As vernacular print cultures and their associated oral forms expanded in the range and depth of their audiences, both served increasingly to define the vernacular public spheres that provided in the decades after 1857 such fertile ground for the development of regional political associations. In fashioning their critiques of colonial policy and their understandings of Indian national culture and identity, these political associations drew not only on pre-colonial discourses about virtuous government, but also on older regional patriotic traditions.

In this setting, regional vernaculars themselves came to represent not merely languages, but vehicles of those local patriotic traditions and regional identities that together constituted India's body politic. On this understanding, as Christopher Bayly has argued, the Indian nation was a composite of 'energized regional cultures', a conception that emerged most

[63] C. A. Bayly, *Empire and Information*, 180–211. See also Rosalind O'Hanlon, 'Speaking from Siva's Temple: Banaras Scholar Households and the Brahman "ecumene" of Mughal India', in O'Hanlon and David Washbrook (eds), *Religious Cultures in Early Modern India* (Delhi, 2011), 174–211.

[64] Naregal, *Language Politics* and Bhattacharya, *Sentinels of Culture*.

clearly in Gandhi's own representation of the Indian nation as an alliance of regional homelands.[65] These arguments emerged strongly in 1920, when Gandhi made his case for the political restructuring of the Indian National Congress around regional vernacular communities, in place of the older administrative divisions of the colonial state. Both in Gandhi's pleas for the cultivation of vernacular languages in place of English, and his appeals for local political support as he toured India's regions during the Non-Cooperation movement, he emphasized the distinctive qualities of people, culture, landscape and history to which each was host. Vernacular languages here were not only languages, but repositories of these regional cultures, each one of them making its own distinctive contribution to the cause of India's freedom: Maharashtra as the land that produced heroes such as Shivaji, Ramdas, and Tukaram; Gujarat as a land of poets, piety, and heroism whose stories still echoed in the hills of Kathiawad; Andhra as a country whose people were spiritually minded and skilled enough to produce fine hand-spun cloth.[66] While the government of India's constitutional reforms of the 1930s perpetuated these administrative divisions as the basis of India's new provincial governments, it was the vernacular language community that emerged again in the 1950s to become the 'natural' and enduring basis for India's state governments, with the formation of independent India's linguistic states.

These long-term shifts had wide-reaching consequences for structures of caste, class, and community. Some of these consequences have been discussed above, particularly in strengthening regionally based scribal elites. However, the development of regional vernacular language communities, and their emerging new political dimensions did not act in any simple way to reinforce the position of local scribal elites. Vernacular print provided much of the framework within which the new forms of caste organization developed, from 'clean' caste associations proclaiming new standards of piety and reformed devotionalism, to the movements for untouchable uplift that became an increasingly prominent part of social reform activity from the 1870s.[67] If these different forms of caste organization offered substantial social advantages in the colonial setting, as Susan Bayly has argued, these were only made possible through vernacular print, in caste histories and the

---

[65] Bayly, *Origins of Indian Nationality*, 120–1.
[66] See e.g. Gandhi, *Collected Writings* (Ahmadabad, 1966), xx. 69, 149, 199.
[67] Mendelsohn and Vicziany, *The Untouchables*, 77–117.

pamphlet and periodical literature through which caste associations sought to disseminate information, enforce social discipline and forge wider networks. The real focus for many caste associations, however, lay not so much in social or ritual convention, but, as we have seen above, in history and identity. The key question for many lay particularly in their status within the regional vernacular communities now emerging as the 'homelands' of the Indian body politic. For Kshatriya reformers in the north, as for non-Brahmans in the south and west, the real question was how far their long local histories as warriors and farmers would enable them to stand as the real embodiments of local patriotic tradition, against those—upper-caste scribal people, landlord elites, rival communities of Muslim artisans or farming people—who might dispute these claims.

These tensions were reflected within the structures and forms of vernacular languages themselves. From its inception, the world of vernacular print had never been completely closed to voices from the margins of colonial society, even if those voices were heard very largely through the medium of missionaries and upper caste reformers. By the 1880s, India's colonial cities were beginning to see the emergence of novel political initiatives amongst the urban poor, particularly those menial and untouchable communities who were drawn so heavily into the service and labouring sectors of the new colonial military and industrial order. These found in print an invaluable political tool. Supported by non-Brahman leaders, representatives of Bombay's Mahar community, for example, launched an association in 1886 whose purpose was to campaign for the removal of the stigma of untouchability, and to persuade the government of Bombay to resume recruitment of Mahars to the army.[68] Nor was the drive to standardization of vernacular languages through print itself uncontested. As Veena Naregal and others have noted, the efforts of intellectuals and literati to develop a 'high' literary style for local vernaculars met with sharp opposition from other vernacular speakers who objected not only to the attempt to develop a 'purer' literary style, but to the wider political agendas of intellectuals and editors seeking to do so.[69]

Perhaps most importantly, the distinction between 'purity' of language and colloquial speech grew more complex as vernacular language communities began to be seen more clearly as repositories of regional patriotic

---

[68] Mendelsohn and Vicziany, *The Untouchables*, 97–8.
[69] Naregal, *Language Politics*, 200–72.

identity. A colloquial idiom in this context could signify less an offence against educated speech, and more a vital guarantee of authenticity, of the writer's deep roots in the homeland of a regional vernacular community. These tensions emerged in different ways in different regional settings. As Sumathi Ramaswamy has described, the complex contests around the end of the nineteenth century over the status and forms of Tamil were pre-eminently contests over the meaning of regional patriotic tradition. Here, 'pure' Tamil was a Tamil cleansed of its Sanskritic impurities and their associations with the alien Aryan Brahmanic Hindu culture of the north, and restored to its proper status as the vehicle for classical Tamil civilization, but also at the same time the intimate language of the home and the family.[70] 'Proper' forms in Marathi were likewise a critical area for contest in western India. The lower caste reformer Jotirao Phule defended his style of Marathi, which used simple words and avoided Sanskrit expressions, as the kind of Marathi language that ordinary farmers and artisans could actually understand.[71] Sumit Sarkar has described the ambivalences that marked the linguistic culture of Bengal's *bhadralok*, committed on the one hand to a modern form of 'purified' Bengali, yet drawn at the same time to the religious figure Ramakrishna Paramahansa, whose 'rustic' speech conjured a lost world of simple rural faith.[72]

It was in the Gangetic regions, however, that these questions of vernacular language communities and regional patriotic traditions presented their greatest complexities. The eclipsing of Persian as the language of India's older Indo-Muslim elites revealed a potential multiplicity of local vernacular successors. Here, the forms of language, and their role as vehicles for the culture of regional homelands, were not only matters of class and caste, but also of religious community identity. For some intellectuals, writers and publicists in this setting, propriety in language lay not in refining a single common vernacular, but in taking the pre-existing composite of Hindustani and splitting it apart into the two separate print languages of Hindi and Urdu. Hindi and Urdu thus emerged as competing vehicles for a regional patriotic tradition defined from the 1860s in increasingly different ways. For

---

[70] Sumathi Ramaswamy, *Passions of the Tongue: Language Devotion in Tamil India, 1891–1970* (Berkeley, 1997), 22–75.

[71] O'Hanlon, *Caste, Conflict and Ideology*, 170.

[72] Sumit Sarkar, 'Renaissance and Kaliyuga: Time, Myth and History in Colonial Bengal', in his *Writing Social History* (Delhi, 1997), 187–215.

Bharatendu Harischandra, the most prominent proponent of Hindi as the 'natural' language of north India's Hindus, Hindi was at once the ancient language of Bharatkhand, and the intimate and familiar language of the home and of local and rustic usage, contrasted to Urdu as the language of Lucknow courts now given unwarranted power and prominence by its use in colonial government offices and law courts.[73] Proponents of Urdu, on the other hand, struggled to reconcile a number of apparently conflicting positions. Thus Sayyid Ahmad Khan's response to the campaign launched from Allahabad in 1868 to get Hindi recognized as the language of the law courts was to insist that Hindi and Urdu were in fact the same language, that Urdu was not an inherently Muslim language, but that substituting Hindi for Urdu would put Muslims at a great disadvantage.[74]

From this perspective, the most significant effect of this longer term shift in the status and political significance of vernacular language communities lay not only in its implications for the power of vernacular scribal elites. It lay also in the way in which some vernacular proponents now found opportunities to begin to excavate the fault lines between language, class, and community. It is to these issues that we turn in the final section.

Region, Language, and Religious Identities

Changing forms of religious community identity in colonial India have been particularly difficult for historians to trace. The violence of India's partition in 1947 invites teleological approaches, and makes it more difficult to maintain a proper sense of the contingency of events over a long period and of India's great regional diversity in forms of religious culture and tradition. One important area of debate for historians has emerged in the extent to which colonial forms of religious community conflict were prefigured in the eighteenth century. Christopher Bayly and others have explored the ways in which India's eighteenth-century states appealed at some times to clearly bounded definitions of religious community, and at others to more syncretic and multiple religious identities.[75] The longer term rise of

---

[73] Vasudha Dalmia, *The Nationalisation of Hindu Traditions: Bharatendu Harischandra and Nineteenth-Century Banaras* (Delhi, 1997), 146–221.

[74] David Lelyveld, *Aligharh's First Generation: Muslim Solidarity in British India* (Delhi, 1996), 98–9.

[75] C. A. Bayly, 'The Pre-history of "Communalism"? Religious Conflict in India, 1700–1860', republished in his *Origins of Nationalism in South Asia*. See also Sanjay Subrahmanyam, 'Before

Hindu scribal elites and of rulers seeking affirmation as dharmic Hindu kingdoms was offset by the need of emerging regional states to attract political, military, commercial, and charismatic religious support of many different kinds. In this setting, monolithic or exclusive definitions of religious community made little sense at the level of popular experience, outside specific moments of conflict.

If pre-colonial states saw in different religious traditions a range of potentially valuable resources on which they might draw, officials of the early Company state tended to see rather different problems and opportunities. Many of the opportunities were intellectual and cultural, particularly in the chance to revive the glories of an ancient literary and learned tradition in Sanskrit, decayed after centuries of alien Muslim overlordship. The problems were both intellectual and practical. The intellectual problem lay in the need to ascertain the law, custom, and culture by which different religious communities should be regulated. The practical problem lay in the development of strategies through which relations between different religious communities at local level could best be managed. The solution in both areas lay in the recruitment of particular local elites: Brahman pandits and Muslim legal experts to interpret law and custom; and in the early colonial urban settings where a role for the state in keeping a balance between competing religious community claims seemed most urgently needed, in recruiting the 'natural' leaders of each religious community to represent them in negotiations with local government. By the 1830s, Company educational policy had turned towards western forms of learning conveyed in English, and to sponsoring the development of regional vernaculars. This was a period, too, of missionary challenge and proselytization in many parts of India, stimulating Hindus and Muslims alike to defend, preach, and rationalize their doctrines.[76]

In the decade after 1857, government of India policy moved in decisively different directions in these areas of law, education, and religious policy. However, the conviction that religious communities were best represented by their 'natural' leaders, and that the state's role lay in acting as a neutral interpreter of the legal precedents through which all competing religious

---

the Leviathan: Sectarian Violence and the State in Pre-Colonial India', in Kaushik Basu and Sanjay Subrahmanyam (eds), *Unravelling the Nation: Sectarian Conflict and India's Secular Identity* (Delhi, 1996).

[76] Kenneth W. Jones (ed.), *Religious Controversy in British India* (New York, 1992).

community claims must be decided, continued to shape colonial policy until the end of the century and beyond. As nationalist challenges and debate about wider issues of constitutional change intensified from the 1880s, a new focus emerged, in the need to build protection for 'religious minorities' into future reforms of Indian government. From the First World War onwards, the government of India increasingly represented itself as the guardian of minority interests, in which the interests of religious 'minorities' were foremost. A wide range of political groupings, from the leaders of the Muslim League to those of non-Brahman and untouchable movements, sought political advantage by casting their own political appeals in these terms.

Thus, the British emerged over the course of the nineteenth century as patrons of religious difference. For some historians, it was essentially from these assumptions and strategies that colonial forms of communal conflict flowed. The contests over ritual precedence in many north Indian towns that emerged strongly from the last decades of the century were exacerbated by colonial legal procedures. Local officials' interference exacerbated existing tensions over cow-slaughter over the same period.[77] In the years after the First World War, religious difference was enshrined within the structures of provincial and central governments themselves, inviting Indians to define themselves first and foremost in religious terms.[78] These arguments contain important insights, yet they need to be placed alongside the longer term reshaping of Indian society by the needs of British colonialism that has been traced out above. Few of the beneficiaries of agrarian sedentarization and the consolidation of new scribal and commercial forms of power were drawn from India's many different and regionally dispersed communities of Muslims. Very often, these beneficiaries expressed their new-found wealth by turning away from the expansive and composite culture of older rural patrician classes and defined their social worth instead in the language of dharmic purity or Kshatriya respectability. The expansive and militant forms of Hinduism that developed from the 1870s and came sharply into conflict with local Muslim communities emerged from these longer term ways in which colonialism reshaped India's regional societies. From

[77] Gyanendra Pandey, 'Rallying Round the Cow: Sectarian Strife in the Bhojpuri Region, c. 1888–1917', in Ranajit Guha (ed.), *Subaltern Studies*, ii (Delhi, 1983).

[78] David Page, *Prelude to Partition: The Indian Muslims and the Imperial System of Control, 1920–1932* (Delhi, 1982).

this perspective, religious conflict in later colonial India was very much a dynamic of particular regions, and the development of Hindu nationalism a search to redefine Hindus as a community in the face of particular regional and caste pressures that were not present in the same way outside India's Gangetic region.

If sedentarization and the emergence of new scribal and commercial elites reshaped the contours of Indian's regional societies, so too did the new political significance of India's regional vernacular communities as repositories of political and religious identity. For north India's Muslim service elites, some of them already defending hard-won local advantages as professionals in colonial administration from the proponents of Hindi, this new understanding of the vernacular regions within India's historical and political landscape represented complicated ideological terrain. As we have seen in Sayyid Ahmad Khan's own approach to the language question, it was less straightforward for proponents of Urdu to assert the same connections between a common colloquial language, a vernacular community, and a clearly defined regional patriotic tradition. It was in part a response to this dilemma that representatives of these Muslim service elites developed their own stronger rhetoric of a Muslim community with a distinctive all-India presence and identity. It is against this longer-term background that we can better understand the more overtly political struggles of the interwar period, as a Congress inclusive in its public rhetoric, but sharing some of its modes of expression and its personnel with militant Hinduism, struggled to deny independent ideological ground to Muslim political organization. William Gould has examined the ways in which these connections with politicized Hinduism weakened the appeal of the Congress to Muslim constituencies in north India.[79] Behind these immediate political struggles, however, lay a deeper challenge emerging from the longer term changes explored above, in an India increasingly viewed as a composite of distinct regional vernacular homelands.

Do these perspectives imply some remorseless trajectory towards more homogenous forms of religious identity? This is certainly not the case. For all their pivotal political influence, the Gangetic heartlands do not encapsulate the whole history of changing forms of religious affiliation in colonial India. There were substantial Muslim and Christian populations in

---

[79] William Gould, *Hindu Nationalism and the Language of Politics in Late Colonial India* (Cambridge, 2004).

many other regions who continued to define themselves primarily in terms of local vernacular culture. From the turn of the twentieth century, Tamil Muslims were substantial contributors to the literary discourses which helped define a Tamil homeland.[80] Studied at the level of popular experience, moreover, it is difficult to find clear evidence in any part of India that monolithic religious identities had radically simplified the ways in which political actors saw themselves. As Nandini Gooptu has argued, the participation of many different social groups in shared activities in north Indian towns in the early twentieth century may convey the impression that wider religious identities were emerging, but such an impression is misleading.[81] A more careful reading of the political language of these public arenas reveals that the urban poor who asserted themselves as the warrior defenders of Hinduism continued to define themselves in multiple and contextual terms, and terms often in tension with the political agendas of local high caste leaders and patrons of Hindu organizations. Christopher Bayly's observation, made some years ago now, that it is in fact difficult to find evidence for the emergence of any 'Hindu' or 'Muslim' identity abstracted from particular regional cultures and more local affiliations of caste and clan, still seems pertinent here.[82] While some of the fault lines that proved significant in 1947 were certainly accentuated over the course of the nineteenth century, there was nothing predetermined about their opening up as the colonial state entered its last stages. This process, as Ayesha Jalal and Joya Chatterjee have argued, lay in shorter term political pressures as local and regional struggles were drawn into the all-India political arena.[83]

Conclusions

The major processes of colonial 'modernity' for India lay in sedentarization, the growth of a new agrarian social order in which caste hierarchies seemed more rigid and more widely applied. At the same time, older scribal and commercial elites consolidated their power within new kinds of vernacular public sphere. These longer term changes continued to shape the Indian

---

[80] Ramaswami, *Passions of the Tongue*, 174–5.
[81] Gooptu, *The Politics of the Urban Poor*, 241–2.
[82] C. A. Bayly, 'Pre-history of "Communalism"?', 233.
[83] Joya Chatterjee, *Bengal Divided*, and Ayesha Jalal, *The Sole Spokesman: Jinnah, the Muslim League and the Demand for Pakistan* (Cambridge, 1985).

social and political order in the decades after 1947. The new linguistic states created in 1956 conferred formal political recognition upon the vernacular language communities shaped over the course of the later nineteenth century and accepted by Congress in the early 1920s. Struggles within the Indian National Congress well into the 1960s continued to be shaped by the politics of dominant peasant castes, and caste affiliations provided both the framework for political mobilization and the language within which what were often hierarchies of class were expressed. Early Congress governments inherited many of the colonial state's approaches to the management of religious community relations, particularly the insistence that disputes over urban public space were matters for the courts, and the colonial state's rhetoric of religious neutrality pursued alongside sometimes openly partisan politics on the ground. At the same time, the fluidity of colonial religious identities survived the upheavals of partition and even the newer forms of Hindu nationalism that emerged from the 1960s had to compromise with still multiple and regionally based religious identities. Noticeably, Muslim constituencies who remained in post-partition India were to become staunch supporters of the Nehruvian Congress Party's vision of a plural and secular India. Finally, colonial forms of political and social exclusion also cast a long shadow. It is possible to see both the mobilization of untouchable communities during the 1950s under Dr Ambedkar, and the dramatic political and cultural challenges of *dalit* and tribal peoples from the 1960s as the longer term outcome of colonialism's narrowing of avenues to social worth for those who did not possess land, capital, or scribal skills.

Select Bibliography

C. A. BAYLY, *Rulers, Townsmen and Bazaars: North Indian Society in the Age of British Expansion, 1770–1870* (Cambridge, 1983).

——*Indian Society and the Making of the British Empire* (Cambridge, 1988).

SUSAN BAYLY, *Caste, Society and Politics in India from the Eighteenth Century to the Modern Age* (Cambridge, 1999).

RITU BIRLA, *Stages of Capital: Law, Culture and Market Governance in Late Colonial India* (Durham, NC, 2009).

RAJNARAYAN CHANDAVARKAR, *The Origins of Industrial Capitalism in India: Business Strategies and the Working Classes in Bombay, 1900–1940* (Cambridge, 1994), 1–20.

PARTHA CHATTERJEE, *The Nation and Its Fragments: Colonial and Postcolonial Histories* (Delhi, 1995).

NICHOLAS DIRKS, *The Hollow Crown: Ethnohistory of a Little Kingdom* (Cambridge, 1987).

Ranajit Guha, *Elementary Aspects of Peasant Insurgency* (Delhi, 1983).
Thomas R. Metcalf, *Ideologies of the Raj* (Cambridge, 1994).
Francesca Orsini, *The Hindi Public Sphere, 1920–1949: Language and Literature in the Age of Nationalism* (New Delhi, 2002).
Gyanendra Pandey, T*he Construction of Communalism in Colonial North India* (Delhi, 1990).
Vijay Prashad, *Untouchable Freedom: A Social History of a Dalit Community* (Oxford, 2000).
Radhika Singha, *A Despotism of Law: Crime and Justice in Early Colonial India* (Delhi, 1998).
Ajay Skaria, *Hybrid Histories: Forests, Frontiers and Wildness in Western India* (Delhi, 1999).

6

Nationalisms in India

Sumit Sarkar

South Asian history-writing about the late colonial era has suffered from both too much and too little engagement with nationalism. Too much, for a single binary opposition between colonialism and nationalism has been dominant for a very long time, revealing a surprising tenacity amidst many changes in forms. Too little has been said of nationalism, at the same time, for the precise and varied meanings of that category in South Asia, its different types, have been seldom explored. The nationalism–colonialism binary often homogenizes both poles, ignoring differences within both categories, and underestimating changes over time. Initiatives and developments get evaluated solely in terms of their placement within this dichotomy.

It might seem that I am oversimplifying, for the distinctiveness of much Muslim political mobilization in the later colonial era is surely obvious, culminating in the emergence in 1947 of not one but two independent nation states. Perhaps, then, it might be argued, the standard framework has been of a triadic rather than a binary pattern, colonialism/Indian nationalism/Muslim nationalism. But in practice, the third element has repeatedly been elided, in otherwise very different, historiographical traditions. In Indian history-writing, Muslim political mobilization, even when on a countrywide scale and perspective, has seldom been acknowledged as 'legitimate' or 'proper' nationalism. The terms preferred have been 'Muslim breakaway', 'Muslim separatism', or 'communalism'. Their counterparts in Pakistani scholarship follow the same assumption, though of course with reversed values. For them, the nationalism that culminated in the realization of Pakistan is the only legitimate claimant to that term. The Indian or anti-colonial nationalism that is written or spoken about and glorified across the border is for them no more than Hindu communalism. The homogenization and the domination of a single narrative framework therefore persists, and along with it the problem which is really my central theme, namely the ways in which nationalism(s) and a host of identity formations mutually inflected each other in late colonial times.

Nationalism has remained far too much a unitary concept. In the words of a recent commentator, South Asian historiography still lacks 'a suitable register within which to locate incipient and formative nationalisms under the conditions of colonial and imperial domination', in significant contrast to nineteenth-century Europe where distinctions between 'primordialist, ethnic, republican and civic nationalisms' have been well established.[1] In both respects, orientalism still flourishes amidst and through its many repudiations, for histories of the non-West often get portrayed in simplistic, unitary terms that would be unacceptable in the historiography of Western countries, and get typecast in entirety under the label of 'nationalism'. There are signs, however, in recent years, that the long persistent binary framework is being complicated through a combination of empirical research and theoretical developments which will be the focus of this chapter. But first I turn to a historiographical and historical survey, taking in briefly the era of the 'Cambridge School' and early Subaltern Studies.

Nationalism: From Cambridge School to Subaltern Studies

In histories of nationalisms, more obviously perhaps than elsewhere, the present keeps moulding the past in ways both fruitful and problematic. Till the late 1960s, the official archives most directly relevant for the study of Indian nationalist movements were unavailable to historians, notably documents about the entire Gandhian era, due to a fifty-year rule. Private paper collections, whether of officials or Indians, were also mostly inaccessible. Academic history-writing about anti-colonial nationalism therefore had a rather late start. Instead, patriotic sentiments—of rather problematic kinds, we shall see—found expression particularly in the literature on movements against medieval Muslim rulers. The study of nationalism emerged in the 1950s, at a time when there was considerable confidence in the possibilities of independent development along 'Nehruvian' lines, and the dominant mood among Indian historians was nationalism of a rather

---

[1] Chetan Bhatt, *Hindu Nationalism: Origins, Ideologies and Modern Myths* (Oxford, 2001), 7.

conventional kind, though complicated by occasional left-oriented writings. Nationalism per se was assumed to be a 'good thing' in a people fighting for independence from foreign domination. That it could also at times be problematic or repressive, in terms of its effects on class, caste, regional, religious, or gender relationships, literature and art, tended to get ignored, provided it could be shown to have been genuinely and sufficiently anti-colonial. Left writings did highlight some kinds of internal tensions, notably of course of class. But there remained, even in the more radical kinds of historiography, a persistent tendency to read elements of conscious, anti-colonial nationalism into otherwise admired figures or movements. Such histories tended to be written 'from above' in terms of leaders or parties mobilizing followers. Left writing was not too different in this respect. What resulted were enthusiastic surveys, usually all-Indian but occasionally region-based, of the achievements of great nationalist heroes effectively energizing the masses. A standard, entirely linear, periodization became firmly established, which still provides the framework for most textbooks. It merits a brief outline. The saga began with a series of anti-British 'popular' movements, of which the 1857 Rebellion was thought to mark the climax. Whether these could be called 'national', and therefore the real beginning of the 'freedom movement', however, was the subject of a rather tedious and sterile controversy. The stimulus to conduct research on 1857 that came about on the occasion of its centenary got bogged down in a debate as to whether it could or could not be called 'The First Indian War of Independence', to the exclusion of other possible questions. In this narrative, the defeat of 1857 was followed after a couple of decades by the nationalism of the educated middle class. Initially quite loyalist, growing sections among them became critical of specific aspects of British rule, notably the 'drain of wealth' and other policies contributing to repeated famines and immiserization, deepening racism, and the refusal to make concessions to middle-class demands for ending discrimination in administrative appointments and a measure of political representation. This was the 'Moderate' phase, from the 1870s until 1905, marked by the foundation of the Indian National Congress (1885), prayers and petitions primarily to win over public opinion in Britain. This was followed by the 'Extremist' phase, from around 1905, most evident in Bengal, Maharashtra, and Punjab. Extremism experimented with new techniques like the boycott of British goods, the promotion of indigenous enterprises (*swadeshi*), and education free of British control—anticipating some Gandhian methods, and occasionally raised a demand for self-government (*swaraj*). But the Extremist phase failed to achieve effective mass mobilization, and, in the face of intensified repression, combined with some limited concessions by the British to win over the Moderates, gave way to revolutionary methods. These meant in practice assassination of officials and occasional conspiracies to get arms from abroad. Extremism and revolutionary terrorism were marked also by a strong Hindu overtone, unlike the broadly social-reformist and secular outlook of their Moderate predecessors.

From 1915 onwards, Gandhi's charisma and skill in developing effective methods of peaceful mass struggle energized large numbers of peasants and important segments of Indian business groups, in three great waves of national upsurge, Non-Cooperation-Khilafat (1919–22), Civil Disobedience (1930–4), and Quit India (1942). There was, however, an unfortunate dimension, which did not quite fit into this triumphalist narrative, and it therefore tended to be played down in conventional nationalist accounts. This was what Indian historians usually described as a 'Muslim breakaway' or 'Muslim separatism', greatly encouraged by British divide-and-rule strategies, to which was attributed the partition of 1947. Their counterparts in Pakistan, equally predictably, described the same phenomena as signs of the growth of a legitimate 'Muslim nationalism'. That chauvinist Hindu-nationalist or communal elements also made a contribution towards the ultimate division of the country, working both outside and within the Congress, was generally ignored on the Indian side of the border.

With access to new sources, such a simple narrative came to be questioned and complicated in the years from the late 1960s to the mid-1980s, and that in two very different and mutually hostile ways. The sudden expansion of access to central and provincial archives, coinciding with the opening up of more and more collections of private papers of British officials and prominent Indians, now stimulated detailed research on political regions and sometimes localities. A group of historians based in Cambridge—labelled the 'Cambridge School'—were the first to make methodologically novel use of these materials which provided an alternative to the standard, eulogistic, and often starry-eyed, and over-generalized nationalist narrative. They imparted a note of cynicism about the idealism and patriotic motivations of many of the cult figures of the national movement. Even Gandhi began to be seen as not much more than an effective political manipulator. Nationalism appeared no more than a cover for the pursuit of selfish group or individual interests of Indian elites. These were initially conceptualized, notably in the pioneering work of Anil Seal, in terms of regional 'elites' based on a blend of Western education and high-caste status. Five years later, the collection *Locality, Province and Nation* disaggregated the category of 'elite' into locality-based 'patron-client' linkages or 'factions', equally animated by selfish interests.[2] This approach aroused very hostile reactions among most Indian historians, some of whom even suspected a 'neo-colonialist' motivation or conspiracy as the basic features of colonial exploitation and domination were obscured by a maze of detail about selfish machinations of rulers and ruled alike. But a cutting-down to size of nationalist icons was perhaps ultimately helpful, and most 'Cambridge' scholars soon moved away from pure faction analysis and excessive cynicism.

Reactions to the Cambridge School took two divergent forms. One was a reassertion of nationalist positions, occasionally backed up by more empirical research than had been possible earlier.[3] The other was the Subaltern Studies project, by far the best-known internationally of all South Asian historiographical trends. Early Subaltern Studies, before the major shift within the project in the late 1980s, made an important contribution by exploring and complicating the relations and tensions between institutionalized political activities and popular initiatives. Effective (or ineffective) mobilization had been studied so far in a top-down, 'elitist' manner, and explained in terms of charismatic patriotic leadership and ideals, skilful manipulations, colonial pressures and stimuli, or (in early Marxist writing) by economic conjunctures and 'correct' or 'incorrect' applications of Marxist strategy. Such interpretations, whether nationalist or orthodox Marxist, were now critiqued for an elitism, and occasionally for their economic determinism. The new approach probed popular (in practice, most often peasant) autonomy, and the emphasis on subjectivity led to efforts at studying subaltern consciousness and culture, no longer assumed to be mere derivatives of 'elite' patterns of thinking.

In the 1970s and early 1980s, South Asian history was simultaneously enlivened, and often obscured, by the polemical fire and smoke which gathered around both the Cambridge School and Subaltern Studies. But major, research-based works of abiding interest did emerge during these

---

[2] Anil Seal, *Emergence of Indian Nationalism* (Cambridge 1968); Jack Gallagher, Gordon Johnson, and Anil Seal, *Locality, Province and Nation* (Cambridge, 1973).

[3] Bipan Chandra, *India's Struggle for Independence* (Delhi, 1988).

years, from both lines of thought, as well as sometimes from historians less easily classed with either. Three themes stand out.

New sources enabled explorations of the social bases of evolving nationalist movements at regional levels. John McLane's carefully nuanced study of the moderate nationalists related their moderation and refusal to encourage mass mobilization amidst poverty, breeding a fear of popular upheavals. My research on early twentieth-century Swadeshi Bengal, while sharply critical of the Cambridge School, also tried to move away from conventional nationalist positions, linking the decline in the open agitation against the partition from around 1907 not primarily to British repression, as had been customary, but to internal, class- and community-related, limits. A movement primarily of higher-caste educated Hindus, often with rentier interests in land, it failed to mobilize the mostly Muslim or lower-caste Hindu peasants, and never extended, for instance, the methods of 'passive resistance' formulated at the peak of Extremist enthusiasm to include no-rent movements. Among Cambridge scholars, the studies of south India by David Washbrook and C. J. Baker combined narrow faction-analysis with interesting suggestions about differences in the structures of politics related to the contrast between 'wet' and 'dry' zones of agriculture.[4] Christopher Bayly's work on late nineteenth-century structures of politics in the Allahabad region, which was included in *Locality, Province and Nation* (1973), the second, revised theoretical statement of the Cambridge School, appears today as a part-critique of that school.[5] It highlighted the links between professional middle-class groups and local bankers and traders, questioned the assumption of invariable connections between moments of agitation and administrative pressures or opportunities, and emphasized rather the quasi-religious dimensions of an emergent nationalist politics which was closely bound up with the growth of Hindu conservative and revivalist sentiments. Here, there is an implicit internal criticism within the Cam-

---

[4] John R. McLane, *Indian Nationalism and the Early Congress* (Princeton, 1977); Sumit Sarkar, *Swadeshi Movement in Bengal 1903–1908* (Delhi, 1973); D. A. Washbrook, *The Emergence of Provincial Politics: Madras Presidency, 1870–1920* (Cambridge, 1976); C. J. Baker, *The Politics of South India, 1920–1927* (Cambridge, 1976).

[5] C. A. Bayly, 'Patrons and Politics in Northern India', *Modern Asian Studies*, 7 (1973), 349–88. Bayly elaborated this line of research through his *The Local Roots of Indian Politics: Allahabad, 1880–1920* (Oxford, 1975), and *Rulers, Townsmen and Bazaars: North Indian Society in the Age of British Expansion, 1770–1870* (Cambridge, 1983).

bridge School of an undue stress on narrow material and factional calculations.

Despite major differences in approach, much of the most impressive work of early Subaltern Studies carried forward this exploration of social dimensions at regional and local levels, notably David Hardiman's micro-study of the major Gandhian base of Kheda (Gujarat).[6] The focus of research on nationalism had by now shifted decisively and permanently to regions or smaller areas, as indicated for instance by the still valuable compendium of studies brought out by D. A. Low in 1977.[7] The trademark of Subaltern Studies in its first phase was the focus on the dialectic between political mobilization by the leadership and autonomous popular initiatives. This was perhaps not entirely as novel as sometimes claimed, for some earlier, orthodox-Marxist work, including R. P. Dutt's pioneering *India Today* (1940), had suggested that Gandhian nationalism appropriated and utilized pre-existing mass militancy. The simultaneous rejection of 'elitism' and 'economism', central to the early Subaltern project, led to explorations of autonomous popular (in effect, primarily peasant) forms of consciousness and culture. Ranajit Guha led the way with a stimulating, if perhaps a bit too structuralist, study of the 'elementary forms' of peasant consciousness in colonial India, and there was important work on, for instance, the construction of images of Gandhi 'from below', and popular mentalities that could be teased out through details of specific events and incidents.[8]

Such initial explorations of culture were still embedded in rigorous studies of material conditions, but soon there developed, both within and beyond Subaltern Studies, a strong culturalist turn in history-writing.[9] This was in tune with worldwide intellectual trends. The early interest in popular movements had ebbed away by the late 1980s, and the minds of peasants and tribals no longer seemed so enthralling. Within Subaltern Studies, there was

---

[6] David Hardiman, *Peasant Nationalists of Gujarat: Kheda District 1917–1934* (Delhi, 1981).

[7] D. A. Low, *Congress and the Raj: Facets of the Indian Struggle, 1917–1947* (London, 1977).

[8] Ranajit Guha, *Elementary Aspects of Peasant Insurgency in Colonial India* (Delhi 1983); David Hardiman, *The Coming of Devi: Adivasi Assertion in Western India* (Delhi, 1987); Ranajit Guha, 'Chandra's Death', in Guha (ed.), *Subaltern Studies*, v (Delhi, 1987); Sumit Sarkar, 'The Kalki-Avatar of Bikrampur: A Village Scandal in Early Twentieth Century Bengal', in Guha (ed.), *Subaltern Studies*, vi (Delhi, 1989).

[9] I have tried to explore the ramifications of the change within Subaltern Studies in my 'The Decline of the Subaltern in *Subaltern Studies*', in Sarkar, *Writing Social History* (Delhi, 1997).

in effect a return to the colonial middle-class intelligentsia, whose culture was after all so much more accessible than the ways of thinking and emotions of a largely illiterate peasantry. Chatterjee's effort to explore colonial middle-class nationalism as an ideology became central to this endeavour. Early Subaltern Studies, despite its primary focus on anti-colonial struggles, had not really tried to explore nationalism as a category: in effect, it had been collapsed into popular movements. To the Cambridge School, nationalism had seemed a ramshackle, occasional, and reactive coming-together of local factions, while stereotypical nationalist writing had remained content to assume their subject to have been a natural given for a subject people.

Chatterjee inaugurated what amounted to a vast expansion, for 'nationalism' now acquired a much wider, 'cultural', set of meanings.[10] The expansion has been a source of strength—and weakness. The wider roots and implications of nationalism, notably ideological and cultural, came under scrutiny, and important work began on its manifestations in diverse realms of late colonial experience: gender images, caste relationships, literature, and art. There was a weakness, too, in terms of an amorphousness, for it is sometimes a puzzle as to who, within the colonial educated intelligentsia, cannot be considered a 'nationalist'. Nowadays virtually any kind of middle-class literati in the colonial era can be described as 'nationalist', even if the people involved had been quite loyalist in their politics—provided hints of a wider 'country', or of a 'modern nation state' can be found somewhere in their writings. Conversely, the cultural domains now being opened up to sophisticated historical investigation tended to be interpreted primarily, at times solely, in terms of the quality of their nationalism, the extent to which they could escape from the burden of colonial modernity.

Why such a big change in the meaning of nationalism attracted so little attention or debate merits some attention. The transformation passed unnoticed because it contained an important continuity: the persistence of a basic colonial/anti-colonial binary. Indeed, the polarity was even accentuated, for, at least in its initial phase, cultural domination by 'modern', 'Western', 'post-Enlightenment' ways of thinking and values was often construed in almost entirely negative ways and juxtaposed against traditional or genuinely indigenous forms. Chatterjee in 1989 famously

---

[10] Partha Chatterjee, *Nationalist Thought and the Colonial World* (Delhi, 1986); Partha Chatterjee, *The Nation and Its Fragments: Colonial and Postcolonial Histories* (Princeton, 1993).

characterized the discourses of the colonized as fundamentally 'derivative', though by 1993 he had quietly abandoned that position and moved towards a disjunction between 'home' and the 'world', where religion, culture, and family values are thought to have retained or developed a certain autonomy. A troubling consequence, at times, was a temptation to characterize the world of the 'home' in predominantly positive ways, occasionally veering towards socially conservative positions.

The degree of efficacy or autonomy vis-à-vis the modern West, political or cultural, becomes often the basic, or even the sole, standard of judgement for evaluating the quality of political or cultural initiatives flowing from the 'colonial' educated middle class. The bigger problem, however, is that the expansion of the term 'nationalist' seems sometimes in danger of swallowing up virtually the whole of late colonial history, even more completely than before. A striking instance would be the evident embarrassment displayed by some feminist historians writing about social reform efforts or measures concerning specific forms of gender oppression, limited and rare as such changes in Hindu law remained under British rule. The laws banning sati, legalizing widow marriage, and imposing a minimum age for consent (1829, 1856, 1891), made by colonial rulers with some persuasion from quite loyalist Indian literati, would be the most obvious instance. The emphasis tends to be on pointing out the limits of such measures, or the possibly suspect quality of British motivations. However, in taking this line, historians have too quickly denied the value of the actual reforms. The history of late colonial India is placed within a simplified mould, and the possibility or even need to explore multiple, even conflictual, narratives, gets brushed aside as too complicated.

A little-noticed paradox needs to be noted. The hallmark of the work of late Subaltern Studies has been a thoroughgoing inversion of the once-standard assumption, shared by liberals, Marxists, and even many Indian nationalists, of 'Enlightened' modernity as, fundamentally, cultural progress, however tainted by its introduction in South Asia through colonial power. But such inversion necessarily retained a similar unilinearity of approach, with unqualified 'progress' only displaced by equally unqualified retrogression, and 'modern' ideas and values being tainted from birth by its undeniably Western origins. Yet rejection alike of unilinearity and of excessive emphasis on origins have been vital to much post-structuralism and postmodernism, and even of some of the more sophisticated strands of postcolonial theory, which see in them some of the worst features of modern

European historicism. Recently, however, something like a new wave seems to be emerging, where, through a combination of concrete research and theoretical analysis, binaries of all kinds are being complicated in very interesting ways. It is to this most recent work on South Asian history and nationalism that I now turn.

New Directions: Nationalism and Multiple Identities

The broader context for the new turn in historical thinking has been constituted by major shifts in both international and South Asian conjunctures through the late 1980s and 1990s. The link between the apparent collapse of movements for radical transformation, and the ascendancy of 'culture' over more materialistic histories has been mentioned already. The other major development, again worldwide, was the displacement of class by diverse forms of 'identity'-based movements, with that term itself coming into wide use only from around these years. Among these the most prominent in India has been 'Hindu nationalism' or 'Hindutva', culminating in the destruction of the Babri Masjid in December 1992, the rise of the Hindu Right to power in the central government between 1998 and 2004, and the bloody, state-sponsored anti-Muslim pogrom in Gujarat in March 2002. But, beginning from the late 1970s and now becoming more visible, there was also the rise of *dalit* and 'lower-caste' formations, in which some have tried to find a kind of counterpoint to the upper-caste-led Hindu Right. Women's movements, previously dependent on organized parties led invariably by men, took more self-conscious theoretically aware feminist forms. A variety of local 'grass-roots' movements around questions of environment helped to constitute yet another new field of intellectual and historical work. The sheer suddenness and evident importance of these largely new movements forced historians of modern India to at last partly overcome the odd inhibitions that had kept them so long on the other side of 1947. Communalism, caste, gender, and environment, themes previously marginal or virtually non-existent in history writing about modern India, became the key subjects of current research. The focus has been on recent times, but there is also a delving back before independence. The net impact was that it has become increasingly difficult to present late colonial history as a single, linear narrative centred solely on anti-colonial nationalism.

The recent work of Dipesh Chakrabarty provides the most sophisticated instance of signs of change within the Subaltern Studies collective. The more empirical chapters of his *Provincializing Europe*, dealing with particular aspects of nineteenth-century middle-class life and sociability in Bengal, still occasionally get limited by the effort to sustain a 'provincializing' project, which seems to demand a continued evaluation in terms of the degree of distance from Western forms of modernity. Chakrabarty's is an effort to work within, and at the same time move beyond, the postcolonial problematic as previously understood by Subaltern Studies scholars. It rejects categorically the possibility of 'shunning European thought', and seeks throughout to hold in creative tension its 'simultaneous indispensability and inadequacy in exploring the mental and emotive world of the colonial intelligentsia'. The concepts it deploys, to use the helpful term coined by Derrida, are usually 'under erasure': one can neither fully accept, nor totally abandon them, but need to work in and through the categories even while never giving up one's critique.[11]

The instances in historical research would be many and extend across very diverse fields. Let me begin with two, drawn from areas less directly related to nationalism. In the new surge in labour history in South Asia after a long period of relative neglect, the rigid polarities around which earlier work had evolved: 'formal' and 'informal' sectors, factory workers and the mass of urban poor, a 'settled' city proletariat and village labourers, histories of labour and of *dalits* and subordinated castes, have all come under fruitful scrutiny. Jan Breman, who pioneered in South Asian studies the questioning of the formal/informal dichotomy back in 1976, formulated later the striking category of 'footloose labour' which cuts across all these distinctions.[12] Here, as in many other contexts, recent developments have forced scholars to rethink in particular the new patterns of 'globalized', neo-liberal capitalism which replaces big factories with a multitude of household-located units tied together by new forms of putting-out, and generally breaks down many of the earlier distinctions. 'Peasant' and 'tribal' movements, sadly, no longer attract much research attention, in sharp contrast to the situation in the 1970s and 1980s. But, once again, over-rigid distinctions are being

---

[11] Dipesh Chakrabarty, *Provincializing Europe: Postcolonial Thought and Historical Difference* (Princeton, 2000), 255–6, and *passim*.

[12] Jan Breman, 'A Dualistic Labour System? A Critique of the "Informal Sector Concept"', *Economic and Political Weekly*, 27 Nov., 4 and 11 Dec. 1976; Jan Bremen, *Footloose Labour: Working in India's Informal Economy* (Cambridge, 1996). For a notable effort at overcoming the long separation between labour history and caste studies, see Peter Robb (ed.), *Dalit Movements and the Meanings of Labour in India* (Delhi, 1993).

questioned, notably that between 'peasant' and 'tribal', and here the burgeoning field of environmental history is making a contribution by going beyond the divides it had constructed earlier between settled cultivators, pastoralists, and forest-dwellers. Studies of 'tribal' and peasant protest are no longer content with romanticized notions of a unified, egalitarian community protesting as a whole against exploitation by intruders, whether British or Indian: internal tensions within such formations are also being probed.[13]

I am aware that work along such lines, stressing indigenous inputs, as well as the collaborative aspects of the colonial encounter, and what sometimes becomes a kind of continuity thesis suggesting that colonial rule may not have constituted any major break with pre-colonial times, can occasionally lay itself open to the danger of becoming an apologia for colonialism. This becomes particularly so when terms like 'dialogue' are used, tending to underplay the ultimately more crucial dimensions of domination and conflict. There is also a need to take full cognizance of the precise time we are speaking of, with the late colonial era certainly marked both by ruptures with pre-colonial conditions not always so evident earlier, and a much-sharpened racial divide.

Research initiated under the aegis of postcolonial theory has repeatedly spilled over its initial limits. One major thrust, beginning with the kinds of colonial discourse analysis that were often narrowly culturalist, over-polemical, and extremely prone to binary formulations, has developed into important studies of colonial/modern statecraft and 'governmentality', bearing the marks of Foucault rather than Said. Everyday details of administration, previously dismissed as tedious or unimportant, have acquired new significance, and their links with processes of identity formation are being intensively probed. Take the two most striking instances. The census had earlier been regarded as no more than an important historical source, and British Indian law was of interest and relevance to specialists of that subject alone.[14] Now both have come under scrutiny for their key roles in the formation of a wide range of more rigid identities, the potentials for

---

[13] 'Forests, Fields, and Pastures', Special Issue, *Studies in History*, 14 (1998), particularly Neeladri Bhattacharya's Introduction, and the articles by Archana Prasad and K. Sivaramakrishnan; Jacques Pouchepadass, *Champaran and Gandhi: Planters, Peasants, and Gandhian Politics* (Delhi, 1986).

[14] Bernard S. Cohn, *Colonialism and Its Forms of Knowledge: The British in India* (Princeton, 1996); Radhika Singha, *A Despotism of Law: Crime and Justice in Early Colonial India* (Delhi, 1998).

which were being constituted around the same time by the qualitative leap in communications integration. From the 1770s onwards, the British erected from more inchoate Mughal foundations a sharp distinction in family law between Hindu and Muslim, helping to make both these categories more homogenous, and forcing a clear choice between them in everyday matters of marriage, death, and inheritance. The introduction of the decennial census a hundred years later accelerated notably solidarities of religion, caste, language, and ethnicity, for enumeration demanded sharp distinctions and uniformity within the categories chosen, once again enforcing firm choices. During the run-up to the 1911 Census, for instance, an official in charge of census operations expressed an inability to locate a particular community in the Gujarat region within either of the two main religious categories, and suggested use of the omnibus term 'Hindu-Muslim'. His superior pulled him up sharply, and asserted that people had to be either Hindus or Muslims.

It needs to be added that the processes of identity formation were not just being imposed by British fiat, and driven solely by administrative convenience and divide-and-rule machinations, as was occasionally implied in the early days of research on such matters. There were important, and growing, Indian inputs in both law and census operations. More and more Indians, beginning with the relatively privileged but spreading downwards, made autonomous and creative use of the new forms of communication introduced in colonial times: improved roads, railways, postal services, a gradual and limited spread of literacy and education and, above all, mechanical print enabling cheap reproduction of all manner of reading and visual material, amounting in their totality to the formation of one or several forms of 'public spheres' not really feasible earlier.

What happened in the late colonial era was a simultaneous crystallization of many collectivities: 'Indian', religious, caste, language and ethnicity, class, gender. But these meant also inevitable processes of mutual inflections of one by the others, interpenetration, undercutting. Identities, one might suggest, were simultaneously becoming 'harder' and more potentially fragile. This in turn stimulated efforts, usually at the instance of leading groups within such communities-in-formation with resources for such projects, to strengthen solidarity through enemy-images of powerful, ever-threatening others. Notable efforts at building a countrywide 'Hindu' unity, for instance, and perhaps widespread internalization of the notion of 'Hinduism' itself, really started from the late nineteenth century, at the initiative mainly of higher-caste groups. Such efforts at what could be termed 'Sanskritization' from above had a clearly conservative and integrative role, aspects often missed out in conventional social-anthropological deployments of that category which, from its initiator M. N. Srinivas onwards, has generally carried only a positive content. There is a sharp contrast here with the more-or-less simultaneous efforts to crystallize identities and organizations of subordinated castes and *dalits*, and figures like Jotirao Phule and later B. R. Ambedkar in Maharashtra and Periyar Ramaswamy Naicker in Tamil Nadu were very suspicious of such moves, and sharply critical of Brahmanical domination. The transition to chauvinistic forms of Hindu nationalism (or what its critics termed 'communalism'), foregrounding Muslims as a perpetual and growing threat, was probably connected with upper-caste efforts in such conjunctures to buttress their slipping hegemony. Unifying moves by some sections of Muslims, becoming increasingly anti-Hindu over time and termed 'Muslim nationalism' by its advocates and 'Muslim communalism' or 'separatism' by others, was similarly an effort to build and consolidate unity within a religious category far from homogenous and linguistically and culturally diverse: as indicated for instance by Jinnah's problems with numerous provincial Muslim politicians in the run-up to Pakistan.[15]

Nor were the conflicts purely political. Two prominent theologians of Indian Islam in the first half of the twentieth century, Husain Ahmad Madani and Maulana Mawdudi, developed sharply different approaches to the problems being faced by Indian Islam in the era of nationalism. Madani, head for several decades of the Deoband training centre for theologians, strongly supported Congress nationalism and the ideal of a 'composite nationalism' within an united India, which he thought would be more conducive to the spread and prosperity of his community over the entire subcontinent than any religious partition. Mawdudi, founder of Jama'at-I-Islami in 1941, came to be recognized in the second half of the century as a principal apostle of a fundamentalist and revivalist Islam, and revered as such by similar groups throughout the Islamic world. But neither liked Jinnah's ideal of Islamic nationalism and a Pakistan that would be non-theological in its political forms.

---

[15] Maulana Madani, *Composite Nationalism and Islam* (Delhi, 2005); Sayyid Vali Reza Nasr, *Mawdudi and the Making of Islamic Revivalism* (New York, 1996).

Perhaps a pattern broadly similar to that noticeable in the narrative of caste can be discerned in the history of gender relationships and images.[16] Social reform efforts here during the nineteenth century had emanated almost entirely from middle-class men, but an increasingly autonomous women's role manifested itself in the course of time, with the gradual empowerment of some through access to literacy and greater possibilities of mutual communication and organization through the emergent public sphere based on print culture. Both discursive and imaginative writing by women, very rare earlier except for some religious poetry, emerged in many parts of the country from the 1860s and 1870s. Women's associations began to be set up from the early twentieth century, raising demands more radical than those voiced by the earlier male reformers. Votes for women, for instance, started becoming an issue from the 1920s mainly at the initiative of some (admittedly elite) women. But, as with caste, counter-thrusts were not slow to manifest themselves, expressed through opposition to reform and assertions that the true role of the 'Hindu', 'Muslim', or 'Indian' woman was to preserve traditional patriarchal values within the home.

Where and how within this welter of crystallizing and yet fragile solidarities are we to locate nationalism(s)? The use of the plural seems advisable, and the term itself clearly requires more precision. The most obvious meaning for the colonial era, and the one that dominated till quite recently would be opposition or resistance to British rule, plus some kind of conception of a nation-state goal. But there have always been ambiguities in the literature, often producing somewhat sterile controversies. Nineteenth-century Indian middle-class thinkers and even the Moderates of the early Congress combined loyalism with a growing sense of India as a national unit. Even the Congress adopted complete independence as its creed only as late as 1929. Many nineteenth-century tribal and peasant protests or rebellions, on the other hand, subsequently eulogized as anti-British and national, were directed initially, and sometimes throughout, against local, mainly Indian, oppressors, and hardly had a sense of a modern kind of nationhood: a problem that would largely apply also to the more complicated instance of

---

[16] Antoinette Burton, *Burdens of History: British Feminists, Indian Women, and Imperial Culture, 1865–1915* (Chapel Hill, NC, 1994); Tanika Sarkar, *Hindu Wife, Hindu Nation: Community, Religion and Cultural Nationalism* (New Delhi, 2001); Mrinalini Sinha, *Colonial Masculinity: The 'Englishman' and the 'Effeminate Bengali' in the Late Nineteenth-Century* (Manchester, 1995).

the major Rebellion of 1857. Hindu or Muslim nationalism/communalism ideologues in the twentieth century thought in terms of uniting co-religionists across the space of India, but believed that it was not colonial rule, but the other religious community, that was the principal or sole enemy.

Perhaps we need a category of nationalism flexible enough to include these diverse expressions, and one that is able to abstract itself from any necessarily and uniformly positive (or, as in some post-colonial thinking, negative) value. The putative imagined space within which such a project is seeking to locate itself would have to be reasonably extensive (as distinct from loyalty to a village, district, or town), and within that the aim is a loyalty superior to differences such as those of class, caste, or gender other than whatever has been taken to be the essential marker for a particular 'nation'. That again has varied widely, often with sharply different implications: common ancestry or ethnicity, language, religion, culture, or an ideal of common citizenship. Narratives of nationalism today have to locate their subject within a complex and shifting field of solidarities. This makes a concentration only on the relations of the colonized with the British rulers increasingly inadequate. In historical practice, studies of particular phases or types of anti-British movements have clearly declined, more specifically work on their popular manifestations which had attained its point of maximum sophistication with early Subaltern Studies. There is considerable scope for regret in this turning away from radical political protest, but there are also compensations. The bulk of recent important research has been not directly on nationalism, but on other solidarities or dimensions of the late colonial era. The remainder of this essay will focus on the reciprocal inflections of nationalism(s) with other emergent solidarities, work which by implication often is illuminating the tensions within 'nationalism', and the variety of meanings of that term, in very interesting ways.

The prism through which such relationships are looked at today is primarily and predictably for our times, 'culture', and so one must start there. The connections of different forms of nationalism with major literary figures, like Bankimchandra, Tagore, or Premchand, have of course provided important themes for quite some time. But with growing research on print-related public spheres, attention is no longer concentrated on prominent thinkers or writers alone. Whole new and more plebeian worlds of production of vernacular writings have been opened up: forgotten plays and farces, tracts and household manuals, and other ephemera. Studies of this 'low-life of literature', to borrow Robert Darnton's phrase, have enabled entry into previously unexplored domains of urban lower-middle-class strata, subordinated castes, less privileged rural Muslims, and, perhaps above all, women, who found through print and a limited but not negligible spread of literacy channels of expression and communication previously denied them.[17]

Print culture over time, to an ever-increasing extent, went hand in hand with a proliferation through mechanical reproduction of diverse visual and aural forms of communications (the gramophone, for instance, reached India in the early twentieth century) which are of obvious importance in what was a predominantly illiterate country. These have become major new foci of historical study in recent years, with important work on the evolution of painting and architecture across the late colonial era, as well as research on the more 'popular' (more precisely, perhaps, mass-cultural, since definitely market-driven and commercialized) forms like lithographs of religious icons, or calendar art. Ravi Varma of Kerala and Bombay, and the Bengal School of Art founded by Abanindranath Tagore, have been perhaps the favoured subjects within 'high' art. Both could claim a relationship with nationalism, and yet the Bengal School sharply condemned its predecessor as denationalized in an artistic conflict roughly corresponding to the Moderate/Extremist rift around the time of the Swadeshi movement. Then, in the early twentieth century came films: silent, with Dadasaheb Phalke's *Raja Harishchandra* (1913), amazingly soon after the Lumière brothers, and 'talkies' from the early 1930s. The gap in time between Western innovation and Indian appropriation was clearly lessening, and yet the early films were often marked by a predominance of mythological themes with a strongly Hindu-revivalist message: 'modernity' and 'tradition' intermingled in complicated and shifting ways, as they still do in what since the 1940s has been by far the most popular art form, the Bollywood film industry.[18]

---

[17] For two instances of such work, see Sumit Sarkar, *Writing Social History*, chs. 6 and 8 and Judith Walsh, *Domesticity in Colonial India: What Women Learned When Men Gave Them Advice* (Oxford, 2004).

[18] For a sample of the rich and growing historical literature on the visual arts, see Christopher Pinney, '*Photos of the Gods*': *The Printed Image and Political Struggle in India* (London, 2004); Tapati Guha Thakurta, *The Making of a New Indian Art: Artists, Aesthetics and Nationalism in Bengal, c.1850–1920* (Cambridge, 1992); Partha Mitter, *Art and Nationalism in India: Occidental Orientations* (Cambridge, 1994); Ashish Rajadhyaksha and Paul Willemin (eds), *Encyclopeadia of Indian Cinema* (Delhi, 1994, 1999); and Madhav Prasad, *Ideology of the Hindi Film: A Historical Construction* (Delhi, 1998).

Of the many emergent solidarities, two have been rather neglected or at least under-theorized. What might loosely be termed 'class' have of course received considerable attention in orthodox Marxist writings, and then in the first phase of Subaltern Studies and the considerable work it helped to stimulate. Marxists for long tended to oscillate between a stress on inevitable conflicts of movements of, or on behalf of, tribals, peasants, and workers with mainstream, bourgeois nationalism, manifested through 'betrayals' by the latter, or need for anti-imperialist unity and consequent rejection of 'sectarian' excesses. Early Subaltern Studies leaned more towards the first approach, but introduced a 'history from below' perspective through categories of the subaltern, most often peasant nationalism distinct from 'elite' forms. Except Dipesh Chakrabarty, subalternists did not take up labour, whether by itself or in relation to anti-colonial movements. Peasant and labour studies then went into a long decline, though there seems to be a revival underway.[19]

The relative poverty of work on the articulations, or their absence, of regional/linguistic/ethnic solidarities with nationalism is cause for some surprise, since for a generation now the bulk of research has concentrated on specific regions. What has been lacking is theoretical and methodological novelty: homogenized notions of nationalism prevail in studies of both all-Indian and regional levels. We have had either a teleological perspective of regional identities ultimately merging with the 'national' mainstream in tighter or looser forms of integration or (at best) 'unity-in-diversity', or occasional assertions of near-independence in which the nationalist model is reproduced at the regional or even local level in an equal and opposite manner, with Indian nationalism replacing British domination as the Other. The articulations between identity formations at the many levels, local, regional, and national, in other words, have remained insufficiently explored. A related problem has been the way entire areas get totally neglected in textbook and pedagogical history: the north-east, most obviously. If modern South Asian history is equated virtually with the growth of anti-colonial nationalism or the freedom struggle, areas that did not visibly

---

[19] Dipesh Chakrabarty, *Rethinking Working-Class History: Bengal 1890–1940* (Delhi, 1989). Dilip Simeon, *The Politics of Labour under Late Colonialism: Workers, Unions and the State in Chota Nagpur, 1928–1939* (Delhi, 1995); Rajnarayan Chandavarkar, *Imperial Power and Popular Politics: Class, Resistance and the State in India, c.1850–1950* (Cambridge, 1998); and Chitra Joshi, *Lost Worlds: Indian Labour and Its Forgotten Histories* (Delhi, 2003).

contribute all that much do not matter: nationalist teleology can hardly go further. But exceptions are there and these are growing. The inter-animations and tensions between anti-Brahmanical impulses, language devotion, and Tamil and pan-Indian nationalisms, for instance, have been the subject of major historical studies. Another recent growth area has been the princely states that had comprised a third of the country before 1947. Kashmir, for instance, has seen some very interesting work recently, highlighting a form of indigenous agency much less attractive than those once explored by Subaltern Studies. The Dogra Raj set up by the British flaunted an alleged Rajput ancestry, and appropriated some of the forms of centralized modern governance to work towards a definitively Hindu state in a Muslim-majority region. This was qualitatively different, Mridu Rai has argued, from the quite common juxtaposition of rulers and ruled differing in religion in many states of pre-colonial India, for then state power could not be concentrated quite so much at a single point.[20]

Caste and Nationalism

Movements critical of Brahmanical hegemony among intermediate castes and *dalits* that we have already touched upon were markedly different from earlier forms of protest, which had had either sought through 'Sanskritization' limited upward mobility, or evolved devotional, *bhakti*, religious forms without seeking this-worldly changes in the social or political order. Gandhian nationalism sought to build bridges with lower castes through humanitarian social work and *bhakti*, but the more radical and this-worldly caste movements of colonial and postcolonial times came to involve complicated, shifting, and often conflictual relations with both pan-Indian and regional nationalisms.

Ideologies and organizations claiming to represent subordinated castes tended to suspect nationalism to be not only higher-caste led (which was largely indisputable), but engaged in promoting basically upper-caste interests. British rule for some among them could seem an asset, with its promise of legal equality, and so preferable to the tighter upper-caste domination which they feared might result from an independence movement led by the

---

[20] Sumathi Ramaswamy, *Passions of the Tongue: Language Devotion in Tamil India, 1891–1970* (California, 1997); Mridu Rai, *Hindu Rulers, Muslim Subjects: Islam, Rights, and the History of Kashmir* (Delhi, 2004).

latter; fears which nationalism in its early twentieth-century Extremist and aggressively Hindu phase did nothing to alleviate. Legal equality, it needs to be added, was extremely limited in practice, through the combination of European racism and continued importance of higher-caste elements in the lower sections of the bureaucracy and educational apparatus.

Regions were the locus of most caste movements till at least the rise of Ambedkar in the 1920s. Lower-caste upthrusts became most effective where they could relate themselves to, and partly merge or take over, regional identity formations. The price was often a certain dilution of the initial, anti-Brahman and anti-caste message. Thus the Satyashodhak Samaj tradition founded by Phule began with powerful denunciations of Brahmans as outsiders who had established their supremacy over the warrior-peasant intermediate caste-cluster of Marathas by force and fraud. By the 1930s, however, a still basically upper-caste Gandhian Congress had been able to establish its hegemony over this initially very anti-caste trend, but only through certain accommodations and limited openings towards lower-caste pressures. In Tamil Nadu, the critique of Brahmanical supremacy was perhaps sharpest, manifesting itself through a 'Dravidian' ideology that condemned Brahmans as conquerors coming from the north. After a moment of extreme radicalism under Periyar during the interwar years, when the critique of upper-caste Hinduism had veered towards atheism, what developed was a regionally unifying cult of Tamil linguistic nationalism which reduced somewhat the sharpness of the attack on Brahmannical domination.

Bengal, and the bulk of the Hindi-speaking belt, was marked by patterns significantly different from Maharashtra or Tamil Nadu. Bengali regional identity remained identified with upper-caste Hindu, *bhadralok* culture, and the occasionally powerful movements of intermediate and lower-caste groups withered away after freedom and partition. A key factor here may have been the large-scale migration of lower castes like the Namasudras from East to West Bengal after 1947, followed by their dispersal as refugees. The Hindi belt, lacking a clear regional focus and more easily identifiable with all-Indian nationalism, was marked by a late development of assertive, politically prominent caste movements—in sharp contrast to the heavily intermediate caste-based politics of more recent, post-independence decades, coalescing under the central plank of extension of affirmative action to the 'Other Backward Castes' (OBCs). Kerala embodies yet another pattern, with its history of peculiarly extreme caste oppression, a powerful movement of lower-caste Ezhavas from the early twentieth century related to the spread of literacy through Christian missionary activity, and eventual partial takeover of that upthrust by the Communists.

In general, upper-caste groups were able to retain their predominance through the late colonial era, but only through certain accommodations, limited openings towards lower-caste and, increasingly, *dalit* pressures. The classic embodiment of such adjustments, in the face of the Ambedkarite near-breakaway of significant sections of *dalits* in the interwar years, was the Gandhian condemnation of untouchability, emphasis on 'Harijan welfare', and reluctant grant of a measure of affirmative action through reserved quotas in government jobs, educational opportunities, and electoral representation. Such concessions came in every case following lower-caste and particularly *dalit* pressure and hard bargaining, as indicated by the Poona Pact of 1932, when Ambedkar gave up his initial support for separate electorates for his community in the face of Gandhi's fast unto death by surrendering the British concession of a separate electorate for *dalits*, but obtained in return a larger number of reserved seats in legislatures.

But the changes brought about through Gandhian nationalism were not insignificant. Extremist nationalism tried to postpone all social reforms concerning caste (and gender relations) till the achievement of political independence. Gandhi in contrast made abolition of untouchability the prerequisite of *swaraj*. But the dissatisfaction felt by many *dalits* found expression through Ambedkar's fluctuating but always tense relationships with the Congress, and more recently through a major political formation (the Bahujan Samaj Party) as well as some significant historical works by *dalit* scholars.[21] Several decades of reservation in government jobs and educational opportunities, won through Ambedkar's movement, have produced today an increasingly restive *dalit* intelligentsia and a political stratum capable of acting effectively on an all-Indian plane.

Gender and Nationalism

Studies of gender relationships and images, which were almost non-existent in Indian history-writing till around the early 1980s, received a major fillip from the rise of self-consciously feminist activism and scholarship, in

---

[21] See e.g. G. Aloysius, *Nationalism Without a Nation in India* (Delhi, 1997), and D. R. Nagraj, *The Flaming Feet: A Study of the Dalit Movement in India* (Bangalore, 1993).

India as well as on a world scale, and today represent a major growth area. The general trajectory here would be familiar already: an initial focus on more material and political dimensions, followed by a culturalist turn towards perceptions and images, studied primarily through women's writings and more recently visual forms. Undoubted advances in scope and sophistication, as elsewhere, was accompanied by certain losses, for the culture brought under scrutiny inevitably pertained to middle-class segments, and studies of labouring women and political movements have tended to lag behind.[22]

Previous accounts of nineteenth-century social reform and twentieth-century nationalism had been generally laudatory about the achievements of reformist or patriotic men, with women occupying at best a marginal position. Even the early 1970s critique of the so-called 'Renaissance model' had failed to foreground very much the 'women's question', focusing rather on the illusions of that era about British rule, and the initial volumes of *Subaltern Studies* included little about gender. Feminist writings made a difference from the beginning, highlighting, notably, the tensions within Gandhian nationalism. On the one hand, large numbers of women came out from domestic confines, faced police repression, went to prison, and even became comrades-in-arms of revolutionary men. On the other hand, the strongly patriarchal elements in much nationalist ideology ultimately relegated women to a marginally modified domestic sphere. Gandhi certainly inspired large numbers of women towards nationalist activism, but primarily through an idiom that emphasized Hindu piety, sacrifice, and the icons of Sita and Sabitri, representing marital devotion. Such icons, drawn from high-Hindu epics, had a predominantly patriarchal ambience. Feminist scholarship, in a development which has been seldom noted, actually anticipated by several years the dialectic that lay at the heart of the early Subaltern Studies breakthrough. The note of criticism sharpened over time, as much writing about women came under the sway of postcolonial moods. Social reform now came to be described as no more than a 'recasting' of patriarchy under colonial conditions, while Partha Chatterjee put forward

---

[22] Two collections of essays, published in the same year, but the first a bringing-together of somewhat earlier articles in the *Indian Economic and Social History Review*, illustrates this contrast: J. Krishnamurty (ed.), *Women in Colonial India: Essays on Survival, Work and the State* (Delhi, 1989), and Kumkum Sangari and Sudesh Vaid (eds), *Recasting Women: Essays in Colonial History* (Delhi, 1989).

what became a very influential generalization about a 'nationalist resolution of the women's question' by the early twentieth century. Questions about women, he suggested, came to be relegated to the private sphere of the 'home' and eased out of the public-political domain, where the struggle against foreign rule and cultural domination was given total priority.

Recently, there are signs of moves away from what had become at times an excessively critical and negative emphasis, amounting to a kind of cultural-nationalistic rejection of all forms that could be branded as 'derivative' from the modern West. Intensive studies of nineteenth-century women's writings are one factor explaining the new shift, highlighting the sheer courage and novelty of women, in small but ever-growing numbers, learning to read and write and so violating age-old taboos, editing journals, beginning to go in for higher and professional education within a generation or so of middle-class Indian men, and braving social ostracism to contract marriages after widowhood. And while the actual impact of the specific legal reforms concerning women during the nineteenth century (the banning of widow immolation in 1829, legalization of widow marriage in 1856, the Age of Consent Act of 1891) was extremely limited and at times shot through with contradictions, there seem to have been some unintended and ultimately far-reaching consequences. What was emerging, it has been recently suggested, was something like a 'pre-history of rights' or individual entitlements: indicated paradoxically by the fact that even conservative opponents of reform from the sati debates of the 1820s onwards repeatedly deployed an argument of 'consent': the bereaved woman voluntarily plunging into her husband's funeral pyre, widows preferring out of love not to marry again, child-brides attracted by the charm of early marriages.[23]

At the same time, the presence of contradictory tendencies cannot be ignored, and Chatterjee's 'nationalist resolution' did contain an important point, though one perhaps presented in a somewhat over-generalized and linear form. Nascent notions of individual rights were (and are) repeatedly sought to be countered through an emphasis on the necessary solidarities of community: Hindu, Muslim, caste, or anti-colonial nationalist. Regional variations are also important: in some parts of the country, notably Kerala and some north-eastern tracts (as well as Ladakh in the far north), prevalent

---

[23] An argument elaborated by Tanika Sarkar: see particularly her 'A Pre-history of Rights? The Age of Consent Debates in Colonial Bengal', in *Hindu Wife, Hindu Nation: Community, Religion and Cultural Nationalism* (Delhi, 2001).

forms of matriliny, possibly permitting more equal status of women, came to be eliminated through the modernizing legal thrust towards monogamy and patrilineal succession.

The counterflows were at their strongest during the Extremist phase, and here a certain continuity can be observed with the subsequent rise of Hindutva nationalism, even an occasional continuity of persons as when some of the erstwhile followers of the best-known extremist leader, B. G. Tilak, helped to set up the core organization of the Rashtriya Swayamsevak Sangh in 1925, with an ideology most clearly formulated by the ex-revolutionary nationalist V. D. Savarkar. But, once again, we have to emphasize contradictory strands. As extremism declined, new intellectual-cultural openings became visible, manifested notably in the post-Swadeshi writings of Rabindranath Tagore in Bengal. Two novels by him, *Gora* and *Home and the World*, vividly portrayed the tensions of that era, while a sheaf of short stories around 1914–15 contained a sharper note of protest about conditions of women than ever before in his writings.[24] Politically, too, the need for mass mobilization in the Gandhian phase of anti-colonial nationalism demanded a degree of openness towards subordinated castes, classes, and women. Meanwhile, reformist groups among women, however small in numbers and elitist, pressed ahead with demands for specific legal reforms on questions like raising the minimum age of marriage, changing elements of Hindu and Muslim family law, and, notably, extending votes to women. Their sustained work helped to lay the basis for the broadly progressive changes in Hindu family laws after independence. The women's question, then, never became a pure matter of the 'home', and the 'nationalist resolution' remained shot through with contradictions.

The relatively few recent works on the era of high nationalism and mass politics, roughly from the early 1920s to the 1940s, indicate a sensitivity towards gender issues largely absent in earlier work. In their totality, the impression which emerges is again the presence of contradictory strands. Space permits only two or three specific instances. Douglas Haynes's study of Surat has explored the ways in which Gandhian ideology meshed with fairly traditional notions of patriarchal *stridharma* (conduct proper to

---

[24] See e.g. the essays of Tanika Sarkar, Sumit Sarkar, and the introduction by Pradip Datta in Datta (ed.), *Rabindranath Tagore's Home and the World: A Critical Companion* (Delhi, 2003).

women).[25] Another local study based on fieldwork in the Darbhanga region of North Bihar in the 1930s by Wendy Singer, however, indicates how in that storm-centre of both Gandhian mass nationalism and left-leaning peasant associations, the Gandhian village centres could at times become much-needed shelters for women oppressed in their homes, and being pressurized to marry men they did not want, so much so that nationalism came to be locally called by women, anti-purdah movement.[26] The additional income earned by village women through the Gandhian stimulus to rural crafts, notably spinning, seems to have been partly responsible for such assertiveness: a pattern noticed also in rural Gandhian centres in parts of Bengal studied by Hitesh Sanyal. But Singer's exploration of oral sources also reveals the existence of tendencies, in the end more effective, towards conservative recuperation. The socially radical moods have been largely forgotten today, and instead the moments of violent anti-British struggle (notably, the 1942 Quit India struggle) are highlighted, in part because the latter is invariably foregrounded in postcolonial, statist evocations of an undifferentiated nationalism bereft of much of the social radicalism it had occasionally possessed. The Congress local activists recuperated in Darbhanga by Singer, for instance, are still honoured, but for their role as militant fighters against British rule in 1942. The 'anti-purdah movement', however, has been almost entirely forgotten, in this still highly patriarchal region.

A not dissimilar pattern, though one marked at times by greater initial rebellion, can be discerned in the mass struggles beyond the constraints and discipline of the Congress led by Left or other radical formations. Telengana, in the highly autocratic princely state of Hyderabad with marked feudal and patriarchal structures of landlordism, represents a striking instance. Here the peasant guerrilla struggle spearheaded by Communists between 1946 and 1951 contributed greatly to the defeat of the Nizam's bid for an independent state and to the merger with India, after which the Indian state suppressed the insurrection through a combination of great repression and a marginal dose of land reform. The revolt had actually been sparked off by the mistreatment of a village washerwoman, Ailamma, in the summer of

---

[25] Douglas Haynes, *Rhetoric and Ritual in Colonial India: Public Culture in Surat City, 1852–1928* (Berkeley, 1991).

[26] Wendy Singer, *Creating Histories: Oral Narratives and the Politics of History-Making* (Delhi, 1997).

1946 by the local landlord. Women participants in interviews conducted several decades later still recalled the days of the insurrection as 'that magic time', imbued with a promise of many forms of equality and comradeship, not excluding gender relationships. But they also spoke with some bitterness of their specific grievances being often sidelined by the overwhelmingly male leaders and cadres, and of conventional division of labour within the household persisting even in life in the forests where guerrillas had been forced to take shelter in the last days of the insurrection. Another, different kind of instance of the radicalism of women comes from the markedly different social milieu of Manipur, where women seem to have been noticeably independent and prominent in everyday social and economic life. Here there were the two 'Nupilals' or Women's Wars, of 1904 and 1939. Despite subsequent efforts to assimilate them into the grand narrative of anti-British freedom struggle, these movements led by women had as their prime targets the local court, which combined exactions with attempts to impose the more rigid norms of orthodox Hindu society on more relaxed local customs, as well as immigrant Marwari traders. The second Nupilal ultimately merged with a Communist-led movement which actually brought about universal suffrage as early as the summer of 1948, several years before the rest of India. The tradition of women's militancy in Manipur lives on: in 2003, they were at the forefront of highly innovative protests against oppression and rape by Indian paramilitary forces.[27]

Religion and Nationalism

Our sketch of the interactions of caste and gender with nationalism have had occasion to touch upon what recent developments have made extremely crucial for India, Pakistan, and Bangladesh today: the questions of religious identity, communalism, and secularism. There is need to clarify that these terms represent specific historically conditioned usages of Indian English. Communalism implies not just an emphasis on community solidarity or consciousness (itself largely a product in South Asia of numerous

---

[27] Vasantha Kannabiran and K. Lalitha, 'That Magic Time: Women in the Telengana People's Struggle', in Sangari and Vaid (eds), *Recasting Women*; John Roosa, 'Passive Revolution Meets Peasant Revolution: Indian Nationalism and the Telengana Revolt', *Journal of Peasant Studies*, 28 (2001), 57–94; Saraj N. Arambam Parrott and John Parrott, 'The Second "Women's War" and the Emergence of Democratic Government in Manipur', *Modern Asian Studies*, 35 (2001), 905–19.

developments in late colonial times, as we have seen) but further assumptions regarding conflicts between (usually religion-defined) communities as inevitable, total, and more vital than any other conflict. For communalism, Hindu or Muslim, such conflicts became far more important than the struggle against foreign rule, for freedom came to mean liberation from a thousand years of alleged Muslim oppression and threat, for Hindus, and re-establishment of the glories of (equally alleged) medieval Muslim domination, for Muslims. Heavily mythologized versions of history provided sustenance for both creeds, at once mutually opposed and analogous to each other. Localized clashes between Hindus and Muslims (as well as occasional quarrels of both with Christians, mostly over proselytization) go fairly far back into the past, and became more frequent from around the 1890s, starting with the riots over cow-protection. In the wake of the breakup of the impressive anti-imperialist unity briefly achieved through the Non-Cooperation-Khilafat upsurge, riots became and remained endemic in South Asian life, and organizations like the Rashtriya Swayamsevak Sangh (RSS), the Hindu Mahasabha, and the Muslim League emerged or became more aggressive. The specific Indian usage of secular also became prominent from around that time. It connotes being not anti-religious or even necessarily indifferent to religion, but anti-communal. The distinctions, it has to be added, have been clearer at the level of theoretical formulation than in actual historical practice. Teleological readings that assume a neat disjunction between secular and communal nationalisms going far back into the past are best avoided. We need to work, rather, with a logic that allows for both real distinctions and frequent affinities and overlaps. Many major Hindu literary figures in the nineteenth century, for instance, had grounded their emergent patriotism in an evocation of medieval Hindu resistance to Muslim kings. They have remained icons for communal and anti-colonial nationalisms alike.[28] The central secular political formation, the Indian National Congress, again, has always contained communal-Hindu elements, prominent particularly at local and provincial levels, despite the undoubtedly anti-communal, if significantly different, standpoints of the devoutly Hindu Gandhi and the agnostic Nehru.

---

[28] Bankimchandra Chattopadhyay would be the most obvious example, with his hymn 'Bande Mataram' that inspired anti-colonial nationalism from the Swadeshi era onwards, but also has frequently served as a rallying-cry for Hindus in anti-Muslim communal riots.

Perhaps the most meaningful way of looking at the secular/communal divide within South Asian nationalisms might be to view them in terms of simultaneous and interpenetrating identity formations, and as distinct ways of imagining the very idea of an Indian nationhood and its history. The Moderate phase of the Congress tried to tackle the question through what in today's terms might be called a narrow public sphere from which divisive issues relating to religion, caste, social reform, regional, and class conflicts would be deliberately excluded. Objections raised by a significant section of Hindu or Muslim delegates, for instance, were made sufficient for exclusion from Congress sessions of any resolution on a matter affecting religious sentiments, while questions of social reform (relating primarily to gender or caste) were left to a separate National Social Conference. The nation, again, was often thought of as a goal to be achieved, still in the womb of the future: Surendranath Banerjea, for instance, gave the title *A Nation in Making* to his political autobiography. These could be termed incipient forms of secular nationalism, and elements going back to the moderate phase remain discernible in postcolonial Indian constitutional provisions and political practices, where secularism is often understood, in a weak sense, as equal proximity to, rather than equal indifference towards, all religious loyalties.

The Social Conference had at first met at the same venue and time as the annual Congress, and often included many of the Congress delegates. Tilak in the 1890s, the foremost leader of Extremism, insisted on its removal as part of his programme of aggressive and orthodox Hindu nationalism, while at the same time organizing a Ganesh festival just at the time of Muharram, as well as an annual celebration of Shivaji, projected as the heroic champion of the Hindu cause against the villainous late seventeenth-century Mughal emperor Aurangzeb. The aim was to mobilize a much wider circle than had been touched by the elitist policies of the Moderates against foreign rule, but the failure to achieve such a breakthrough often led Extremists to pass over to methods of revolutionary terrorism. In practice, these remained equally elitist, with activists drawn entirely from the middle-class Hindu literati of regions like Bengal, Maharashtra, and Punjab, though not devoid of wider imaginative appeal through its undoubted heroism and self-sacrifice. By the 1920s, some among the extremists and revolutionaries, notably Savarkar and a section of the erstwhile followers of Tilak, had come to constitute the core of what today is Hindutva nationalism, with one significant departure. Muslims had now displaced the British as the enemy that had to be overcome in the cause of achieving true Hindu freedom.

An opposite but analogous trajectory from a prioritization of Muslim religious community to aggressive Muslim communalism took place around the same time. The nation, Hindu or Muslim, came to mean for communalists an already existent sacred entity, grounded in fetishized and chauvinistic constructions of religion and culture. Savarkar's *Hindutva: Who is a Hindu* (1923) summed up this basic communal creed through defining the Hindu as possessed of a unique identity of fatherland and holy land. The Muslim or Christian might also claim or think themselves to be patriots, but their holy land, for this Hindutva ideologue, had to be Palestine or Mecca. True membership of the nation, therefore, was determined by religious and cultural origin alone. Non-Hindus could exist only on sufferance, on unequal terms, and Golwalkar, the second supreme head of the RSS, subsequently ridiculed as an 'amazing doctrine' the idea, central to all forms of secular nationalism, that the nation was an entity in the process of formation, 'composed of all those who, for one reason or another happen to live at the time in the country'.[29] For Hindu and Muslim communalism alike, other communities were to be cowed into submission by threat and periodic use of force. Such ideals and strategies would also help to overcome all divisions of caste, gender, ethnicity, or class internal to the religious communities, without seriously modifying their often deeply unjust and hierarchical patterns. Their outcome, in practice, became the violent partition of the country, continuing tensions and occasional wars between these successor states, periodic riots, and, in more recent times, events like the destruction of the Babri Masjid in 1992 and the state-sponsored pogrom in Gujarat in 2002.

The anti-communal alternatives to such exacerbation of identity conflicts have taken two different forms. From the 1920s onwards, left-leaning formations—Communist, Socialist, the section within the Congress close to Nehru (particularly in his more radical, 1930s phase)—have sought to undercut religious and other loyalties thought to be divisive through emphasizing the united interests and aspirations of toilers and radical socioeconomic change through class struggle. Their evident decline or stagnation by the 1990s sometimes led to a too hurried and over-generalized dismissal of such possibilities, that had been, and might still become, quite effective in some areas and times. Numerous powerful movements of peasants and

---

[29] M. S. Golwalkar, *We or Our Nationhood Defined* (1939; 3rd edn., Nagpur, 1945), 64.

workers—Telengana between 1946 and 1951, for instance—indicate the occasional existence of such potentials.

It is not difficult, and perhaps as inadmissibly presentist, to adopt a similar total skepticism towards the Gandhian way, too. Gandhi's lifelong prioritization of the question of non-violence, and conflict-resolution through effective peaceful methods, can only be explained in terms of an agonized realization of the great potential of escalation of violence in late colonial India—between British rulers and Indian subjects, but also notably among Indians themselves—as well as in what he thought were the inevitable evils of contemporary industrial civilization. Resolution of conflict through *ahimsa* (non-violence) and *satyagraha* (mass but strictly peaceful struggle) sought a very difficult combination of rejection of violence and total confrontations, and real, if limited, change in relationships which Gandhi recognized to be deeply unjust, without the exacerbation of conflicts, barriers, permanently hardened identities. Gandhi's basic text, *Hind Swaraj* (1909), represents the opposite pole to Savarkar's programme and values, and it was not an accident that its author was murdered by a close associate of the latter who had once been in the RSS.[30]

Such methods did help to constitute what at its peak moments could become one of the biggest of mass movements of the twentieth century. Its limits and failures in practice remain equally clear. The old left and early Subalternist critique, that Gandhian non-violence also rejected methods like labour strikes or peasant no-rent that had nothing intrinsically violent about them (any more than picketing of foreign goods, which he advocated), and that therefore Gandhism had a pronounced tilt towards propertied groups in its conception of the Congress as an all-embracing umbrella, still has considerable resonance. The tilt, many have felt, was also towards higher castes (rejection of untouchability being combined with refusal to repudiate caste in its entirety), and high-Hindu strata and values. By the 1930s, there was an important and worrying breakaway by considerable sections among the *dalits*, led by Ambedkar, while Gandhi's continued reliance on Hindu imagery and symbols, even while emphasizing their syncretistic and non-violent elements, also aroused suspicion among many Muslims. His 'double-edged use of Hindu imagery', seeking to utilize Hindu symbolism to push for reform from within, was also not understood

---

[30] See Antony Parel's Introduction to Gandhi, *Hind Swaraj* (Cambridge, 1997).

or internalized by possibly the bulk of his followers, who took that language as uncritically celebratory.[31] Not too dissimilar patterns manifested themselves with respect to questions of family and gender relationships, leading to considerable later feminist criticism.

But perhaps there still is a need to distinguish between Gandhi as a specific historical figure, conditioned by his location in given class, social, religious, and patriarchal structures and values, and the long-term and continued relevance of some among his ideals and methods. Nothing else can explain how certain strands related to Gandhian values live on, both in India (not because but despite his erection into a statist icon, and mainly through the surge in recent times of a variety of 'grass-roots' activists and environmentalist movements) and abroad (the early African National Congress, the civil rights movement in the United States in the phase of the Students Non-Violent Coordination and Martin Luther King).

Political Legacies

As for the continued significance of Indian nationalism as a whole, I would like to suggest in conclusion that this lay not so much in the achievement of independence (which, given the weakening of British military and political power after the Second World War, would have happened even in the absence of such a countrywide movement, as the experience of some colonies indicate), or even the heroism and self-sacrifice of its activists. What was remarkable was the capacity for internal debate, change, and auto-critique, even at the height of anti-colonial movements. Such debates, combined with a persistent concern for mass poverty from the early Moderate phase onwards and the need for mass mobilization that was heightened by the adoption of Gandhian methods (as distinct from conspiratorial armed struggle where only some could be active), led to a progressive broadening of the meanings of freedom. One need only note that none of the four features central to the Constitution adopted by independent India in 1949—democracy based on universal suffrage, secularism, elements of federalism, and social justice through affirmative action—had been present in the early programmes of mainstream nationalism. They came to be incorporated only through a dialectic of change through internal

---

[31] A perceptive point made by a Dalit intellectual: D. R. Nagaraj, *The Flaming Feet: A Study of the Dalit Movement in India* (Bangalore, 1993), ch. 1.

debates, pressures, conflicts. Hindutva nationalism, in sharp contrast, has changed little in its basic objectives since the 1920s, and is also marked by the absence of any deep concern with mass poverty. Here there is a fit, though, with present-day elite attraction for neo-liberal values the world over. Perhaps most remarkable of all, there was a persistent realization among many of the key figures of the dangers of narrow forms of nationalism, and a quest in different ways for a combination with broader internationalist and humanist critiques. This was most evident in three of the most outstanding figures of the nationalist era. Gandhi's *Hind Swaraj* was utterly different from a conventional nationalist tract, Tagore around the same time launched a powerful critique of the dangers of nationalism, Nehru—though perhaps the most 'statist' among them—still sought to introduce and retain an internationalist dimension. It is precisely such strands that are in danger of getting lost through the current domination of linear and homogenized views about nationalism, where its icons are projected as unchanging and uniform knights in shining armour. Few nationalisms, it needs to be emphasized, have been capable of such change through internal tensions, and of working simultaneously within, yet beyond, the confines of its chosen ideology.

Select Bibliography

Shahid Amin, *Event, Metaphor, Memory: Chauri Chaura, 1922–1992* (Berkeley, 1995).
Bipan Chandra, *India's Struggle for Independence* (Delhi, 1988).
Partha Chatterjee, *The Nation and Its Fragments: Colonial and Postcolonial Histories* (Princeton, 1993).
Ian Copland, *The Princes of India in the Endgame of Empire, 1917–1947* (Cambridge, 1997).
William Gould, *Hindu Nationalism and the Language of Politics in Late Colonial India* (Cambridge, 2003).
Ranajit Guha, *Elementary Aspects of Peasant Insurgency in Colonial India* (Delhi, 1983).
——and Gayatri Chakravorty Spivak (eds), *Selected Subaltern Studies* (Oxford, 1988).
David Hardiman, *Gandhi in His Time and Ours: The Global Legacy of His Ideas* (New York, 2004).
Mushirul Hasan, *Nationalism and Communal Politics in India, 1885–1930* (Delhi, 1994).
——*A Moral Reckoning: Muslim Intellectuals in Nineteenth-Century Delhi* (Delhi, 2005).

Douglas Haynes, *Rhetoric and Ritual in Colonial India: The Shaping of a Public Culture in Surat City, 1852–1928* (Berkeley, 1991).

——and Gyan Prakash (eds), *Contesting Power: Everyday Resistance in South Asian Society and History* (Berkeley, 1991).

Christophe Jaffrelot, *The Hindu Nationalist Movement in India, 1925–1993* (New York, 1995).

——*Dr Ambedkar and Untouchability: Fighting the Indian Caste System* (New York, 2005).

Ayesha Jalal, *The Sole Spokesman: Jinnah, the Muslim League and the Demand for Pakistan* (Cambridge, 1985).

David Lelyveld, *Aligarh's First Generation: Muslim Solidarity in British India* (Delhi, 1996).

D. A. Low (ed.), *Congress and the Raj: Facets of the Indian Struggle, 1917–1947* (London, 1977).

——*Britain and Indian Nationalism: The Imprint of Ambiguity, 1929–1942* (Cambridge, 1997).

Dilip M. Menon, *Caste, Nationalism and Communism in South India: Malabar, 1900–1948* (Cambridge, 1994).

Sumathi Ramaswamy, *Passions of the Tongue: Language Devotion in Tamil India, 1891–1970* (Berkeley, 1997).

Francis Robinson, *Islam and Muslim History in South Asia* (Delhi, 2000).

Sumit Sarkar, *The Swadeshi Movement in Bengal, 1903–1908* (Delhi, 1973).

——*Modern India* (London, 1989).

Peter van der Veer, *Religious Nationalism: Hindu and Muslims in India* (Berkeley, 1994).

7

Law, Authority, and Colonial Rule

Sandra den Otter

British-administered law had far-reaching, long-lasting, and often paradoxical consequences for the Indian subcontinent. Legal reform, and the moral conquest it claimed to represent, was a principal justification enumerated by defenders of British conquest and dominion who believed that law would systematize the relationships of the marketplace and entrench a market economy; law would introduce notions of individual rights and freedom of contract upon which civilized societies rested; law would guarantee security of property and person. But legal reform was not merely a broad vision under the eye of the imperium; law intruded into individual lives in an immediate and far-reaching manner. Marriage, inheritance, contractual employment, and land tenure cases came before the colonial courts, and decisions made in the courts of the interior, in the presidency towns, and in the Privy Council in London bound millions of inhabitants across the subcontinent. New codes of civil and criminal procedures and a new law of evidence generated a formal administration of justice. Legal interventions descended into the fabric of indigenous society, and the courthouse, and law books powerfully shaped imperial and indigenous identities by patrolling the boundaries of public/private and articulating new and often-contested meanings of subject and citizen. Law was also the instrument that enabled the colonial state to insist that it 'alone had the right to a legitimate exercise of violence' and provided the state with legal tools to define delinquency, to stifle sedition, and to suppress challenges to its supremacy.[1]

Colonial laws embodied multiple, often contradictory, requirements and expectations that changed throughout the colonial period. For the colonial state, the overriding desire to secure and maintain order dictated the shape

---

[1] R. Singha, *A Despotism of Law: Crime and Justice in Early Colonial India* (Delhi, 1998), 33.

of judicial administration, especially as the British fought wars of conquest and consolidation. The mayoral courts established in 1753 in Madras, Bombay, and Calcutta administered English law to Europeans, and their successor supreme courts dispensed primarily English and occasionally Roman law in most civil and criminal cases. The parallel courts of the East India Company continued to some degree the tradition of legal pluralism of the Mughal empire, and accordingly, William Hastings, in a plan for the administration of justice in Bengal, provided in 1773 that 'in all suits regarding marriage, inheritance and caste, and other religious usages and institutions, the laws of the Koran with respect to Mahomedans, and those of the Shaster with respect to Gentus [Hindus] shall be invariably adhered to'.[2] By separating Hindu and Muslim personal laws from public law, the colonial state sought to harness existing legal structures and to diminish the upheaval thrown up by the conquest, but dividing Hindu and Muslim personal laws from public law had long-lasting implications. Judicial administration, and legal cultures more broadly, also emerged in response to capitalist development and the demands for governance of the market. Laws were determined by economic interests that required a legal system to govern economic relations, to enable the extraction of revenue from the subcontinent, to ensure the stability of markets, and so to extend and consolidate colonial rule. Although Governor-General Cornwallis separated judicial and revenue powers in Bengal in 1793 along Whiggish principles, revenue and judicial functions increasingly overlapped in the Bengal Presidency, as they had long been merged in the Madras Presidency, and collectors both ruled in suits over rent and acted as local magistrates.

While law equipped the colonial state with the visible authority to dominate, to command, and to control, this authority rested on volatile and insecure foundations. Knowledge of indigenous laws and customs was essential to the legal pluralism that the Raj claimed to uphold. But despite the insatiable appetite of the colonial administration for knowledge, understanding of indigenous law and society more broadly was starkly limited. This produced an often contradictory and inconsistent system of law, so that notwithstanding the powerful ideology that called for India to be civilized through the rule of law, colonial legal administration was tentative, regionally variable, ambiguous, and arguably an arrested move-

[2] East India Regulating Act of 1773.

ment through indigenous social practices rather than securing a triumphant march of civilization. Colonial courts and their technologies of rule made a marked incursion into Indian society; they were also much more partial, more ambiguous, and more strongly resisted and manipulated than the liberal ambitions to civilize India through law acknowledged. The utilitarians of the early nineteenth century pledged 'rule of law' based on universal principles, but even the most ardent utilitarian saw how much the particularity of Indian society undercut this universalism and how effectively various groups and interests unsettled the universalism of colonial assumptions about freedom of contract and individual rights.

The utilitarian ambition to translate indigenous law into codes of law loomed over many of the legal transformations of the long nineteenth century. I consider briefly this natural history of ideas and practice, negotiation, compromise, and eventual retreat to take a closer look at the legal revolution that British brought and to re-examine the encounter between indigenous customary law and English law, and between colonial administrators and South Asian legal scholars and officers and litigants. Colonial jurisprudence elucidates the tensions and paradoxes of empire partly because law affected indigenous society more directly than almost any other aspect of British rule, and partly because it highlights a transnational flow of ideas and legal cultures, at the same time as pointing out the conflict between these liberal principles and the demands of a despotic state, and the legal identities that litigants and Indian legal scholars articulated.

I. Law, Custom, and Colonial Knowledge

From the outset, the administration of law in colonial India depended on an accommodation with indigenous law and practice that was without precedent in the British empire.[3] The provisions that indigenous law was to be followed in cases governing marriage, inheritance, and succession and that courts would rule according to 'justice, equity and good conscience' was repeatedly intoned, for instance in Queen Victoria's declaration in 1858 that the colonial state would not tamper with the religious and cultural sensibilities of its subjects. In practice these assurances did not prevent incursion into the religious life of the population, nor a far-reaching legal

---

[3] See L. Benton, *Law and Colonial Cultures: Legal Regimes in World History 1400–1900* (Cambridge, 2002).

transformation. In order to follow indigenous law, the colonial state had first to locate and define it, and understanding what constituted law on the subcontinent depended on the constantly shifting practical realities of colonial administration which varied greatly by region, by changing conceptions of imperial rule, and by consultations with indigenous law officers and elites. The thousands of cases coming before the early colonial courts showed how little colonial officers knew of Indian law and society.

Indian law officers were initially indispensable to colonial legal machinery and early colonial judges relied on indigenous legal experts, clerks, and interpreters adept in Persian and Arabic to determine the law and deliver judgement. Sir William Jones's massive *Digest of Hindu Law*, produced between 1788 and 1797, depended on the expertise of the renowned scholar Jagganatha, and also on Radhakanta Tarkavagisa, Savoru Trivedi, and others who were selected by Jones in part for their knowledge of diverse local practice and custom.[4] Jones and Colebrooke regarded law as a blend of custom and natural reason that varied according to local circumstance and region. But later colonial administrators, who required an unambiguous body of law to administer, were inclined to regard these and other digests as authoritative and uniformly binding statements, and thereby distorted, truncated, and misrepresented the complexity and regional diversity of indigenous law. By favouring the most ancient legal scriptures, these later officials neglected both later interpretations of these laws and overlooked the vast array of customary law. Furthermore, as colonial officials and British scholars translated indigenous law into written form and entrenched them in legal decisions, the evolutionary fluidity of pre-colonial law and custom was ossified. As the legal scholar and colonial administrator H. S. Maine reflected, 'its spontaneous growth was suddenly arrested by the administration of the country passing into the hands of the English, and a degree of rigidity was given to it which it never before possessed'.[5] This was compounded by the fact that colonial judges were often poorly equipped to navigate Hindu or Islamic jurisprudence and often used their own

---

[4] J. Wilson, *The Domination of Strangers: Modern Governance in Eastern India, 1780–1835* (London, 2008); R. Rocher, 'The Career of Radhakanta Tarkavasiga: An 18th Century *Pandit* in the British Employ', *Journal of the American Oriental Society*, 109/4 (1989), 527–633; D. Davis, 'Law in the Mirror of Language: The Madras School of Orientalism on Hindu Law', in T. Trautmann (ed.), *The Madras School of Orientalism: Producing Knowledge in Colonial South India* (Delhi, 2009).

[5] H. S. Maine, *Village Communities in the East and West* (London, 1881), 53.

interpretation of 'justice, equity and good conscience' to fill in the missing parts of their understanding, though not all colonial officers were so poorly equipped and made good use of training at Haileybury or at the College of Fort William to learn Sanskrit, Arabic, and Persian and to study indigenous jurisprudence. Imbued with common law thinking and seeking further aids to navigate an alien legal landscape, judges depended on digests of earlier decisions made by colonial courts and followed these 'currents of authority' established by precedent unless they held a very strong opinion the other way. This early reliance on case law meant that not only were misinterpretations and errors perpetuated in later decisions, but the elasticity of indigenous jurisprudence was lost as legal decisions no longer came from careful arbitration between conflicting construals and consideration of the particularities of each case. Colonial judges continually debated whether or not correcting erroneous judicial interpretations justified the uncertainty brought to law by departing from case law traditions.

Volume upon volume of Indian case law reveals a protracted attempt throughout the nineteenth century to bring indigenous custom under the legal arm of the state and to adjudicate between apparently competing customs and their interpretation. While early colonial courts depended on indigenous legal experts to define which customs were legally binding, conventions emerged throughout the first part of the nineteenth century on how to decide which customs were to be judicially recognized. Here, as in other areas, the colonial state came to place a high premium on ancient authority, especially textual authority. Customs could only stand above written law if they were proven to be 'ancient, invariable, uniform and constant...in short be part of the legal conscience of all those whom it is said to bind'.[6] Judges did not invariably depend on the antiquity of a custom as evidence of its authority, so long as a custom appeared to be so well known as to be tacitly understood by the community. A quasi-ethnological or anthropological knowledge was part of judicial administration and this meant that at least in the early colonial period, recognition of the regional variation in customary law.

Indigenous law officers investigated local custom but they tended to consult texts of sacred law rather than local communities with their variable customs, and this tended to contribute to the Brahminization of Hindu

---

[6] Vayidinada v. Appu, 9 *Madras High Court* 44, F.B.

customary law. Even so, the colonial state increasingly throughout the 1840s and 1850s restricted these local consultations and judges often disregarded the opinion of law officers on the grounds that they could not always be reconciled with those textual authorities upon which courts relied. Dependence on *qazi* and pandits and *maulvi* had long mingled with colonial fears or suspicions of duplicity, and the conviction that the state required its own command of legal knowledge to minimize their vulnerability to deceit and corruption had prompted the production of colonial digests of Indian laws. In 1864 the office of pandit was abolished on the assumption that a record of Hindu law had been established which could be consulted independently of the pandits' interpretation. Ending this exchange between indigenous legal experts and a largely foreign judiciary had a long-term, detrimental impact on judicial interpretation. Colonial judges no longer had access to the oral traditions by which law evolved and the loss of this fluidity of revising interpretation which indigenous experts had brought to colonial administration contributed to the ossification of Hindu law, and, at least at the level of appeal courts, a diminution of regional variation. But while the courts agreed that in Hindu systems of law, written law should not be given priority over customary law, the burden to prove authentic and binding custom was so great that in practice only ancient customs were recognized and written law acquired much greater weight. As the late nineteenth-century jurist Trailokyanath Mitra warned, 'The dry bones of ancient law, unless viewed in connection with the customs which have grown out of them, and, in some cases, have supplanted them, can never correctly represent the conditions or feelings of the people.'[7] Increasingly the authority of custom turned upon case law and textual authorities. This had grave consequences, for it fettered indigenous societies to an ossified jurisprudence and compromised the capacity of colonial law to bend to changes in those societies.

The colonial legal system tended to categorize complex religious identities into the two monolithic categories of 'Hindu' and 'Muslim': Hindus were to be governed by Hindu law, and Muslims by Muslim law. But indigenous society was much more heterodox and much more variegated than the simple categories of colonial legal knowledge allowed. Some Muslim communities, like the Sunni Borahs in Gujarat, followed Hindu

---

[7] T. Mitra, *The Law Relating to the Hindu Widow* (Calcutta, 1881), 84.

inheritance laws, and other Hindu converts to Islam, notably the Khojas and Cutchi Memons, continued to follow Hindu patterns of succession, and in some cases, special customary laws.[8] Colonial courts were forced to recognize this heterodoxy as they heard suits from parties who claimed complex religious and ethnic identities. Courts arbitrated on when a custom was sufficiently well established to override the general presumption that Muslims and Hindus were to be governed by their own law and custom, and in which cases customs specific to one family could be regarded as binding on local communities. These attempts to adjudicate in specific cases the force of indigenous custom produced a contradictory and obfuscating body of case law. Sometimes custom was deemed binding even if it conflicted with statute law, while in other cases statute law was given precedent over custom. There were vast regional differences, partly because much customary law had a particularistic and local character, and because many courts had distinctive legal cultures and accordingly interpreted law and custom differently.

The rhetorical separation of indigenous personal from colonial public law obscured how much colonial reluctance to change personal law frustrated developments in public law. The conservatism of colonial legality was markedly shown in agriculture, where customary law continued to dominate through the colonial period. By constructing and entrenching tradition in civil law, the colonial state hampered the move towards a market economy, and frustrated indigenous demands for innovation. On the other hand, late nineteenth-century colonial anxieties about indigenous capitalism led the colonial state to use law to confine indigenous economic relations to the private realm of the family rather than a public domain.[9] The attempt to define and patrol the margins of custom also led the colonial state to intrude in indigenous social practices. Although successive governments pledged that domestic and family questions were outside the state except as the state administered specific communal and religious law, the colonial state none the less selectively intervened in multiple ways in those areas supposedly cordoned off from their direct intervention. Some of the earliest cases to come before the new colonial courts entailed marriage and inheritance questions, and courts decided the cases using an amalgam of

---

[8] Abraham v Abraham 9 *Moore's Indian Appeals* 195; Bai Baizi v Bai Santok *Indian Law Reports* 20 Bom 53. This was formalized in the Cutchi Memons Act, 1938.

[9] R. Birla, *Stages of Capitalism: Law, Culture, and Market Governance in Late Colonial India* (Durham, NC, 2009).

customary laws and sacred texts, as well as appeals to 'the dictates of nature, reason and natural justice'. The sheer number of cases that came before colonial courts on marriage, succession, betrothal, and inheritance give some indication of how far this largely alien legal system stretched into indigenous society. Colonial courts heard case after case that turned on issues of family inheritance and marriage; simply by hearing these suits, indigenous law on these cases was transformed; with very little statutory law affecting marriage and inheritance, the danger of judge-made laws based on partial understanding of existing customary laws became greater. Marriage and adoption customs, interpreted by colonial judges, for example, entrenched domestic slavery, for it became difficult to incorporate slaves, notably as mothers, into kin structures, when birth and marriage were so closely defined by the colonial legal corpus, even as the British state abolished slavery more generally.[10]

Colonial reformers had sought to raise up the building blocks of civil society out of what they saw to be a stagnant status-bound society, and accordingly sought to 'introduce' notions of contract and individual rights. But by constructing and upholding tradition in their administration of personal law, they also limited individual rights in far-reaching ways, as Tanika Sarkar and others have argued.[11] Although British rule swiftly extended the practice of writing wills and testaments in Bengal, colonial judges in many instances, especially in Madras, supported the tradition of male joint ownership over individual property rights that might have left more space for women's property rights.[12] There are numerous examples of colonial judges ruling against willing property to daughters.[13] Colonial courts also enforced such personal laws as made the widow's inheritance and maintenance contingent on her chastity. Wives had little recourse to escape from cruel marriages, though in pre-colonial jurisprudence marriages were dissolved in some instances of cruelty. The programme of civilization through law hung on assumptions that civilization was measured across the empire in part by how gender roles were prescribed

---

[10] I. Chatterjee, *Gender, Slavery and Law in Colonial India* (Oxford, 1999); S. Chandra, *Enslaved Daughters: Colonialism, Law and Women's Rights* (Delhi, 1998).

[11] T. Sarkar, *Hindu Wife and Hindu Nation* (Bloomington, Ind., 2001); D. Ghosh, *Sex and the Family in Colonial India: The Making of Empire* (Cambridge, 2006). R. Majumdar, *Marriage and Modernity: Family Values in Colonial Bengal* (Durham, NC, 2009).

[12] T. Strange, *Notes of Cases at Madras* (Madras, 1827), ii. 79 J. Cochrane, *Hindu Law: A Defence of the Daya Bhaga* (London, 1873), 175-7.

[13] See Mahomed Sidick v Haji Ahmed and others, ILR 10 Bom 1, p 18.

and observed, and colonial laws on marriage and age of consent, as well as judicial decisions, were predicated in part on these assumptions. The supreme courts and the Privy Council made judgements that shaped the personal laws governing millions of inhabitants across the subcontinent on marriage and inheritance and adoption practices. Because legal judgements passed into something akin to the common law, these incursions had a seemingly permanent quality. A constellation of statutes—the abolition of sati (1829) and infanticide (1870), the Widow's Remarriage Act (XV of 1856), the Succession Act (X of 1865), Converts' Remarriage Act (XXI of 1866), Indian Special Marriages Act (III of 1872), and amendments to the Penal Code raising the age of consent in 1891 to 12 years and then in 1929 to 14 years—extended this judicial incursion into the personal laws of South Asians, ostensibly so long cordoned off from the interference of the colonial state. This amounted to the first steps towards a civil code, a project imagined but never completed under colonial rule. Recent scholarship has suggested that Indian litigants manoeuvred through the courts to articulate judicial interpretations of personal laws that had a significant impact on colonial legal administration.[14]

II. *The Codification of Law and Custom*

I have been tracing how the colonial state took upon itself the authority to adjudicate indigenous customary law, and have highlighted some implications of this ostensibly neutral legal sovereignty. Nowhere was the incursion of the state into the juridical culture of the subcontinent most vividly exemplified than in the colonial attempt to codify Indian law, nor was the conflict between a legal pluralism and a universalism demanded by a civilizing mission accentuated so sharply. Liberals and utilitarians, who by the 1820s were gaining an authoritative voice in Britain and India, advocated codes of law that they argued would answer all of India's legal requirements. In the place of the chaotic jumble of English common law, the hundreds of regulations enacted by the East India Company, local customs, diverse parts of Hindu sacred law which earlier British officials had canonized, much of

---

[14] See e.g. the special issue of *Law and History*, 28/4 (2010), notably C. Mallampalli, 'Escaping the Grip of Personal Law in Colonial India: Proving Custom, Negotiating Hindu-ness', 1043–65; M. Sharifa, 'The Marital Patchwork of Colonial South Asia: Forum Shopping from Britain to Baroda', 979–1009.

Islamic criminal law, simple and uniform codes of law would be written. These codes would not need armies of lawyers or indigenous experts to interpret them but would be encapsulated in a small pocket-size book. Between 1859 and 1861 three major codes framed by the Indian Law Commissioners were passed and by this time most of Indian public law had been translated into codes, leaving Indian law much more codified than English law ever became; many of these codes in modified forms remain in force.[15]

Proponents of codification could turn to Jeremy Bentham for its philosophical defence, for Bentham had campaigned internationally for codes of law premised on universal principles of utility, and in a widely influential essay 'On the Influence of Time and Place' chose Bengal as a hypothetical setting for a bold legal revolution.[16] But closer examination of both metropolitan and Indian juridical discourse calls into question the radical transformation either envisioned or engineered by Benthamite principles. Even Bentham, despite the radical and unequivocal force of his proposals to codify all law, recognized the weight of strong local customs and the limitations of political authority to execute radical legal change. His influential coterie of supporters, both in the East India Company on Leadenhall Street in London, and across the subcontinent, were yet more modest in their expectations and reinterpreted Benthamite theories in the light of their experience of colonial governance. Although Bentham exerted a persuasive influence on legal reform in the 1820s, his recommendations for a broad-sweeping codification of common law did not meet a receptive audience within Britain.[17] Critics of the current state of law, like Thomas Starkie, John Millar, and John Reddie followed Bentham's campaign for greater clarity in rules and procedure, but not his disdain for the common law or his paeans to codes.[18] The two Royal Commissions headed by the Benthamite Lord Chancellor Henry Brougham concluded in recommendations not for codes but a digest that would unite statute and common law, thereby

---

[15] See E. Stokes, *The English Utilitarians and India* (Oxford, 1959); E. Kolsky, 'Codification and the Rule of Colonial Difference: Criminal Procedure in British India', *Law and History Review*, 23/3 (2005), 1–38.

[16] J. Bentham, 'Essay On the Influence of Time and Place', in *The Works of Jeremy Bentham*, ed. John Bowring (Edinburgh, 1843), i. 180; J. Pitts, *A Turn to Empire* (Princeton, 2005), ch. 4.

[17] See *Law Magazine*, 1 (1828–9), 613–37 and *Edinburgh Review*, 54 (1831), 183–238.

[18] See M. Lobban, *The Common Law and English Jurisprudence* (Oxford, 1991), 187; see e.g. J. Miller, *Civil Law of England* (London, 1825), 481–507; D. Lieberman, 'From Bentham to Benthamism', *Historical Journal*, 28 (1985), 199–124.

avoiding what the commissioners regarded as the dangerous oversimplification of the ever-evolving repository of natural reason and custom, refined by generations of legal argument.[19]

In contrast, many London utilitarians regarded India as a 'magnificent field for codification', for legal experiments not possible or even desirable in Britain.[20] But from the start, there was a presumption against radical change, and Governor-General Bentinck ruled against any code that would 'sweep away at one stroke the laws of our Hindo and Moslem subjects'.[21] When the Charter of the East India Company was renewed in 1833, an Indian Law Commission was established to frame law codes with the ostensible stipulation to respect indigenous customs and laws. T. B. Macaulay in the role of scientific legislator went out to India in 1834, intending to write codes quickly and expeditiously and thereby create a framework for his understanding of progressive civilization. But even this proponent of a radical legal revolution for India acknowledged the obstacles and qualified the boldness of his proposals. Too many considerations militated against a universal code of laws patterned on abstract principles of utility, and even at the height of the utilitarian enthusiasm for reform of the subcontinent, a Benthamite revolution in the law was not widely defended. The universalism of law though continued to justify colonial legal administration for several important reasons, not least because universalism strengthened the legitimating myth of colonial laws and cloaked the more naked need of the state to use law to maintain its authority. But in these early utilitarian attempts to write law codes for India, a dominant universalism was consistently mingled with attention to how particularity and difference limited or constrained the applicability of universal principles.

The genesis of the codes lay as much in frustrations with the existing legal system as in Benthamite ideas. By the late 1820s, Indian courts were plagued by lengthy delays as they administered a bewildering array of laws and regulations. A chaotic pottage of Hindu and Muslim law and usage, Hindu scripture, government regulations, letters patent from the Crown,

---

[19] Lobban, *The Common Law*, 199–206. See both the 4th and 7th reports of Her Majesty's Commissioners on Criminal Law. *Parliamentary Papers* (1839), 168, XIX, 6, and (1843), 448, XIX, 4.

[20] Cambridge University Library. J. F. Stephen MSS 7349/14/f4. 16 Mar. 1876. Stephen to Lytton. James Mill, *History of British India* (London, 1817), v. 361.

[21] C. E. Grey and E. Ryan, 'Some Observations on a Suggestion of a Code of Laws', submitted 13 Sept. 1830 to the Governor-General in Council. Bentinck to Grey and Ryan, 9 Oct. 1831. *Parliamentary Papers* (1831), VI, 144.

and circulars from various courts formed the law of India, and this confusion led to inconsistent decisions and stimulated even more litigation. Judges and administrators maintained that law was uncertain and its interpretation and execution varied widely across the subcontinent. The infamous trial and execution of Nandakumar for forgery in 1775 and the subsequent impeachment hearings of Sir Elijah Impey, Supreme Court judge, illustrate the early disordered application of English common law to India, the misunderstanding of Indian evidence and litigation, the jurisdictional disputes between the judicial and executive branches of the colonial state, and the disrepute of the Supreme Court in the late eighteenth century.[22] Indian courts had been reorganized several times by the 1820s and numerous digests of Indian law had been produced, but the administration of justice was hardly swift, accessible, or invariably equitable. Judicial procedure was also uncertain, and no less than nine different systems of civil procedure were simultaneously in effect in Bengal before 1859.[23] British claims to bestow the rule of law on India, with all its apparent attendant virtues, increasingly seemed hollow, not only to the critics of imperial rule in Britain and India, but also to its own administrators and to some indigenous elites, notably Rammohun Roy, who urged the colonial state to frame codes of law to remedy the worst abuses of colonial jurisprudence.[24]

The codes were not simply the transportation of English law to India, though contract law was the most heavily anglicized of the codes, partly because by the mid-nineteenth century English contract law had largely superseded Hindu law of contract. Roman law was a major source for law codes, as it was in case law produced by some Indian courts and certainly also by appeals to the Privy Council.[25] The single uniform system of law its proponents celebrated was never realized. While it is true that English law was inexorably implemented across India, the intended uniformity of the codes broke apart as indigenous groups contested the unifying impulse of utilitarian legal reform in different ways. The Indian Succession Act

---

[22] J. F. Stephen, *The Story of Nuncomar and the Impeachment of Sir Elijah Impey*, 2 vols. (London, 1885). J. Duncan Derrett, 'Nundakumar's Forgery', *English Historical Review*, 75 (1960), 223–38.

[23] B. K. Acharyya, *Codification in British India* (Calcutta, 1914), 86.

[24] Rammohun Roy, *Exposition of the Practical Operation of the Judicial and Revenue Systems of India* (London, 1832).

[25] J. D. M. Derrett, 'Roman Law in India', in *Essays in Classical and Modern Hindu Law* (Oxford, 1963), ii. 66–196.

of 1865, for example, had multiple exceptions on confessional grounds and was accompanied by legislation that further restricted its reach. Similarly, the Contract Act provided for the continued operation of customary rules on contractual obligation and that contract in presidency towns could be regulated by the personal law of the party.[26] Although the demand for uniformity lay behind codification, in practice uniformity was constantly broken by existing custom and law, in all its regional expressions. While the brevity and simplicity of the codes satisfied Benthamite nostrums of simplification, the new codes generated extensive case law to clarify their meaning. Almost every section of the Code of Civil Procedure was the subject of an appeal to a higher court. Similarly the 1872 Law of Evidence which its framer J. F. Stephen claimed would bring simplicity and integrity and transparency to criminal and civil procedure resulted in enormous litigation as colonial courts continued to struggle against the limitations of their knowledge of indigenous laws and society. Even the illustrations of the new codes generated litigation, notwithstanding Macaulay's conviction that Indian illustrations were essential to their clarity.[27] Courts at all levels continued to be plagued by lengthy delays, and both the delays and the cost continued to be an obstacle to equitable and speedy justice.

Earlier plans to codify personal law were largely abandoned by the 1870s. Personal law remained uncodified, despite the original intention of utilitarian reformers in the 1830s to translate all of Indian laws into simple uniform codes. In the end, the colonial state lacked both the will and the authoritarian power to compel a social transformation of this magnitude. Both early and latter-day utilitarians like Macaulay and Stephen assumed that despots were singularly well equipped to implement codes of law, but the absolutism of the British colonial state itself was circumscribed and many South Asians challenged a project of this magnitude and chiselled away at its universalist presumptions. Moreover, utilitarians both in Britain and India were more ambivalent about codification than some of their grander claims of scientific engineering allow, and were much more mindful of how time and place shaped the universal principles of law. Ambivalence within utilitarian ideas of legal revolution, the inherent conservatism of common law, an attachment to the solidity of custom contributed as much as practical administrative factors to explain the face of colonial legality.

---

[26] Sec 2 Act IX of 1872.
[27] Nanak Ram v Mehin Lal *Indian Law Reports* 1 All. 487.

III. Indigenous Legal Knowledge

From the beginning of colonial rule, colonial courts ran alongside indigenous systems of justice that continued long after the establishment of extensive courts, and from the start, colonial legal machinery was dependent on South Asian legal officers. The East India Company, as we have noted, was for a while dependent on indigenous tribunals of arbitration, panchayats, and on indigenous intermediaries as *vakils*, muftis, pandits, and *ulma* (Muslim legal scholars). Colonial courts were staffed by Indian law officers, jurors, low-ranking clerks, and assistant judges. Indigenous elites navigated the legal changes inscribed by the colonial state in different ways, sometimes to reassert patriarchy, other times to advance social reforms and sometimes to challenge colonial rule. More South Asians were employed in the administration of law than in any other branch of the colonial state. The subordinate court officials, collectively gathered under the rubric *amla*, were the linchpin of the colonial courts—*sarishtadars* (head ministerial officer), translators, and *muharrir* (scribes) collectively undertook essential clerical duties, assisted the magistrate, kept records, executed the magistrates' orders, wrote and copied *perwanahs* (court orders).[28] The salaries of *amlas* in the subordinate courts was less than that earned by agricultural labourers, although they were skilled legal officers, knowledgeable in the laws and practice of the court, and higher grade *amlas* frequently carried out the duties of European colonial officers. These low salaries opened the possibility of corruption and compromised the efficiency of legal administration, and repeated but ultimately frustrated calls for improving the pay of indigenous court officers as an incentive for recruitment and as a barrier to corruption and abuse were heard.

Dependence on indigenous law officers was dictated by expediency but also by ideology. Central to the idea of the rule of law as a civilizing force was the notion that modern and sophisticated legal systems were a kind of moral education; the rule of law would help prepare Indians for self-government by training them in the art of citizenship. Pragmatic reasons to utilize indigenous legal knowledge contrasted with reluctance in some quarters to be dependent on indigenous officers or legal bodies. The

---

[28] A. Shakespear, 'Court Establishments, Low Salaries and Corruption', in N. Bhatia, *The Origin and Development of the Legal and Political System in India* (New Delhi, 1978), 201–16.

shifting status of the panchayat illustrates this ambivalence. Village councils or panchayats were the primary pre-colonial site for judicial arbitration, and, although they continued after the conquest to decide on small claims, as well as caste disputes, in many areas they lost much of their traditional vigour or authority, partly because their rulings tended not to be enforced by the colonial state. The decline of the panchayat, already evident in the 1820s, was regretted by some colonial administrators like John Malcolm who saw these local tribunals as a way to make justice speedier and less costly and to bring law closer to the customs and practices of local societies: 'no law of the state can so effectively reach the moral character of the natives as the *panchayat*'.[29] But scepticism about the effectiveness and impartiality of the panchayat was also widely expressed; the Bengal Government argued in the 1830s against suggestions by the Court of Directors to recognize formally the authority of local village leaders and their councils to settle disputes, replying that local leaders were too likely to pursue their own interests and that such a scheme would leave *raiyots* at the mercy of predatory zamindars holding the scales of justice.[30] The panchayat was 'rediscovered' by the liberal Ripon administration in the 1880s, and its retrieval figured prominently in Mahatma Gandhi's writings and in the post-independence attempts to restore indigenous law, although its reconstituted form was unlike pre-colonial panchayats.[31] Successive attempts to introduce Indian juries met with similar mixed responses, with judges of the Supreme Court opposing the creation of English-style juries on the grounds that Indian minds lacked the requisite ability to discern and make difficult decisions unaffected by prejudice or pre-existing assumptions.[32] On the other hand, Indian juries had powerful early champions, not least Scottish Enlightenment men like Sir Thomas Munro and John Malcolm, who saw the merits of shaping law to suit local communities and reverting 'to an ancient usage to temper our great and unprecedented innovations!'[33]

---

[29] African, Asian and Pacific Collections, British Library (hereafter APAC), F/4/629f9. 29 July 1818. Extra Judicial Letter from Bombay.

[30] Bengal Government to the Court of Directors, 22 Feb. 1827. *Parliamentary Papers: East India Company Affairs. Judicial* (1831–2), XII, appendix, No. 11.

[31] M. Galanter, 'The Aborted Restoration of "Indigenous Law" in India' and 'Panchayat Justice: An Indian Experiment in Legal Access', in *Law and Society in Modern India* (Delhi, 1989), 37–99, U. Baxi, *The Crisis of the Indian Legal System* (Delhi, 1981).

[32] APAC, F/4/1007/27328 f1-13. Judicial Department to Court of Directors, 22 Apr. 1828.

[33] Malcolm to Wynn, 24 May 1828, *The Correspondence of Lord William Cavendish Bentinck*, ed. C. H. Phillips (Oxford, 1977), 35. See also Malcolm to Lord Meville, 1 June 1828, 42.

Arguments in favour of Indians filling senior judicial positions in the 1820s (an under-examined precursor to the Ilbert Bill controversy in the early 1880s) closely paralleled arguments in favour of representative government in Britain: 'nothing so certainly degrades the character of a people as exclusion from a share in the public affairs of a country'.[34] The entire original jurisdiction in civil suits in Bengal and Bombay Presidencies were Indian judges, and in Madras all suits below the value of 10,000 rupees. In criminal justice and revenue, deputy magistrates and deputy collectors had broad authority, many were South Asian. The Charter of 1833 had removed all racial bars to the Indian civil service by mandating that no indigenous subject 'shall, by reason only of his religion, place of birth, descent, colour or any of them, be disabled from holding any place, office or employment under the Company'.[35] None the less, indigenous judges were blocked from high office for much of the nineteenth century; pleaders and other court officials were most often regarded as avaricious, venal, and a threat to the rule of law, and indigenous juries were regarded with suspicion. Even the attempt to place Europeans and Indians under the same courts was a contentious issue, and proposals to raise indigenous judges in judgement over European subjects even more so. Separated by almost half a century, the Black Act and the Ilbert Bill provided the locus for a polemical and sometimes vitriolic debate about imperialism and the rule of law. Act XI of 1836, which earned the sobriquet Black Act because of its unpopularity among a small number of vocal British settlers, ended the right unique to Europeans to bypass the *mofussil* courts in the interior and to use instead the Supreme Court.[36] Both Indians and Europeans living outside the presidency towns became subject to the civil jurisdiction of the Company courts.

Successive attempts to place both Indians and Europeans under the same criminal jurisdiction faltered, however. While earlier drafts of the Criminal Procedure Code extended the principle of uniformity before the law to the criminal as well as civil courts, the mutinies of 1857–8 led to a questioning of this liberal expectation, and the provision was abandoned. In 1872 when Europeans were finally brought under the same criminal courts in the interior as Indians, the provision had became racially charged—Europeans

---

[34] Minute on extending trial by jury to natives in criminal cases by Sir Thomas Munro (1827). *Parliamentary Papers* (1833), XXVI, 35.
[35] III and IV. William IV.c 85.
[36] Dharker, *Lord Macaulay's Legislative Minutes* (Oxford, 1946), 47–64; Minute 10, 176.

would appear in the same courts but could not be tried by Indian judges. It was this long-standing debate about the administration of justice in the interior which set the stage for the Ilbert Bill controversy of 1883. The Ilbert Bill sought to remove a racial bar by providing that all district magistrates and sessions judges would have criminal jurisdiction over Europeans. The furore that this proposed reform awakened, both in India and in the metropole, and the bigotry that its very public debate showcased, pointed to the hollowness of universalism so pivotal to civilizing mission at the same time as intensifying critiques of the Raj. South Asians in the colonial legal administration—judges, barristers, lawyers, *vakils*, and others—formed a professional cadre that shaped a public sphere where effective challenges to British rule were articulated. Newspaper articles, public meetings, and petitions followed controversial legal cases, and decisions and law became an arena for a contested debate about social reform. The legal machinery of the colonial state employed cadres of professionally educated Indians well versed in legal procedure and in colonial laws. By the 1880s, indigenous lawyers and legal scholars were articulating a distinctive and highly critical interpretation of colonial laws. Badruddin Tyabji, judge of the High Court of Bombay, developed a forceful critique of colonial interpretations of Islamic jurisprudence.[37] The jurist Rajkumar Sarvadhikari in his withering appraisal of colonial interpretations of personal law, argued that the very identification of authoritative schools of law, notably the Dahabhaga and Mitakshara, overlooked the fluidity of Hindu law and the colonial emphasis on legal texts erased the essential connection that ought to exist between the law and society, both in symbiotic evolution.[38] While the litigiousness of the Bengali was a familiar colonial stereotype, the late nineteenth-century jurist Mitra disputed this essentialist explanation and instead attributed increased litigation to the uncertainty of colonial laws, created by the constant misinterpretation of customary laws by colonial judges.[39]

---

[37] See L. Futehally, *Badruddin Tyabji* (Delhi, 1994); M. Umar, *Badruddin Tyabji: A Political Study* (Bangalore, 1997). See Faiz Tyabji, *Principles of Muhammadan Law* (Bombay, 1940) for a critique of colonial interpretations of Islamic law and M. Mukherjee, *India in the Shadows of the Empire: A Legal and Political History 1774–1950* (Oxford, 2010).

[38] R. Sarvadhikari, *The Principles of the Hindu Law of Inheritance* (Calcutta, 1882), 243.

[39] T. Mitra, *The Law Relating to the Hindu Widow* (Calcutta, 1881), 84.

IV. The Violence of 'The Rule of Law'

Historians of criminal law have highlighted the selective and shifting ways in which the colonial state defined and prosecuted crime, noting that it elected to accentuate crimes that challenged security of property or that threatened to spill over into acts of insurgency against the state, rather than, for example, sexual crimes or domestic murders or violence by Europeans.[40] By defining challenges to state authority as 'criminal', the colonial state translated political activism into individual acts of criminality, even if these acts did not entail crimes against property or person.[41] Through the rubric of a colonial legality, challenges to colonial rule were interpreted not as collective political acts but as crimes, judged not in the public arena but in courtrooms and interrogation cells. Eliding political insurgency and crime took a further toll on the culture of judicial liberalism, which had been such a touchstone of liberal civilizing ideas earlier in the nineteenth century. Establishing the 'rule of law' was one of the centrepieces of the civilizing mission but the imperatives of maintaining the control of the colonial state repeatedly ran counter to the principles of the 'rule of law'. Fitzjames Stephen vividly illustrated the conflict between the lofty principles of the rule of law and the despotism of the imperial state: 'Our law is in fact the sum and substance of what we have to teach them. It is, so to speak, the gospel of the English, and it is a compulsory gospel which admits of no dissent and no disobedience.'[42] This contradiction was exemplified in censorship laws and in repression of acts of civil disobedience but looked back to much earlier laws to extirpate *thagi* in the 1840s. In a campaign to suppress rural crime, William Sleeman and his special police force, the Thuggee and Dacoity Department, had erected new standards of evidence to identify and convict criminals who were very difficult to contain under the usual administration of law. Colonial courts accepted the testimony of approvers (former dacoits turned informers in exchange for suspension of

---

[40] E. Kolsky, *Colonial Justice in British India: White Violence and the Rule of Law* (Cambridge: 2010); M. Wiener, *An Empire on Trial: Race, Murder and Justice under British Rule, 1870–1935* (Cambridge: 2009).

[41] U. Baxi, '"The State's Emissary": The Place of Law in Subaltern Studies', in Partha Chatterjee and Gyanendra Pandey (eds), *Subaltern Studies*, vii (Delhi, 1992), 257.

[42] Stephen, 'Legislation under Lord Mayo', in W. W. Hunter (ed.), *The Life of the Earl of Mayo*, ii. 169; see R. Kostal, *A Jurisprudence of Power* (Oxford, 2006).

their own sentence) as irrefutable evidence of criminality, even without any other corroborating evidence.

These earlier coercive measures against hereditary crime were extended in the Criminal Tribes Act of 1871 which gave broad-sweeping powers to the colonial state to contain and discipline thousands of people solely because they belonged to hereditary groups deemed to be 'criminal'. Members of tribes which the colonial state had designated as 'criminal', because of criminal activity by some of its members, were required to be registered, and thereafter their lives were monitored and invigilated. Local governments assumed the authority to restrict movement by allocating passes, holding roll calls and daily inspections; they had the power to resettle tribes with the aim of reform, to search homes, to arrest without warrant, and other discretionary powers. No evidence of individual criminality was required, other than a suspected inherited propensity to commit crime, for as one district officer reported of criminal tribes in Berar, 'crime is their trade and they are born to it and must commit it'.[43] The Act removed individual autonomy and responsibility and deemed members of these tribes to be compelled by their birth and caste occupation to crime rather than motivated by deprivation, the fluctuations of the market in land and grain, famine, or political defiance. Ethnographic research in the history of wandering, traditional social practices such as polygamy or bride price, were used to categorize tribes as criminal. These were a more potent and authoritarian response to parallel metropolitan anxieties about the urban residuum as irredeemably criminal, expressed in the Habitual Criminals Act of 1869. As in the metropolis where science was employed to define the pathology of criminality, anthropometric measurements were used to identify criminality; a history of nomadic wandering and the width of nose, shape of ears, contours of skulls marked these tribes as criminal, and these ethnological and racial particularities were then used to justify abandoning the principles of justice elsewhere defended as universal. But unlike the habitual criminals in London where the state did not have such sweeping powers to act on their anxieties about the dangerous urban classes, criminal tribes in India were imprisoned in penal colonies, children confined to reformatories, and whole tribes resettled as the state attempted to inculcate the virtues of agricultural labour and settled farming, and to neutralize

---

[43] Cited in S. Nigam, 'Disciplining and Policing the "Criminals by Birth"', *Indian Economic and Social History Review*, 27/2 (1990), 135.

feared threats to the colonial order.[44] Although these resettlement schemes were unsuccessful, the Criminal Tribes legislation, revised in 1911, lasted up until 1947 in spite of nationalist critiques and international pressure to abolish coerced labour.

The glaring disjuncture in imperial jurisprudence was most harshly and dangerously exemplified in a battery of measures aimed at controlling emergent nationalism and asserting British supremacy. Amendments to the Indian Penal Code and various press acts gave the state the authority to control the press by prohibiting publication of articles intending 'to bring into hatred or contempt His Majesty or the Government established by law in British India or the administration of justice in British India'.[45] These powers were extended in the Prevention of Seditious Meetings Act of 1911 which enabled District Magistrates to prohibit public meetings if 'such meeting is likely to promote sedition or disaffection or to cause a disturbance of the public tranquillity',[46] and the Criminal Conspiracy Act of 1913 which strengthened even further the powers to control sedition by amendments to the penal code and code of criminal procedure. These enactments led to the prosecution and imprisonment of such leading critics of the British Raj as the newspaper publisher and journalist Bal Gangadhar Tilak who was found guilty in the Bombay High Court in 1908 of advocating the bomb as an instrument to defy the current political order, and sentenced to transportation for six years.[47] What constituted the crime of sedition was not at all self-evident and judgements in Indian courts, and Privy Council sought to construct its parameters and to assert the legitimacy of its visible and overwhelming authority. This entailed sometimes elaborate reflections on the differences between British and Indian society to justify repression in India that would have been unthinkable in metropolitan Britain. In a measure passed in 1878 to gag the vernacular press, Viceroy Lytton deflected objections that such repression departed too far from British standards of

---

[44] Meena Radhakrishna, *Dishonoured by History: 'Criminal Tribes' and British Colonial Policy* (Hyderabad, 2001); S. Freitag, 'Sansiahs and the State: The Changing Nature of "Crime" and "Justice" in Nineteenth-Century British India', in Anderson and Guha (eds), *Changing Concepts of Rights and Justice in South Asia* (New Delhi, 2000), 82–113.

[45] Indian Press Act, Act 1 of 1910; N. Bhatia, *Acts of Authority, Acts of Resistance: Theater and Politics in Colonial and Postcolonial India* (Ann Arbor, 2004), ch. 2.

[46] Prevention of Seditious Meetings Act, 1911, Act X of 1911; Criminal Conspiracy Act, Act VIII of 1913.

[47] W. R. Donagh, *The History and Law of Sedition* (1911; Calcutta, 1917), 144, 156.

liberty by maintaining, 'Now I think that there is no use in ignoring the plain fact that the existence of a Free Press in a country whose Government is not based on free institutions or carried on upon representative principles is a great political anomaly, and that the relations between such a Government and such a press must necessarily be somewhat peculiar.'[48] Elaborate ethnological observations about the consequences of free speech on an excitable and easily impassioned race were employed to justify the harsh legislation.

A similar view was used to justify the sweeping powers assumed by the colonial state under the Defence of Empire Act to attempt to suppress the nationalist movement during the First World War, powers continued temporarily into peacetime under the aegis of the Rowlatt Act. The right to trial by jury was abolished in cases of alleged sedition, and instead three judges decided on cases; the right of appeal was abrogated, and the testimony of accomplices did not require corroboration (a precedent established under the Dacoity and Criminal Tribes legislation). As one of the critics in the Legislative Council, Kamini Kumar Chanda, noted, these provisions 'have certainly no precedent in the jurisprudence of any other civilised country'.[49] These so-called 'emergency measures' to prevent sedition would, as the Rowlatt Committee admitted, 'involve some infringement of the rules normally safeguarding the liberty of the subject'.[50] Notwithstanding the opposition of Congress and all the Indian members of the Viceroy's Council, these measures were passed into law, remaining deeply unpopular and occasioning Gandhi's *swaraji* against it in 1919. As the Jallianwala Bagh Massacre and the martial law declared in its aftermath exemplified, colonial laws against sedition were a 'performative violence', to exhibit state domination as much as to minimize specific threats to the state.[51]

Following the outbreak of the Second World War and the emergence of the Quit India movement, the colonial state strengthened special instruments of suppression that enabled the government to arrest and detain a person without trial, to try cases before special criminal courts which had special powers, and to restrict appeal to higher courts.[52] Suppressing

[48] Cited ibid. 206.
[49] 'Legislative Council Debate on the Rowlatt Bill, 6 February 1919', in H. N. Mitra (ed.), *Punjab Unrest: Before and After* (Calcutta, 1920).
[50] Sedition Committee, 1918, Report (Calcutta, 1973), sect. 187.
[51] N. Hussain, *The Jurisprudence of Emergency: Colonialism and the Rule of Law* (Ann Arbor, 2003), 118–31.
[52] Defence of India Act, Special Criminal Courts Ordinance of 1942.

sedition through criminal law meant nationalist challenges were defined by the state as criminal rather than political acts.[53] By 1942 roughly sixty thousand supporters of the Quit India *satyagraha* movement had been arrested. Almost immediately, the high courts challenged these repressive measures, first Justice A. N. Sen of the Calcutta High Court in April 1943, and thereafter other courts and other judges, both Indian and British, declared the anti-sedition legislation (Ordinance 2) ultra vires.[54] When these and other high-profile attacks on the government campaign against sedition were echoed by the law member of the Indian government, Sir Asoke Ray, a new ordinance was drafted, obliging the government to give reasons for arrests and giving detainees the right to make representations against their arrest; once again, basic legal rights enjoyed in Britain.[55] Reversals in the law courts and criticism of government policy on repressing sedition by high-profile Indian and British justices left provincial governments scrambling to find new legal powers to detain and prosecute suspects, most infamously in Lahore Fort.[56]

Parallel to attempts at strengthening legal powers to suppress sedition, colonial prisons were constructed to punish, contain, and in some cases rehabilitate those convicted of sedition. One such, erected in the wake of the mutinies of 1857–8 to incarcerate rebels and isolate them from loyal Indians, was the infamous penal colony on the Andaman Islands. Following the agitations around the partition of 1905, nationalist prisoners were imprisoned in the newly constructed Cellular Jail, and by 1947 hundreds of nationalists were incarcerated there and forced into punitive labour, notably V. V. D. Savarkar, those convicted in the Second Lahore Conspiracy, and the nationalists of the Chittagong Revolt of 1930.[57] Here both the punitive and

---

[53] S. Amin, *Event, Metaphor and Memory: Chauri Chaura, 1922–1992* (Berkeley, 1995); Baxi, '"The State's Emissary"', 257.

[54] See e.g. Keshav Talpade v Emperor (C. J. Gwyer, SW. Varadachariar and Zafrullah Khan J. J. (22 Apr. 1943), AIR 30 (1943). 1–9. [Federal Court Calcutta].

[55] P. S. Gupta, *Power, Politics, and the People: Studies in British Imperialism, and Indian Nationalism* (Oxford, 2002), 171; Ordinance 3 of 1944.

[56] See e.g. Sardul Singh Caveeshar, *The Lahore Fort torture camp; being the first hand account of physical and mental torture and persecution of political detainees kept in the Lahore Fort under the Defence of India rules during the war* (Lahore, 1946).

[57] Satadru Sen, *Disciplining Punishment: Colonialism and Convict Society in the Andaman Islands* (Delhi, 2000); Clare Anderson, *Legible Bodies: Race, Criminality and Colonialism in South Asia* (Oxford, 2004); P. K. Srivastava, 'Resistance and Repression in India: The Hunger Strike at the Andaman Cellular Jail in 1933', *Crime, histoire & sociétés*, 7/2(2003), 81–102.

moral faces of colonial law were bizarrely embodied. The penal colony attempted to rehabilitate criminals and nationalists through the rituals of 'honest' labour and attempted to inculcate loyalty by making the administration of the penal colony dependent on 'self-supporters', that is, on inmates of the penitentiary.

In contrast to the encomiums to a legal revolution, the colonial administration of law was at once ambiguous, contradictory, regionally-diverse, and partial, shaped by an incomplete and limited knowledge of indigenous societies, by the contradictions between a liberal jurisprudence and the requirements of an authoritarian state, and by the manoeuvring of indigenous litigants and defendants. None the less, colonial laws and the courts, which sought to enforce them, reached deep into Indian society and brought imperial conquest into the lives of millions, and in so doing, imperial jurisprudence generated those formidable powers of opposition that were to contribute to the disintegration of the imperial rule of law.

Select Bibliography

S. AMIN, *Event, Metaphor and Memory: Chauri Chaura, 1922–1992* (Berkeley, 1995).

U. BAXI, '"The State's Emissary": The Place of Law in Subaltern Studies', in R. Guha (ed.), *Subaltern Studies*, vii (Delhi, 1993).

L. BENTON, *A Search for Sovereignty: Law and Geography in European Empires, 1400–1900* (Cambridge: Cambridge University Press, 2010).

RITU BIRLA, *Stages of Capitalism: Law, Culture, and Market Governance in Late Colonial India* (Durham, NC, 2009).

B. S. COHN, *Colonialism and Its Forms of Knowledge* (Princeton, 1996).

ELIZABETH KOLSKY, *Colonial Justice in British India: White Violence and the Rule of Law* (Cambridge, 2010).

H. S. MAINE, *Village Communities in the East and West* (London, 1881).

K. MANTENA, *Alibis of Empire: Henry Maine and the Ends of Liberal Inperialism* (Princeton, 2010).

T. METCALF, *Ideologies of the Raj* (Cambridge, 2002).

R. SINGHA, *A Despotism of Law: Crime and Justice in Early Colonial India* (Delhi, 1998).

E. STOKES, *The English Utilitarians and India* (1959; Oxford, 1990).

R. TRAVERS, *Ideology and Empire in Eighteenth Century India* (Cambridge, 2007).

D. WASHBROOK, 'Law, State and Agrarian Society in Colonial India', *Modern Asian Studies*, 15 (1981), 649–721.

JON WILSON, *The Domination of Strangers: Modern Governance in Eastern India, 1780–1835* (London, 2008).

8

Networks of Knowledge

Science and Medicine in Early Colonial India, c.1750–1820

Mark Harrison

Francis Bacon's fable *New Atlantis* (1627) envisaged a godly civilization that had acquired unparalleled mastery over nature. It was a mature, dignified, and rational society, supported by an institution called Salomon's House, or the College of Six Days' Works, in which knowledge of the natural world was harnessed for the purposes of enlightened government. This knowledge was acquired chiefly by means of experimentation and by voyages of discovery: every twelve years, two ships set sail for distant lands to gather knowledge of their arts, sciences, and manufactures, and to bring back curiosities likely to be useful to the advancement of knowledge. These ingenious people organized the acquisition of knowledge hierarchically, with collectors and experimenters passing on their findings to compilers, abstracters, and analysts. Those who ventured overseas in search of useful information, Bacon termed 'Merchants of Light', underlining the growing sense that commerce and knowledge were mutually beneficial.[1]

It was a vision that was to prove enduring, appealing to the Puritan idealists of the Commonwealth and later to many philosophers and statesmen in the eighteenth century.[2] Indeed, by the late eighteenth century, the scientific relationship between Britain's colonies and the imperial metropolis approximated to Bacon's ideal. Much of the knowledge gathered from overseas was acquired by the servants of a commercial organization, the East India Company, which, within its territories, was the sole sponsor of

---

[1] Francis Bacon, *The Advancement of Learning and New Atlantis*, ed. A. Johnston (Oxford, 1974).
[2] Charles Webster, *The Great Instauration: Science, Medicine and Reform 1626–1660* (London, 1975).

scientific activity. The dominance within this framework of a handful of scientific patrons such as Sir Joseph Banks—president of the Royal Society of London and scientific adviser to the Company—further inscribes the impression of a Baconian division of labour, with data gathering in the colonies complemented by analysis by august scientific bodies in Britain.

For many years, this relationship was construed in terms of the 'core-periphery' model propounded by George Basalla in his seminal essay on 'The Spread of Western Science'. He saw science in the former colonies as evolving through several stages, from a metropolitan-directed phase of resource exploitation through to eventual scientific independence. This model, which had a profound influence on several generations of scholars, posited a hierarchical and centralized system of science, in which data was extracted from the colonies while new scientific methods and technologies were, in turn, exported overseas.[3] Writing when modernization theory was in the ascendant, Basalla viewed science as the key to the development of the former colonies and saw its importation into non-Western countries as relatively unproblematic.[4]

Today, the process of scientific 'diffusion' no longer seems quite so straightforward. While Basalla's idea of a progression through stages is generally acknowledged as a valuable heuristic device, its generalizations have been difficult to apply in such radically different contexts as India and the settler colonies of Australia and Canada. Moreover, his model of colonial science has been criticized for seeing the colonies as a kind of neutral space, neglecting the ways in which the development of science and technology may have been distorted by colonial power relations. Most scholars of colonial science in India now prefer to stress the ways in which science and technology worked in the service of colonialism, as both a 'tool of empire' in the practical sense and as a vehicle for cultural imperialism. In other words, science developed in India in ways that reflected colonial priorities, tending to benefit Europeans at the expense of Indians, while remaining dependent on and subservient to scientific authorities in the colonial metropolis.[5]

---

[3] George Basalla: 'The Spread of Western Science', *Science*, 156 (1967), 611–22.

[4] See Mark Harrison, 'Science and the British Empire', *Isis*, 96 (2005), 56–63.

[5] Daniel Headrick, *The Tools of Empire: Technology and European Imperialism in the Nineteenth Century* (Oxford, 1981); Daniel Headrick, *The Tentacles of Progress: Technology Transfer in the Age of Imperialism* (Oxford, 1988). For India specifically: Radhika Ramasubban, *Public Health and Medical Research in India: Their Origins and Development under the Impact of British*

Recent scholarship has also highlighted the ways in which Western science was resisted, appropriated, and modified following its introduction into India. Historians have long argued that Indian engagement with Western science and technology was selective and discriminating, both before and after formal colonial rule.[6] At one extreme, some religious revivalist movements rejected Western science outright, seeking instead to regenerate their country's scientific and medical traditions. At the other, secular modernizers dismissed much of their own culture as 'superstition', seeking a basis for national renewal in Western science and rationality. But most responses to Western science lay somewhere in between. Some Indians sought to 'naturalize' science by placing it within a universal 'scientific' tradition, to which India had previously contributed, and attempted to find analogues of Western sciences such as chemistry within their own culture.[7] Gyan Prakash, for instance, has gone so far as to claim that Indian scientists created 'hybrid' forms of knowledge that subverted the dominance of the West, although as Pratik Chakrabarti reminds us, this attempt to legitimize science by incorporating it within Indian traditions was supplanted in the twentieth century by the dominant discourse of scientific industrialism.[8]

Recent scholarship on the history of science in British India has therefore revealed many difficulties with conventional models of scientific diffusion, yet some aspects have proved enduring. Most historians of science in India continue to view its development as a linear progression from a 'Baconian' period of exploration, mapping, and resource-identification, to the emer-

---

Colonial Policy (Stockholm, 1982); Deepak Kumar, *Science and the Raj 1857–1905* (Oxford, 1995); R. MacLeod and D. Kumar (eds), *Technology and the Raj: Western Technology and Technical Transfers to India, 1700–1947* (New Delhi, 1995).

[6] Ashan Jan Qaisar, *The Indian Response to European Technology and Culture AD 1498–1707* (New Delhi, 1982); Saptal Sangwan, 'Indian Response to European Science and Technology 1757–1857', *British Journal for the History of Science*, 21 (1988), 211–32.

[7] Dhruv Raina and S. Irfan Habib, 'The Unfolding of an Engagement: "The Dawn" on Science, Technical Education and Industrialisation: India, 1896–1912', *Studies in History*, 9 (1993), 87–117; S. Irfan Habib, 'Science, Technical Education and Industrialisation: Contours of a *Bhadralok* Debate, 1890–1915', in MacLeod and Kumar (eds), *Technology and the Raj*, 235–49; Kapil Raj, 'Knowledge, Power and Modern Science: The Brahmins Strike Back', in D. Kumar (ed.), *Science and Empire: Essays in India Context (1700–1947)* (New Delhi, 1991), 115–25; John Lourdusamy, *Science and National Consciousness in Bengal 1870–1930* (Hyderabad, 2004).

[8] Gyan Prakash, *Another Reason: Science and the Imagination of Modern India* (Princeton, 1999); Pratik Chakrabarti, *Western Science in Modern India: Metropolitan Methods, Colonial Practices* (New Delhi, 2004).

gence of more formal colonial institutions, and ultimately to independence.[9] The same is true of many of the assumptions traditionally made about each of these 'stages', such as the notion that early colonial science was driven by a metropolitan elite which collected and processed raw data from subordinate scientists in India. Although scientific work in India was not directed by the state, as it was in the French colonies, it has been shown that the East India Company's Court of Directors, and the likes of Joseph Banks, acquired immense authority through their standing in metropolitan societies and through the exercise of patronage.[10] Notwithstanding efforts to recognize a measure of autonomy in colonial institutions, even the most eminent scientists who worked for the Company in India have been described as mere 'fact-gatherers', dependent on senior figures in Britain for the analysis of their data.[11]

Some historians have already begun to question this picture of subservience,[12] and this chapter takes their arguments further, showing that many of those engaged in scientific and medical work in India used their experience to challenge metropolitan orthodoxies. The first section of the chapter examines how the British tapped local networks of knowledge and how they attempted to evaluate information obtained from Indian sources. The second section of the chapter considers the networks through which this knowledge was communicated to Britain and other countries, and the impact that it made. Particular attention is paid to the informal networks that existed alongside official pathways of information, networks that linked

---

[9] David Arnold, *Science, Technology and Medicine in Colonial India* (The New Cambridge History of India, iii/5; Cambridge, 2000), 12.

[10] James McClellan, *Colonialism and Science: Saint Domingue in the Old Regime* (Baltimore, 1992); John Gascoigne, *Science in the Service of Empire: Joseph Banks, the British State and the Uses of Science in the Age of Revolution* (Cambridge, 1998); id., *Joseph Banks and the English Enlightenment: Useful Knowledge and Polite Culture* (Cambridge, 1994).

[11] Roy MacLeod, 'On Visiting the "Moving Metropolis": Reflections on the Architecture of Imperial Science', in N. Reingold and M. Rothenberg (eds), *Scientific Colonialism: A Cross-Cultural Comparison* (Washington DC and London, 1987); Deepak Kumar, *Science and the Raj 1857–1905* (New Delhi, 1995).

[12] e.g. Kapil Raj, 'Surgeons, Fakirs, Merchants, and Craftspeople: Making L'Empereur's Jardin in Early Modern Asia', in L. Schiebinger and C. Swan (eds), *Colonial Botany: Science, Commerce, and Politics in the Early Modern World* (Philadelphia, 2005), 252–69; Satpal Sangwan, 'Natural History in Colonial Context: Profit or Pursuit? British Botanical Enterprise in India, 1778–1820', in P. Petitjean et al. (eds), *Science and Empires* (Dordrecht, 1992), 281–98; Dhruv Raina, *Images and Contexts: The Historiography of Science and Modernity in India* (New Delhi, 2003).

British men of science to a community of scholars that transcended national boundaries. While some scientific information was jealously guarded because of its commercial or military utility,[13] the Company's servants aimed to contribute to the gentlemanly public culture of Enlightenment Europe.[14] As might be expected in view of recent work by Richard Drayton and John Gascoigne, their publications and correspondence reveal a deep commitment to the idea of 'Improvement', with its roots in mercantilist doctrine and Christian theology.[15] However, the radicalism of those engaged in scientific pursuits in India has seldom been appreciated, nor has their willingness to challenge institutions and orthodoxies within Britain. These radical convictions—sometimes internationalist in their scope—underpinned a web of communications that stretched from the Indian to the Atlantic oceans.

I

Scholars of Portuguese, Dutch, and French colonial expansion in the East Indies have shown that Europeans derived much of their medical and botanical information from local sources,[16] and this continued to be the case under the British. In science and medicine, as in the realms of politics and commerce, the British relied extensively on information networks

---

[13] Londa Schiebinger, *Plants and Empire: Colonial Bioprospecting in the Atlantic World* (Cambridge, Mass., 2004), 35–46.

[14] T. C. W. Blanning, *The Culture of Power and the Power of Culture: Old Regime Europe 1660–1789* (Oxford, 2002), ch. 5; Jan Golinski, *Science as Public Culture: Chemistry and Enlightenment in Britain, 1760–1820* (New York, 1992); Andrew Grout, 'Geology and India, 1775–1805: An Episode in Colonial Science', *South Asia Research*, 10 (1990), 1–18.

[15] Gascoigne, *Science*, 147–63; Richard Drayton, 'Knowledge and Empire', in P. J. Marshall (ed.), *Oxford History of the British Empire*, vol. ii (Oxford, 1998), 231–52; Richard Drayton, *Nature's Government: Science, Imperial Britain, and the 'Improvement' of the World* (New Haven, 2000); S. Sivasundaram, 'Natural History Spiritualized: Civilizing Islanders, Cultivating Breadfruit and Collecting Souls', *History of Science*, 32 (2001), 417–43.

[16] Richard Grove, 'Indigenous Knowledge and the Significance of South West India for Portuguese and Dutch Constructions of Tropical Nature', *Modern Asian Studies*, 30 (1996), 121–44; M. N. Pearson, 'The Thin End of the Wedge: Medical Relativities as a Paradigm of Early Modern Indian-European Relations', *Modern Asian Studies*, 29 (1996), 141–70; Kapil Raj, 'Histoire d'un inventaire oublié', *La Recherche* (July–Aug. 2000), 78–83; id., 'Surgeons, Fakirs, Merchants and Craftspeople'; Harold J. Cook, 'Global Economies and Local Knowledge in the East Indies: Jacobus Bontius Learns the Facts of Nature', in Schiebinger and Swan (eds), *Colonial Botany*, 100–18.

inherited from the Mughal empire and its successor states.[17] In addition to gathering information on botany and other economically useful sciences, the Company sought political legitimacy by patronizing indigenous learning. European visitors marvelled at Sawai Jai Singh's famous astronomical observatories at Jaipur, Delhi, Mathura, and Varanasi, and, although Indian astronomy was still regarded as less advanced than that of the West, they were impressed by the technical skills demonstrated by Indian astronomers.[18] The *Asiatic Researches*, the organ of the Asiatic Society of Bengal, carried thirteen articles on Indian astronomy between 1784 and 1835, making it one of the one most popular scientific subjects considered at the Society's meetings.

The interest displayed by Europeans in Indian astronomy was chiefly of an antiquarian nature and, in his second discourse to the Asiatic Society of Bengal, its founder and guiding light, Sir William Jones, told its members that in 'science, properly so named...the Asiatics, if compared with our Western nations, are mere children'.[19] By 'science', Jones meant 'an assemblage of transcendental propositions discoverable by human reason, and reducible to first principles...from which they may all be derived in a regular succession'.[20] He believed that there was little evidence of such reasoning in Indian philosophical traditions, and most of his contemporaries appear to have concurred, but he did see in the 'vague' notions of Indian philosophy some metaphysical ideas that were compatible with science as he understood it, not least the concept of the *Aditya*, or 'attractor', which seemed to illuminate Newton's otherwise mysterious theory of gravitation.[21] Jones's interest in Indian metaphysics was not therefore to improve Western science but to complete 'the history of universal philosophy'.[22] This dimension of orientalism tends to be glossed over nowadays, but it is important to take it seriously as an objective in its

---

[17] C. A. Bayly, *Empire and Information: Intelligence Gathering and Social Communication in India, 1780–1870* (Cambridge, 1996). On colonial surveys of India, see: Marika Vicziany, 'Imperialism, Botany and Statistics in Early-Nineteenth Century India: The Surveys of Francis Buchanan (1762–1829)', *Modern Asian Studies*, 20 (1986), 625–60; Mathew H. Edney, *Mapping an Empire: The Geographical Construction of British India, 1765–1843* (Chicago, 1997).

[18] Kumar, *Science*, 21–4; Bayly, *Empire*, 247–52.

[19] Discourse II, 24 Feb. 1785, in *Sir William Jones's Discourses* (London, 1821), 16.

[20] Discourse X, 20 Feb. 1794, ibid. 36.

[21] Ibid. 49–50.

[22] Ibid. 40.

own right. Jones's scholarship was not merely an instrument of imperial rule but expressed the Enlightenment's sense of a common humanity and its shared intellectual heritage.[23] Indeed, it is only by taking this endeavour seriously that we can account satisfactorily for the many articles on astronomy and sciences without obvious utility in the proceedings of the Asiatic Society of Bengal—the only forum for scientific discussion in India until the foundation of medical and physical societies from the mid-1820s.[24] Articles of an antiquarian nature are almost as frequent as those on evidently 'useful' sciences such as botany, agriculture, and medicine. But this is not to suggest that Jones and other orientalists felt that nothing useful could be gleaned from ancient Indian texts. Rather, in empirical sciences like medicine and botany, as in agriculture and manufacturing, useful knowledge could be obtained by judicious sifting of fact, philosophy, and superstition. In medicine, for example, Jones declared that 'we can expect nothing so important from the works of Hindu or Musselman physicians, as the knowledge, which experience must have given them, of simple medicines'.[25]

In most cases, however, scientific knowledge was acquired not from ancient texts—of which knowledge was still very limited—but from living sources. Dr Patrick Russell, who undertook natural history studies in the Carnatic, relied heavily on local knowledge in compiling his works on plants and reptiles. Using anonymous Indian informants, he recorded local names for snakes and plants, in addition to Linnaean genera and species; he also made a point of noting folklore concerning their properties, behaviour, and uses, while subjecting such information to scientific scrutiny where possible. Having already gained experience in the Near East, as a servant of the Levant Company, and having connections throughout India and Sri Lanka, Russell's approach was comparative in nature, cross-referencing local sources of knowledge with those from Europe and elsewhere in Asia.[26]

---

[23] Rosanne Rocher, 'British Orientalism in the Eighteenth Century: The Dialectics of Knowledge and Government', in C. A. Breckenridge and P. van der Veer (eds), *Orientalism and the Postcolonial Predicament: Perspectives on South Asia* (Philadelphia, 1993), 215–49.

[24] Mark Harrison, 'Was There an Oriental Renaissance in Medicine? The Evidence of the Nineteenth-Century Medical Press', in D. Finkelstein and D. M. Peers (eds), *Negotiating India in the Nineteenth-Century Media* (London, 2000), 233–53.

[25] *Discourses*, 13.

[26] P. Russell, *Account of Indian Serpents collected on the Coast of Coromandel* (London, 1796); Russell to Joseph Banks, Vizagapatam, 20 June 1789, Russell Papers, MS 1788, Royal College of Physicians, Edinburgh (hereafter, RCPE); Russell's catalogue of plants, MSS Eur E 54, Oriental India and Office Collection, British Library (hereafter OIOC).

This comparative and flexible methodology was employed by many naturalists working for the Company, possibly reflecting some doubts about the practical uses of the Linnaean system of classification. For ease of identification, it was normal to record vernacular, Sanskrit, Persian, and Arabic names for most species, in addition to their European equivalents, in so far as these could be ascertained.[27] Such practices were common in most of the European colonies,[28] although the cross-cultural fusion characteristic of the Creole societies of Spanish America had no parallel anywhere in the British empire.[29]

Borrowing from Indian sources was even more evident in the case of medicine. Although Western medicine had progressed in significant ways since the Renaissance—especially in its understanding of anatomy and physiology—there were still important links with the medical traditions of classical antiquity, which had their basis in the humoral system. The indigenous medical traditions of Ayurveda, *unani*, and *siddha* were essentially humoral, too, and Western practitioners shared with Indian counterparts certain basic ideas about the causes of sickness. More importantly, Western practitioners felt that they could learn much about the treatment of diseases in India, which seemed to differ in form and intensity from those in Europe.[30] But respect for Indian traditions went only so far. Even the most ardent orientalists believed that Indian science and medicine were mired in superstition and, as early as the mid-seventeenth century, European visitors such as François Bernier were making disparaging comments about Indian anatomy and physiology. It was only in the realm of therapeutics that admiration for indigenous traditions proved enduring.[31]

It is now generally accepted that Europeans gleaned much from Indian sources but little is known about how medical and scientific information

---

[27] e.g. James Kerr, 'A Description of a New Plant from which the Terra Japonica of the Shops is extracted', 1773, Papers of Dr James Kerr (1738–82), MSS EurE11, OIOC.

[28] Schiebinger, *Plants and Empire*, 55.

[29] Susana Pinar, 'Little-known Travellers and Natural Systems: Francisco Noroña's Exploratory Voyage through the Islands of the Indian Ocean (1784–1788)', *Archives of Natural History*, 24 (1997), 127–44; Antonio Lafuente, 'Enlightenment in an Imperial Context: Local Science in the Late-Eighteenth Century Hispanic World', in MacLeod (ed.), *Nature and Empire*, 155–73.

[30] Mark Harrison, *Climates and Constitutions: Health, Race, Medicine and British Imperialism in India 1600–1850* (New Delhi, 1999).

[31] Mark Harrison, 'Medicine and Orientalism: Perspectives on Europe's Encounter with Indian Medical Systems', in B. Pati and M. Harrison (eds), *Health, Medicine and Empire: Perspectives on Colonial India* (Hyderabad, 2001), 37–87.

was obtained and evaluated. One difficulty faced by the historian of eighteenth-century India is that indigenous informants are seldom named in European texts, in marked contrast to some earlier works. We find no equivalent to Hendrik Adriaan Reede tot Drakenstein's monumental *Hortus Malabaricus* (1678–93), in which the Dutch botanist prominently named four Indians who assisted him.[32] The British were sometimes prepared to acknowledge debts to local 'physicians', 'black doctors', and 'learned pundits', but in most cases, even this limited information is absent; at least until the expansion of formal 'orientalist' studies of medical texts by British practitioners in the early nineteenth century.[33] One reason for the anonymity of Indian practitioners may be that Europeans were becoming increasingly committed to emphasizing the intellectual distance separating European and Asian cultures. Informants in the fields of medicine and natural history therefore lacked the authority of those in areas such as politics and trade, where the provenance of intelligence still mattered.

Another reason why Indians were seldom named may be that a great deal of medical and botanical knowledge was acquired in bazaars, through commercial transactions rather than through prolonged interaction. By the mid-eighteenth century, the Company's hospitals (established from the 1660s) were relying increasingly on local remedies, not only on account of their popularity, but also because supplies from Britain were irregular and frequently damaged. Surgeons had to bid for contracts to supply their own hospitals from local sources in order to make good the deficiency. The Company's hospitals in major settlements like Madras, Bombay, and Calcutta were often located adjacent to bazaars and, in the course of the eighteenth century, as Company surgeons became increasingly involved in the inland or 'Country' trade, their sources of information grew more diverse and the opportunities for purchasing new drugs ever greater. But while the bazaar served as an important social nexus,[34] it seems unlikely that British surgeons and Indian merchants would have developed close

---

[32] Ray Desmond, *The European Discovery of the Indian Flora* (Oxford, 1992, ch. 2).

[33] J. F. Royle, *An Essay on the Antiquity of Hindoo Medicine* (London, 1837), 25. See also George Playfair, *The Taleef Shereef, or Indian Materia Medica, Translated from the Original* (Calcutta, 1833), p. iii.

[34] C. A. Bayly, *Rulers, Townsmen and Bazaars: North Indian Society in the Age of British Expansion 1770–1870* (Cambridge, 1993); Eugene F. Irschick, *Dialogue and History: Constructing South India, 1795–1895* (Berkeley, 1994); Anand A. Yang, *Bazaar India: Markets, Society, and the Colonial State in Bihar* (Berkeley, 1998).

relationships, especially as the purveyors of some remedies tended to be itinerant. The British also found themselves dependent on foreign intermediaries such as Armenian traders and Danish/German Protestant missionaries, who introduced the British to merchants and practitioners of medicine.[35] It is also important to note that Company surgeons were not simply gaining access to Indian materia medica but to remedies from across Asia and the Indian Ocean.[36] Hospital indents and medical publications show that articles from as far away as Zanzibar and China were to be found in some Indian bazaars.[37]

Most of the remedies adopted by the British in India were used locally and did not make a major impact on Western pharmacopoeia, but in a few cases what began as local remedies spread much further. One particularly important example is the use of mercury to treat a range of hepatic and digestive disorders, a practice that began in the Company's hospital in Madras in the 1750s, under the direction of two surgeons, John Wilson and Gilbert Pasley. The use of mercury to treat such diseases may have had its origin in the *siddha* medical tradition of southern India, in which a variety of minerals were used to relieve 'obstructions' of the humours and cure fevers. Pasley and Wilson had a contract to supply their hospital with bazaar medicines and would have been familiar with local practices. At their initiative, a laboratory was established in the Madras hospital to manufacture remedies, and Indian practitioners were engaged to work there as compounders of medicine.[38]

---

[35] Holden Furber, *John Company at Work: A Study of European Expansion in India from the Late Eighteenth Century* (Cambridge, Mass., 1948), 160–1; Pratik Chakrabarti, '"Neither of meate nor drinke, but what the Doctor alloweth": Medicine amidst War and Commerce in Eighteenth-Century Madras', *Bulletin of the History of Medicine*, 80 (2006), 1–38; Pratik Chakrabarti, *Materials and Medicine: Trade, Conquest and Therapeutics in the Eighteenth Century* (Manchester, 2010).

[36] Denys Lombard and Jean Aubin (eds), *Asian Merchants and Businessmen in the Indian Ocean and the China Sea* (New Delhi, 2000); Ashin Das Gupta, *The World of the Indian Ocean Merchant 1500–1800* (Oxford, 2001).

[37] Russell to Sir Joseph Banks, 25 Nov. 1788, Russell Papers, MS 1788, RCPE; Whitelaw Ainslie, *Materia Indica, Or, Some Account of Those Articles which are Employed by the Hindoos, and Other Eastern Nations, in their Medicine, Arts, and Agriculture* (London, 1826); John Forbes Royle, *An Essay on the Antiquity of Hindoo Medicine* (London, 1837); Furber, *John Company*, 175.

[38] Madras Public Consultations: No. 177, 26 Feb. 1762, P/240/20; No. 155, 9 Mar. 1762, P240/20; No. 192, 3 May 1763, P/240/21; No. 491, 18 Oct. 1765, P/240/23, OIOC.

By the 1780s mercury in the form of calomel pills had come to dominate British medical practice in India, where it was used in high doses to treat many common ailments, including dysentery and fevers.[39] In Britain, by contrast, mercury was used predominantly for venereal complaints and most physicians regarded its liberal use in cases of hepatitis and fevers as dangerous and unsophisticated, preferring less drastic and more individualized therapies. Although Company surgeons may not have seen eye to eye with metropolitan physicians, their close links with surgeons in the armed forces of the Crown were important for the dissemination of practices originating in the Company's hospitals. It was through such connections that calomel came to be widely used in the West Indies to treat a range of diseases, including the deadly yellow fever. Links between Company surgeons and those in the Army and Navy also account for the spread of this practice to Britain. By 1800 calomel was being touted as a remedy for numerous diseases at home, ranging from liver disorders—where Indian expertise was making a real contribution to pathology and therapeutics—to common childhood ailments.[40]

II

It has been said that British colonial science was dominated by an 'interlocking directorate' based in London and Edinburgh,[41] and most of those engaged in scientific work in India certainly looked to eminent patrons like Banks for approval and preferment. They also maintained close links with physicians and natural philosophers at institutions such as Edinburgh

---

[39] e.g. 'J.M.', *The Medical Museum: Or, A Repository of Cases, Experiments, Researches, and Discoveries Collected at Home and Abroad by Gentlemen of the Faculty* (London, 1764), 611–12; Gilbert Pasly to Hon. Court of Directors, 29 Mar. 1771, Madras Public Proceedings, P/240/3, OIOC; James Lind, 'An Account of the Efficacy of Mercury in the Cure of Inflammatory Diseases, and the Dysentery', *London Medical Journal*, 8 (1787), 53–4.

[40] Mark Harrison, *Medicine in an Age of Commerce and Empire: Britain and its Tropical Colonies 1660–1830* (Oxford, 2010), 146–71. See also: William Saunders, *A Treatise on the Structure, Economy, and Diseases of the Liver* (London, 4th edn 1809); William Wright, 'Practical Observations on the Treatment of Acute Diseases; particularly those of the West Indies', *Medical Facts and Observations*, 7 (1797), 23–4; Colin Chisholm, *An Essay on the Malignant Pestilential Fever introduced into the West Indian Islands from Boulam, on the Coast of Guinea, as it appeared in 1793 and 1794* (London, 1795), 163; J. Mabit, *Essai sur les maladies de l'armée de St.-Domingue en l'an XI, et principalement sur la fièvre jaune* (Paris, 1804), 17.

[41] Roy MacLeod, 'Passages in Imperial Science: From Empire to Commonwealth', *Journal of World History*, 4 (1993), 127.

University, which was attended by many of the Company's surgeons.[42] Indeed, the Scottish Enlightenment is generally acknowledged to have had a formative impact upon the governance and intellectual culture of early British India.[43] Yet there were other important channels of influence besides those emanating from Edinburgh or London. The remainder of this chapter examines these linkages, exploring connections between practitioners of science and medicine in India and the 'scores of intellectual enclaves' that were dispersed across the British Isles.[44] These enclaves—the clubs and coffee houses of Georgian Britain—provided much of the impetus behind the Enlightenment, although their significance has only recently been appreciated.[45]

One important network that linked men of science in India to their counterparts in Britain was the Lunar Society of Birmingham. The Society was an extraordinary monthly gathering of experimental philosophers which counted among its members the physician, poet, and evolutionary theorist Erasmus Darwin (1731–1802), the chemists Joseph Priestley (1733–1804) and James Kier (1735–1820), and James Watt (1736–1819) of steam-engine fame.[46] Like the East India Company's surgeons, members of the Lunar Society tended to come from backgrounds that excluded them from the universities of Oxford and Cambridge, usually by dint of their religious beliefs. Many were dissenters in politics as well as religion, and all opposed tyranny in matters of the intellect.

A number of Company men had links to well-known figures in the Lunar Society or those on its periphery. One such was the physician James Lind (1736–1812), not to be confused with his more famous kinsman, the naval surgeon of the same name (1716–94).[47] Lind was a cousin of James Kier, a

---

[42] This trend continued well into the 19th cent.: Mark Harrison, *Public Health in British India: Anglo-Indian Preventive Medicine 1859–1914* (Cambridge, 1994), ch. 1.

[43] Martha McLaren, 'From Analysis to Perception: Scottish Concepts of Asian Despotism in Early Nineteenth-Century British India', *International History Review*, 15 (1993), 469–501; Douglas M. Peers, 'Soldiers, Scholars, and the Scottish Enlightenment: Militarism in Early Nineteenth-Century India', *International History Review*, 16 (1994), 441–65. For science and medicine specifically, see Grove, *Green Imperialism*, chs. 7–8; Harrison, *Climates*, ch. 3.

[44] E. P. Thompson, 'The Peculiarities of the English', in his *The Poverty of Theory and Other Essays* (London, 1978), 58.

[45] Roy Porter, *Enlightenment: Britain and the Creation of the Modern World* (London, 2000), 12.

[46] Jenny Uglow, *The Lunar Men: The Friends Who Made the Future* (London, 2002).

[47] *The Genealogy of the Family of Lind and the Montgomeries of Smithton*, written by Sir Robert Douglas Baronet (Windsor, 1795), 4, 7.

close friend of James Watt, and an acquaintance of Erasmus Darwin. He knew Watt from his time in Glasgow, where he worked as a surgeon prior to joining the Company, and their correspondence shows enthusiasm for many aspects of natural philosophy such as electricity and steam power.[48] Lind appears to have made up his mind to seek employment with the East India Company in 1763, after attending lectures on geometry, science, and medicine at Edinburgh University. In December 1765 he left for India, taking with him an electrical machine, a sextant ('I have turned longitude mad', he declared), a telescope, and a microscope.[49]

When he arrived in India, Lind worked as a surgeon on the Bengal establishment, where he collected meteorological data and made astronomical observations, in addition to clinical studies of various Indian diseases. He returned to Britain in 1767, in ill health, whereupon he resumed studies at Edinburgh University, gaining an MD degree in 1768. His thesis—which proclaimed the influence of the moon on fevers—proved controversial in Britain, but was enthusiastically embraced by Erasmus Darwin, whom he met in Edinburgh.[50] There, too, he continued his astronomical work, publishing a paper on the transit of Venus in the *Transactions of the Royal Society* in 1769. The following year, he was made a Fellow of the Edinburgh College of Physicians and in 1772 he made a voyage to Iceland with Joseph Banks and other natural philosophers, serving as the party's astronomer.[51] He was now a man of some standing and was appointed physician to the royal household. On settling in Windsor, he continued his scientific work and was elected a Fellow of the Royal Society in 1777.

Although few of the Company's employees were as closely involved with the Lunar Society as Lind, some had dealings with figures on its periphery, like the radical physician Thomas Beddoes (1760–1808). An ardent supporter of the French Revolution, Beddoes believed that chemistry had the potential to alter medicine fundamentally and make effective treatments

---

[48] Watt to Lind, Glasgow, 6 Nov. 1764; 30 Nov. 1764; 5 Oct. 1768; Lind to Watt, Edinburgh, 3 Sept. 1765; Papers of James Watt (1736–1819), JWP C1/15, Birmingham City Archives.

[49] Lind to Watt, Edinburgh, 29 Oct. 1763; London, 9 Dec. 1765, JWP C1/15. For Lind's career, Lind, *Sketch for a Medical Education* (Windsor, 1800), 5–6.

[50] Erasmus Darwin, *Zoonomia: Or, the Laws of Organic Life* (London, 1794–6), ii. 375–7, 453, 460, 588, 625.

[51] Uno von Troil, *Letters on Iceland, containing Observations on the Civil, Literary, Ecclesiastical, and Natural History; Antiquities, Volcanos, Basaltes, Hot Springs; Customs, Dress, Manners of the Inhabitants, etc., etc.* (London, 1780).

available to the whole of society. To this end, he resigned his Readership in Chemistry at Oxford University and in 1799 established a 'Pneumatic Institution' in Bristol, which counted nearly all the members of the Lunar Society among its subscribers.[52] Beddoes took a keen interest in similar attempts to introduce pneumatic chemistry into medicine, including work conducted in the colonies, and it was through Beddoes that the work of some Company surgeons was brought to the attention of the Lunar Society.

One such was Dr Helenus Scott (1757–1821) of the Bombay Medical Service. For some years, Scott had corresponded with Sir Joseph Banks on a range of topics including the therapeutic uses of chemicals and methods for cleaning and dyeing cotton.[53] At the same time, he had attempted—with little apparent success—to arouse the interest of the Company and its Directors in the alkali deposits he had found in India, alluding to their various commercial and medical uses.[54] In 1796, however, Scott sent Banks an article he had written in the *Bombay Courier*, in which he described a number of clinical trials with nitrous acid in the treatment of venereal disease; all had been conducted at the Company's military hospital in Bombay. Scott believed that nitrous acid was effective because it possessed high quantities of 'vital air' (oxygen), which had therapeutic properties.[55] As venereal disease was a persistent cause of sickness in the Army and Navy, Scott's claim to have found a safer and more effective treatment than mercury elicited an enthusiastic response. Banks thought the matter sufficiently important to have Scott's article republished in the new medical journal, the *Annals of Medicine*.[56] As soon as Scott's work came to light, Beddoes seized on the Bombay trials as evidence of the therapeutic potential of pneumatic chemistry, urged others around the country to conduct similar experiments, and wrote to Watt to encourage him to endorse the

[52] Michael Neve, 'Thomas Beddoes 1760–1808)', *Oxford Dictionary of National Biography*; Roy Porter, *Thomas Beddoes and the Sick Trade in Late-Enlightenment England* (London, 1992); Mike Jay, *The Atmosphere of Heaven: The Unnatural Experiments of Dr Beddoes and His Sons of Genius* (New Haven, 2009).

[53] Scott to Banks, 7 Jan. 1790, Banks Correspondence, 1765–1821, vol. iii, fos. 1–13; 14 Mar. 1792, fos. 127–30, BL Add. MSS 33979.

[54] Scott to Governor of Bombay, 2 Apr. 1790, Bombay Public Department Diary, 1790, No. 96, Part II, pp. 228–9; Scott to Hospital Board, 9 Feb. 1792, Public Department Diary, No. 100, Part II, pp. 222–5, Maharashtra State Archives.

[55] Scott, 'Account of the Effects of the Nitrous Acid on the Human Body', *Bombay Courier*, 30 Apr. 1796, enclosed in a letter to Banks, 6 May, fo. 18, BL Add. MSS 33979.

[56] *Annals of Medicine*, 1 (1796), 373–86.

practice.[57] Scott's remedy was subjected to extensive trials throughout Britain, with surgeons at the Royal Naval Hospital, Plymouth, for example, writing excitedly to Beddoes about their positive results.[58] Beddoes published or otherwise publicized numerous attempts to duplicate Scott's experiments and the latter's claims were widely discussed in medical journals from 1796 through to 1804. Trials with nitrous acid were conducted outside Britain too, in the Germanic countries, for example, and in the West Indies.[59] After 1800, however, there were a growing number of negative reports and the therapy fell increasingly into disrepute.[60]

It is a peculiarity of the first phase of British imperialism in India that many of its key intellectual figures were dissenters or radicals in politics and religion. Some, like J. Z. Holwell, had deistical leanings and claimed to find in Indian religious philosophy certain 'Primitive Truths'.[61] Others, like William Jones, were orthodox and theistical, but more radical in politics, Jones being a staunch Whig.[62] Indeed, India attracted a number of important, though still largely unknown figures, whose scientific ambitions harmonized with a reformist outlook in politics and religion. Though the Company was increasingly criticized for its adventurism and lack of accountability, India offered the prospect of unfettered enquiry and access to new sources of knowledge. The Company surgeon Charles Maclean

---

[57] Beddoes to Watt, (undated) Feb. 1798, enclosing circular letter on nitrous acid, 5 Sept. 1797, JWP W/9.

[58] Thomas Beddoes (ed.), *Reports, principally concerning the Effects of the Nitrous Acid in the Venereal Disease, by Surgeons of the Royal Naval Hospital at Plymouth, and other Practitioners* (Bristol, 1797); Letter from Mr Hammick, Royal Naval Hospital, Plymouth, to Beddoes, 29 Sept. 1797, enclosed in letter to Watt, JWP W/9.

[59] *Medical and Physical Journal*, 3 (1800), 465; Thomas Dancer, *The Medical Assistant; Or Jamaica Practice of Physic* (Kingston, 1801), 82; Colin Chisholm, *A Manual of the Climate and Diseases of Tropical Countries* (London, 1822), 74–6.

[60] John Pearson, *Observation on the Effects of Various Articles of the Materia Medica in the Cure of Lues Venerea* (London, 1800); Mark Harrison, 'Medical Experimentation in British India: The Case of Dr Helenus Scott', in H. Ebrahimnejad (ed.), *The Development of Modern Medicine in Non-Western Countries: Historical Perspectives* (London, 2009), 23–41.

[61] J. Z. Holwell, *Interesting Historical Events, Relative to the Provinces of Bengal and the Empire of Indostan* (London, 1766–71), iii. 225.

[62] S. N. Mukherjee, *Sir William Jones: A Study in Eighteenth-Century British Attitudes to India* (Hyderabad, 1987), 46–67. It is worth noting that Jones was connected to the Lunar Society through one of its members, Esther Day, who participated in the reform agitation of the 1780s and shared a platform with John Wilkes; Uglow, *Lunar Men*, 337.

(1765–1826)[63] left contemporaries in no doubt of this when he proclaimed that

> The great independence of mind, which prevails among the faculty in the East and West Indies, but more especially in the former, from the superior organization of the East India Company's extensive medical establishments... not only admit[s] of, but even enjoin[s], an increased freedom of investigation; of which a more efficacious, as well as a more discriminating practice are the inevitable result.[64]

Maclean began his career as surgeon on an East Indiaman in 1788, but in the 1790s, found employment at the European general hospital in Calcutta. A radical by instinct and conviction, Maclean was expelled by the Governor-General, Wellesley, in 1798, ostensibly for criticizing a magistrate.[65] This may well have been a pretext, however, as Wellesley had already identified Maclean as part of a 'tribe' of newspaper editors in Calcutta who professed the 'boldest spirit of Jacobinism', and singled him out as 'a most audacious and turbulent demagogue'.[66] Maclean had also annoyed the medical establishment in Bengal by his advocacy of the unorthodox medical doctrines of John Brown (1733–88), which ran counter to some of the basic principles of medical practice in India.[67] After his expulsion from India, he continued to denounce Wellesley's administration (despite the latter's return to Britain in 1805), likening the Governor-General to Bonaparte for his attack on liberties in India, and professing concern for the corrosive effects of Indian 'despotism' on British politics. 'Asiatic influences', he asserted, were corrupting the nation's morals and eroding the desire for liberty.[68]

---

[63] Many details of Maclean's life are obscure and dates of birth and death are approximate.
[64] Charles Maclean, *Practical Illustrations of the Progress of Medical Improvement, for the last Thirty Years: Or, Histories of Cases of Acute Diseases, as Fevers, Dysentery, Hepatitis and Plague, treated according to the Principles of the Doctrine of Excitation, by Himself and Other Practitioners, chiefly in the East and West Indies, in the Levant, and at Sea* (London, 1818), p. xiii.
[65] Maclean, *To the British Inhabitants of India* (Calcutta, 1798).
[66] Wellesley to Henry Dundas, 21 Mar. 1799, in E. Ingram (ed.), *Two Views of British India: The Private Correspondence of Mr Dundas and Lord Wellesley: 1798–1801* (Bath, 1969), 235. During 1798–9, on the eve of the war with Mysore, there was great concern about political agitation in Calcutta amidst fears of a global republican conspiracy; Bayly, *Empire*, 146.
[67] Charles Maclean and William Yates, *A View of the Science of Life* (Philadelphia, 1797).
[68] Charles Maclean, *The Affairs of Asia considered in their Effects on the Liberties of Britain* (London, 1806).

Maclean was far more outspoken than most of his colleagues but many set themselves against what they perceived as tyranny in the realms of politics and medicine. The intermingling of these political and intellectual convictions helps to account for the affinity between Company men and bodies such as the Lunar Society. It is also noteworthy that Company surgeons are to be found among the members of other literary and philosophical societies, which blossomed in provincial towns from the end of the eighteenth century. Such organizations played an important role in the development of 'scientific careers' for those who could not, for religious or other reasons, gain entry into elite institutions; their meetings and their published transactions were also important in converting natural and experimental philosophy into popular culture.[69] These attributes may have made the societies attractive to men engaged in scientific pursuits in India; Helenus Scott, for example, was a corresponding member of the Manchester Literary and Philosophical Society, as were others in India and the West Indies. Of all the provincial societies, the Manchester 'Lit and Phil' had the strongest reformist inclinations, counting among its members the likes of Watt and Priestley from the Lunar Society, and the Republican, Edinburgh-trained physician Benjamin Rush of Philadelphia, whose medical and political views were similar to those of Maclean.[70]

It is easy to see the appeal of such societies to men of science in India, but news of experiments conducted there and in other exotic locations also attracted attention in Britain, where there was a growing appetite for such items in newspapers and periodicals.[71] Articles on science and medicine from the *Asiatic Researches* were reprinted in periodicals such as the *Philosophical Magazine*,[72] and there were numerous pieces on India in the London-based journal *Medical Facts and Observations*.[73] Several articles written by British surgeons in India are also to be found in the New York

---

[69] I. Inkster and J. Morrell (eds), *Metropolis and Province: Science in British Culture 1780–1850* (London, 1983).

[70] Membership lists, *Memoirs of the Manchester Literary and Philosophical Society*, 3 (1790), pp. x–xi; 5, pt. I (1798), pp. xi; 5, pt. 2 (1802), p. iv; NS 2 (1813), p. iv.

[71] Jeremy Osborn, 'India and the East India Company in the Public Sphere of Eighteenth-Century Britain', in H. V. Bowen, M. Lincoln, and N. Rigby (eds), *The Worlds of the East India Company* (Woodbridge, 2002), 201–22.

[72] John Williams, 'On the Cure of Persons bitten by Snakes in India', *Philosophical Magazine*, 13 (1799), 191–6.

[73] Entry of 8 Sept. 1792, Journal of Sir Paul Jodrell, MD, FRS, MSS Eur/Photo Eur 136/1, OIOC.

journal, the *Medical Repository*,[74] alongside articles by West Indian surgeons and Benjamin Rush, highlighting another dimension of the connections that existed between British expansion in India and the troubled history of the Atlantic colonies.[75] Even on the basis of this limited selection, it is clear that Company men were part of an international network of like-minded individuals, who commonly professed their disdain for medical and scientific orthodoxies, and delighted in an experimental approach to natural philosophy. Indeed, one striking feature of the articles in these new journals is their interest in pneumatic chemistry and its medical applications, including the mercurial and nitrous treatments pioneered in India.[76] As Jan Golinski has observed, those in the medical profession who were drawn to pneumatic chemistry were what Humphry Davy termed, 'liberal and enlightened physicians', committed to the reform of medical practice and the promotion of experimental science.[77]

The journals mentioned above drew their readership largely from the Anglo-Saxon world and it is here that the strongest connections with India existed. Nevertheless, those engaged in medicine and science in British India were familiar with work in Continental Europe and in the colonies of other European powers. War and rivalry with France meant that intellectual connections with its savants were limited, but the religious affinity between the British and the missionaries at Tranquebar in southern India, together with Denmark's benevolent neutrality, served to foster close and important connections between the Protestant nations.[78] In addition to acting as intermediaries between the British and indigenous informants, the missionaries played a crucial role in communicating British scientific work to a wider European audience. The importance of the Tranquebar connection is

---

[74] S. Ffirth (Calcutta), 'Practical Remarks on the Similarity of American and Asiatic Fevers; and on the Efficacy of Black Henbane and White Vitriol in curing Intermittent Fevers and Dysenteries', *Medical Repository*, 4 (1807), 145–8.

[75] Peter Marshall, *The Making and Unmaking of Empires: Britain, India, and America c.1750–1783* (Oxford, 2005).

[76] George Davidson, 'Practical and Diagnostic Observations on Yellow Fever, as it occurs in Martinique, and the Remedial Effects of Calomel and Opium in the same; together with some Remarks on the Glandular Disease of Barbadoes', *Medical Repository*, 2 (1805), 244–52; Joseph Comstock (Rhode-Island), 'Remarks on the Bilious, or Yellow Fever, with some Hints for the more free and frequent use of Mercurial Medicines therein', *Medical Repository*, 4 (1807), 21–7.

[77] Golinski, *Science as Public Culture*, 161.

[78] C. S. Mohanavelu, *German Tamilology: German Contributions to Tamil Language, Literature and Culture during the Period 1706–1945* (Madras, 1993).

clearly evident in the case of William Roxburgh (1751–1815), who was among the most eminent of the Company's botanists. His close friendship with the missionary, Father Christopher John, enabled Roxburgh to dispatch specimens to scientists across northern Europe in order that they might investigate the properties of Indian plants.[79] Due to Denmark's ostensible neutrality in the wars of the eighteenth century, this traffic continued even during periods of hostility, in much the same way as the Company was able to conduct its commerce under the protection of the Danish flag.

Conclusion

Rather than focusing on official channels of direction and influence, this chapter has examined some of the less formal networks that sustained scientific work in early British India. It has looked at connections between British men of science and local informants, the scientific societies and periodicals of the Anglophone world, and the physician-naturalists of European nations. The existence of so many diverse but overlapping networks suggests that it might be more appropriate to view early colonial science as a 'polycentric communications network', rather than simply as a wheel, with Banks or the Company's Court of Directors at its hub.[80] An equally fruitful approach may be to take specific objects of knowledge (such as the therapies discussed above) as the focus of historical enquiry, tracing diverse flows of information from many sources and contexts.[81] This is not to deny the significance of Banksian patronage or the Company's sponsorship of science, but to recognize that there were other channels of communication in which indigenous knowledge sometimes blended with that of the imperial powers.

In stressing the importance of these informal networks—especially those that connected men in India to an international 'Republic of Letters'—this chapter has sought to correct the view that 'colonial science' was defined solely by the requirements of empire. It was the East India Company, of

---

[79] John to Roxburgh, 26 July 1792; 17 Aug. 1792; 26 Nov. 1792.

[80] The phrase is borrowed from David Wade Chambers and Richard Gillespie, 'Locality in the History of Science: Colonial Science, Technoscience, and Indigenous Knowledge', in R. MacLeod (ed.), 'Nature and Empire: Science and the Colonial Enterprise', *Osiris*, 15 (2000), 221–40.

[81] Sujit Sivasundaram, 'Trading Knowledge: The East India Company's Elephants in India and Britain', *Historical Journal*, 48 (2005), 27–63.

course, that enabled scientific research to be conducted in India and the work that it sponsored was likely to benefit it commercially and to improve knowledge of its newly acquired territories. However, the utilitarian origins of what is often termed 'colonial science' ought to be the starting point rather than the conclusion of historical inquiry. It is equally important to acknowledge that those engaged in scientific work in India drew their inspiration from medical practitioners and natural philosophers across the world and contributed much that was original and important to debates in medicine and sciences such as botany and zoology. The networks and societies to which they belonged, and the journals to which they regularly contributed, voiced internationalist aspirations for political reform, free trade, and an experimental approach to science and medicine.

It may seem paradoxical that agents of a colonial power should champion the cause of liberty, but few of the Company's servants felt any tension between their intellectual and political aspirations and the Company's rule in India, although some like Maclean were evidently critical of the pomp and grandeur of Wellesley's administration. On the whole, as Peter Marshall has recently reiterated, contemporaries saw no contradiction between an empire of free English-speaking peoples and one in which they exercised dominion over other races.[82] Such complexities are by no means untypical of what Roy MacLeod has recently termed the 'multiple engagements' of colonial science;[83] and while science was inextricably woven into the fabric of empire, its threads were more colourful and diverse than are normally allowed.

Select Bibliography

DAVID ARNOLD, *Colonizing the Body: State Medicine and Epidemic Disease in Nineteenth-Century India* (Berkeley, 1993).

——*Science, Technology and Medicine in Colonial India* (The New Cambridge History of India, iii/5; Cambridge, 2000).

PRATIK CHAKRABARTI, *Western Science in Modern India: Metropolitan Methods, Colonial Practices* (New Delhi, 2004).

——*Materials and Medicine: Trade, Conquest and Therapeutics in the Eighteenth Century* (Manchester, 2010).

---

[82] Marshall, *The Making and Unmaking of Empires*, 379.
[83] MacLeod, 'Introduction', *Nature and Empire*, 6.

RICHARD H. GROVE, *Green Imperialism: Colonial Expansion, Tropical Island Edens and the Origins of Environmentalism, 1600–1860* (Cambridge, 1995).

——VINITA DAMODARAN, and SATPAL SANGWAN (eds), *Nature and the Orient: The Environmental History of South and Southeast Asia* (New Delhi, 1998).

MARK HARRISON, *Public Health in British India: Anglo-Indian Preventive Medicine 1859–1914* (Cambridge, 1994).

——*Climates and Constitutions: Health, Race, Environment and British Imperialism in India 1600–1850* (New Delhi, 1999).

——*Medicine in an Age of Commerce and Empire: Britain and Its Tropical Colonies 1660–1830* (Oxford, 2010).

DEEPAK KUMAR (ed.), *Science and Empire: Essays in Indian Context (1700–1947)* (New Delhi, 1991).

——*Science and the Raj 1857–1905* (New Delhi, 1995).

——and ROY MACLEOD (eds), *Technology and the Raj: Western Technology and Technical Transfers to India, 1700–1947* (New Delhi, 1995).

JOHN LOURDUSAMY, *Science and National Consciousness in Bengal 1870–1930* (Hyderabad, 2004).

BISWAMOY PATI and MARK HARRISON (eds), *Health, Medicine and Empire: Perspectives on Colonial India* (Hyderabad, 2001).

GYAN PRAKASH, *Another Reason: Science and the Imagination of Modern India* (Princeton, 1999).

ASHAN JAN QAISAR, *The Indian Response to European Technology and Culture AD 1498–1707* (New Delhi, 1998).

9

Environment and Ecology Under British Rule

Mahesh Rangarajan

Historical studies of environmental change in colonial India, once a novelty, are now flourishing. The literature, though vast, is mostly focused on the later colonial period, from around the mid-nineteenth century.[1] A powerful motivation has been the growing awareness of the environmental legacies of British rule: even those who differ widely on the nature and impact of colonialism, such as whether or not it marked a distinct break with the past, do not differ in their focus. Another obvious issue has been the interplay of ideas, material interests, and political imperatives in the formation of colonial environmental policy in general and of key departments, like those of Forests or Irrigation, in particular. Of late, there has been an additional interest in the pre-colonial period that places more recent events against a long-term backdrop.

Three features are worthy of note, but they make sense only if placed within the context of influential research works in diverse fields with which they remain in constant dialogue. First, it has been asserted that the colonial period saw a major break in terms of the destructive impact of imperial policy on forests, land, and water. This in turn sparked popular protest or resistance movements that were precursors to present-day popular struggles. While these ideas have been very insightful, they are in the process of being tested, qualified, and questioned for empirical validity. There are now a number of regional ecological histories that probe these general issues from the perspective of whole provinces or large regions, paying considerable attention to land tenure, vegetation, and livelihood. Second, there are

---

[1] K. Sivaramakrishnan, 'Nationalism and the Writing of Environmental History', *Seminar*, 522 (2003), 25–30; Mahesh Rangarajan, 'Polity, Ecology and Landscape: Fresh Writing on South Asia's Past', *Studies in History*, 17 (2002), 135–48.

still many critical issues that have to be re-examined in the light of environmental concern. These include urbanization and industry, mining and housing, water access and sanitation. Finally, there has historically been a division between the older stream of work on agriculture and the newer strands of works on land and ecosystems beyond the cultivated arable.[2] Such a divorce is in the process of being overcome, but remains a matter of concern. One consequence has been the influence of anthropological studies that view cultures and ecologies as static and unchanging, and attribute their disruption entirely to external political or economic forces. Even pioneering works on India's ecological past, while rich in insight, tend towards such perspectives.[3] Recent regional histories demonstrate a willingness to go beyond such models and approaches. Works focusing on specific ideological debates and disciplines help to examine contested and rival forms of knowledge more critically.[4] Whether such works are representative of the macro-region of India/South Asia remains to be seen. One of the problems of drawing larger conclusions is the diversity of conditions, agro-ecological and social, in the various regions of the subcontinent.

A brief attempt to synthesize and look beyond existing work cannot but reflect as well as exemplify such limitations. Yet there is no doubt that the ecological history of colonial India is now a subject of growing interest for historians of other regions. Scholars of rural protest against statist conservation in rural America have drawn on studies of South Asia, especially with regard to the hidden histories of resistance and sabotage that undermine earlier more triumphal accounts of official conservation. Comparisons with Dutch-ruled Indonesia, where colonial rule had a longer history, have also surfaced.[5] A dialogue with southern African history is long overdue and there are now serious attempts to draw contrasts and comparisons. In the

---

[2] Arun Agrawal and K. Sivaramkrishnan (eds), *Social Nature, Resources, Representations and Rule in India* (Delhi, 2000), pp. vii–viii. Archana Prasad, *Against Ecological Romanticism: Verrier Elwin and the Making of an Anti Modern Tribal Identity* (Delhi, 2003).

[3] M. Gadgil and R. Guha, *This Fissured Land: An Ecological History of India* (Delhi, 1992). The first major monograph was by Ramachandra Guha, *The Unquiet Woods: Ecological change and Peasant Resistance in the Western Himalaya* (Delhi, 1989, 2000).

[4] A. Pathak, *Legislating Forests: Ideology, Strategies, Policy* (Delhi, 2001). Richard Drayton, *Nature's Government: Science, Imperial Britain and the Improvement of the World* (Cambridge, 2000).

[5] Paul Sutter, 'What U.S. Historians Can Learn from Non-US Environmental History', *Environmental History*, 8 (2003), 109–35; Peter Boomgaard, *Frontiers of Fear, the Tiger in the Malay World, 1600–1950* (New Haven, 2001).

latter case, a narrow elite of white settlers overwhelmed a large local population. Colonialism in India was very different in character, with white settlers limited to a few enclaves. Furthermore, in India as opposed to southern Africa, colonial ecological intrusion had more to do with forests than with soil erosion and loss of livestock.[6] Such comparisons might be more apt than drawing simply on British, more specifically English history. South Asia was a land of continental proportions with variations of climate, ecological diversity, and heterogeneous landscapes. Comparisons and contrasts with other regions like South East Asia can be fruitful, especially given the commonalities of shared colonial pasts and the divergences of the imperial experience. It may also explain how far the issues of the environment, its contestation and control, and divergent attitudes on who was or was not damaging or repairing it, were specific to India.

Closing the Inner Frontiers, 1760–1870

There is little ground to believe that there was a pre-colonial equilibrium where the use of land, water, wildlife, or trees was mediated by custom in a homeostatic manner. Landscapes and community boundaries were in flux at the local level. The geographical movements of certain groups over long distances in time are also an established fact. Small endogamous groups did not occupy the same location for long periods of time, and even when they did, they lacked exclusive access to particular resources.[7] In general, the picture of the subcontinent prior to the eighteenth century was one of islands of intensive agriculture in a vast sea of secondary forest and savannah. New estimates for the acreage under permanent tillage in Mughal times have pushed the figure down to around one-fourth of the total land. There were significant pockets of intensive resource use as in the Ganga-Yamuna Doab but these were the exception and not the rule.[8]

---

[6] Mahesh Rangarajan, 'Parks, Politics and History: Conservation Dilemmas in Africa', *Conservation and Society*, 1 (2003), 77–98; William Beinart, *The Rise of Conservation in South Africa: Settlers, Livestock and the Environment, 1770–1950* (Oxford, 2003).

[7] Sumit Guha, *Environment and Ethnicity in India, 1200–1991* (Cambridge, 1999), 43.

[8] K. K. Trivedi, 'Estimating Forests, Wastes and Fields c.1600', *Studies in History*, 14 (1998), 301–11; For other, older estimates, see Shireen Moosvi, *The Economy of the Mughal Empire, c. 1595: A Statistical Analysis* (Delhi, 1987), 42, 45. Also see Irfan Habib, *Atlas of the Mughal Empire* (Cambridge, 1983).

Divisions of occupation in the past could be less rigid than they appear in colonial records. The Banjaras, for instance, were cattle keepers in the sixteenth century with huge herds of pack bullocks, but they were also important merchants in Mughal India. Itinerant cattle keepers and traders—like the Banjaras or Lambadas—moved grain and salt, serviced armies, and sold their heifers to settled agriculturists.[9] The complex interweaving of settled agriculture and animal husbandry, hunting and slash and burn cultivation, trade and labour, the building of forts and tanks, all suggest a far more complex economy than can possibly be accounted for by ecologically ordered endogamous divisions of labour. Those on the fluid frontier of jungle and cultivated land, usually known as 'tribals', used their strategic knowledge and logistical skills in hunts or warfare to bargain with their neighbours. Tribal peoples even seized power, founding royal lineages: this was the story of Gonds in central India or the Bhils in the west.[10] In the south, the Bedas—another itinerant people—served in Haidar and Tipu's armies (1761–99) and kept their armed power intact. Across much of the west and north, all armies, even those of the East India Company, till the mid-nineteenth century were serviced by trains of thousands of pack bullocks.[11] Similarly, the Tondaimman rulers of Pudukottai in the Tamil country were a princely house tracing their lineage to an ancestor who tamed a wild elephant. Even in the late nineteenth century, the family 'looked at the forest from the inside out'. Velaiyan tribal hunters were indispensable to court ritual: venison, herbs, and honey from the Palni hills reaffirmed the links with the forest, seeing it not as primeval chaos but as a place at the heart of power. A clear hierarchy dividing the forest from the plains, and nature from civilization, did not exist.[12] A similar kind of relationship made the tiger a cult-like animal in the regime of Tipu Sultan. He was perhaps guided by the 'prevalence of the tiger in south

---

[9] Irfan Habib, 'Merchant Communities in Pre-Colonial India' in J. D. Tracy (ed.), *The Rise of the Merchant Empires: Long Distance Trade in the Early Modern World* (Cambridge, 1987), 371–99.

[10] Christopher A. Bayly, 'Knowing the Country, Empire and Information in Asia', *Modern Asian Studies*, 27 (1993), 3–43. On the Bhils and Gonds, Sumit Guha, *Environment*, 138–49.

[11] C. A. Bayly, *Indian Society and the Making of the British Empire* (The New Cambridge History of India, ii/1; Cambridge, 1989), 138–45.

[12] J. P. Wagehorne, *The Rajah's Magic Clothes, Revisioning Kingship and Divinity in England's India* (Philadelphia, 1994), 168–74, 182–5, 186. Also Carla M. Sinopoli, 'From the Lion Throne: Political and Social Relations of the Vijaynagar Empire', *Journal of the Economic and Social History of the Orient*, 43 (2000), 364–98.

Indian life' especially in popular lore and religion. He may have been aware also of its centrality in older south Indian royal lineages like the Chola and Hoysala dynasties.[13] The search for legitimacy thus often entailed complex cultural and social arrangements between aspiring rulers and peoples of the forest margins and hills which were continuously renegotiated.

There was therefore no long spell of pre-colonial equilibrium. Still in large parts of South Asia, there was a significant break with the past under the early Company state. It has been argued that the British settled mobile populations, and this simply completed a process of sedentarization begun by Indian rulers. However, this process was never as linear as some have supposed.[14] The creation of a *cordon sanitaire* around tribal areas and the tightening of pressures on itinerant activity were the logical corollary of tying down peasants to fixed plots of land which the British accelerated but did not invent. This not only made assessment of revenues easier. It also encouraged the spread of a settled, cultivated, and ordered landscape. The development of survey techniques was integral to such a process. But it was easier said than done. Often such projects were difficult to execute on the ground. Allied to these changes in the highlands and forests were developments in irrigation. Old canals were repaired and in some cases, new canal networks were laid out. Earlier canals, like the Shah Nahr near Delhi, had been inundation canals. Now in the north as well as in the deltas of the peninsular rivers, perennial canals were built.[15] Such attempts to consolidate settlements or to expand cultivation through the patronage of irrigation were not new. But the scale and scope of the exercise was without precedent.

The tea and coffee plantations in Assam in the east and in the southern High Ranges by the 1840s were strikingly new, with plantation crops requiring wholesale forest clearance and importation of new groups of labourers.[16] Raids by those on the fringe of the cultivated land were more

---

[13] Kate Brittlebank, *Islam and Kingship in a Hindu Dominion: Tipu's Sultan's Search for Legitimacy* (Delhi, 1997), 144–5.

[14] David Ludden, *An Agrarian History of South Asia* (The New Cambridge History of India, ii/1; Cambridge, 1999).

[15] David Ludden, 'Patronage and Irrigation in Tamil Nadu: A Long-Term View', *Indian Economic and Social History Review*, 16 (1979), 347–65; B. Easwara Rao, 'Colonial Discourses on Dam Technology and Its Consequences: A Study of the Godavari Anicut', paper presented at the Conference on the Environmental History of Asia, Jawaharlal Nehru University, New Delhi, Dec. 2002.

[16] Jayeeta Sharma, 'From Jungle to Garden: Colonial Assam in the 19th Century', paper presented at the Conference on the Environmental History of Asia, 2002.

firmly put down and their avenues to gain political power via military means choked off. Thugs, bandits, and tigers were hunted alike. Earlier rulers had stalked large wild animals, but none had set a precedent of setting out large bounties as was done soon after the conquest of Bengal in 1757. By the early 1800s, bounties covered even the elephant, until then rarely killed though routinely captured for use in captivity. The capture of wild elephants had long been a matter of strategic vital interest since the sixth century BCE for their importance in transportation and warfare. Their capture, training, and upkeep were highly skilled tasks. But in the colonial era, elephants were less valuable to the state and hence their physical elimination was without precedent.[17]

Yet the agrarian frontier did not move ahead in an inexorable fashion, nor were colonial irrigation and water management plans always that consistent. A critical ingredient of successful and sustained crop growing was the availability of water. British policy was shaped in part by fears of desiccation, as orchestrated by the Company's scientific networks centered on the Botanical Gardens at Dapuri and Saharanpur, Pune, and Calcutta. This cadre of surgeons and botanists formed an early technocratic elite, loosely tied to the colonial state. Botanists like Hugh Cleghorn and Alexander Gibson denounced unregulated use of the catchments and hills for it would denude the earth of its green mantle, erode the topsoil, and upset the hydraulic cycle. They however met with limited success in changing policy, at least in the first half of the nineteenth century. In the 1850s, conservation would still be on the cheap with minuscule departments in the Bombay and Madras presidencies. In areas like the Sahyadris, western India, where older small dam systems existed and which had been funded by the Marathas, the British did not help in their repair and reconstruction. By the second half of the century, conservationist thought was having a bigger impact. Whereas swidden farming had been earlier viewed as an acceptable form of cultivation, it was now criticized for its low productivity as well as the damage done to the land itself. This

---

[17] Dhriti Kanta Lahiri Choudhury (ed.), *The Great Indian Elephant Book: An Anthology of Writings on Elephants and the Raj* (Delhi, 1987), pp. xiv–xvii. For early periods see Simon Digby, *War-Horse and Elephant in the Delhi Sultanate: A Problem of Military Supplies* (Karachi, 1974); Thomas R. Trautmann, 'Elephants and the Mauryas', in S. N. Mukherjea (ed.), *India, History and Thought: Essays in Honour of AL Basham* (Calcutta, 1982), 254–81.

demonstrates how economic interests deepened science's penetration into the colonial state.[18]

There were, however, limits to the reach and ability of the new rulers. Internal divisions in the administration played no small role. Despite having the ear of high officials, the botanists and early foresters found it tough to back their nascent administrative machine with enough cash or men to police the woods.[19] Their work was also conditioned and constrained by shifts in imperial ideology and perceptions of India. India was increasingly viewed as being synonymous with poverty, dearth, pestilence, and famine, which went well with a 'more cruel capricious view of nature', a view described by David Arnold as 'tropicalization'.[20] Despite these differences in policy and perspective, two major trends can be identified. One was the impetus to break the cycle by which lands lapsed into forest and to expand the agrarian frontier. The other was the attempt to persuade decision makers to give a conservationist edge to their policies of land control and regulation.

Remaking the Forest: 1870s to the 1930s

In environmental terms, the 1870s and 1880s were decisive decades with regards to both legislative enactment and executive action. These changes did not take place in a vacuum but evolved out of the debates of the previous decade. Many legislative changes and administrative reforms actually took effect on the forest floor only in the last decade of the nineteenth century. But this period, as Gadgil and Guha noted, was critical in defining an 'ecological watershed'. Until then, intrusion into uncultivated lands had been fitful and intermittent.[21] What was altered by the 1870s was the attitude of the new rulers who had a very different notion of political power, one with profound and varied ecological consequences.

The most significant changes were undoubtedly the expansion of the government's own forested estate and the growth of vast irrigation networks. After the Rebellion of 1857, the strategic ring of jungles around the

---

[18] R. H. Grove, *Ecology, Climate and Empire: Colonialism and Global Environmental History* (Cambridge, 1997). For a different view, Pathak, *Legislating Forests* (2001).

[19] Sumit Guha, *Environment and Ethnicity in India, 1200–1991* (Cambridge, 1999) 164–5.

[20] David Arnold, 'India's Place in the Tropical World, 1770–1830', *Journal of Imperial and Commonwealth History*, 26 (1998), 1–21.

[21] Sivaramakrishnan, 'Nationalism and the Writing of Environmental History', 25–30.

forts of the *talukdars* was denuded. Earlier, the landed intermediaries had strictly regulated their use for grazing and lopping, mainly to guard their forts. Now, not only in Awadh but also in Bihar, officials encouraged the rapid destruction of these forests as part of their plans to disarm the countryside, a campaign that reflected the increasingly racialized politics and security concerns of the post-1858 era.[22]

The second great change came with the railways. By the time of the First World War, India had over 50,000 miles of track. But in its early days, railway construction sparked a timber famine. A mile-long rail track needed over 2,000 logs per mile. It was the problem of securing a regular supply of timber that provoked the creation of the Imperial Forest Department in 1864. The last decades of the nineteenth century also saw the start of underground coal mining in Jharia and Raniganj. Coal reduced firewood consumption by steam engines, but the mines needed wood for pit props and were therefore often sited in forested areas. The supply of timber for the railways led to extensive over-felling by contractors and fears of a timber famine further encouraged the creation of the Imperial Forest Department in 1864. A Forest Act quickly followed in 1865, but it was quickly deemed inadequate and new legislation, which gave Forest Officers wider powers, was enacted in 1878.[23]

Between 1864 and the turn of the century, the forest estates of the government grew to encompass well over a fifth of the land area of British India. Revenues from forestry were partly responsible for keeping the budget of the empire in the black after the early 1900s. The forester in India, initially a military man, later an official trained in forestry, aimed to increase the output of revenue of forest products. But civil officials who saw forest regulations as a recipe for disaffection and public disorder often resisted the expansion of the authority of the forest department. Revenue officials also saw foresters and forestry as placing limits on areas they controlled.

Dilemmas were evident with respect to what were increasingly, if not always accurately, viewed as 'forest peoples'. While imperial foresters had

---

[22] David Omissi, *Sepoy and the Raj: The Indian Army, 1860–1940* (London, 1995), 133. D. Arnold, *Colonizing the Body: State Medicine and Epidemic Disease in Nineteenth Century India*, 64.

[23] R. Guha, 'An Early Environment Debate: The Making of the 1878 Forest Act', *Indian Economic and Social History Review*, 27 (1990), 65–84.

hoped to free the woods of troublesome swidden cultivators, ethnographers found the practice a mark of an older, simpler way of life. The efforts to set aside special enclaves for such people, which eventually took the form of Scheduled Areas, was a specific approach to an older question of how the hill and forest regions and their inhabitants would relate to the wider society. They had never really been that isolated from larger society but the previous half-century had seen epochal changes, although the impact was uneven. In his work on the Rajmahal hills, Pratap shows how the Paharias were adversely affected, while the Santhals were favoured as pioneer cultivators.[24] Skaria has revealed how Bhils and Koknas in the Dangs in western India were affected by leases for timber, large-scale appropriation of teak-growing lands, and interference in slash and burn agriculture.[25] Perhaps the most powerfully evocative image of tribal swidden cultivator was that of the Baigas of central India: the restrictions on hunting deprived them of a major mode of support.[26]

Scholarship is divided on many critical issues, such as the precise kind of production or the modes of power in these various regions, and their process of incorporation.[27] The Raj bore down hard, not only due to the specialized nature of production of key *adivasi* or tribal groups, but also by curtailing and changing the wider context in which they lived and worked.[28] Interestingly, the use of the term *adivasi* for the original inhabitants, though traceable to the late nineteenth century, became part of wider usage and political lexicon in the twentieth century. The very fact that enclaves for tribals or forest people were a matter of debate was a measure of how far the situation had evolved. A crucial part of the remaking of the forest was the bid to transform not only its floral composition but also the way it was drawn upon for production and habitation. There were conflicting impulses operating by the late colonial period. Accommodation found advocacy among officials as they came to realize the limits to their power. In Himachal and Uttarakhand, foresters struggled to enforce a regime of control over the 'intricate tapestries' of competing and collaborating claims. Buffalo herders migrated across sub-Himalayan tracts; shepherds took sheep up to

---

[24] Ajay Pratap, The *Hoe and the Axe: An Ethno History of Shifting Cultivation in Eastern India* (Delhi, 2000).
[25] Ajay Skaria, *Hybrid Histories, Forests, Frontiers and Wildness* (Delhi, 1998), 114–15.
[26] Prasad, *Ecological Romanticism*, 67.
[27] Guha, *Environment*, 142–3.
[28] Prasad, *Ecological Romanticism*, 67; Rangarajan, *Fencing the Forest*, 182–3.

the alpine meadows in summer, to the pine forests on lower slopes in winter. Though timber mattered, non-timber produce like bamboo could produce up to a fifth of forest revenues. A wave of environmental alarmism swept through the ranks of government: sheep were denuding the hill slopes of vegetation, threatening the agrarian stability and security of the fertile plains. A generation earlier, German forest experts had been enlisted to help demarcate and survey the woods. The forest was to be reshaped to increase the output of pine and deodar as against the oaks and hornbeams, the former spelling cash for the Department and the latter the economic base of village sustenance.[29]

There is mounting evidence that the process of bounding the land with the creation of vast wooded estates of the government was only one episode in continuing contests for control. Private forests in east and central India saw multi-cornered conflicts between foresters, civil officials, and peasants who were locked in struggles with each other and the rent receivers or *zamindars*.[30] Even as state power expanded across the subcontinent, there were constraints and dilemmas to be faced. As the power of the state extended into hills and forests, the problems of transmuting power into authority seemed to multiply. In fact, the early years of the twentieth century found more candid admissions among officials about how their older policies had often failed to meet stated objectives. Practices like swidden farming by the Karens had been incorporated into teak growing cycles in Burma, teak saplings and rice being sown together.[31] In the great forest belt from south-west Bengal into the central Indian massif, fire and intensified grazing was encouraged, if only to open the forest to the planting of commercially valuable *sal*, *shisham*, and teak. As with different cultures or peoples, the forest also was not so easy to sort out into 'commercially valuable' and 'useless' species and later workplans often began to take note of the existence of multi-species forests that could not be reduced to monoculture.[32] After decades of bearing down hard on local users to protect

---

[29] Vasant Saberwal, 'Environmental Alarm and Institutionalized Conservation in Himachal Pradesh, 1865–1994', in Agrawal et al. (eds), *Social Natures*, 68–87.

[30] K. Sivaramakrishnan, 'Co-Managed Forests in West Bengal: Historical Perspectives on Community and Control', *Journal of Sustainable Forestry*, 7 (1998), 23–51.

[31] Raymond Bryant, 'Shifting the Cultivator: The Politics of Teak Regeneration in Colonial Burma', *Modern Asian Studies*, 28 (1994), 225–50; Jenna Rae Carl, 'Empire, Science and Forestry in Colonial Burma', Unpublished BA thesis, Cornell University, 2002.

[32] Sivaramakrishnan, *Modern Forests*, 227, 240.

and build up stocks of game animals and birds, foresters also tried to make them allies though very subordinate ones. Fears that species, like the greater one-horned rhinoceros, might become extinct spurred selective but significant accommodation of local interests. For instance, locals in Assam were allowed to graze their buffalo in a wet savannah grassland reserve in return for their help in apprehending rhinoceros poachers.[33]

The caution with regard to forest and game conservation had their counterparts in irrigation. The debates over irrigation were more strident than any rumpus over the forest. By 1900 canals irrigated a fifth of the cultivated lands. Among the most spectacular were the Canal Colonies of the Indus, where wheat was grown by peasant colonists, most of whom were in the list of 'martial races', providing recruits for the British Indian Army that policed the border and were deployed across half the globe.[34] The Ganges and Sharda canals in north India were equally significant. Critics within the colonial administration argued that irrigation in many cases increased waterlogging and the incidence of malaria. The debates were often inconclusive, especially because the stakes were so high and the experiences often diverse.[35] Further, costs and benefits of irrigation were constantly under scrutiny from Revenue Officers and engineers. Even in the Punjab, there were constant tensions between the new settlers and older residents, many of whom lived off a mix of dry land farming and cattle rearing. Engineers, like foresters, also often disagreed vehemently with the civil servants who ranked higher and professed to know better than those in a lower ranking service.[36] Such tensions were not as sharp in much of peninsular India where the new irrigation systems blended in and built on older works like tanks and wells. Further east, as in the delta of the Mahanadi and the flood relief works on the Kosi, the record was poor if not disastrous. In such regions, the annual floods had long been an accepted

[33] A. J. W. Milroy, 'The Preservation of Wildlife in India: Assam', *Journal of the Bombay Natural History Society*, 37 (1934), 97–105; European planters were a major force in game protection by this time, see Swati Sresth, 'Hunters and Protectors, British Rule and Indian Wildlife', unpublished MPhil thesis, Jawaharlal Nehru University, New Delhi, 2001.

[34] Imran Ali, *The Punjab under Imperialism, 1885–1947* (Delhi, 1987).

[35] Elizabeth Whitcombe, 'The Environmental Costs of Irrigation, Water Logging, Salinity, Malaria', in Arnold and Guha (eds), *Nature, Culture*, 237–59.

[36] David Gilmartin, 'Scientific Empire and Imperial Science: Colonialism and Irrigation Technology in the Indus Basin', *Journal of Asian Studies*, 53 (1995), 1127–54. Indu Agnihotri, 'Ecology, Land Use and Colonization: The Canal Colonies of Punjab', *Indian Economic and Social History Review*, 33 (1996), 37–58.

part of the landscape and efforts to banish them through elaborate engineering solutions only worsened matters.[37]

Despite these instances where forest conservation and water management policies advanced haltingly, Pax Britannica by the early twentieth century did mark an ecological watershed in the millennia-old recorded human history of South Asia. In particular, the new kind of state system and the way it privileged sedentary over itinerant lifestyles was a turning point even before the Forest Laws of the 1860s and 1870s. By the last quarter of the nineteenth century there were a series of qualitative transformations in the way most humans related to the land and indeed to each other. Without romanticizing peasants, artisans, grazers, or game trappers in any way, it is possible to assert that complex systems of land use and husbandry were placed under enormous strain due to legislative enactment, executive policies, and larger economic changes. Many of the new systems of forestry and water use struggled to come to terms with ecosystems, land and soil regimes that were far more intractable than early foresters or engineers were perhaps willing to concede. Not only were the rival resource users not as thriftless, wasteful, or idle as portrayed by colonial officials, many of their practices were to be incorporated, if on a highly selective basis, into the new systems of control as the twentieth century wore on. Historians will continue to debate how far the years 1860–80 were really decisive decades. While there is much evidence to warrant such a conclusion, there is a need for caution in an empire that covered 4 million square kilometres and to acknowledge that many changes were staggered: there were no push-button mechanisms to bring about wholesale change.

The Tiger in Transition: From 'Devilish Brute' to 'Large-Hearted Gentleman'

Transitions of a similar nature were taking place in the remaking of human relations with the faunal world. In the history of the tiger between the 1870s and 1930s, for instance, the period was a decisive one. At its outset, the government of India began to collect figures on the killing of vermin across its provinces. Each year, efforts were made to improve the efficacy of rewards for anyone who would kill or snare tigers and other 'dangerous

[37] Rohan D'Souza, 'Canal Irrigation and the Conundrum of Flood Protection: The Failure of the Orissa Scheme of 1863 in Eastern India', *Studies in History*, 9 (2000), 42–68.

beasts'. The explicit parallel drawn was with the wiping out of the Thugs and Pindaris earlier in the century. By the mid-1920s, such schemes were no longer being coordinated from the centre and initiatives were left to the provinces and the princely states. The river basins of the Indus, Brahmaputra, and Ganga were a historic stronghold of tigers. Tigers had come to be classed as vermin who competed with sportsmen for hoofed quarry. For a fifty-year period ending in the mid-1920s, over 1,500 tigers were killed in British India and a few princely states *every* year for bounties.[38] There was an inherent contradiction in such policy, for villagers' use of snares to kill tigers was considered cruel while hunting for bounties or sport was not. The 80,000-odd tigers killed for bounties were in addition to those hunted for sport.[39] In the Indus basin, by the First World War, bounty hunting and agrarian expansion finished off the species in a region where its presence had left a mark on human cultures even five millennia ago.[40] Such changes were slower to take effect in the east. Unlike in much of north India, the greater one-horned rhino, swamp deer, and wild buffalo flourished in the silt-laden islands in the great rivers of eastern India until well into the twentieth century. These isolated areas were used once a year by herders who set fire to the grass to force a fresh crop of green grass, benefiting cattle and wild herbivore alike. The arrival of immigrants from Nepal and East Bengal in the 1920s obliterated vast tracts of habitat. Cultivators raised subscription funds to fund professional expert hunters to rid them of tigers.[41] Eventually, the creation of Reserved Forests helped to arrest agrarian expansion and secured some of the remaining forest for the tigers.

Contrasting the fate of the tiger and two other large cats, the lion and the cheetah, illuminates a crucial feature of the imperial impact. The former lives in relatively wetter, denser, and more rugged terrain, and much of its habitat remained intact until 1947. The lion and cheetah prefer the plains and scrub forest that are more accessible to hunters on horseback and later by motor car. Such lands were also easier to plough. By 1891 there was only

---

[38] Mahesh Rangarajan, *India's Wildlife History: An Introduction* (Delhi, 2001), 22–35.

[39] Kailash Sankhala, *Tiger! The Story of the Indian Tiger* (London, 1978), 132–3.

[40] David Arnold, 'Disease, Resistance and India's Ecological Frontier, 1770–1947', in J. Scott and N. Bhatt (eds), *Agrarian Studies: Synthetic Studies at the Cutting Edge* (Delhi, 2002), 186–205.

[41] Stuart Baker, *Wild Beasts and Their Ways* (London, 1891), 108–9; A. J. W. Milroy, 'The Preservation of Wildlife in India: Assam', *Journal of the Bombay Natural History Society*, 37 (1934), 97–105.

one small community of lions in western India. Cheetahs would linger on into the 1960s but in ever-decreasing numbers. The tree-dotted savannahs were irrevocably transformed much earlier than the mature tree forest.[42]

It was only in the early twentieth century that the war on the tiger eased up. It won some support as a friend of the farmer that held down crop-raiding deer.[43] Several princes made tiger hunting a privilege, using hunts to curry favour with British officials. Princes in Junagadh, western India, protected lions from 1900, allowing a few to be shot on invitation and compensating loss of domestic stock.[44] Tigers were sometimes depicted as guardians of the monsoon forests against marauding cattle, and a guarantor that the green mantle would clothe the hills. By the end of the 1920s, most provinces had abolished general bounties. Laxman Singh, the ruler of Dungarpur, western India, even reintroduced the tiger in 1928. This was certainly the first known case of reintroducing the species in any part of its range.[45] Some princes subsidized early nature studies, perhaps to reinforce local patriotism. Well-known sportsmen naturalists like Jim Corbett publicized fears of extinction. From a devil-like creature of the night, the tiger was on the way to rehabilitation, though the process was far from complete. Corbett saw the tiger as 'a large hearted gentleman of the forest' that became a man-eater almost wholly due to force of circumstances.

Nationalists and the Environment

Indian public and political opinion on issues of the environment were complex and often beset with contradictions. Gandhi's response to Edward Thompson on the matter of vanishing wildlife was typically witty. Wildlife may be decreasing in the villages and jungles but was on the increase in the towns.[46] From the 1880s on, the Congress had consistently been very critical of the imposition of the Forest Law on the peasantry. In this it had inherited

---

[42] Divyabhanusinh, *The Story of Asia's Last Lions* (Bombay 2005), 146; The *End of a Trail: The Cheetah in India* (Delhi, 1995), 215–33.

[43] G. P. Sanderson, *Thirteen Years among the Wild Beasts of India* (1874; Delhi, 1983), 307, 312.

[44] For details, see M. Rangarajan, 'From Princely Symbol to Conservation Icon: A Political History of the Lion in India', in Mushirul Hasan and Nariaki Nakazato (eds), *The Unfinished Agenda: Nation-building in South Asia* (Delhi, 2000), 399–442.

[45] M. K. Ranjitsinh, *Beyond the Tiger: Portraits of Asia's Wildlife* (Delhi, 1995), 22–4.

[46] E. Thompson, 'Mainly about Lions' (1944), repr. in M. Rangarajan (ed.), *The Oxford Anthology of Indian Wildlife*, ii. *Watching and Conserving* (Delhi, 1999), 96–9.

older critiques of the handling of famine, forest, and game issues. Historians have unearthed far more diverse and often more militant forms of protest from the 1870s (the Gudem Rampa risings) in the Northern Circars to the Bastar rebellion of 1910 in which the ban on swidden cultivation was a central issue.[47] But a variety of forms of less spectacular protest have also come to light. The selective firing of pine monoculture plantations in the foothills of the Himalayas by hill peasants in 1919–21, even as they protected mixed broad leaf forests, suggested a sharp opposition to the forester's view of how to reshape the land. Similarly, poaching, squatting, and sabotage of the game law were widespread in both princely and British India.[48]

The larger picture was a complex one. The reining in of more militant strands of opposition was a feature shared by Gandhi and his associates. During the forest *satyagarahas* in central India, provincial Congress leaders had a tough time restraining militant tribals who wanted to cut down large swathes of forest.[49] Earlier, displaced peasants in Mulshi Peth had opposed the Tata Power Company's dam near Pune. Gandhi himself rejected the idea of all-out opposition to the dam. He argued that the project had already commenced work and that opponents were not unified in rejecting compensation in cash or in land grants. Divisions between the Kunbi Maratha peasantry and the landless untouchable Mahars fractured protest.[50] By the early twentieth century, even as popular protest was intertwined with middle-class nationalism, its more strident tones were muted.

A predilection on the part of some nationalists for technology had major environmental implications. The left-wing Congressman V. V. Giri favoured the wholesale adoption of modern technology to utilize 'every acre' of land. Expansion of the cultivated arable was an antidote to poverty, even if his estimates were extraordinarily optimistic.[51] The scientist Dr Meghnad

---

[47] David Arnold, 'The Gudem Rampa Risings, 1839–1924', in Ranajit Guha (ed.), *Subaltern Studies*, i (Delhi, 1982), 88–142; Nandini Sundar, *Subalterns and Sovereigns: An Anthropological History of Bastar* (Delhi, 1997), 104–55.

[48] Guha, *Unquiet Woods*, 114–20.

[49] David Baker, '"A Serious Time": Forest *Satyagraha* in Madhya Pradesh, 1930', *Indian Economic and Social History Review* 21 (1984), 71–90.

[50] L. Rodrigues, *Rural Political Protest in Western India* (Delhi, 1998), 108–34.

[51] V. V. Giri, *Jobs for the Millions* (Madras, 1944), 39, 41. For a different view Bibuthibhushan Bandhopadhyay, *Aranyak of the Forest* (1938) translated from Bengali by Rimli Bhattacharya (Calcutta, 1992).

Saha saw industrial production as the only way to provide a politically independent India with economic means to protect itself. B. R. Ambedkar saw large dams as an antidote to floods. Modern technology would hasten the demise of caste-based distinctions and exploitation.[52] Men like Ambedkar or Nehru were not alone in seeing big as beautiful. Diwan Visweswaraya of Mysore had led in the building of a dam on the Kaveri. Ganga Singh of Bikaner was the first to conceive of irrigating the western Thar Desert with waters from the Punjab. The new irrigated, intensively cropped landscapes would sustain far higher numbers of people per square kilometre than the systems of production they supplanted. This was a fact not lost on decision makers as the population growth rates rose above 1 per cent after 1921. No wonder that peasants and literati alike eulogized dam builders in the south Indian countryside.[53] There were, however, other strands of thought. The economist J. C. Kumarappa saw decentralized renewable energy as less destructive but such critics of high technology were outnumbered.[54]

After 1947, these tensions would only multiply as Indian industry, mining, and hydropower would advance their own claims. At a time of mass poverty and limited investment in irrigation or industry, the biggest issue seemed quite simply to be how to make two ears of corn grow where one grew before. The first two decades after independence saw remarkable continuities in policies on land use with the measures initiated during the Second World War (1939–45). Land colonization was a means to settle the refugees of Partition in north and central India. Roads and malaria control opened up south India's highlands.[55] Large dams were given priority not only for irrigation or flood control but also to generate large amounts of cheap power. States upstream and downstream of the Indus tributaries and the Kaveri became locked in conflict over dividing the waters, just as across the centuries kings had tried to gain control of the fertile lowlands. The attitude to wildlife and forests did have the impress of scientific concerns as

---

[52] Gail Omvedt, *Ambedkar: Toward an Enlightened India* (Delhi, 2004), 111–12; Meghnad Saha, 'A Scientist's Philosophy of Industrialization', *Modern Review*, 64 (1938), 145–9. Also see Basudev Chatterjee (ed.), *Towards Freedom: Documents on the Freedom Movement in India, 1938*, Part 1 (Delhi, 1997), 846–52.

[53] S. Guha, *Health*, 68–9; Easvara Rao, 'Colonial Discourses on Dam Technology'.

[54] See Ramachandra Guha, *Mahatma Gandhi and the Environmental Movement*, The Parisar Annual Lecture, Pune, 1993.

[55] B. H. Farmer, *Agricultural Colonization in India since Independence* (Delhi, 1974), 40–5.

in Dr Salim Ali's intervention that helped protect the wetland of the Keoladeo Ghana, a former princely hunting ground from being drained for agriculture.[56] Such cases were exceptional, however. The replacement of certain landscapes seen as unproductive was an enduring feature of land use policy for the first two decades of freedom. The first Indian Inspector General of Forests, M. D. Chaturvedi, had questioned the grandiose hopes of land colonization, as he pointed out how many of such lands were better suited to grazing, horticulture, and forestry. But he was firm that all new foresters must demand guns, not gold from future in-laws. How else would they be able to pass the ultimate test that was essential to be able to run a forest division: namely to shoot dead a tiger in their first year in office.[57] Old habits died hard.

Conclusion

The pioneering historians of ecological change in India's history were right to assert that there was a watershed between the pre-colonial and the colonial eras. But the breaks look less polarized in the light of further work. In forests, water use, and pastures, a set of flexible arrangements with a hierarchy of user rights long pre-dated colonialism. Any sense of a neat division of labour or resource partitioning would be an anachronism. At the same time, there were a series of breaks in the colonial era, both under the Company and the Crown, which do stand out. The unprecedented interventionist Company state tried to sedentarize those who had earlier been on the move. The old ways of life in forests and highlands did not die out but became more marginal. Modern science, both in its idiom of desiccation and its production-driven land management regimes of the late nineteenth century, vilified competing resource users while vesting control, if not ownership, in a narrow set of land managers. The latter term is ambiguous for it included civil forest officials, often at loggerheads over how far and how fast to go. There was an increasing concentration of power over the forest and pasture between the Rebellion of 1857 and the end of the Great War (1918). A very different trend was evident in the same time period in the agrarian sector at large where peasant resistance to revenues

---

[56] Salim Ali, *The Fall of a Sparrow* (Delhi, 1987), 150–1.
[57] M. D. Chaturvedi, *Land Management in the United Provinces* (Allahabad, 1946) and Sankhala, *Tiger!*, 19.

and demands of tenants for rights against rent receivers loosened the degree of control.

The colonial era left a complex legacy, one with which Indians are still grappling. Displacement by and for large development projects is an explosive political issue in several Indian states today.[58] The Indian record in wildlife preservation is impressive in comparison with several Asian countries, but contests for land in national park and forest estate has become sharper.[59] Bureaucratic agendas, political pressures, a growing middle class and the assertiveness of the underprivileged are all reflected in battles over the environment, and discussion on the colonial era frequently features in these debates and struggles.

Select Bibliography

ARUN AGRAWAL and K. SIVARAMAKRISHNAN (eds), *Social Nature, Resources, Representations and Rule in India* (Delhi, 2000).

DAVID ARNOLD and R. GUHA (eds), *Nature, Culture, Imperialism: Essays on the Environmental History of South Asia* (Delhi, 1995).

AMITA BAVISKAR (ed.), *Waterscapes: The Cultural Politics of a Natural Resource* (Ranikhet, 2007).

MEENA BHARGAVA, *State, Society and Ecology: Gorakhpur in Transition, 1750–1830* (Delhi, 1999).

MARLENE BUCHY, *Teak and Arecanut: Colonial State, Forests and People in the Western Ghats, 1800–1947* (Pondicherry, 1996).

DIVYA BHANUSINH, *The Story of Asia's Lions* (Bombay 2005).

RICHARD GROVE, V. DAMODARAN, and S. SANGWAN (eds), *Nature and the Orient: Essays on the Environmental History of South and South East Asia* (Delhi, 1998).

RAMACHANDRA GUHA, *The Unquiet Woods: Ecological Change and Peasant Resistance in the Himalaya* (Delhi 1989).

——*Savaging the Civilized: Verrier Elwin, His Tribals and India* (Delhi, 1999).

SUMIT GUHA, *Environment and Ethnicity in India, 1200–1991* (Cambridge, 1999).

AJAY PRATAP, The *Hoe and the Axe: An Ethno History of Shifting Cultivation in Eastern India* (Delhi, 2000).

HARIPRIYA RANGAN, *Of Myths and Movements: Writing Chipko into Himalayan History* (Delhi, 2001).

MAHESH RANGARAJAN, *Fencing the Forest: Conservation and Ecological Change in India's Central Provinces, 1860–1914* (Delhi, 1996).

---

[58] 'Shades of Green', special issue of *Seminar*, 516 (Aug. 2002).

[59] Vasant Saberwal and Mahesh Rangarajan (eds), *Battles Over Nature, Science and the Politics of Conservation* (New Delhi, 2003).

Mahesh Rangarajan, *India's Wildlife History, An Introduction* (Delhi, 2001, 2005).

——and K. Sivaramakrishnan (eds), *India's Environmental History*, i. *Ancient Times to the Early Colonial Period*; ii. *Colonialism, Modernity and the Nation* (Ranikhet, 2012).

Vasant Kabir Saberwal, *Pastoral Politics: Shepherds, Bureaucrats and Conservation in the Western Himalaya* (Delhi, 1998).

——and M. Rangarajan (eds), *Battles Over Nature: Science and the Politics of Conservation* (Delhi, 2003).

Arupjyoti Saikia, *Forests and Ecological History of Assam* (Delhi, 2011).

Ghazala Shahabuddin, *Conservation at the Crossroads* (Ranikhet, 2010).

Chetan Singh, *Natural Premises: Ecology and Peasant Life in the Western Himalaya, 1800–1950* (Delhi, 1998).

K. Sivaramakrishnan, *Modern Forests: State-Making and Environmental Change in Colonial Eastern India* (Delhi, 1999).

Ajay Skaria, *Hybrid Histories: Forests, Frontiers and Wildness* (Delhi, 1998).

Ajantha Subramanian, *Shore Lines: Space and Rights in South India* (Stanford, 2009).

Sudha Vasan, *Living with Diversity* (Shimla, 2006).

10

The Material and Visual Culture of British India

Christopher Pinney

> Empire follows Art and Not Vice Versa as Englishmen suppose
> William Blake

Cultural historiography has increasingly focused on the material and visual dimensions of colonial rule. A key question remains undecided: can traditions of visual representation, the restructuring of the built environment, and transformations in modes of consumption be reduced to 'cultural technologies' of colonial control, or does their very complexity demand a new algorithm through which to understand their intricate mechanics?

An old duality is at the point of exhaustion. This offered an impoverished menu of affirmation or negation to the question of culture's relation to power. Dramatized most starkly in Edward Said's work and in an Indian context in more fruitful ways through the Cohnian school (that is the work initiated by Bernard Cohn and developed by Ronald Inden, Nicholas Dirks, and Arjun Appadurai),[1] this historiography has sought narratives of connectivity between colonial interest and cultural practice. Pitched in a battle against other historiographies deemed to be complicit with colonialism by virtue of the alibi they grant colonial knowledge, Saidian and Cohnian historiography has little room for 'disinterest' and disconnection. Although Said gestures to the complex desires that underlay orientalist knowledge production ('a battery of desires, repressions, investments, and projections'), the bulk of his analysis advances a confident systematicity—a

---

[1] Arjun Appadurai, *Modernity at Large: Cultural Dimensions of Globalization* (Minneapolis, 1997); B. S. Cohn, *Colonialism and Its Forms of Knowledge: The British in India* (Princeton, 1996); Ronald Inden, *Imagining India* (Oxford, 1990); Edward Said, *Orientalism* (London, 1985 1st pub. 1978); Edward Said, 'Orientalism Reconsidered', *Cultural Critique*, 1 (1985), 89–107; Edward Said, *Culture and Imperialism* (London, 1992).

world of 'racial, ideological and imperialist stereotypes'—apparently devoid of self-doubt and contradiction.[2]

Here I will outline a different way of viewing the relationship between power and cultural practice which I hope can more adequately engage its complexity. However, mine is not a wholesale rejection of the paradigm invoked above. Indeed there is one central aspect of it that I wish to amplify: the Nietzschean/Foucauldian stress on the elision of knowledge and power, and the possibility that art (or more properly, the visual and material) may constitute a primary form of 'knowledge'. One of my key concerns is the need to engage material and visual practices not as 'superstructure' (as an *after*-effect of what has already been achieved socially or politically) but as a formative zone of debate. This idea lies explicitly at the heart of Said's work, for the phantasmatic entities of the Orient and the Occident are essentially works of the *imagination*. Cohn's work on the Census and the Darbar illuminated how spatial structures of hierarchy and precedence constituted key nodes of engagement through which both Indians and Britons redefined themselves. Dirks—a student of Cohn's—subsequently explicitly theorized this, in his study of Puddokatai, through Clifford Geertz's suggestion that (within what he called the 'theatre state'), power might serve pomp.[3] This inverted the conventional assumption that pomp would serve power, that is that cultural practice and representation should be seen only as a mere appendage, a supplement to a pre-existing and already consolidated structure of power.

Until recently the historiography of Empire has had little time for questions of materiality. Empire was discussed largely in the absence of the visual art, statuary, public architecture, costume, and interior decor that have sustained all empires. Ideologies seemed to originate and find sustenance in minds which appeared not to engage with paintings, theatrical performances, photography, or film. If one assumes that this domain of 'representation' was simply a secondary elaboration of what had already been determined in a more important sphere of 'politics', 'society', or 'culture', the omission would be minor, and of little consequence. However, if one sees the 'material history' of the British empire as more than simply a 'supplement' to—or a set of illustrative embodiments of—a history with which we are already familiar, we face not an omission so much as the

---

[2] Said, *Orientalism*, 8, 328.

[3] N. B. Dirks, *The Hollow Crown: Ethnohistory of an Indian Kingdom* (Cambridge, 1987).

deletion of an alternative mode of historiography. We can approach this question through the following formulation: does the visual serve simply as an illustration of what we already know, or can a history be written through the visual and material? Can we escape from the process Carlo Ginzburg describes in which 'the historian reads into images what he has already learned by other means'?[4]

Sometimes the visual appears to us with a message that we have *not* already learned. Consider for instance the striking pictorial celebration of violent revolutionary opposition to British rule, which still figures visibly in India's popular imagery, including both chromolithography and Hindi film.[5] Focusing especially on Bhagat Singh who was executed in 1931, these images constitute a 'visual archive' which narrates a history quite unlike that to be found deposited in the textual archive. Bhagat makes only a fleeting appearance in Nehru's autobiography, and most textbooks of Indian history have room for little more than a footnote. Yet they have endured in the visual imaginary of India since the 1930s, embodying an enduring preoccupation with the nature of action, identity, and freedom that is far more 'visible' in the everyday than Gandhi's quite different resolutions of this triad.

With respect to this question of the possibility of a 'visual history' we can identify an unexpected alliance between orthodox histories and many postcolonial critiques, since although the latter are likely to be of a more culturalist persuasion and preoccupied with representation, they share with the former the Platonic assumption that these are essentially reflections of something, more important, happening elsewhere. Representations are in this way deemed to be representations 'of' something and it is that something, that Idea, which is endowed with primary explanatory power. This is one further reason to see Edward Said's *Orientalism* as a challenge to engagement and supersession rather than simply as negation. The binary choice that usually characterizes the debate around *Orientalism* can be sidestepped by a different analytic strategy that invokes the notions of 'transculturation', 'purification', and 'autonomy'. These terms are chosen as potentials of specific moments and spaces, and reflect a desire to avoid having to be *tout court* for or against a particular paradigmatic approach.

---

[4] Carlo Ginzburg, 'From Aby Warburg to E. H. Gombrich: A Problem of Method', in his *Clues, Myths and the Historical Method* (Baltimore, 1989), 35.

[5] The most recent being Rakeysh Omprakash Mehra's *Rang de Basanti* (2006).

'Transculturation' is derived from its usage by Mary Louise Pratt and James Clifford to signify a 'contact zone'[6] characterized by co-presence and interaction. This exchange can flow in both directions (from colonizer to colonized and vice versa) as is the case with the bungalow's dissemination as a global architectural form, and Indians' enthusiasm for the technology of photography.

'Purification' takes its character from Bruno Latour's use of the term. This is purification in the sense of titration: the creation of two putatively 'entirely distinct ontological zones'.[7] This purification is also characterized by a bi-directionality: at times it involves a purification towards European idioms (as with the prevalence of Palladian civic architecture) and at others, purification serves to essentialize Indianness as with certain aesthetic styles associated with chromolithography which derived part of their cachet from their rejection of European conventions, the pan-Asian aesthetic associated with Abanindranath Tagore,[8] or the musicological Hindu purism of Vishnu Narayan Bhatkhande.[9] However, aspects of visual and material culture frequently embody aspects of both the transcultural and the purificatory (as with, for instance, the bungalow which became a central element in exclusionary enclave settlement patterns, or Gandhian anti-industrialism which was indebted to John Ruskin and Lockwood Kipling, but was mobilized in the cause of an essentialized India).

'Autonomy' is a provisional and unsatisfactory term intended to mark the limits of the above two terms through a recognition that vast swathes of the visual and material culture of British India stemmed from enduring traditions and developed in ways that were not significantly impacted by colonialism. The recognition of this domain, which, if not quite autonomous, was largely independent of empire, is intended as a recognition that Indian cultural production was vast and complex and much of it was capable of creating its own history free from the shadow of colonialism.

---

[6] Mary Louise Pratt, *Imperial Eyes: Travel Writing and Transculturation* (London, 1992), 6; see also James Clifford, *Routes: Travel and Translation in the Late Twentieth Century* (Cambridge, Mass., 1997), 192.

[7] B. Latour, *We Have Never Been Modern* (Cambridge, Mass., 1993), 10.

[8] See Partha Mitter, *Art and Nationalism in Colonial India, 1850–1922: Occidental Orientations* (Cambridge, 1995), 283–314.

[9] Janaki Bakhle, *Two Men and Music: Nationalism in the Making of an Indian Classical Tradition* (New York, 2005).

Image Flows

The material and visual culture of the British presence in India came to operate in a field that was already structured by *other* empires, technologies, and regimes of taste. With some of these they directly engaged, with others they found themselves in confrontation, and some they simply bypassed. As an example of the complex transformations that were occurring alongside the British encroachment we might briefly consider the fate of traditions of court painting in north India. Here we find transformation, rupture, and reinvention, traditions that were 'lost and found'. Robert Skelton has traced the dispersal of those artist communities that formed around Akbar's great court, where over a hundred painters were employed under the tutelage of Persian masters, noting the diverse outcomes as their metropolitan hybridity was exported to remote regions of Rajasthan. In Bikaner, Mughal influence persisted, and elsewhere it was 'quite remarkable how rapidly Mughal-trained artists... reverted in style to the essential characteristics of the pre-Mughal Hindu school'.[10] For Skelton, the styles which subsequently became identified with Mewar and Bundi had more in common with 'early 16th century precursors than with the more worldly and academic art of the Mughal court'.[11]

Was this the continuation of a tradition, a restoration to a normalcy of practices that had been 'contaminated' by interaction with the aesthetic practices of the Mughal empire? Or do we see here a 'reinvention', a 'rediscovery', a reconstitution which parallels similar nostalgic 'returns' to modes of cultural production that would characterize India in the late nineteenth century? In this latter understanding 'locality' and 'tradition' appear in their most tangible and self-conscious formulations as a strategy of return, or a going back to what has been lost. Either way, we are confronted with the need to engage spheres of cultural production whose logic is not that of British mercantile or colonial presence. We can understand the emergence of what we might term 'neo-Mewar' aesthetics (which in the early twentieth century would come to play an extremely important political role—see below) as a 'purificatory' manoeuvre within a Mughal paradigm: its valency is inextricably linked to a movement away from Mughal aesthetics of individuation and

---

[10] Robert Skelton, *Rajasthani Temple Hangings of the Krishna Cult from the Collection of Karl Mann* (New York, 1973), p. 27.

[11] Ibid.

contingency. In relation to the British presence, however, we would have to characterize this through a logic of separation or of non-engagement. The space of Mewar painting—at least in the seventeenth century—was not determined in any significant way by Britons.

The genre which has become known as 'Company Painting' stands in stark contrast, for these are images produced in a very intimate space of hybrid transculturation. Described by Mildred Archer as 'an attempt by Indian artists to work in a mixed Indo-European style which would appeal to Europeans',[12] many of the images within this diverse genre (especially those from Murshidabad and Calcutta) manifest their desire to mediate an Indian reality with a European aesthetic expectation through the marked use of shadowing to produce an illusion of depth. This might be seen as an early example of the 'xeno-real', an attempt to reproduce the codes of a European naturalism/realism through certain stylized practises that amount to what Geeta Kapur terms 'an enabling technique'.[13] In Company Painting these were the heavy shadows which all objects seemed to throw onto the ground beneath them and the attempt to transcend the incipient symmetry of Indian aesthetics to a realigned and contingent colonial time-space, or chronotope.

In late eighteenth-century Bengal, Lucknow, and Arcot, conversely, Mughal and British aesthetic schemata engaged in a complex dance of transculturation and purification. We can see in the European longing for Mughal miniatures a transculturating desire, and in Indian ambivalence about British portraiture we can trace a purificatory strategy of distance. Natasha Eaton alerts us to the complex politics and aesthetics of the commissioning and prestation of, and payment for, portraits in late eighteenth-century Indian courts. She describes the East India Company's attempt to replace Mughal gifts of rulers' robes (*khil'at*) and tribute money (*nazar*) with 'symbolically potent portraits'.[14] Both *khil'at* and painted portraits 'aimed to transmit the "presence" of the donor to the recipient',[15] but they were aspects of aesthetic regimes which misunderstood and misrecognized each other. Warren Hastings's enthusiastic patronage of

---

[12] Mildred Archer, *Company Paintings: Indian Paintings of the British Period* (London, 1992), 11.

[13] Geeta Kapur, 'Ravi Varma: Representational Dilemmas of a Nineteenth Century Indian Painter', *Journal of Arts and Ideas*, 27–8 (1989), 60.

[14] Natasha Eaton, 'Between Mimesis and Alterity: Art, Gift and Diplomacy in Colonial India, 1770–1800', *Comparative Studies in Society and History*, 46 (2004), 818.

[15] Ibid.

portraitists such as Tilly Kettle[16] and Johan Zoffany, and his dissemination of his own likeness as 'image-gifts' was in part designed to negotiate the strictures of the Regulating Act of 1773 which had prohibited the acceptance of money, land, and jewels from Indians.[17] But British and Indian expectations of portraiture were often opposed: Eaton cites the case of the Scottish artist James Wales in the Maratha court in Pune in the 1790s whose idea of how to depict Shinde conflicted with the sitter's own. Shinde himself, as reported by the Resident Charles Malet, 'expressed a desire that his picture may be drawn on horseback, observing that every man's character and way of life should be painted in his picture and that his whole life had been present in the field'.[18] Wales, by contrast, was intent on depicting a man who was 'of mean appearance and rather low stature, fat and lame of one leg'.[19]

The residue of a similar divergence of representational expectation may be apparent in Mihr Chand's gouache depicting Shuja ud-daula, the Nawab of Oudh, painted c.1772 (Figure 1). The central figure of the Nawab is undoubtedly closely copied from an oil painting by Tilly Kettle. There are at least two possible contenders for prototype, both of which also date from 1772. The first of these (currently in the Paul Mellon Collection, Yale Centre for British Art) is a three-quarter-length portrait of Shuja ud-daula standing alone, in front of an indistinct backdrop. The second (currently in the Victoria Memorial, Calcutta) presents the Nawab full-length surrounded by numerous other figures. Titled *Shuja ud-daula, Nawab of Oudh, and Four Sons with General Barker and Military Officers*, it was sent by Kettle to London to be shown at the Society of Artists.[20] The sons cluster to the Nawab's right and on his left, holding the Nawab's hand, stands Robert Barker, the Company commander-in-chief with whom he had completed a treaty of alliance. This latter image—commissioned by Barker—subsumes the identity of the Nawab in his relationship with the Company. Mihr Chand's elaboration, by contrast, positions him outdoors with the appurtenances of power: with attendants and an

---

[16] H. De Almeida and G. H. Gilpin, *Indian Renaissance: British Romantic Art and the Prospect of India* (Aldershot, 2005), 68.
[17] Eaton, 'Between Mimesis and Alterity', 820.
[18] Cited ibid. 836.
[19] Cited ibid. 837.
[20] Almeida and Gilpin, *Indian Renaissance*, 74.

Figure 1. Mihr Chand, Shuja ud-Daula, Nawab of Oudh. Goauche *c*.1772, after an oil painting by Tilly Kettle. Courtesy Victorian and Albert Museum.

elephant with howdah in the background.[21] Here in the 'native copy' we can see the positioning of the Nawab within a very different space.

From the British point of view, the late eighteenth century is a key point in the visual culture of the colony for it was then that the first landscape painters (Hodges during 1780–3 and the Daniells between 1786 and 1793)

---

[21] See Mildred Archer, *Company Paintings: Indian Paintings of the British Period* (London, 1992), 116–17.

toured India and made visible to a wider British audience the nature of the country. In the case of Hodges who had earlier travelled as an artist on the second Cook voyage, much critical weight has been placed on his documentation as a pivotal moment in the movement from highly conventionalized representation to a *plein-air* empiricist sensibility. In Bernard Smith's powerful account[22] of his career in both the South Pacific and India, Hodges emerges as a 'provincializer of Europe' *avant la lettre*. From the colonial periphery he appears to invent a new revolutionary aesthetic—better suited to the atmospheric realities of these unfamiliar places—which precedes Turner's by twenty-five years.

By the end of the eighteenth century Calcutta was a major clearing house for pictures. It has been argued that the frequent auctions of the effects of those Europeans who succumbed to the high mortality rates led to the rapid diffusion of printed images through a wider population. In 1788 Thomas Daniell could observe that 'the commonest bazaar is full of prints—and Hodges *Indian Views* are selling off by the cart loads'.[23] In evaluating the impact of different genres and modalities of colonial representation, the nature of the different audiences they invoked is all too often forgotten. Hodges and the Daniells largely produced images for mass reproduction: their incomes depended on the ability of aquatint and engraving technologies to disseminate their images to large audiences.[24] In Hodges's case this was tragically unsuccessful: he died in penury, possibly committing suicide. Most portraitists addressed far smaller audiences—these might be the moderately sized audiences that encountered official portraiture in the sacred spaces of the colonial administration (banquet halls, government offices, and so on), or much smaller numbers of viewers in the case of privately commissioned domestic portraiture. Official portraiture had been encouraged by Hastings and was commonly used in courts in exchange for the Indian miniature paintings that Europeans craved. Large formal portraiture was used 'performatively' in key colonial spaces. The Banqueting Hall of the Government House in Madras which opened in 1803 became one such site. Built in Doric style in imitation of a Greek temple, there were

---

[22] Bernard Smith, *European Vision and the South Pacific* (New Haven, 1976). See G. H. R. Tillotson, *The Artificial Empire: The Indian Landscapes of William Hodges* (Richmond, Surrey, 2000) for a contrary view.

[23] W. G. Archer, *Bazaar Paintings of Calcutta* (London, 1953), 7–8.

[24] See Geoff Quilley and John Bonehill (eds), *William Hodges 1744–1797: The Art of Exploration* (London, 2004).

Figure 2. Nawab Walajah with Stringer Lawrence. Engraving from H. D. Love, *Descriptive List of Pictures in Government House and the Banqueting Hall, Madras.* Madras: Government Press, 1903.

spoils from Seringapatam at the north end and from Plassey at the south. Bishop Heber, writing in 1826, noted that the building was 'in vile taste... It contains some paintings of Coote, Cornwallis, Meadows and other military heroes,... all fast going to decay in the moist sea-breeze'. During the course of the nineteenth century, the images acted as physical traces of incorporation into the Raj: the painting of Nawab Walajah with Stringer Lawrence

(Figure 2) was acquired from the Carnatic Palace in 1859 following the abolition of the Carnatic *musnud*.[25]

Domestic portraiture addressed a still different audience and operated within different phenomenological regimes of viewing. Beth Fowkes Tobin has argued that such portraiture can be read as embodiments of changing conventions of colonial domesticity. She contrasts earlier images (such as those by Francesco Renaldi) which depict hybrid concubinage (and represent a serious cultural and moral challenge to English national identity and colonial culture)[26] with later visual affirmations of 'racial estrangement' by painters such as Johan Zoffany. In 1793 Governor-General Cornwallis, in response to growing anxieties about emergent hybrid identities, excluded Indians and those of mixed race from government and military office. Tobin maps this changing political history onto the changing forms of domestic portraiture. These questions of iconography, performativity, and circulation, are all necessary dimensions of any coherent understanding of visual culture in eighteenth-century India.

'The Museum Gone Wild'

Visualization, objectification, and categorization undoubtedly played an important role in rendering an India that was 'consumable' and governable. The elision of knowledge and power is fundamental to the Foucauldian and Saidian paradigms. However, it is not necessary to concur with every element of those paradigms to concede that from the late eighteenth century India was the focus of an immense project of visualization, driven by a desire to make what was 'pictured' knowable. Popular panoramas, history paintings treating of the death of Tipu Sultan, a profusion of lithographs, aquatints and engravings, exhibitions, and photography, constructed a new India—one that was graspable by distant viewers—and gave birth to new classes of artists, curators, archaeologists, and photographers 'whose careers were sustained by manipulating objects in their various categorical

---

[25] H. D. Love, *Vestiges of Old Madras, 1640–1800: Traced from the East India Company's records preserved at Fort St. George and the India Office and from other sources* (London, 1913), 54, 53, 98.

[26] Beth Fowkes Tobin, *Picturing Imperial Power: Colonial Subjects in Eighteenth-Century British Painting* (Durham, NC, 1999), 114. However, see Prakash's review of William Dalrymple entitled 'Inevitable Revolutions', *The Nation*, 30 Apr. 2007.

incarnations'.[27] The Archaeological Survey of India, for example, was founded in 1861 with Alexander Cunningham as director. These categorical incarnations were also exported to India, through various pedagogical devices such as the museum, but in the process of translation museological hierarchies and separations were frequently transformed. Natasha Eaton has documented how collections of images—which in a European context provided a means of exemplifying a collector's discerning sensibility—created 'complex spaces' within India. Framed and glazed prints became 'reflecting surfaces to be either superimposed or replace elaborate marble and [metal & mirror] decoration'.[28]

A similar hybridization of a colonial space and taxonomy is elucidated by Gyan Prakash in his discussion of the museum 'gone wild'. India here becomes the site of 'inappropriate' translations as a European museology and classification is imported into India. In part this was due to the inherent ambivalence of the 'man' that figured in colonial knowledge: incarnated as specimen in 'living ethnological' displays this man ceased to be a mere specimen and 'the staging of the science of man was inevitably "contaminated" by objects in which it inhered'.[29] In addition to this intrinsic performative ambivalence, we must also consider the spectrum of spectatorial practices that were brought to bear on displays. Prakash documents a wondrous subaltern curiosity that converted the museum into the *ajaibghar* and the *jadu-ghar* (house of wonder and house of magic) and had the Allahabad Exhibition of 1910–11 resounding to cries of 'Kolossal!, Jya ajib! [how amazing], Bápre báp [akin to O my God], Wah! [splendid]'.[30] The museum, evolved from the Renaissance *wunderkammer*, was imported into India as part of a technology of pedagogic disenchantment: many subaltern viewers reconstructed it as a cabinet of marvels.[31]

In the eighteenth century, little thought had been given to what form British architecture in India should take: the prevailing classical models that

---

[27] Carol A. Breckenridge, 'The Aesthetics and Politics of Colonial Collecting: India at World Fairs', *Comparative Studies in Society and History*, 31 (1989), 206.

[28] Eaton, 'Between Mimesis and Alterity', 839.

[29] Gyan Prakash, 'Science "Gone native" in Colonial India', *Representations*, 40 (1992), 159.

[30] An account in the *Pioneer* cited ibid. 163. Parentheses by Prakash.

[31] Prakash notes that the Indian National Congress began to hold exhibitions from 1901. For Prakash this was the natural co-option by an Indian elite of elite colonial practices. See also Lisa N. Trivedi, 'Visually Mapping the "Nation": Swadeshi Politics in Nationalist India, 1920–1930', *Journal of Asian Studies*, 62 (2003), 11–41.

prevailed in Britain were simply imported with pragmatic adjustments made for climatic difference. The enthusiasm for Greece and Rome, which gripped Europe, formed the basic template for many buildings in Madras and Calcutta. The painter William Hodges, arriving in Madras in 1780, noted that the buildings arising from Fort St George with their long colonnades and open porticoes 'offer to the eye an appearance familiar to what we may conceive of a Grecian city in the age of Alexander'.[32] This neoclassical aesthetic would be ramped up for key edifices of British power such as Lord Wellesley's Government House in Calcutta (Figure 3)—a swollen copy of Robert Adams's Kedleston Hall in Derbyshire—which embodied in the opulence and scale of their conception the idea that India would henceforth be ruled 'from a palace, not a counting house; with the ideas of a Prince, not with those of a retail dealer in muslins and indigo'.[33] Bombay's somewhat later urban development has left it with a predominantly Gothic architecture, reflecting the dominance of Gothic in Britain at that time.

Following the Revolt of 1857 and the subsequent consolidation of British rule, a debate emerged about the appropriate architectural form of the new imperialism and whether in the words of the Madras Government architect R. F. Chisholm, 'we are to have a style suited to the requirements of this country, or whether we are to be the mere copyists of every bubble which breaks on the surface of European art, and import our architecture with our beer and our hats, by every mail-steamer which leaves the shores of England'.[34] The 'Saracenic' aesthetic drew upon what were deemed to be the architectural forms produced by the various Muslim dynasties which had ruled in India and came to be understood—given its association with the empire that preceded the British—as 'simply [...] the most suited for the representation of empire'.[35] It was, as Thomas Metcalf has argued, no coincidence that museums would in the 1870s become the site for the

---

[32] William Hodges, *Travels in India During the Years 1780, 1781, 1782 & 1783* (London, 1893), 2.

[33] Cited in Metcalf, 'Architecture', 40. See also Thomas R. Metcalf, *An Imperial Vision: Indian Architecture and Britain's Raj* (Delhi, 2002), 12–14.

[34] Cited in Metcalf, 'Architecture', 42–3.

[35] Ibid. 42. The art historian Shivaji Panikkar has recently traced how the early temples built by Gujarati followers of Swaminarayan were 'marked by Victorian arches, Corinthian columns, and gigantic clock towers in the Indo-Saracenic style'. In the late 20th century these structures were 'purified' and made to exemplify the 11th-century Solanki style (see Atreyee Gupta at www.mattersofart.com/Featurese83.html).

Figure 3. Government House, Calcutta, c.1870. Photographer unknown. Private Collection.

canonization of the Indo-Saracenic, a hybrid architectural style which, after much conflict, had emerged as one of the solutions to the question as to 'how Empire ought best to be translated into stone'.[36] It was appropriate that museums—in which India's past was classified—would be given a form that reflected a 'museological' understanding of its past architecture.[37]

Drawing on the hybrid styles of buildings in Agra and Fatehpur Sikri, and reconceptualized as the 'Indo-Saracenic', this style would leave its impress on many key buildings in the later nineteenth century such as Major C. Mant's Mayo College in Ajmer (1877–85) (Figure 4) and Swinton Jacob's Albert Hall Museum in Jaipur (1878–86). Fusing British engineering with a 'native' aesthetic, these buldings and others would be criticized (in 1913) by the art school director E. B. Havell for the manner in which they clothed

---

[36] Thomas R. Metcalf, 'Architecture and the Representation of Empire: India, 1860–1910', *Representations*, 6 (1984), 46.

[37] Ibid. 50.

Figure 4. Mayo College, Ajmer. Photograph by Lala Deen Dayal, c.1880s.

structures with 'external paper-designed adornments borrowed from ancient buildings which were made for purposes totally foreign'.[38]

The ornate fusion of Jacob's Indo-Saracenic was largely rejected in the design of the new capital at Delhi.[39] Herbert Baker, who would be brought in to counterbalance Luytens, writing to *The Times* in 1912, declared the desirability of putting the 'stamp of British sovereignty' on the new capital and opined that the Indo-Saracenic 'has not the constructive and geometrical qualities necessary to embody the idea of law and order which has been produced out of chaos by the British Administration'.[40] His Secretariat Buildings fused the classical colonnades which he had used earlier in the Union Buildings in Pretoria with 'Indian' features such as *chattris* (canopied turrets) and *jaalis* (pierced stone screens) whose presence was largely justified functionally and climatically.[41]

Lutyens's Viceroy's House placed a massive dome, modelled on the Buddhist stupa at Sanchi (compete with railing) on top of huge colonnades

---

[38] Cited in Metcalf, 'Architecture', 60.

[39] Swinton Jacob was appointed architect of New Delhi, along with Luytens and Baker in Mar. 1913, largely to counterbalance what Hardinge saw as Luyten's unwillingness to 'Indianise' his designs. Jacob resigned six months later. See Metcalf, *Imperial Vision*, 229.

[40] Ibid. 222.   [41] Ibid. 224.

from which protruded a stone cornice, all of this scattered with sundry *chattris* of his own austere design. Metcalf reads this building as a final, futile 'device to mask a growing insecurity by shouting forth an assertive magnificence': sheer size filled the void of authority.[42] Lutyens's incorporation of Indic elements may seem somewhat surprising in view of his contempt for most Indian architecture ('silly Moghul-Hindu stuff') but his refuge from the hybridity of the previous two millennia of Indian history found an intriguing echo in the Bengali archaeologist Rakhaldas Banerjee who had likewise sought escape from a 'contaminated' Indian modernity in a utopian Buddhist past. In Rakhaldas's case he chose Barhut. By placing Barhut carvings and architecture as the key monument in the Indian Museum, Rakhaldas sought 'to extract the monument from the clutches of the white man's exclusive authority and make it available to a new national community... as a "stone of India"'.[43]

Metcalf reads the history of British colonial architecture in India in a highly 'Cohnian'[44] manner, seeing the form given to stone as reflecting British desires and claims to have 'mastered' India: 'they asserted a claim to knowledge, and hence to power, from within'.[45] This history can also be refigured as an oscillation between purification and transculturation. We can see in the form of the bungalow a transculturation of form, and in the cantonment culture, which usually accompanied it, a purification of space. In early Calcutta's neo-Palladianism we can see purification, in Swinton Jacob we can see an enthusiastic transculturation, in Luytens, an ambivalence in which Sanchi appears as a *deus ex machina*, providing escape from a history which has become simply too complex to mediate, but which as Metcalf rightly notes, is headed nowhere.[46]

---

[42] See Metcalf, *Imperial Vision*, 236.

[43] Tapati Guha-Thakurta, *Monuments, Objects, Histories: Institutions of Art in Colonial and Postcolonial India* (Delhi, 2004), 135.

[44] I do not say 'pre-Saidian' although it is this too, since Bernard Cohn's work prefigures much of the nexus of colonial knowledge and power which Said would later formalize. However, Cohn's work presents a much more detailed and powerful account of the material mechanism of power. See Christopher Pinney, 'Colonialism and Culture', in Tony Bennett and John Frow (eds), *A Handbook of Cultural Analysis* (London, 2007).

[45] Metcalf, 'Architecture', 62.

[46] Metcalf, *Imperial Vision*, 239.

Pedagogy, Performance, and Technology

We can see parallel essentializations and their introduction into Indian society in the work of colonial art schools and museums. Art schools in Bombay, Madras, and Calcutta were started with a variety of motives but were quickly co-opted by the colonial state as instruments of an optimistic strategy to alter an Indian sensibility[47] and to preserve what were perceived to be threatened artisanal skills. In Madras a surgeon, Dr Alexander Hunter, founded two schools in 1850 and 1851 with 'fine art' and 'industrial' rationales; in Bombay, the Parsee industrialist, Jamsethji Jijibhai, established an institution for the promotion of the 'arts and manufactures [and] habits of industry of the middle and lower classes'; in Calcutta, in 1854, the Society for the Promotion of Industrial Art founded a school in order to 'supply skilled draughtsmen, designers [and] engravers...to promote taste and refinement...among the upper classes'. Ultimately these incompatible aims would collide as middle-class aspirant artists edged out impoverished artisans. Within ten years all these schools were under government control, engaged in a new aesthetics in which—as Partha Mitter pointedly notes—'the scientific scrutiny of nature was a sacred act'. For some such as Richard Temple, art education was at the vanguard of a colonial 'perceptual' revolution ('which constantly corrects the initial formula by means of observation')[48] designed to supersede a 'conceptual' mode of India art dependent on hierarchical inculcation. Through the inculcation of new modes of perception, its aim was a latter-day Baconian colonial empirical revolution. Art schools, Temple opined, 'will teach them one thing, which through all the preceding ages they have never learnt, namely drawing objects correctly, whether figures, landscape or architecture'.[49] This mimetic perfection would serve to transform a broader perception, for 'Such drawing tends to rectify some of their mental faults, to intensify their powers of observation, and to make them understand analytically the glories of nature which they love so well'.[50]

---

[47] Partha Mitter, *Art and Nationalism in Colonial India, 1850–1922: Occidental Orientations* (Cambridge, 1995), 29.
[48] Ibid. 30.   [49] Cited ibid. 32.   [50] Ibid.

However, colonial art pedagogy was fractured from the start: although some sought an aesthetic imperialism through the mimicking of European art forms, key figures like Henry Cole and George Birdwood looked to Indian craft production for the sustenance and revival of 'traditional' forms which they perceived were threatened by colonialism's transnational commodity flows. Birdwood (who returned permanently to Britain in 1868) sought the continuance of a purified Indian craft practice in which although everything is 'more or less a work of art', nothing attained the status of fine art.[51] Later figures associated with the art schools such as E. B. Havell and W. E. Gladstone Solomon saw their task as the rescue of an Indian 'fine art' from the contamination of Western illusionism. These seemingly opposed options shared certain ideas in common: Birdwood deprecated the 'evil' polluting transculturation in Indian artisanal manufacture; Havell disparaged the corruption of a pan-Asian aesthetic by colonial illusionism.

Outside the art schools a vibrant popular visual culture thrived. In the mid to late nineteenth century, Kalighat *pats*, characterized by strong and fluid draughtsmanship, catered to a popular market seeking devotional pilgrimage souvenirs, and subsequently, visual commentary on Bengal's colonial modernity. In Kalighat *pats* we can see copious evidence of a society in flux: women enter a new public visibility, the pretensions of anglicized *babus* are mocked, and the sense of a dangerous and new upside-down world is attested to by many images depicting women beating their husbands. These images invoke an inversion of appropriate gendered behaviour, an inversion which conjures the *kaliyug*, the present base epoch which in Hindu cosmology signifies a degenerate modernity. The colonial dimension of this decay and disorder is made explicit in a small number of images such as one depicting the Jackal Raja's Court (Figure 5). According to W. G. Archer's exegesis, this is a visualization of the Bengali proverb that 'In the jungle even a jackal is king'. The image depicts a jackal seated on a royal *gaddi* and smoking a hookah, and in the lower half of the image the same jackal 'now seated in a Western-style chair, [pronouncing] judgement on two tied and bound animals which are led before him by a jack tailor, dressed in black top-hat and midshipman's uniform'.[52]

---

[51] 'The spirit of fine art is everywhere latent in India, but it has yet to be quickened into creative operation'. George Birdwood, *Paris Universal Exhibition of 1878: Handbook to the British Indian Section*, (London, 1878), 56.

[52] W. G. Archer, *Kalighat Paintings: A Catalogue and Introduction* (London, 1971), 55.

Figure 5. *The Jackal Raja's Court.* Kalighat painting, c.1870. Courtesy Victoria and Albert Museum. 08144(b).

Jyotindra Jain is obliged to place them in a 'changing world' to sidestep the aesthetic adjudications of early commentators such as the nationalist ICS folklorist Gurusaday Dutt (1882–1941) for whom Kalighat *pats* lacked 'the inner spiritual motive or *rasa*' and could only be viewed as 'commercial art devoid of any high spiritual significance'.[53] Gurusaday's sentiments

---

[53] Jyotindra Jain, *Kalighat Painting: Images from a Changing World* (Ahmedabad, 1999); Gurusaday Dutt, 'Traditional Artisans and Their Arts and Crafts', in *Folk Arts and Crafts of Bengal: The Collected Papers* (Calcutta, 1990), 84.

reflected the new nationalist aesthetics associated with Abanindranath Tagore (who succeeded Havell at the Calcutta School of Art) which would exert a powerful influence on elite thinking about the arts for much of the twentieth century. Jain stresses the inter-visuality within which Kalighat *pats* were enmeshed and relates the frontality and symmetry apparent in certain Kalighat images to the formation of new kinds of subjects pictured in the act of 'looking at' a camera or an audience that lay on the other side of the proscenium stage. Jain stresses the circularity of influence: painted styles influence photographic conventions which in turn fed back into photographic aesthetics, this all occurring against the burgeoning of photographic studios in Calcutta: by 1860 there were nearly 130 Bengali photographers in Calcutta, and a further 200 European ones.[54]

The early fruits of lithography, as practised by graduates of the School of Art in Calcutta, were highly transculturated: Nala and Damayanti were exiled in a European pastoral; Shiv meditated in a Himalayas forested with European trees. However, this new technology would soon be used in powerfully purifying strategies. In part this can be seen as a manifestation of the inherent volatility and instability of a colonially inculcated 'xeno-real' in which realism was merely an 'enabling technique'. The Calcutta Art Studio, founded in 1878 by four graduates of H. H. Locke's School of Art, competed with other Calcutta lithography presses for a burgeoning market which came increasingly to desire images with a devotional utility. Many of these images also record a complex entanglement with popular mythological theatre, and one can trace a commonality of subject matter and mode of address. The 'xeno-real' fused with conventions associated with the proscenium arch was to confound Temple's conversional agenda, for the gods were becoming progressively *more*, not less, 'real'.[55]

In the same year (1878), Vishnu Shastri Chiplunkar, an associate of B. G. Tilak, founded the Chitrashala Press in Poona. Its rationale was overtly political—indeed its own official history boasts that it was on its premises that the first bomb in the Deccan was assembled—and sought mass political mobilization through image circulation as a complement to Tilak's interventions. Chitrashala evoked a historical past of resistance and political

---

[54] Jain, *Kalighat Painting*, 113.
[55] Anuradha Kapur, *Actors, Pilgrims, Kings, and Gods: The Ramlila at Ramnagar* (Calcutta, 1990).

power, through Shivaji and the Peshwas, whose allegorical intent was obvious to Maharashtrian consumers.

The Calcutta Art Studio's aesthetic experiments and Chitrashala's political aspirations found a complex repose in the work of the painter Ravi Varma who was persuaded to start mass-reproducing his work in the early 1890s. Declared the 'first modern Indian painter' by his supporters—a 'stealer of fire' because of his appropriation of oil as medium—Ravi Varma was the first individual cultural producer in India capable of bearing the sign of gentleman 'artist'. Undoubtedly important for his role in nationalizing a popular aesthetic, his work owed much more to his Calcutta and Chitrashala forebears than is commonly accepted, and his legacy was far less permanent than many commentators assume. However, together with the film-maker D. G. Phalke, he occupies centre stage in the articulation of popular media practices with a new cultural nationalism. What Abanindranath Tagore and his circle enacted at an elite level in Bengal, the Ravi Varma aesthetic and the rise of mythological film would do for a popular pan-Indian imaginary (see Figure 6).

In this respect it is not surprising that Phalke worked as a block maker in the Ravi Varma Press at Lonavala (several years after Ravi Varma's death). Just as Ravi Varma had given India (which by now was conceptualized as possessing 'a public') 'their' gods, so Phalke self-narrates a mythic moment of the birth of national cinema. In about 1910 he is watching a European silent film *The Life of Christ* and in a moment of epiphany takes onto himself the national duty of allowing Indians to see 'their' own filmic gods and goddesses: 'Could we, the sons of India, ever be able to see Indian images on the screen?'[56] He produces his first film in 1913, and within the next few years produces a slew of mythological films, cinematically empowering Krishna, Hanuman, and other deities.

Phalke's sense that new representational technologies could be co-opted in the service of a particular 'national' and ideological cause had been long ago prefigured in relation to photography. This is most clearly evident in the architectural historian James Fergusson's extraordinary rebuke of the Bengali antiquarian, and founder member of the Bengal Photographic Society, Rajendralal Mitra, in which the 'proper' use of photography

---

[56] See Christopher Pinney, *Camera Indica: The Social Life of Indian Photographs* (London, 1997), 96–7.

Figure 6. *Kirat & Bhilli*, Ravi Varma. The god Shiva is disguised as a tribal hunter. Ravi Varma's images were first mass-produced as chromolithographs and subsequently circulated as postcards. Postcard c.1905. Private Collection.

becomes an idiom for a larger—and politically charged—debate about protocols of evidence. In 1884 Fergusson published an astonishing *ad hominem* attack on Mitra in a book entitled *Archaeology in India with Especial Reference to the Works of Babu Rajendralal Mitra*.[57] Fergusson had first gone to India as an indigo planter and had made such an enormous

---

[57] James Fergusson, *Archaeology in India, With Special Reference to the Works of Babu Rajendralal Mitra* (London, 1884).

fortune that he was able to retire after ten years.[58] Fergusson's indebtness to the exploitation of the rural poor of Bengal and Bihar and Mitra's outspoken statements against the suffering inflicted by the indigo system[59] clearly inform the antagonism between the two, but it is the use of the photograph as evidence, the ability to read photographs, and the very nature of 'being there' through which this conflict is articulated. Ferguson was a great enthusiast for the inviolable nature of photographic evidence and used photographs extensively in his publications, but being no photographer himself he relied on Gill, Burgess, Pigou, and others. Mitra by contrast was a competent photographer.[60] He had prefaced his 1875 *Antiquities of Orissa* by explaining that one of his prime objectives was to 'carry out the directions of the late Lord Canning...to secure an accurate description—illustrated by plans, measurements, drawings, or photographs, and by copies of inscriptions'.[61] It was this publication, *Antiquities of Orissa*, which would so infuriate Fergusson who complained that 'these works have become practically gigantic pamphlets written for the purpose of exposing my iniquities and ignorance'.

One point of dispute between Fergusson and Mitra concerned whether Indians (having initially built in wood) had copied stone techniques from the Bactrian Greeks. However, Fergusson focuses on the methodological uses of photographs. Fergusson's problem was how to retain the authority of the photograph as index (and as a proof for his own argument) when faced with a photographic counter-practice. His solution was not to challenge Mitra's photographs, but to question his ability to 'see' them properly. At the heart of Fergusson's complaint is the claim that Mitra's eye was 'uneducated'. He may have been a good photographer but he could not see what was really in his photographs, he muddled his locations, and claimed to have been to places that he had never in fact visited. Mitra's

---

[58] Major-Gen. Sir Frederic Goldsmid, obituary in *Proceedings of the Royal Geographical Society* (Feb. 1886), 114.

[59] Which had led to his expulsion from the Bengal Photographic Society in 1857. See Malavika Karlekar, *Re-Visioning the Past: Early Photography in Bengal 1875–1915* (Delhi, 2005), 136–48.

[60] An anonymous writer in a pamphlet entitled 'A member To the Members of the Photographic Society of Bengal', 28 July 1857, conceded that the President of the Society had said that he was 'one of the few practical Photographers of whom the Society could boast' and 'had worked well for the Society, and had done so when Europeans had hung back'.

[61] Rajendralal Mitra, *The Antiquities of Orissa* (Calcutta, 1961; 1st pub. 1875), vol 1. p.i. See also Kalyan Kumar Dasgupta, *Indian Historiography and Rajendralal Mitra* (Calcutta 1976), 28.

work was, Fergusson claimed in a resonant metaphor, 'an attempt to throw dust in the eyes of the public'.[62] Mitra—like other Indians—Fergusson suggested, excelled in the arts of memory, but could not see properly. 'I perfectly understand the uneducated eye of the Babu not perceiving' a particular detail, he writes, and concludes that since 'the Babu had no system and no story to tell, one photograph in his eyes was as good as another'—even with a photograph 'staring him in the face' his 'uneducated eye' prevents him from seeing what he really should see, Fergusson claims.[63]

For Fergusson the issue at stake was more than simply a debate between wood and stone. Rather, as he explicitly states, the question was about evidence and whether Indians could be trusted to assess it justly. 'The real interest', he wrote, 'in these days of discussions of Ilbert Bills, [is] the question of whether the natives of India are to be treated as equal to Europeans in all respects.'[64] The Ilbert Bill would have allowed senior Indian magistrates to preside over cases involving British subjects; Fergusson also mentions that his nephew Frederick Fergusson was barrister in the Supreme Court in Calcutta. According to Ferguson, Mitra was 'a typical specimen of one of the proposed class of governors', and Fergusson's message is that, inured in the arts of memory and lacking the ability to read 'photographic truth', Indians were not fit to judge Europeans.

This astonishing dispute permits us to see how technologies of representation entered into and structured broader debates. It also reveals the key role that Indians played in the development of photography in the subcontinent. News of photography reached India within a few months of its announcement in Europe: in October 1839 William O'Shaughnessy (who, significantly was also the originator of India's telegraphic network) reported to a meeting of the Asiatic Society in Calcutta on his experiments with 'photogenic drawing'. However, it was not until the 1850s that photography was practised in any systematic manner in India. In 1855 the Elphinstone Institution opened a photography class which attracted forty pupils including Hurrychund Chintamon who would soon open his own commercial studio. In the same year the Bombay Photographic Society had already attracted over 250 members (see Figure 7).

Indians demonstrated a very early enthusiasm for photography's potential for what has been called 'sentimental realism': the British in India shared this desire but also invested much in photography's potential for an 'instrumental

[62] Fergusson, *Archaeology in India*, 99.
[63] Ibid. 56, 59.   [64] Ibid. p. vi.

Figure 7. Reverse of a cabinet card photographic portrait created by S. Hormusji. Numerous photographic studios clustered around Kalbadevi Rd in Bombay. Many, like Hormusji, were Parsee-run and Parsees were enthusiastic commissioners of photography, c.1880s. Private Collection.

realism'.[65] Chief among these was *The People of India*, the delayed fruit of Canning's interest in photography. Published in eight volumes starting in 1868, this idiosyncratic survey struggled to understand the diversity of the Indian population. As the most ambitious of all colonial photographic projects, it also marks the limits of colonial anthropological knowledge.[66]

Initially photography appeared to be a cure for all the inadequacies of earlier representational practices but it would soon also manifest a poisonous dimension. Its 'truth' was desirable so long as it was controlled by the colonial state. As photographic apparatus became more mobile, and more easily affordable, it became detached from the colonial 'habitus' which had previously ensured complicity between photographer and colonial authority. Curzon's promotion of the 1903 Delhi Durbar as a spectacle

[65] The terms are Leslie Shedden's, cited in Geoffrey Batchen, *Burning with Desire: The Conception of Photography* (Cambridge, Mass., 1997), 9.

[66] For the best account of its genesis and compilation see John Falconer, '"A Pure Labor of Love": A Publishing History of *The People of India*', in Eleanor M. Hight and Gary D. Sampson (eds), *Colonialist Photography: Imag(in)ing Race and Place* (London, 2002), 51–83.

available to any foreign press that cared to record it established public space as the new domain of photography. What the foothills of the Himalayas had been to mid-nineteenth-century photography, the street was to the twentieth-century practice. In 1922 the Guru-ka-Bagh riot in Amritsar was photographed and filmed by an American cinematographer, A. L. Varges, precipitating a profound anxiety in the colonial state and provoking discussions about how photography in public spaces might be policed, or even forbidden. Photography had slipped from the slippery hands of the colonial state: no longer a handmaiden to power, it became a dangerous weapon of scrutiny.

Music would also become in the twentieth century a vector of anticolonial critique. The Swadeshi Movement in Bengal took its cue from Rabindranath Tagore's July 1904 Swadeshi Samaj in which he suggested that 'festivals, open-air folk entertainments like the *jatra*, and song should be used to reach out to the masses'.[67] At the same time Subramanya Bharathi, the Tamil poet, started to produce 'nationalistic lyrical poetry in a simple and lucid style suitable for singing'.[68] But behind this overt politicization a number of different developments were being played out which complexly exemplified purification and 'autonomy'. Autonomy is an awkward notion in a colonial world of intimate connections. Nevertheless, some kind of label is required to describe cultural practices which appear to proceed in a state of what might be described as 'indifference'. Indifference stands opposed to the investment that drives 'purification'. Purified cultural production consciously valorizes 'authentic' and 'traditional' cultural practice as a direct response to what is seen to threaten it.

Despite a century-long tradition of what Janaki Bakhle terms 'nation, notation and religion',[69] it is striking how 'un-transculturated' early sound recordings of Indian music are. Following the first recordings of Indian music in London by Gramophone and Typewriter Ltd in 1899, Fred Gaisberg travelled to India in 1902 both to make recordings and to establish the basic infrastructure of a market for recorded music.[70] As Gerry Farrell has noted, this was no ethnomusicological project, but a strictly commercial

---

[67] Theodore Bhaskaran, *The Messsage Bearers* (Madras, 1981), 47.
[68] Ibid.
[69] Bakhle, *Two Men and Music*, 52.
[70] Farrell, *Indian Music and the West* (Oxford, 1998), 114–15.

endeavour and one which was dependent on Indian intermediaries—Amarendra Nath Dutt and Jamshedji Framji Madan—for Gaisberg was unable to find Europeans with a serious interest in Indian music. Gaisberg was 'at the mercy of local entrepreneurs' and, as the Gramophone and Typewriter Ltd's Calcutta agent said, 'the baboos here are slick'.[71] His first recording was of two *nautch* girls, Soshi Mukhi and Fani Bala, singing extracts from popular theatre, but soon after he was able to record the legendary Gauhar Jan and during the course of a six-week stay was able to produce over five hundred wax matrices for despatch to a pressing factory in Hanover.[72] He would initiate a remarkable intensity of recording activity and the overwhelming bulk of early recordings manifest almost no residue of a broader colonial context.[73] Yet the impact of different technologies associated with colonialism can be surprising: the communications revolution effected in part by the railways in mid-nineteenth-century India was one of the factors encouraging the formation of *gharanas*—the 'guilds' which subsequently came to define style and genre in 'classical' performance traditions.

But outside the recording studio, different and explicitly purifying forces were at work. The leading musicologists Vishnu Narayan Bhatkande and Vishnu Digamber Paluskar played a key role in the 1920s in demarcating distinct 'Hindu' and 'Muslim' musical traditions and spheres, privileging the former as the 'traditional' and 'textual' embodiment of an Indian 'classical' practice. Amanda Weidman complicates this further, suggesting that south Indian Karnatic music's attempt to define itself within a colonial and technological modernity involved the transculturating appropriation of a Western classical set of signs (such as notation, composers, conservatoires) and a simultaneously purifying invocation of an essentialized 'voice' which incarnated an Indian authenticity.[74] This is an immensely complex cultural landscape in which a vulgar elision of power and knowledge has no purchase.

---

[71] Ibid. 117.
[72] M. S. Kinnear, *The Gramophone Company's First Indian Recordings, 1899–1908* (Bombay, 1994), 12.
[73] Farrell, *Indian Music and the West*, 112.
[74] Amanda J. Weidman, *Singing the Classical, Voicing the Modern: The Postcolonial Politics of Music in South India* (Durham, NC, 2006).

Art and Empire

The material and visual dimensions of British India have heretofore been marginalized in accounts which privileged politics, economics, and culture. The prevailing assumption has been that the material and visual was a secondary reflection of something else more important. This expectation was variously incarnated as a distinction between infrastructure and superstructure, and a sociological consensus that representation was a kind of screen onto which more primal determinants were projected. Why study the monkey, when one could engage the organ grinder? In concluding this account we might note how representation—material and visual artefacts and practices—is increasingly understood as much more than mere secondary reflection. Ample evidence of its causative potential has already been invoked above, but here I will merely mention three strong instances in which the material and visual serve as motors of change or agents of transformation.

First consider the impact of an Indian aesthetic on European Romanticism. Almeida and Gilpin have recently marshalled convincing evidence that India was the *uroffenbarung* (moment of revelatory insight) of Romanticism.[75] They propose that visual images from India opened, in the words of James Forbes, 'a new scene... to the intellectual view'. Images produced by the likes of Tilly Kettle, William Hodges, and Edward Moor introduced Britain to a fantastical, sublime, and enchanted India. Hodges was acknowledged by Joshua Reynolds in a presidential address to the Royal Academy to have provided 'hints of composition and general effect, which could not otherwise have occurred'.[76] For the poet and artist William Blake, Reynolds's neoclassical aestheticism sustained the evil of empire. In his copy of Reynolds's *Works* of 1798, Blake wrote that 'The Arts and Sciences are the Destruction of Tyrannies and Bad Governments... Empire follows Art and Not Vice Versa as Englishmen suppose.'[77] In formulating an Art opposed to Empire, Blake drew heavily on Indian sources—Charles Wilkins's 1785 translation of the *Bhagavad Gita* affected him greatly and an Indian aspiration seems to be at work in a number of his images. Almeida and Gilpin have provocatively suggested that Blake's celebrated *Nebuchadnezzar*

---

[75] Almeida and Gilpin, *Indian Renaissance*, 61.
[76] Ibid. 125.
[77] Ibid. 271.

'resembles not so much King Lear as a sadhu or Hindu ascetic'[78] and that his *Spiritual Form of Pitt Guiding Behemoth* (c.1805–9) derives much of its structure and iconographic detail from the Daniells' depictions of monumental carvings of Buddha and Shiva. Blake's *Jerusalem* (c.1804–20) is clearly iconographically indebted to Moor's *Hindu Pantheon* (which was published by his friend Joseph Johnson[79]), just as many of its ideas owe much to Wilkins's translation of the *Gita*.[80] More generally it seems plausible that Blake's repeated creation of complex 'friezes'—surfaces covered with elaborate mythological forms—owes much to his engagement with depictions of Indian cave-temples.

Consider also the role of aesthetic practice in the constitution of Gandhi's highly efficacious political 'somatics' and political theorization. A complex network connects John Ruskin, William Morris, John Lockwood Kipling, and the aesthetician Ananda K. Coomaraswamy to Gandhi. Lockwood Kipling (inspired in part by George Birdwood) and Coomaraswamy both articulated within the sphere of art pedagogy and aesthetic theory, positions that prefigured Gandhi's own essentialization of the village, of artisanal—as opposed to industrial—production, and of a political ethic rooted in a civilizational 'craft'. But this flow of ideas—triangulating India, Britain, and South Africa—would form the basis of a much more significant aesthetic 'intervention' in the form of Gandhi's somaticization of a political theology. His increasingly naked body became an aesthetic surface which exemplified the ethics of anti-colonial practice, and when this body was in turn positioned next to the *chakra* (the spinning wheel which symbolized the self-production of *swadeshi*), it made visible the performative dimensions of his politics (see Figure 8).

A similar aesthetic excess can be seen in a genre of mass-produced images—motors of 'national feeling'—whose popularity mirrored Gandhi's ascendancy in the 1920s and 1930s. Produced by Brahman artists from the Pushtimarg pilgrimage centre of Nathdvara in Rajasthan, these images foregrounded deities in fecund landscapes. Pictorially animating the lush topography of Krishna's Braj, these images depicted landscape as

---

[78] Ibid. 274.

[79] Joseph Burke, 'The Eidetic and the Borrowed Image: An Interpretation of Blake's Theory and Practice of Art', in Franz Philipp and June Stewart (eds), *In Honour of Daryl Lindsay: Essays and Studies* (Melbourne, 1964), 124. Almeida and Gilpin demonstrate in much greater detail the visual influence (271–86).

[80] Almeida and Gilpin, *Indian Renaissance*, 281–6.

260   CHRISTOPHER PINNEY

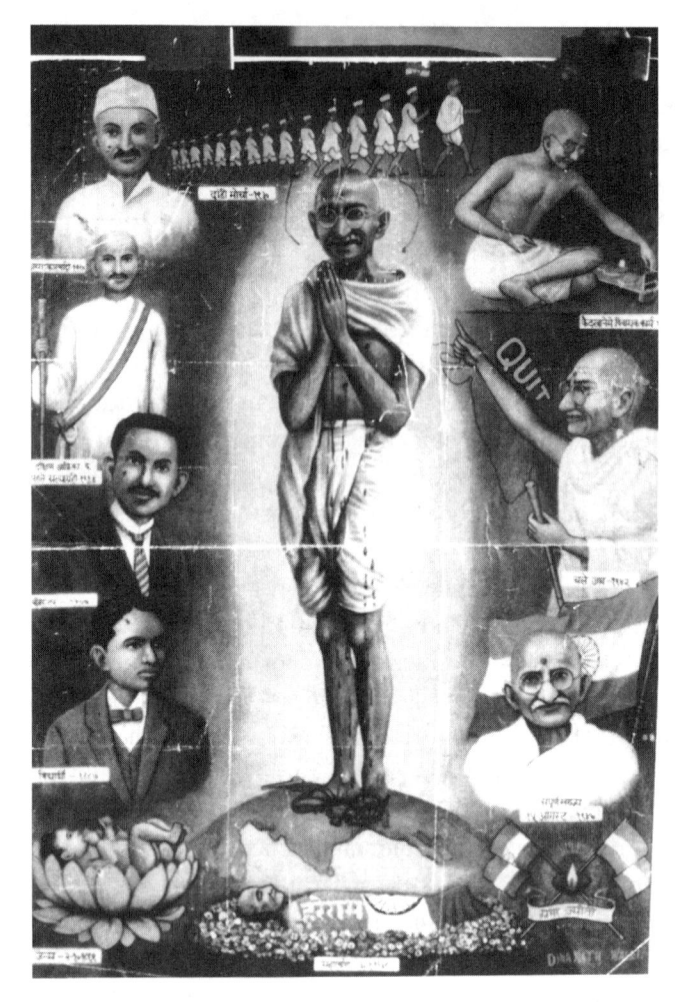

Figure 8. *Evolution of Gandhi*, a chromolithograph by the artist 'Dinanath', tracing Gandhi's performance of an aesthetic of austerity.

an emanation of the gods. Waterfalls cascaded, parrots and peacocks festooned every tree, and a melancholic moon shone an unearthly light.[81] Reproduced in their millions these ubiquitous images manifested a utopian 'elsewhere'—making itself present in a flash of recognition—which paralleled Gandhi's pastoral utopia. Much more than mere illustrations of a yearning that had already been resolved in 'society', these images constituted

---

[81] See Christopher Pinney, *'Photos of the Gods': The Printed Image and Political Struggle in India* (London, 2004), 92–103.

their own immensely powerful and affective force-field. Empire and anti-Empire did indeed follow Art.

Select Bibliography

HERMIONE DE ALMEIDA and GEORGE H. GILPIN, *Indian Renaissance: British Romantic Art and the Prospect of India* (Aldershot, 2005).

MILDRED ARCHER, *India and British Portraiture, 1770–1825* (London, 1979).

JANAKI BAKHLE, *Two Men and Music: Nationalism in the Making of an Indian Classical Tradition* (New York, 2005).

TAPATI GUHA-THAKURTA, *The Making of a New 'Indian' Art: Artists, Aestheticians and Nationalism in Bengal, 1850–1920* (Cambridge, 1992).

——*Monuments, Objects, Histories: Institutions of Art in Colonial and Postcolonial Art* (New York, 2004).

JYOTINDRA JAIN, *Kalighat Painting: Images from a Changing World* (Ahmedabad, 1999).

MALAVIKA KARLEKAR, *Re-visioning the Past: Early Photography in Bengal 1875–1915* (Delhi, 2005).

THOMAS METCALF, *An Imperial Vision: Indian Architecture and Britain's Raj* (Berkeley, 1989).

PARTHA MITTER, *Much Maligned Monsters* (Chicago, 1977).

——*Art and Nationalism in Colonial India 1850–1922: Occidental Orientations* (Cambridge, 1995).

CHRISTOPHER PINNEY, *'Photos of the Gods': The Printed Image and Political Struggle in India* (London, 2004).

AMANDA J. WEIDMAN, *Singing the Classical, Voicing the Modern: The Postcolonial Politics of Music in South India* (Durham, NC, 2006).

11

Literary Modernity in South Asia

Javed Majeed

I

On the basis of scholarship on modern South Asian literatures, we can identify three broad problems which constitute the field of South Asian literary studies. The first is the standardization of written forms of the 'vernaculars', partly resulting from the impact of print culture,[1] ranging from the periodical press to the printing of textbooks. These forms of printed literature influenced the development of genres of literature, such as the novel, and new forms of poetry. For example, Kamil Zvelebil has detailed the impact of printing and the growth of journalism on the development of modern Tamil literature, while Vasudha Dalmia discusses the importance of the periodical press in the nineteenth century as providing a space for new forms of writing in Hindi.[2] Francesca Orsini considers the role of textbooks in the growth of Hindi literature, and Dusan Zbativel has studied the role of textbooks and journalism in the development of modern Bengali literature from the early nineteenth century onwards.[3]

The second theme which scholarship on modern South Asian literatures has addressed is the location and constitution of texts in the relationships

---

[1] Sheldon Pollock has argued that for some Indian languages standardization in orthography and grammar, and unification into a literary language, were preprint achievements, and so standardization can only be partly attributed to the impact of print. Sheldon Pollock (ed.), *Literary Cultures in History: Reconstructions from South Asia* (Berkeley, 2003), 22.

[2] Kamil Zvelebil, *The Smile of Murugan: On Tamil Literature of South India* (Leiden, 1973), ch. 17; Vasudha Dalmia, *The Nationalization of Hindu Traditions: Bharatendu Harischandra and Nineteenth-Century Banaras* (Delhi, 1997), 224–51.

[3] Francesca Orsini, *The Hindi Public Sphere 1920–1940: Language and Literature in the Age of Nationalism* (Delhi, 2002), 92–115; Dusan Zbativel, *Bengali Literature* (Wiesbaden, 1976), 208–21, at 283.

between Indian society and the colonial state. This includes the ways in which the colonial state intervened in the development of the vernaculars and their literary cultures, as well as the processes through which languages became symptomatic of the constitution of identities in the public realm. A number of scholars have considered how South Asian languages came to stand for communal and religious identities, the most important case here being the Hindi movement and its developing association with a nationalist Hindu identity.[4] The important studies of Dalmia and Orsini, referred to above, deal with this in considerable detail, as does Christopher King, who examines how Urdu and Hindi became two different languages in the course of the nineteenth century.[5] Scholars have also considered how the educational and cultural institutions established by the British state in India played a key role in the development of nineteenth-century South Asian literatures.[6]

The third broad area is the rupture between a modern and pre-modern poetics. By poetics I mean the choice of words, figures, and devices used by authors to create literary language or, in other words, the collection of linguistic and formal properties which distinguish literary texts from non-literary texts. The nature of the rupture between a modern and pre-modern poetics in South Asian literature has been explored less fully in the secondary literature and, consequently, it will be addressed here. I will suggest ways in which the critical ground in relation to the question of South Asian literary modernity might be shifted. The terms 'modern' and 'pre-modern'

---

[4] See O'Hanlon's essay in this volume for a further discussion of the interplay between region, language, and nationalism.

[5] C. R. King, *One Language, Two Scripts: The Hindi Movement in Nineteenth Century North India* (Bombay, 1994). In addition, Paul Brass, *Language, Religion and Politics in India* (London and New York, 1974); C. Shackle and R. Snell, *Hindi and Urdu since 1800: A Common Reader* (London, 1990). Also C. A. Bayly, *Empire and Information: Intelligence Gathering and Social Communication in India, 1780–1870* (Cambridge, 1996).

[6] e.g. Zbativel, *Bengali Literature*, 209 ff. on the role of Fort William College in the development of Bengali literature, and R. S. McGregor, *Hindi Literature of the Nineteenth and Early Twentieth Centuries* (Wiesbaden, 1974), 64–70, for the role of the same college in the case of Hindi literature. See also David Kopf, *British Orientalism and the Bengal Renaissance: The Dynamics of Indian Modernization* (Berkeley, 1969), 43–108 for a detailed account of Fort William College and C. M. Naim, 'Prize-winning *adab*: A Study of Five Urdu Books Written in Response to the Allahabad Government Gazette Notification', in Barbara D. Metcalf (ed.), *Moral Conduct and Authority: The Place of Adab in South Asian Islam* (Berkeley, 1974), 290–314 for the role of prizegiving in the encouragement of new forms of Urdu literature.

used here correspond roughly to colonial and pre-colonial India in terms of chronology, yet I am more concerned with how South Asian poets, writers, and thinkers used the category 'modernity' as an attempt at self-definition. The term became a way of defining what they perceived to be the newness of their present as distinct from their literary predecessors, whom they tended to group under the rubric of 'tradition'. Ultimately, though, the term 'modern' does not have (and perhaps cannot have) any fixed historical reference, a point which has been persuasively made by both Jürgen Habermas and Paul de Man.[7] In this essay, then, I am concerned with 'literary modernity' in South Asia, that is, with how the self-conscious sense of being 'modern' was used by South Asian writers as an ideology of aesthetics in order to distinguish themselves from their 'traditional' predecessors.

II

A useful starting point to consider modern South Asian literature, and especially poetry, is Faiz Ahmed Faiz's Urdu poem of 1943, 'Mujh se pahli si mahabbat miri mahbub na mang' (which might be translated as 'My beloved, do not ask of me my former love').[8] This poem's subject matter is the poet's self-conscious reflection on his predicament, his oscillation between the pull of the self-reflexive world of the *ghazal*,[9] with its hermeneutically enclosed and self-referring poetics, and a modern realism, where literary texts engage with and construct the everyday world.[10] The last three lines sum up the poet's predicament: 'aur bhi dukh hain zamane men mahabbat ke siva | rahaten aur bhi hain vasl ki rahat ke siva | mujh se

---

[7] Jürgen Habermas, 'Modernity: An Incomplete Project', in Hal Foster, *Postmodern Culture* (London, 1993), 3–15 and Paul de Man, 'Literary History and Literary Modernity', in *Blindness and Insight: Essays in the Rhetoric of Contemporary Criticism* (London, 1983), 142–65.

[8] This poem first appeared in *Naqsh-e Faryadi* (1943). I have taken the text of the poem from *Poems by Faiz*, trans. V. G. Kiernan (London, 1971).

[9] The *ghazal* is a short love poem. In its classical form, the two halves of the first couplet and the second line of the remaining couplets rhyme. There is also a convention generally adhered to, according to which the poet inserts his pen name in the closing couplet as a kind of signature. See D. J. Matthews and C. Shackle, *An Anthology of Urdu Love Lyrics* (London, 1972), 1, 8.

[10] Francis Pritchett has analysed the poetics of the *ghazal* in terms of how it creates its world according to its own laws of metaphor, which preclude any mimetic function of the text in relation to the 'natural' world. See Francis W. Pritchett, *Nets of Awareness: Urdu Poetry and Its Critics* (Berkeley, 1994), 104.

pahli si mahabbat meri mahbub na mang' (which might be translated as 'There are other sufferings in the world besides those of love | There are other pleasures besides those of union | Do not, my beloved, ask me for my former love').

The content of the poem is its enactment of a rupture from pre-modern poetics, willed by the poet himself; but by the same token the poem incorporates within itself this pre-modern aesthetic realm with which it seeks to break. The aesthetics of the *ghazal*, the resonance of its key figures of the 'beloved' and 'love',[11] loom large as the background to the poem. This background invests the foregrounding of the poet's predicament with significance, and gives him the choice which defines him as a poet.

There are three other aspects to the play between continuity and discontinuity in this poem. In its typically classical form, each couplet in the *ghazal* is self-contained.[12] Faiz's poem is continuous in the sense that it has a unified subject matter, an integrating plot, yet the theme of the poem is discontinuity. The poem is a unified *ghazal* whose theme is rupture. Each couplet refers to the other couplets, but the poem as a whole enacts a break from the pre-modern poetics which it reinscribes on another level. Secondly, in the classical *ghazal*, the poem ends with a couplet in which the poet uses his *takhallus*, or pen name. In Faiz's poem, the poet's persona has a different presence, in terms of his predicament with regard to the demands and techniques of writing, and the different referential possibilities open to him. What makes the poem a textual whole is the persona of the poet himself, defined in relation to his creative dilemma as an artist which is the subject matter of the poem. Finally, Faiz's poem is written in the *ramal* metre, a common metre with a regular pattern of three identical feet of four syllables each, followed by a similar foot of three syllables. In metrical terms, the poem announces its continuity with literary tradition, while in terms of its subject matter it is innovative in breaking from literary tradition.

Muhammad Iqbal's epic poem *Javed Nama* (1932) also manifests this tension between continuity and discontinuity. As in Faiz's poem, the nature

[11] For these features, see Matthews and Shackle, *Anthology of Classical Urdu Love Lyrics*, introd.

[12] The autonomous status of the individual verse in relation to a textual whole is a key feature of Sanskrit and traditional Tamil literary culture also, and is not limited to the *ghazal* alone. Norman Cutler, 'Three Moments in the Genealogy of Tamil Literary Culture', in Sheldon Pollock (ed.), *Literary Cultures in History: Reconstructions from South Asia* (Berkeley, 2003), 316. As such, it seems to be a broader feature of pre-modern South Asian literary cultures as a whole.

of the poet's identity is at issue. His journey through the cosmos is the enactment of that identity as well as his quest for it. On one level, the text signals its continuity with the Persian literary tradition by having the figure of the great Persian poet Rumi (1207–73) as the poet's guide through the cosmos.[13] Some of the lines in the *Javed Nama*, including its first line, also echo lines of Rumi's *Masnavi*. Moreover, the *Javed Nama* is written in the same metre as Rumi's *Masnavi*. But the two texts could not be more different in other ways. Rumi's *Masnavi* is a compendium of different stories, each with its own moral, which can be read on a multiplicity of levels, from the mundane to the esoteric. In contrast, the *Javed Nama* is tied together through the linear progression of the poet's journey, with a starting point and a destination, in which each episode is linked to the other episodes in the poet's travel through the cosmos. This explicitly integrating plot of the poet's persona is generally absent from Rumi's *Masnavi*.

This dialectical interplay between a mutually sustaining modern and premodern poetics constitutes the form and content of modern South Asian literatures.[14] For instance, the 'new poetry' of modern Tamil literature, inaugurated by the publication of a volume entitled 'New Voices' in October 1962, had its roots in the 'prose-poems' of Subrahmanya Bharati (1882–1921).[15] These poets shared a disregard for traditional forms and prosodic structures, and made innovative use of the basic prosodic properties of Tamil. They also eschewed the stock formulae of medieval Tamil poetry. At the same time, as Kamil Zvelebil has argued, the self-conscious modernity of these poets can be read as a return to the terseness and brevity of early classical Tamil poetry. The work of specific poets, such as that of T. S. Venugopal, is also reminiscent of the classical Tamil poetry of the *Cankam* age.[16] We have seen above that Faiz's poem and Iqbal's *Javed Nama* do not experiment with metrical forms, but employ a common metre used

---

[13] Rumi is considered to be one of the greatest Sufi mystic poets in the Persian language. He is famous for his lyrics and for his epic poem, *Masnavi-ye Ma'navi* or 'Spiritual Couplets', which consists of some 26,000 verses.

[14] For a detailed analysis of this interplay in Muhammad Iqbal's poetry and prose, see Javed Majeed, *Muhammad Iqbal: Islam, Aesthetics, and Postcolonialism* (New Delhi, 2009).

[15] Zvelebil, *Smile of Murugan*, 313–14.

[16] According to Zvelebil, the term *cangam* is best translated as 'classical'. It refers to a 'frozen' corpus of texts, probably of the 5th to 7th century AD, which had not been expanded upon since it ceased to be part of a live oral tradition. As a result, the term also refers to linguistic, stylistic, and prosodic excellence. Ibid. 49–50, and ch. 2.

by both pre-modern and modern poets. A similar instance of innovation and tradition in Tamil 'new poetry' is partly reflected in the tension between the traditional metrical form of their texts and their radically new content. The 'new' Tamil poets' experiments with metre and prosody enact this interplay. Zvelebil argues that the novelty of this 'new poetry' lies in its innovative and forcible use of traditional material, especially in its application and utilization of the basic prosodic and formal properties of Tamil poetry, rather than in its complete rejection.[17] He gives other detailed examples of how such innovative experiments can be seen to emerge from literary tradition, but he also stresses that there is one fundamental 'high-level' feature which marks a definitive break with tradition. Previously Tamil poetry was sung or at least scanned in a sing-song manner, whereas the 'new poetry' is meant to be read or recited.

Thus, Tamil 'new poetry' is marked by a self-conscious mingling of literary tradition and modernity, both in its metrical form and in terms of the tensions between metrical form and content. Modern Bengali poetry demonstrates similar traits. Michael Madhusudan Dutt's (1824–73) *Meghnadavadha Kavya* of 1861 is both a retelling and a subversion of an episode from the *Ramayana*. Critics have called attention to Dutt's skilful narrative structuring as he both echoes and subverts the main story of the *Ramayana*. They have also discussed his weaving together of diverse episodes from the *Mahabharata* within his subversion of the *Ramayana*.[18] Dutt's work experiments with innovation and tradition in both form and content.[19] As Seely has argued, even Dutt's complex narrative structuring in *Meghnadavadha Kavya* can be read in terms of the tradition of his Sanskrit poetic predecessors, because its multi-semic narrative is in keeping with Sanskrit narrative tradition, particularly in the latter's deployment of euphonic assimilation to produce two or more stories in the same text.[20] Dutt's handling of the *Ramayana* exemplifies the defining feature of modern South Asian poetry, which is its reinscription of tradition even as it subverts it. Dusan Zbativel also refers to the epic poem of Hemchandra Bandyopadhyay (1838–1903)

---

[17] Zvelebil, *Smile of Murugan*, 312–32.
[18] Clinton Seely, 'The Raja's New Clothes: Redressing Ravana in *Meghnadavadha Kavya*', in Paula Richman (ed.), *Many Ramayanas: The Diversity of a Narrative Tradition in South Asia* (Berkeley, 1991), 137–55.
[19] Zbativel, *Bengali Literature*, 232–4.
[20] Seely, 'The Raja's New Clothes,' 142–3.

entitled *Brtrasamhar* ('The killing of Vrtra', 1875–7) in which Hemchandra freed his *payar* of rhyme but retained the rhythmic structure of traditional verse. Similarly, Tagore's verse drama *Chitrangada* (1891) deals with an episode from the *Mahabharata* but reworks it in original ways, and is written in free verse.[21]

Like poetry, prose narrations of modern South Asian literatures represent or are marked by a combination of continuity with and discontinuity from tradition. Here the question of realism as a 'Western' form in relation to South Asian literary traditions is crucial. Meenakshi Mukherjee in particular has drawn attention to the way in which the modern novel in South Asia is complicated by pre-novel narrative traditions, to the extent that many of them can be called 'narrative amalgams'. She draws attention to the continuing influence of works from the Puranic tradition,[22] oral narratives, and the *Ramayana* and *Mahabharata*, on the modern South Asian novel. This includes stylized set pieces in the early novel and the elaborate *nakha-sikha* depictions of the heroine's beauty in the Sanskrit *kavya* tradition.[23] The persistence of pre-novel narrative conventions are evident in Chandu Menon's *Indulekha* (1888), in spite of the novelist's conscious adoption of what he saw as the European mode of realism and his deliberate debunking of the mythic imagination.[24] The earlier novel *Sau anjan aur ek sujan* ('A hundred fools, and one wise man', 1892) by Balkrsna Bhatt is dependent on an earlier literary tradition, in this case the elaborate rhetorical devices of later medieval poetry. This includes the conventions of *barahmasa* descriptions (Bengali folk poetry describing human feelings in the perspective of changing seasons) in terms of the months of the year, or of *nakha-sikha*

---

[21] Zbativel, *Bengali Literature*, 235, 253. The term *payar* refers to a rhymed couplet of essentially narrative verses of equal length; see ibid. 123.

[22] The Puranas refer to a collection of sacred treatises, legendary in character, discussing the nature of the universe and the genealogy of the gods and patriarchs, amongst other topics. Theos Bernard, *Hindu Philosophy* (New York, 1947), 186.

[23] Meenakshi Mukherjee, *Realism and Reality: The Novel and Society in India* (Delhi, 1994), 9–10. *Kavya* is generally understood to refer to poetic or literary composition, as opposed to shastra which comprises texts that do not fall under the rubric of 'poetry' or 'literature', such as history, logic, scripture, philosophy, and science. A. K. Warder, *Indian Kavya Literature* (Delhi, 1972), 7 vols, vol. i, p. x, and Amaresh Datta (ed.), *Encyclopaedia of Indian Literature* (New Delhi, 1989), 6 vols, iii. 2038–9. *Nakha-sikha* refers to stylized depictions of feminine beauty, conveying a sense of overall grace as well as the beauty of individual limbs; see ibid. iii. 2850–3.

[24] Mukherjee, *Realism*, 15, 77–9, 84–5.

descriptions of the persons of heroines and heroes.[25] Similarly, the novel *Lilavati* (1901) by Kisori lal Gosvami (1865–1932) disclaims any ability to emulate Sanskrit poets in the description of the heroine's charms and then proceeds to give such a description in the manner of *srngara* (erotic or amorous) poetry of the eighteenth century.[26]

Another dimension to this narrative amalgam was the influence of the *dastan* or *qissa*[27] narrative of the Perso-Arabic tradition on realist prose fiction. Mukherjee has shown how the emergence of the historical novel in South Asia needs to be seen in terms of the combined impact of this tradition with the Sanskritic tradition of *itihasa*,[28] while Orsini has discussed early historical novels in Hindi in terms of their deployment of the narrative conventions of the *dastan* tradition.[29] McGregor has drawn attention to the multiple sources in the early development of the novel in Hindi as a whole, ranging from the prose tales and fables of Sanskrit sources to the *dastan* narratives of early Urdu literature, and translations of Bengali novels from the 1880s onwards.[30] The interplay between a literary modernity and literary tradition is clearly evident in the tensions between form and content in a number of *dastan* and *qissa* narratives which combine social realism and commentary with the marvellous mode of the romance narrative.[31] This is the case with the *Kissa moti ka per* ('The pearl tree') and *Kissa danav des* ('The land of the demons') in which there is an interpenetration of realistic and marvellous preoccupations.[32] This interpenetration is evident in the very character of Hatim in *Qissa-e Hatim Ta'i* who, while being an

---

[25] McGregor, *Hindi Literature*, 100. R. S. McGregor, 'The Rise of Standard Hindi, and Early Hindi Prose Fiction', in T. W. Clark (ed.), *The Novel in India: Its Birth and Development* (London, 1970), 153–4.

[26] McGregor, 'The Rise of Standard Hindi, and Early Hindi Fiction', in Clark (ed.), *The Novel in India*, 164.

[27] These terms refer to forms of orally recited prose romances, created and transmitted by professional narrators, which had its roots in Persian folk narratives. Frances W. Pritchett, *Marvellous Encounters: Folk Romance in Urdu and Hindi* (New Delhi, 1985), 1.

[28] Mukherjee, *Realism and Reality*, 40–2, 46. Itihasa refers to a genre of narrative which presents an account of the events of a remote past, and is generally equated with 'history'; Datta, *Encyclopaedia of Indian Literature*, ii. 1754–5.

[29] Orsini, *Hindi Public Sphere*, 211–12.

[30] McGregor, *Hindi Literature*, 98.

[31] The definitive work on the *qissa* and *dastan* narrative of the 19th and 20th centuries in South Asia is Frances W. Pritchett's *Marvellous Encounters: Folk Romance in Urdu and Hindi* (New Delhi, 1985).

[32] Ibid. 30–3.

archetypal *qissa* hero, also suffers from doubts, fears, and anxieties, and is capable of being petty.[33] The mixing of realist and romance modes is also at work in Ratan Nath Sarshar's *Fasana-i Azad*, which in terms of its form is in a direct line of descent from the *dastan* tradition, but its hero is a champion of modernism and social reform. Moreover, its temporal and geographical setting is contemporary, rather than an imaginary and marvellous time and place.[34] This combination of romance with realism also marks some of the novels of Bankim, particularly in the use of the figure of the holy man as a *deus ex machina*, and the introduction of the chance accident, especially in *Debichaudhurani*.[35] It is also a feature of the Tamil novels of R. Krishnamurti (1899–1954).[36] It is further evident in the combination of the plausible with the fantastical in the Hindi social romances of the 1920s and 1930s, which deployed the mode of the romance alongside social critique and used verisimilitude to provide the setting for extraordinary events.[37]

Critics such as McGregor and Clark have tended to see the instability in realist modes of modern South Asian fiction in terms of the authors' uncertain handling of an alien mode of writing.[38] While we need to continue to draw on their scholarship, we also need to reassess the problematical relationship between modern South Asian fiction and realism as a literary mode of writing. The tendency in the secondary literature as a whole is to measure the realism of South Asian fiction and the novel in particular, against a ready-made category of the realist novel as a Western form. This begs the question of what realism might be in the first case. There are a number of points which need to be made here. First, the European novel is continually changing in form, but more importantly, it is itself a hybrid literary genre, which participates in other genres, such as confessions, the philosophical tract, the diary, epistles and letters, and political manifestos.[39]

---

[33] Pritchett, *Marvellous Encounters*, 41–3, 50.

[34] Ralph Russell, 'The Development of the Modern Novel in Urdu', in Clark (ed.), *The Novel in India*, 110–11.

[35] T. W. Clark, 'Bengali Prose Fiction up to Bankimcandra', in Clark (ed.), *The Novel in India*, 71.

[36] Zvelebil, *Smile of Murugan*, 290–1.

[37] Orsini, *Hindi Public Sphere*, 287–9.

[38] McGregor, *Hindi Literature*, 100–1; Clark, 'Bengali Prose Fiction', in Clark (ed.), *The Novel in India*, 71–2.

[39] This point is emphasized by Mikhail Bakhtin, *The Dialogical Imagination: Four Essays by Mikhail Bakhtin*, ed. Michael Holquist (Austin, 1981), 33.

To measure (either explicitly or implicitly) the hybridity of the South Asian novel and fiction in general against the category of the European novel as though it were not itself a hybrid form is therefore a misplaced critical exercise. The hybridity of the South Asian novel and its narrative amalgamations need to be approached differently and assessed on other grounds. Secondly, if there is a defining feature of the novel, it is its malleability. As Bakhtin has emphasized, the novel has built in 'plastic possibilities', which is why as a genre it continues to develop, and is yet uncompleted, as opposed to the European epic, which is 'as closed as a circle, inside it everything is finished, already over'.[40] The novel has been and continues to be 'a genre-in-the-making', 'the most fluid of genres'.[41] The open-ended nature of the South Asian novel as a hybrid construct needs to be seen in terms of the novel's plastic possibilities as a form. The South Asian novel is also a genre-in-the-making, a work in progress, rather than a category that should be measured against the 'Western' novel as a completed and fully developed end point. To use Bakhtin's evocative words, 'the generic skeleton of the novel is still far from having hardened, and we cannot foresee all its plastic possibilities'.[42]

If we take these points into account, the aesthetic achievement of South Asian novels can be reassessed. For example, in the case of what is usually taken to be the first Hindi novel, *Pariksaguru* (1882),[43] rather than seeing the tensions between its didacticism and the 'realism' of the life of the protagonist as a mark of aesthetic failure, we can begin to view this in terms of a text whose aesthetic is that of a work in progress. Amrik Kalsi notes that Srinivasdas's handling of characterization changes as the novel progresses, so that he begins to find a via media between narrative, dialogue, and characterization as the text develops. But this might be less a sign of possible aesthetic failure,[44] and more an indication of how *Pariksaguru* exemplifies the nature of the novel as a genre-in-the-making. Such an approach could also be applied to the contradictory course the Hindi novel was to take in the early twentieth century,[45] and indeed to the development of the South

---

[40] Ibid. 3, 16.   [41] Ibid. 11.
[42] Bakhtin, *Dialogic Imagination*, 3.
[43] A. S. Kalsi, '*Pariksaguru* (1882): The First Hindi Novel and the Hindu Elite', *Modern Asian Studies*, 26/4 (1992), 763–90.
[44] Kalsi, 'Pariksaguru', 788, 790.
[45] For which, see ibid. 790.

Asian novel and fictional narrative in the nineteenth and twentieth centuries as a whole.

Moreover, modern South Asian writers clearly signal an awareness of how realism is an unstable literary artifice. The formulations of realism as a utopian aspiration in Menon's work, or as 'idealistic realism' in Premchand's work,[46] capture the paradoxical nature of realism as a literary mode. Realist texts are not unproblematic reflections of a given and non-verbal social reality, but are imaginative and fictive recreations of that reality. They sometimes strive to disguise their status as fictions in order to create the effects of naturalistic realism. As George Levine has stressed, inherent in any 'realist' effort is the struggle to avoid the inevitable conventionality of language in pursuit of the 'unattainable unmediated reality'. We get close to the texture of realism, if we recognize that narratives touched by the 'realist impulse try to resist or circumvent the formal conventions of realism'.[47] Realism is as much an ideal and aspiration for European writers as it is for Indian authors. While the realism of the South Asian novel and modern fictional narrative was generally in tensely productive relationships with the romance mode, this is also the case with the nineteenth-century English novel as a whole, given the place of what might be called the novel of domestic realism, such as *Middlemarch* (1871–2), alongside the novelistic romance of the adventure narrative, often set in the extra-European territories of colonial and imperial spaces, such as *Kim* (1901). The relationship between the two was best summed up by Andrew Lang in 1887, when he described nineteenth-century English fiction as 'a shield with two sides, the silver and the golden: the study of manners and of character, on one hand; on the other, the description of adventure, the delight of the romantic narrative'.[48] There were also some novels which had a dual form and multiple geographical locations. They combined domestic realism with the romance of the adventure narrative, the obvious example being Wilkie Collins's *The Moonstone* (1868). The implications of this for realism as a mode of writing in the nineteenth-century English novel have been explored

---

[46] These are Menon's and Premchand's own formulations of realism, as cited in Mukherjee, *Realism and Reality*, 80–1, 165, and app. 2.

[47] George Levine, 'The Realist Imagination', in Dennis Walder (ed.), *Approaching Literature: The Realist Novel* (London, 1995), 240.

[48] Cited by Patrick Brantlinger, *Rule of Darkness: British Literature and Imperialism, 1830–1914* (Ithaca, NY, 1988), 231.

in detail by critics.[49] The simultaneously disruptive and rejuvenating relationships between realism and romance were as much part of the history of the nineteenth-century English novel as they are of the modern novel in South Asia.

The uncertainty of realism in modern South Asian fiction, then, is a mark of aesthetic profundity rather than a deviation from some stable and pre-given aesthetic norm. We can develop Mukherjee's important point about the difficulties of reconciling the realist novel as an alien form to the intransigence of Indian social realities,[50] to suggest that realism, already an uncertain literary mode, is rendered doubly unstable by the additional tensions generated between its presuppositions about social reality and the category of the individual, and the very different nature of Indian societies. If realism has always been a self-conscious mode of writing,[51] then it is more so for South Asian writers, not only because of the general tension discussed by Mukherjee, but also because of the continuing presence and valency of a whole repertoire of pre-novel narrative conventions from the Sanskrit and Perso-Arabic literary traditions. It is this doubly self-conscious handling of realism which marks the South Asian novel and fictional narrative as experiments with realism in progress rather than deviations from an apparently stable aesthetic.

It is precisely the transgressions of realism which constitute the imaginative force of the South Asian novel and fictional narratives. In modern South Asian literatures, it is realism itself that is being measured, assessed, and relativized in relation to a whole range of pre-novel narrative conventions, both written and oral. This perspective also help us to understand the peculiarly disappointing effect which the staunch realism of some of the Progressive Writers' texts has on the reader. The Progressive Writers and the authors they have influenced strain not so much against realism as a mode of writing, but against transgressing that mode. The overt didacticism of some of their texts is an indication of their attempt to rein in their transgressive instincts. They attempt the impossible task of converting realism as a self-conscious mode of writing into an unselfconscious mode

---

[49] Ibid. 12–14, 36, 231; Martin Green, *Dreams of Adventure, Deeds of Empire* (London, 1980), 58, 341; and Robert Fraser, *Victorian Quest Romance: Stevenson, Haggard, Kipling, and Conan Doyle* (Plymouth, 1998), 11–14.
[50] Mukherjee, *Realism and Reality*, p. vii.
[51] Levine, 'The Realistic Imagination', 241.

of representing social reality.[52] In this attempt, their texts sometimes read not just as fables at odds with their realist aims,[53] but almost as parodies of realism.

There is another way in which the critical ground needs to be shifted regarding our general approach to modern South Asian literatures. There is a tendency among critics to stress the nature of the difficulties faced by Indian writers in adapting modern or Western literary forms to Indian conditions.[54] But the difficulties faced by modern South Asian writers are less those of constrictions imposed on them by working with what was initially an alien form, and more those of managing expansiveness. The technical problem they face is that of negotiating an expansive range of material and literary traditions. In Faiz's poem, the subject matter is not how constricted the poet is, but how he is faced with a choice. It is the burdensome nature of that choice which he contemplates, rather than the imposition of any constrictions. This choice reflects the cosmopolitan nature of modern South Asian literatures, which in their genesis and development reflect the freedom of Indian authors to move across and appropriate the resources and conventions of a variety of literary traditions.

The cosmopolitan eclecticism of modern South Asian literatures is evident in the case of Iqbal's *Javed Nama*. The poet draws upon Rumi's *Masnavi* as a model, as well as Dante's *Divine Comedy* and Milton's *Paradise Lost*.[55] The fifth-century Sanskrit poet Bhartrihari,[56] who was renowned for his epigrams, appears in the highest region of the cosmos which is represented in the poem. Dalmia has shown how the models for early Hindi

---

[52] For example, I am thinking here of Premchand's 'Kafan', in *Tera Urdu afsane*, ed. Athar Pervez (Aligarh, 1987), 17–26 and Mazhar ul Islam's 'Sargosiyon ki ot men baitha khakrob' ('The sweeper sitting in the whispers' shadow'), in *Guriya ki ankh se shehr ko dekho* ('See the city through the doll's eye') (Lahore, 1988), 102–12. The conflict between an attempted unselfconscious realism and romance writing is evident in the short stories of Krishan Chander, for example in 'Mahalakshmi ka pul' ('Mahalakshmi's bridge') in *Tera Urdu afsane*, 27–46, and his story of the sweeper 'Kalu Bhangi', trans. Jai Ratan in *Krishan Chander: Selected Urdu Short Stories* (New Delhi, 1990), 19–33.

[53] For an excellent analysis of how the social realism of some Progressive Writers' texts slides into fable, see Mukherjee, *Realism and Reality*, 145–9, 151–2, 154.

[54] Ibid. p. vii. Also McGregor, *Hindi Literature*, 98–101.

[55] Annemarie Schimmel, *Gabriel's Wing: A Study into the Religious Ideas of Sir Muhammad Iqbal* (Leiden, 1963), 52–3.

[56] Although this date is not beyond dispute, B. S. Miller argues that this is the most likely. See B. S. Miller, *Bhartri and Bilhana: The Hermit and the Love-Thief* (1978; New Delhi, 1990), 3.

drama ranged from Kalidasa to Shakespeare,[57] while Vidyasagar adapted both Kalidasa's *Shakuntala* (1854) and Shakespeare's *Comedy of Errors* (*Bhrantibilas*, 1869).[58] Similarly, *Fasana-e Azad* was a reworking of the *dastan* narrative alongside a complex engagement with *Don Quixote*,[59] while Sarshar's later book, *Khudai Faujdar*, is a free adaptation of *Don Quixote*.[60] The Tamil novelist Natesa Sastri (1859–1906) also adapted some English texts in his own works (see his *Tailaiyanai mantiropatecam*, 1903, based on Douglas Jerrold's *Mrs Caudle's Curtain Lectures*)[61] while L. S. Ramamirthan's novel *Putra* has been called a tongue-in-cheek experiment which draws upon both Italian models and the English metaphysical poets.[62] This cosmopolitanism is also evident in some key works of Bengali literature, for example in the work of Madhusudan, with its reworkings of the *Ramayana* and the *Mahabharata*, as well as his elaboration of a Greek myth in 'an Indian garb' in *Padmavati* (1860).[63] The poet Satyendranath Datta (1882–1922) experimented with metrical forms and diction alongside translations of European and Asian poems, while the work of the poets Buddhadeb Basu (1908–74) and Bisnu Dey (1909–82) also involves a complex engagement with world literature.[64] This cosmopolitan eclecticism is also enacted on the level of metrical form. The members of the 'modern school' of Sindhi poetry, in addition to reviving traditional Sindhi forms of verse, also created new ones, some of which were modelled on European forms, such as free verse and the sonnet.[65] This cosmopolitan mixing of forms and subject matters is in some ways an extension of the hybrid formations of other literary texts, which drew upon both the Persian and Sanskritic traditions. The poet Harivamsray Bachchan's *Madhusala* (1935) combined *ghazal* imagery with 'an easy diction' in Khari Boli utilizing the form of the *ruba'i* (or quatrains).[66]

---

[57] Dalmia, *Nationalization of Hindu Traditions*, 300–1; see pp. 300–14 for her analysis of Hindi drama. Also McGregor, *Hindi Literature*, 77–9, 97.

[58] Clark, 'Bengali Prose Fiction', 33.

[59] Ralph Russell, 'The Modern Novel in Urdu', in Clark (ed.), *The Novel in India*, 111–12.

[60] Ibid. 111.

[61] R. E. Asher, 'The Tamil Renaissance', in Clark (ed.), *The Novel in India*, 200–1.

[62] Zvelebil, *Smile of Murugan*, 309–10.

[63] Zabavitel, *Bengali Literature*, 232–4.

[64] Ibid. 288–90.

[65] Ali S. Asani, 'At the Crossroads of Indic and Iranian Civilizations: Sindhi Literary Culture', in Sheldon Pollock (ed.), *Literary Cultures in History*, 629.

[66] Orsini, *Hindi Public Sphere*, 88.

The range of conventions and poetic systems, both indigenous and European, which are available to South Asian writers underpins the imaginative experimentation of modern South Asian literatures. The variety of models appropriated by writers for their own creative purposes are starting points for departure and experimentation, rather than simply sites of emulation. In many cases, as Mukherjee has stressed, these ostensible models are quickly surpassed, as in the case of *Indulekha*, which begins as an adaptation of Disraeli's *Henrietta Temple*, but soon moves beyond it. This is also the case with the relationship between Bankim's *Rajani* and Bulwer Lytton and Wilkie Collins.[67] It is almost as though the invocation of these models becomes a legitimizing pretext for these authors' own creative experiments in the colonial period, especially if we are to accept that in these cases what was being staged were the very instabilities of realism as a 'Western' mode. In this sense, the choice of such English models which can be very quickly emulated, described by Mukherjee as a 'strange irony,'[68] perhaps becomes less strange and more understandable.

The cosmopolitan eclecticism of modern South Asian writers is also apparent in two important works of twentieth-century South Asian thought, Muhammad Iqbal's *The Reconstruction of Religious Thought in Islam* (1934) and Vasudeva J. Kirtikar's *Studies in Vedanta* (1924). What is striking about both works is their style of argumentation, in which they discuss their respective philosophical traditions in relation to modern European thought. In Kirtikar's *Studies in Vedanta* (1924), there is a wide range of references to European philosophers, both ancient and modern, and to the texts and commentaries of the Vedanta tradition.[69] This comparative approach underpins the complexity of his argument. He begins with Hegelian critics of the Vedanta, remarking that their criticisms are surprising because in fact both systems have much in common.[70] He then seeks to rebut these critics by reconciling their Hegelianism with the Vedanta, and in doing so, illuminates both, bringing out more profoundly their

---

[67] Mukherjee, *Realism and Reality*, 77–8.
[68] Ibid.
[69] *Vedanta*, literally 'the end of the Vedas' or the last consideration of the Vedas, refers to interpretations of the system of thought and philosophical teachings of the Upanishads concerning the nature of and relationship between ultimate reality, the world, and the soul. See Bernard, *Hindu Philosophy*, 116–28.
[70] Vasudeva J. Kirtikar, *Studies in Vedanta* (Bombay, 1924), 7–8.

respective distinctive characters. Kirtikar identifies the key problem here as the Hegelian objection that the notion of Absolute reality in the Vedanta is an empty abstraction.[71] He first cites Hegel to delineate what an empty abstraction is, then he considers Hegel's own notion of an ultimate reality, and finally he shows how this notion is already present in the Vedanta.[72] In doing so, he also challenges Hegel's explicit criticisms of the Indian conception of Brahma,[73] so that he deftly uses Hegelian thought against Hegel to vindicate the Vedanta system and counter Hegel's misconceptions of ancient Indian philosophy.[74] The complexities of Kirtikar's comparativism are especially evident when parallels are drawn between Hegelian criticisms of the notion of Brahma, and the criticisms by other European thinkers of Kant and Herbert Spencer when their work first appeared.[75] Critical battles within the European tradition are seen as parallels to the philosophical struggles between European and Indian traditions. The uncomprehending reception of ancient Indian philosophy when it first appeared in Europe is likened to the equally uncomprehending reception of such original thinkers as Kant and Spencer by their own contemporaries. Kirtikar's argument culminates in the point that if the '*Brahma* of the Indian *Vedanta* is a false and empty abstraction, the idea of the Absolute Being in the Hegelian system would be no less so'.[76] For Kirtikar, Hegelianism and the Vedanta either stand together or fall together.

Iqbal's *The Reconstruction of Religious Thought in Islam* (1934), like Kirtikar's text, marshals an impressive array of references to thinkers from both his own intellectual tradition and that of Europe. This includes drawing specific comparisons between thinkers.[77] The aim is to reconcile and validate earlier Islamic thought with modern European thought and science,

---

[71] Ibid. 8.   [72] Ibid. 8–10.

[73] In this philosophical context, Brahma refers to an ultimate principle or an ultimate reality, beyond the play of appearances.

[74] Ibid. 13, and esp. 15 where he cites Hegel's comments on the notion of Brahma, and then shows how in 'the language of Hegelianism', the notion of *Maya* takes away from it 'the character of an empty abstraction'.

[75] Ibid. 14.

[76] Ibid. 27.

[77] For example, he draws comparisons between Ghazali and Kant, Ibn Khaldun and William James, and Ibn Khaldun and Henri Bergson. In the context of discussing responses to Zeno's arguments on the unreality of motion, he refers to al-Ash'ari, Ibn Hazm, Henri Bergson, and Bertrand Russell. See Muhammad Iqbal, *The Reconstruction of Religious Thought in Islam* (1934; Lahore: Institute of Islamic Culture, 1986), 4, 14, 113, 29.

and as such, the work moves fluently between intellectual traditions as it seeks to answer the question which forms the title of the last chapter, 'Is religion possible?'. The cosmopolitan eclecticism of the text underpins the search for the grounds of religion as a whole, rather than of Islam alone, although there is often a slippage between the two.[78] Specifically, Iqbal tries to show how the intellectual revolt against Greek thought by Muslim thinkers, and especially against the speculative nature of Aristotelian logic, paved the way for the experimental and empirical attitudes which underlay the development of modern science.[79] While there are clearly differences between Kirtikar's and Iqbal's texts, Kirtikar's lucid exposition of his aims serves just as well for both texts. He wants to show how well developed and sophisticated his own chosen intellectual tradition is, so as to correct the misconceived ideas European intellectuals have of it. He also wants to ensure that it receives its 'due share of appreciation' from them. His intention is to expound the Vedanta in 'a language familiar to modern European thought', and to show how far 'it finds confirmation in parallel currents of Western thought—ancient and modern—and likewise in the discoveries of modern science'.[80] Both Kirtikar and Iqbal are anxious to legitimize their intellectual traditions through modern European thought, and in part they do so by (to quote Kirtikar again) trying to 'read modern thoughts into archaic writings'.[81] The logic of their argument can be read in other ways too. By stressing that their intellectual traditions prefigure modern European thought, they are undercutting the supposedly unprecedented nature of that thought and its originality. The subtext of their works articulates an alternative intellectual history in which ancient Indian and Islamic thought become enabling reference points for understanding modern European intellectual endeavour. This is underpinned by an intellectual cosmopolitanism which takes for granted that different philosophical traditions can be compared and related to each other, and moreover that these traditions are open to perusal and appropriation by those who are not originally located in them. At the same time, this leads to an irreconcilable tension, even an impasse, in their works, because they radically relativize

---

[78] See Iqbal, *The Reconstruction of Religious Thought in Islam*, pp. xxi–xxii, 2, 6, 78.
[79] Ibid. 102–3.
[80] Kirtikar, *Studies in Vedanta*, 1.
[81] Ibid. 10.

philosophical traditions as a means to valorize and elevate one tradition alone. There is a contradiction between the means and the conclusions of their argument. It is also clear that their cosmopolitan eclecticism exceeds the strict demands of their argument. Rather than a means to an end, it becomes an end in itself, displaying the burdensome plenitude of choice and hermeneutic freedom open to the South Asian thinker for whom a variety of intellectual and literary traditions are available for selective appropriation.[82]

I have argued that modern South Asian literary texts need to be seen as works in progress, rather than finished products. The notion of a text as a creative process rather than a finished product is deeply embedded in Indian literary traditions, and to a certain extent, reflects what Ong has referred to in another context as 'the resilience of oral forms in a society where literacy is highly valued'.[83] Scholars who have studied Indian oral and performative traditions have shown how these involve distinctive notions of authorship and originality. Essays in the collection edited by Paula Richman have analysed the plurality of the *Ramayan* narrative tradition in its various tellings and performances, both in Sanskrit and in a variety of other South Asian languages.[84] The essays as a whole stress that the *Ramayana* is less an ur-text in relation to which all other tellings can be located, and more a set of resources for narrators and performers to draw upon. Similarly, in his study of Tulsidas's *Ramcharitmanas* and its enactment in different kinds of performance, Lutgendorf shows how this epic poem is framed through narratives which provide cues for performance.[85] He argues that performance is constitutive of the text itself, so that the text has an emergent quality. The text is a means rather than an end, a blueprint rather than a finished artefact.[86]

Moreover, a salient feature of South Asian literary traditions is the way printed and oral forms of literature coexist in a variety of ways. In the development of modern South Asian print culture, sometimes this relation-

---

[82] For a discussion of cosmopolitanism in South Asia, see Kris Manjapra and Sugata Bose (eds), *Cosmopolitan Thought Zones: South Asia and the Global Circulation of Ideas* (Basingstoke, 2010).

[83] Arjun Appaduria, Frank J. Korom, and Margeret A. Mills (eds), *Gender, Genre, and Power in South Asian Expressive Traditions* (Philadelphia, 1991), 3.

[84] Paula Richman (ed.), *Many Ramayanas: The Diversity of a Narrative Tradition in South Asia* (Berkeley, 1991).

[85] Philip Lutgendorf, *The Life of a Text: Performing the Ramcaritmanas of Tulsidas* (Delhi, 1994), 18–29.

[86] Ibid. 36.

ship is a tense one, as in the case of the formation of the Tamil novel. According to one scholar, while between 1879 and 1900 about a dozen Tamil novels were published, this did not produce the sensational effects of a print revolution, in part because of the misapplication of the technique of oral storytelling to print technology.[87] In the case of modern Tamil literature, rather than dislodging orality as the primary medium of storytelling, printed stories introduced a new public dimension to oral narration.[88] The interaction between printed text and oral narrative has also been analysed by Frances Pritchett, who shows how the modern printed *qissa* overlaps with oral narrative. This extends to the physical nature of these printed texts which are as ephemeral as individual oral performances. The text of each story is also subject to modification in successive reprintings, so that the printed *qissa* represents the continuation of oral narrative traditions in a newly available mode.[89] In South Asia, then, there are many possibilities for the interaction between print culture and oral storytelling, from the 'misapplication' of oral storytelling in the printed novel, to the emulation of oral storytelling in some of the printed versions of the *qissa*. This spectrum includes taking into account how institutions such as the press, publishers, literary associations, and the education system, helped to reshape the production, transmission, and consumption of literature, without displacing orality, but rather investing it with new meanings and significances.[90] Ong wrote of the 'electronic age' of the television, radio, and telephone as an age of 'secondary orality', which depends on writing and print for its existence.[91] The transition of some Indian genres from a pre-modern oral and performative literary tradition to the milieu of a secondary orality is evident in the case of the *ghazal*, which has made a transition from its original courtly milieu to the cassette and film song in north India.[92] Moreover, the milieu of orality is often reinscribed in the novelistic worlds

---

[87] Stuart Blackburn, 'The Tale of the Book: Story Telling and Print in Nineteenth-Century Tamil', in Rachel Dwyer and Christopher Pinney (eds), *Pleasure and the Nation: The History, Politics and Consumption of Public Culture in India* (Delhi, 2001), 115–37, at 130.

[88] Ibid. 132.

[89] Pritchett, *Marvelous Encounters*, ch. 8.

[90] Orsini, *Hindi Public Sphere*, 31–2, 51–2, 57.

[91] Ong, *Orality and Literacy*, 3.

[92] But not without some aesthetic cost. Peter Manuel, 'The Popularization and Transformation of the Light-Classical Urdu *Ghazal*-Song', in Arjun Appadurai et al., *Gender, Genre, and Power*, 347–61. See also David Llelyveld, 'Eloquence and Authority in Urdu: Poetry, Oratory, Film', in K. P. Ewing (ed.), *Shari'at and Ambiguity in South Asian Islam* (Berkeley, 1981), 98–113.

of the modern novel, with a number of authors drawing upon conventions of oral narration in their texts.[93] In the case of Rusva's *Umrao Jan Ada* (1899), the translation of orality into the printed form of the novel constitutes the latter's very genesis as well as its subject matter, given that it centres on the transcription of the voice of a courtesan who was the embodiment of the performative and courtly provenance of a specific literary tradition. Seen from this perspective, we might interpret *Umrao Jan Ada* in general terms as consciously enacting its interplay with a performative literary tradition, and transcribing that form into print as its own genesis. This simultaneous appropriation, interplay, transcription, and even competition, is resonant of the wide range of possibilities open to the modern South Asian author in terms of the interaction between orality and performance and printed text.

Conclusion

In modern South Asian literatures, then, the self-conscious enactment of a break from literary tradition simultaneously opens up new lines of continuity. The category of 'literary tradition' becomes a site of experimentation and innovation, a point of departure, and a set of resources. T. S. Eliot's formulation of literary tradition in his 'Tradition and the Individual Talent', of the 'existing monuments' of art forming 'an ideal order among themselves, which is modified by the introduction of the new... work of art among them', is useful as a point of contrast here. Eliot's contention that after the arrival of the new work of art, the 'whole existing order must be, if ever so slightly, altered; and so the relations, proportions, values of each work of art toward the whole are readjusted; and this is conformity between the old and the new',[94] would not be wholly applicable to the interplay between literary modernity and literary tradition in South Asia. Here tradition is not seen in terms of readjustments which secure the conformity between the old and the new, so that the 'new' is somehow reabsorbed into the literary system of tradition. Rather, the paradox of literary modernity in South Asia is that its genuine innovations consist in ruptures from tradition which require that tradition to be kept in play so that the 'newness' of literary modernity can be displayed.

---

[93] Mukherjee, *Realism and Reality*, 79, 128, 132.

[94] T. S. Eliot, 'Tradition and the Individual Talent', in *The Sacred Wood: Essays on Poetry and Criticism* (1920; London, 1997), 39–49, 41.

While drawing on the scholarship of scholars of South Asian literature, I have tried to shift the critical ground in a number of ways by suggesting perspectives to open up the creative horizons of modern South Asian literatures. In particular, these horizons were much wider than simply responding to, in however a sophisticated way, colonialism and the colonial state. It is important not to read back into the formation of modern South Asian literatures a postcolonial teleology which sees colonialism and the colonial state as omnipotent. This ultimately becomes a disguised celebration of European colonialism itself, as the only possible reference point for South Asian authors and thinkers. If anything, the colonial predicament was one starting point for literary experimentation, and only one reference point amongst many for South Asian writers. In the colonial period modern South Asian writers had a set of creative choices which were often reflected in the cosmopolitan eclecticism of their works. This essay has tried to draw attention to these choices and the aesthetic profundity of modern South Asian literature as a whole, by suggesting how modern South Asian texts might be more fruitfully approached as works in progress in their own right, rather than as attenuated versions of ready-made European literary and aesthetic categories, engaging with European colonialism as their only possible referent.

Select Bibliography

ARJUN APPADURI, FRANK KOROM, and MARGARET MILLS (eds), *Gender, Genre, and Power in South Asian Expressive Traditions* (Philadelphia, 1991).

PAUL BRASS, *Language, Religion and Politics in India* (London, 1974).

T. W. CLARK (ed.), *The Novel in India: Its Birth and Development* (London, 1970).

VASUDHA DALMIA, *The Nationalization of Hindu Traditions: Bharatendu Harischandra and Nineteenth-Century Banaras* (Delhi, 1997).

A. S. KALSI, '*Pariksaguru* (1882): The First Hindi Novel and the Hindu Elite', *Modern Asian Studies*, 26/4 (1992).

PHILIP LUTGENDORF, *The Life of a Text: Performing the Ramcaritmanas of Tulsidas* (Delhi, 1994).

R. S. MCGREGOR, *Hindi Literature of the Nineteenth and Early Twentieth Centuries* (Wiesbaden, 1974).

JAVED MAJEED, *Muhammad Iqbal: Islam, Aesthetics, and Postcolonialism* (New Delhi, 2009).

KRIS MANJAPRA and SUGATA BOSE (eds), *Cosmopolitan Thought Zones: South Asia and the Global Circulation of Ideas* (Basingstoke, 2010).

MEENAKSHI MUKHERJEE, *Realism and Reality: The Novel and Society in India* (Delhi, 1994).

FRANCESCA ORSINI, *The Hindi Public Sphere 1920–1940: Language and Literature in the Age of Nationalism* (Delhi, 2002).

SHELDON POLLOCK (ed.), *Literary Cultures in History: Reconstructions from South Asia* (Berkeley, 2003).

FRANCES W. PRITCHETT, *Marvellous Encounters: Folk Romance in Urdu and Hindi* (New Delhi, 1985).

——*Nets of Awareness: Urdu Poetry and Its Critics* (Berkeley, 1994).

PAULA RICHMAN (ed.), *Many Ramayanas: The Diversity of a Narrative Tradition in South Asia* (Berkeley, 1991).

DUSAN ZBATIVEL, *Bengali Literature* (Wiesbaden, 1976).

KAMIL ZVELEBIL, KAMIL, *The Smile of Murugan: On Tamil Literature of South India* (Leiden, 1973).

12

Gendering of Public and Private Selves in Colonial Times

Tanika Sarkar

Colonial modernity was marked by a ceaseless constitution and reconstitution of individual subjectivities and collective identities. New social groups like factory workers or owners emerged, while older social categories like peasants, artisans, and landlords experienced sweeping changes in their modes of being and work. Paradoxically, much of the older ways of working and thinking often inflected what seemed to be very new. Modernity in India, thus, was a complex interweaving of past and present compulsions, often jostling together within the same person or group. I would argue that changes were wrought very substantially by what Indians did and thought: by how they related to one another and to the state. They did so, however, under great constraints: those imposed by the state as well as by their own conflicting needs and interests, their pasts. Much of the experience of change was captured in the arguments and conversations that Indians carried on among themselves in the new public sphere created by novel modes of communication: print, newspapers, vernacular prose writings, tracts and pamphlets, public theatre and novels, and, later on, the cinema and the radio. Vastly enhanced communication and transport resources brought local, national, and global identities into interaction. They also allowed for a questioning of the fundamental premises of the ideologies of gender difference, both past and present.

First, though, a few words on dominant frameworks for looking at the constitution of modern Indian selves. Postcolonial historiography has shifted the understanding of problems of modernity onto the terrain of cultural colonization, away from the Marxian accent on class or on the political economy of imperialism. Colonial power-knowledge, so the thinking goes, has constructed an inflexible iron cage of attributed selves for the colonized, from which an escape is possible only through covert, over-the-shoulder glances at pre-colonial and pre-modern habits. Some, like Ronald Inden, would contest even this possibility. In his understanding, colonialism achieved an epistemic break, after which no recuperation of self knowledge was possible.[1] Partha Chatterjee has similarly argued for entirely derivative and mimic knowledge forms even in the politics of resistance to colonialism, since nationalism itself is a Western construct.[2]

Other kinds of readings of colonialism and postcolonialism would offer, instead, a far more vibrant sense of self-making. In their different ways, nationalist, Leftist, and the early Subaltern Studies school shared a strong perspective on the contestatory agency of poor people. A recent crop of studies of Indian labour has recuperated the sense of agency and selfhood in more complex and nuanced ways.[3] Sumit Sarkar shifts the gaze back to different categories of Indians, whose mutual interactions, he thinks, should be traced more attentively than an exclusive emphasis on the colonizer/colonized binary.[4] Despite the reinterpretation of the colonial encounter offered by postcolonial scholars, they continue to harbour fixed and closed notions of the colonizer and the colonized. Homi Bhabha, for instance, stays with a situation where both colonizer and colonized—both conceived of in the singular—look at each other. He, however, constructs the gazing in supple ways: not simply as an effect of power that flows from the colonizer, but as the power-laden look of the colonizer that the colonized absorbs and sends back. The return of the gaze is disconcerting and not fully controlled.[5]

A formidable slice of postcolonial feminist thinking subscribes to the notion of an emulative and doubly oppressive modernity. The paradigmatic collection of essays, *Recasting Women: Essays in Colonial History*, was the first feminist effort to configure a single conceptual framework for colonial

---

[1] Ronald Inden, *Imagining India* (Oxford, 1990).

[2] Partha Chatterjee, *Nationalist Thought and the Colonial World: A Derivative Discourse?* (London, 1986).

[3] Among others, Chitra Joshi, *Lost Worlds: Indian Labour and Its Forgotten Histories* (Delhi, 2003).

[4] Sumit Sarkar, *Beyond Nationalist Frames: Relocating Postmodernism, Hindutva, History,* (Delhi, 2002).

[5] Homi Bhabha, 'Dissemination: Time, Narrative and the Margins of the Modern Nation', in Bhabha (ed.), *Nation and Narration* (London, 1990).

history under which all significant developments in gender relations could be enfolded.[6] The unifying assumption was that the installation of capitalism in India through colonial agency resulted in the dissemination of notions of Victorian gentility and domesticity among the modern Indian middle classes who realigned their patriarchal norms to Western bourgeois forms of gender relations. In this reading, Indian women came under what I would designate as double negative teleology: while patriarchy was refurbished, it simultaneously became de-indigenized and alien. Historians of Indian political economy, however, do not see that kind of wholesale transition to capitalism. Domestic and gender changes, therefore, were highly mediated, opaque socio-cognitive processes. The Indian middle classes did not throw up only an attachment to new, Western ways of domesticity. The identical social group also produced the orthodoxy, tenaciously defending tradition. Nor were middle-class reformers merely emulating Victorian standards. In contrast, the volume assumes—quite problematically—that modern times witnessed a mere reordering of the discipline of patriarchy, now more under Western inspiration. Obviously, patriarchy as a broad framework of relations was not overthrown. By restricting some of the economic options for poor women, colonialism certainly worsened the state of female dependency. At the same time, patriarchy was named as a structure of oppression and injustice, and multiple sites of interrogation and resistance were evolved. Women, moreover, appeared in the new public sphere as radical critics of orthodox norms and practices. By the turn of the twentieth century, they had organized themselves into political organizations, soon to be deeply involved in issues of education, health, franchise, marriage reform, nationalism, and Left movements. A sense of their political agency—perhaps, one of the most significant signs of modern times—does not indent the framework of the volume. If we need to explain Indian feminism as a modern Indian phenomenon, and not simply as a foreign implant, then the relationship between gender and modernity requires a far more complex framework of understanding.

Gender and Political Action

We must identify a social location for the subject of feminism within the processes of modernity, and also locate new social imaginaries about

---

[6] Kumkum Sangari (ed.), *Recasting Women: Essays in Colonial History* (Delhi, 1989).

masculinities. Colonial rulers stereotyped Indian men as inherently conservative and often effeminate, except for the designated martial races, like the Sikhs of Punjab.[7] This view had points of rupture as well as points of collaboration with Indian patriarchal designs. Some of the new Indian gender imaginaries were thought out within parameters of modern politics. Gandhi's vision of gentle, patiently constructive, non-violent, self-abnegating, practically androgynous manhood can be juxtaposed against the masculinity of revolutionary terrorists, dedicated to violence and self-destruction in equal measure, to non-introspective, action-oriented passion, and to the cult of fury and death. Revolutionaries equated maleness with youth alone, holding no imaginative reserves for a masculine self that was younger or older than that required for the violent act or for modes of being that lay beyond it. At the same time, the opposition between Gandhians and revolutionaries would be somewhat mitigated by the unified commitment to an ideal outside the narrow confines of the self. Self-abnegation and self-destruction shared certain common features. For both, a renunciation of erotic desire was a necessity, even though, for both, that which was extinguished would be recuperated at a different level: for Gandhi, in unremitting struggles against sexuality that denoted presence rather than absence, and for revolutionaries, in a displacement of sexual desire for women onto a passionate love for a feminized and deified Motherland. For revolutionaries, too, the abdication of marriage and domesticity, and the formation of strong and emotional male bonding denoted an anxiety about heterosexuality. Moreover, the notion of highly controlled and disciplined non-libertarian selves was shared by both visions of masculinity. This ideal was strongly opposed by Rabindranath Tagore's preference for individuated selves: fuller and fulfilled selves elevated by sacrifice rather than selves attenuated by political commitment. At the same time, with some exceptions, Rabindranath's writings acknowledged a moral, emotional, and aesthetic autonomy for womens' lives but they also accepted a gendered division of private and public spheres.[8]

In nationalist political practice, the deployment of women was multiple and conflicted, a deployment whose terms were increasingly set by women themselves. For late nineteenth-century Hindu revivalist-nationalists, the

---

[7] Mrinalini Sinha, *Colonial Masculinity: The 'Manly Englishman' and the 'Effeminate Bengali' in the Late Nineteenth Century Bengal* (Manchester, 1995).

[8] Pradip Datta (ed.), *The Home and the World: Critical Notes* (Delhi, 2003).

Motherland was imagined as a Mother Goddess. Hindu female chastity and the woman's fidelity to strict Hindu domestic discipline were configured as traces of a past freedom and the resource for a future nationhood, untainted by foreign ways and hence unvanquished. The woman thus figured as the passive icon of the desired nation. In contrast, during the first anti-colonial popular movements against the partition of Bengal between 1905 and 1908, women were encouraged to become more actively involved, boycotting British goods, buying indigenous Swadeshi products for domestic use, and in some cases sheltering revolutionary terrorists. Gandhi expanded anti-colonial agitations into formidable movements of peasants, tribal, and middle-class people in the early twenties. He at first hesitated to call women into active forms of agitation. Women, however, poured into them from all social ranks, forcing open the entire spectrum of Congress organizations. Sometimes, open and active female defiance was powered by a strategic use of traditional kinship practice and affect. The mother of two Khilafatist leaders in 1921, a woman coming from an orthodox Muslim family, began to address large crowds of Muslims protesting British dethronement of the Turkish Caliphate after the War. This revolutionary abjuration of the principle of female seclusion was managed by the fact that she at first spoke from behind the veil and addressed the crowds as her children. There came a time, however, when she unveiled her face in public, since all were her sons.[9]

By the time of the Civil Disobedience movement of 1930–4, peasant women had emerged as 'dictators' of local organizations and movements, they courted arrest and led demonstrations, they faced police terror and made contraband salt. During the Quit India struggle of 1942, women led the underground networks in different places. Most of these struggles did not pause to develop a gender ideology that would fit the dimensions of the new political woman. Gandhi and many other nationalist leaders clung to the image of the self-sacrificing, self-abnegating mother, nurturing and modest. At the same time, the very inundation of the movement by women activists distinctly altered womens' actual location within the family, opening up new possibilities and problems in domestic relationships, just as they had to forge an altogether new range of gender interactions with their male comrades. Autobiographies of such women talk of unprecedented

---

[9] Gail Minault (ed.), *The Extended Family: Women and Political Participation in India and Pakistan*, introd. (Delhi, 1981).

relationships, predicaments, and exhilaration. The wife of a senior Bengali bureaucrat, for instance, followed Gandhi into Noakhali in Bengal in 1946, a district then devastated by Hindu Muslim violence. She left her children behind and they were brought up by their father, while she lived for nearly a year in a remote village with her baby daughter to organize relief and rehabilitation for victims of rape. Her political choice abruptly tore her out of her own social and familial matrix. It also created a new familial role for her husband in a way that could not have been imaginable earlier.[10]

By casting nationalist masculinity as in some ways androgynous—non-retaliatory and non-violent, covertly undoing oppression through defiance of unjust laws rather than through attacks, as women sometimes tend to do within their homes—Gandhi's ideology attempted to transcend the gulf between gender norms. By insisting that men do what women often do at homes—cleaning, spinning, healing—he also sought to bridge the gap between gender practices. At the same time, by applauding feminine qualities as the hallmark for the ideal patriot, in a paradoxical way he doubled the force of conventional feminine norms and values: self-sacrifice, submission, and self-denial.[11]

Other Congress leaders like Jawaharlal Nehru and Subhas Chandra Bose were committed to a more extended, explicit, and activist notion of the political woman. They invited women to form their own organizations and volunteer corps within the Congress; they were enthusiastic about female franchise in independent India; and they forcefully questioned domestic constraints. When he constituted the Azad Hind Fauj, an army of prisoners of war under Japanese occupation in 1941, Bose encouraged the formation of an all women's militia.[12] Certain groups of revolutionary terrorists in Bengal began to admit women into their ranks from 1930: they participated in violent raids on the British armoury at Chittagong and they also took part in assassination attempts against colonial officials.[13]

Women's organizations, functioning in large cities with recruits from rich, educated women from all religious communities, were divided about their choice: whether to utilize colonial enquiry commissions into the

---

[10] Ashoka Gupta, *In the Path of Service: Memories of a Changing Century* (Calcutta, 2005).

[11] Tanika Sarkar, 'Political Women', in Bharati Ray (ed.), *Women of India: Colonial and Post Colonial Periods* (Delhi 2005).

[12] Geraldine Forbes, 'Mothers and Sisters: Feminism and Nationalism in the Thought of Subhas Chandra Bose', *Asian Studies*, 2 (1984), 23–32.

[13] Manini Chatterjee, *Do and Die; The Chittagong Uprising, 1930–1934* (Delhi, 1999).

franchise and cooperate with new constitutional openings in provincial legislatures, or to throw themselves into anti-colonial mass movements, shelving issues of female franchise for the moment to wait for independence and the Congress promise of universal adult franchise. Their participation in the Congress agitations brought them into closer touch with poor 'low caste' women on more equal terms than was possible in their own rather elitist women's organizations. It also introduced another major dilemma. As the Congress and the Muslim League drew apart, involvement in Congress movements meant a separation from Muslim women colleagues, whose presence had been a remarkable feature of their otherwise socially elitist and politically non-confrontational organizations.[14]

By and large, the Congress avoided involvement with struggles of peasants and workers on issues of class power, even though it had extremely large worker and peasant contingents. From the 1920s, Leftist and Communistic political groups—very often banned and severely repressed by the state—filled up this space, cooperating with or leading rural and working class movements. Women workers would often adopt confrontational tactics during working-class strikes in Bombay, Calcutta, and Kanpur: attacking the police and shaming blacklegs who broke strikes. But their needs and demands were rarely a prominent part of the workers' charter of demands. Nor were they usually accommodated within the trade unions. In the 1940s, there were huge peasant and tribal upheavals in Bengal and in the Telengana region within the princely state of Hyderabad. The Tebhaga movement in Bengal was a struggle of landless cultivators, asking for a larger share of the harvest and for rent. The Telengana movement was an armed struggle against landlord and state oppression. Women were especially prominent in moments of intense repression, when male leadership could not function very effectively. However, the militancy was not translated by the Communist Party into more effective and leading positions for women in Party life once the struggles were crushed. Often, the Party would expect them simply to return home as if nothing had happened. The struggles thus were experienced by women as their entry into history, even as they were left stranded in a renewed domesticity as the movement receded.[15]

[14] Jana Everett, *Women and Social Change in India* (New York, 1979).
[15] Peter Custers, *Women in the Tebhaga Uprising* (Calcutta, 1987); Stree Shakti Sangathana, *We Were Making History* (Delhi, 1987).

Even though the Party did not explicitly address gender issues, in practice it was often transgressive, easily accepting intercaste and intercommunity love matches as the norm, and forming mixed communes. Communist women were very active in asking for marriage reform, equal property and inheritance rights, and the right to divorce. Muslim women in the Leftist Progressive Writers' movement wrote deeply critical accounts of Muslim social conservatism in Urdu.[16]

Women also became involved in religious organizations and movements were often drawn more tightly into their closely integrated community life. During periods of intensified communal competition, the Rashtriya Swayamsevak Sangh allowed women from its families to form the Rashtrasevika Samiti in 1936, and the Muslim League formed a female cadre in 1940.[17] The public and political identity that right-wing politics allowed to their women would have partially reformulated the domestic balance of power. However, the organizations continued to valorize the cultural texts of gender inequality. They did not provide legal counselling for women in distress, nor did they initiate movements for better gender laws. Masculinity was recast on markedly militant lines, and political methods were devised to inculcate a will to mutual communal aggression and violence.

Gender, Religion, and Social Reform

Some of the gender imaginaries and practices would unfold within the agenda of religious and social reform. The agency of middle-class reformers has been the source of two distinct kinds of discomfort among postcolonial historians. First, their reformism often went together with political quietism that failed to confront colonial power. Second, they were generally middle-class and upper-caste Hindu or Sharif Muslim men from courtly elites and landed gentry, now deeply influenced by the new colonial education.[18] Their links with their own culture, therefore, were presumed to be slender, and their agency is seen as a mask for Western cultural hegemony. There is

---

[16] Renu Chakravartty, *Communists in Indian Womens' Movement* (Delhi, 1980).

[17] Tanika Sarkar, 'Heroic Women, Fierce Goddesses', in T. Sarkar and U. Butalia (eds), *Women and the Hindu Right* (Delhi, 1995). Gail Minault, 'Sisterhood or Separatism?', in Minault (ed.), *The Extended Family*.

[18] Barbara Metcalf, 'Reading and Writing about Muslim Women in British India' and Faisal Devji, 'Gender and the Politics of Space: The Movement for Womens' Reform 1857–1900', in Zoya Hasan (ed.), *Forging Identities: Gender, Communities and the State* (Delhi, 1994).

some truth as well as some misreading in these interpretations, some of which I will address later. However, historical change is frequently derived from 'impure' origins: in this case, it did so from agents whose class-caste milieu was privileged and whose perspective was deeply limited. The process of interrogation of social power initiated by their restricted efforts, nonetheless, could take unexpected turns.

The reformist vocabulary of the Indian middle classes was modestly liberal, but it was nonetheless transgressive when set against orthodoxy. Straining against the grain of Hindu and Islamic orthodox hegemony, liberal reformist efforts to achieve female education, mobility in public spaces, and, later, female political activism, had implications that exceeded what such gestures would represent today: pallid and timid reforms. In the nineteenth and early twentieth century, these reforms were proposed within a context where strict female seclusion, illiteracy, celibate widowhood, and domesticity were expected. Hindu orthodoxy at this time openly proclaimed that women were naturally fickle, thus lending support to widow immolation and infant marriage as both scriptural and social necessity while also opposing female education.

Undoubtedly, reforms bred their own antithesis. Rammohun Roy, in his eagerness to save Hindu widows from the ritual of burning alive, insisted that they were fully capable of chaste widowhood and, therefore, should be allowed to survive their husbands. He thus tried to purchase their lives at the cost of affirming the norms of chaste widowhood. This created great problems for the next generation of Hindu reformers who wanted to legalize widow remarriage, and they had to do so by playing on fears of immoral widowhood, foeticide, and infanticide. At the same time, they violated the codes that were central to caste, patriarchy, and Hindu nationalism: first, that of female monogamy, supposed to last beyond the death of the husband, and second, that of celibacy and the need to negate female sexuality in widows. Their pleas for male monogamy were based on notions of companionate marriage. On the one hand, this produced visions of romantic conjugality, but, on the other hand, this romanticism was premised on an inflexible mutual monogamy in sentiments and, in practice, made the forging of other relationships unthinkable. However, they also reconfigured the wife as an intellectual companion who denoted female intelligence and a radically different mode of socialization. Education for Muslim women was justified on the ground that this would segregate them from a world of false ritual and custom that was shared by Hindu women. It was simultaneously a ploy for the communalization of Muslim women as well as a plea for an intellectually and morally self reliant female identity.[19] The pace of change, however, was often slow, protracted, and self-limiting.

Gender and the Law

Social reform was often translated into movements for change in the 'Personal Laws' of the religious communities. It is important, therefore, to look at social and legal change together. The colonial legal apparatus had made a sharp distinction within civil law from the early days of the Company's rule. Production relations and economic activities were governed by a new set of Anglo-Indian norms, neither fully derived from English law, nor following older Indian precedents substantially, but developed through responses to the shifts in the Company's politico-financial requirements. In the entire arena of other private matters—marriage, divorce, inheritance, succession, caste, belief, and custom—the different religious communities were to be governed by their scripture and custom. Laws would be enacted only if it could be proved that current practices violated more authentic religious scripture and custom. At first, there were three sets of personal laws that were demarcated: Hindu, Muslim, and Christian. Parsees and Sikhs were subsumed under Hindu laws. In the 1850s, Parsees protested and extracted a separate code for themselves that was remarkably advanced for the times. It abolished polygamy, allowed divorce and widow remarriage, and disallowed infant marriage.[20] Tribal practices—with their widely varying gender regimes—were slotted under the category of customary law.[21] Thus the state enclosed an arena of personal laws that would be governed by the opinion of Indian authorities. This, then, was a residual sovereignty, lost elsewhere for colonized Indians. Before the birth of organized nationalism, this was a rare site for self-fashioning where Indian initiative could be decisive, even transformative. No wonder then that domestic issues came to dominate debates in the public sphere. In Bengal, on the whole, ancient and written scripture—a sign of India's advanced civilizational status, at

---

[19] Barbara Daly Metcalf, *Perfecting Women: Maulana Ali Thanawi's Bihishti Zewar* (Berkeley, 1990).

[20] Archana Parashar, *Women and Family Law Reform in India* (Delhi, 1992).

[21] Virginius Xaxa, 'Women and Gender in the Study of Tribes in India', in Sumit and Tanika Sarkar (eds), *Gender and Social Reform in Colonial India* (Delhi, forthcoming).

least according to early orientalists—was considered as a more reliable basis for judgements than oral custom which varied from caste to caste, and whose provenance and authenticity were difficult to validate.[22] Hindu texts were, however, notoriously variegated. This triggered debates on different textual and exegetical traditions, on strategies of authentication, which would uphold one or other competing truth claims. Wherever scriptural law was in the ascendant, a tendency existed to Brahmanize gender practices, since scripture reflected upper-caste norms: or to align practice to classical Islamic injunctions as found in the medieval text *Hedaya* or in the Hanafi school of law. In such instances, the divergent and varied marriage and inheritance traditions among Khojas, Memons, or Mapillas were considered non-Islamic. At the same time, it is important to recognize that neither were they disallowed.[23] In fact, the uncertainty about the relative weight of text and custom, about the precise meaning of each, lingered throughout the colonial era. It allowed for very interesting reformulations of traditional injunctions and practices. Courts were used extensively by Hindu widows and by upper-class Muslim women for whom litigation became a mode of altering domestic practice. Even Muslim women in deep seclusion found ways of speaking in courts without violating the purdah.[24]

An interesting bargain was struck by Muslim women in 1939, desirous of the right to initiate dissolution of marriages which was difficult under Hanafi law. They threatened apostasy and this persuaded Muslim leaders to concede to the application of Maliki law in order to enlarge their base of political support. Similarly, in the 1880s, Rukmabai, an educated girl from the carpenter caste in Bombay, refused to live with her illiterate and dissolute husband who demanded his conjugal rights over her. She argued her case on the basis of her caste custom which, she said, allowed her the right to dissolve her marriage.[25] Lower-caste widows would argue in court that their caste custom allowed them to inherit the first husband's share of

---

[22] Neeladri Bhattacharya, 'Remaking Custom: The Discourse and Practice of Colonial Codification', in R. Champakalakshmi and S. Gopal (eds), *Tradition, Dissent and Ideology: Essays in Honour of Romila Thapar* (Delhi, 1996), 20–54.

[23] Janaki Nair, *Women and Law in Colonial India: A Social History* (Delhi, 1996).

[24] Gregory Kozlowski, 'Muslim Women and the Control of Property in North India', in J. Krishnamurty (ed.), *Women in Colonial India: Essays on Survival, Work and the State* (Delhi, 1989), 114–32.

[25] Sudhir Chandra, *Enslaved Daughters: Colonialism, Law and Womens' Rights* (Delhi, 1998).

property even on remarriage, which both Brahmanical scripture and colonial law denied to them. Law was trapped in a dilemma here, since the new colonial legislation of 1856 allowed widow remarriage on condition that widows would forfeit rights to the first husband's property. Colonial rulers were not yet entirely familiar with lower-caste norms which allowed different forms of remarriage along with inheritance rights. Some High Courts ruled in such cases that the entire community be governed by a single set of laws and follow the letter of the 1856 law which denied them inheritance rights while allowing remarriage. The Allahabad Court, however, decided that law should be 'most enabling': it granted entitlements that did not exist before, such as the right to remarriage for upper-caste widows. But it could not take away any existing entitlements, such as inheritance claims of lower-caste widows whose custom had already allowed remarriage and hence who stood to gain nothing and to only lose from the new law.[26]

Despite the timid and highly circumscribed possibilities of legal reform, law often stimulated the creation of new and daring social imaginaries. Over the widow remarriage debates, for instance, arguments over the specific issue refused to stay in place: they irresistibly prompted wide and radical reviews of gender norms and invoked an ethic of equality as natural or divine law. They also challenged scriptural and social convictions about the absolute chastity and monogamy of the good woman who can have only one sexual relationship in her lifetime and who cannot move into a new relationship even if her first husband had been polygamous, impotent, ill, or dead. Our discussion of the consequences of legal change remains attenuated if we look only at the nature of the proposed legislation and its specific application. The collateral effects were unruly and productive of new cognitive possibilities.

Even as the Brahmanical orthodoxy replied with a renewed defence of textual injunctions, they, too, had to realign their ethical standards to meet the force of arguments of compassion and justice that advocates of equality invoked. For instance, in the debates over widow immolation in the early nineteenth century, both defenders and opponents of the practice built their cases on claims to representing the woman's 'own will and pleasure'. Unnoticed and unintended, female consent had slipped into the legal regime as a test of the validity of regulations that governed her. The

---

[26] Lucy Carroll, 'Law, Custom and Statutory Social Reform: The Hindu Widows' Remarriage Act of 1856', in J. Krishnamurty (ed.), *Women in Colonial India*, 1–26.

orthodoxy had referred to 'willing satis' who defied dissuasion and followed their husbands to the pyre. To meet their claim, Rammohun Roy then needed to reconfigure woman's socialization that had hitherto subjected her to a life structured by exploitation, humiliation, and inequality. He composed the first ethnography of women's everyday life—for the upper caste as well as for the lower caste woman and for the wife as well as for the widow—providing a thick description of labour, incarceration in the kitchen, insulation from education, punishments, lack of property rights, and sexual double standards.[27]

We have here the composition of a new male gaze of female lifeworlds. While classical and folk literature abounded with elaborate and detailed erotic descriptions of woman, we now have a discussion of her labour and her punishments, but which insists, at the same time, on her intellectual and moral resources, thus saving her from victimhood. This is linked to the growth of a reformist and introspective masculinity that reflects upon male privileges and norms. Moreover, in the course of the continuous debates among reformers and orthodoxy, both religious prescription and state law lost their axiomatic character. Such unintended consequences of reformist laws exceeded their immediate and practical effects. Very few widows remarried, even in the south where the remarriage issue constituted the exclusive field of reformist campaigns. At the same time, these debates opened up discursive and critical possibilities.[28]

Early orientalist administrators deeply admired scriptural traditions and this, combined with the paramount imperative of 'political expediency', made them extremely wary of change through state diktat. The real arena for conflict lay among Brahman pandits; the state played a monitoring role while the rules of the game were derived from scripture and custom. In 1890, a young Bengali girl died an agonizing death after marital rape. The colonial court had to free the husband since she was more than 10 years old and thus just above the statutory age limit, below which intercourse counted as rape under the Indian Penal Code. The Age of Consent Act that was passed as a result of this death in 1891 raised the age of consent within and outside

---

[27] Tanika Sarkar, 'The Fire Eaters: Why Widow Immolation Became a Question in Colonial Bengal', in *Rebels, Wives, Saints: Designing Selves and Nations in Colonial Times* (New Delhi, 2009).

[28] Tanika Sarkar, 'Enfranchised Selves: Women, Culture and Rights in Nineteenth Century Bengal', *Gender and History*, 13 (2001), 546–65.

marriage from 10 to 12. It met with outraged Hindu nationalist agitations in Bengal and Bombay on the grounds that a foreign state could not legislate religious practice.[29] In 1929, however, a new kind of nationalism had replaced revivalism with a liberal emphasis and could count on more widespread popular support. The legislature had come to include a substantial segment of elected Indians. They debated the child marriage issue and raised the minimum age of marriage with staunch support from womens' organizations, even though the new law clearly defied scriptural injunctions.[30] Female suffrage—albeit on a very limited scale—came to be debated and granted only when provincial legislatures and ministries came to be run by elected Indians, and when an organized womens' movement had established itself as a force of some weight. Indians, thus, could defy their own traditions and initiate social change with far greater readiness than did their colonial masters. In this context, it is noteworthy that Indian universities formally admitted women and granted them degrees decades earlier than did English universities.

In their representations of widow immolation, ascetic widowhood, or infant marriage, Western records did not display unmitigated horror at alleged Indian barbarity. When widows insisted on concremation, colonial and even missionary observers would often marvel at her moral victory over pain and terror. One likened a sati to Christian martyrs. Child brides were also romanticized, their innocence turning marriage into play, and overwriting the reality of their subsequent loss of childhood and freedom. In womens' autobiographical writings, however, enforced patrilocality in infancy and the total absence of her consent and will were common subjects of concern. This deepens our sense of the complicity between the colonial state and Indian patriarchal orthodoxy. Hence, the colonial period was often more of a stasis in terms of legislative intervention in domestic matters, the laws punctuating the status quo were extremely few and more often the results of Indian reformers, male and female.

Ultimately, government policy was driven more by political and financial expediency than cultural imperialism. A brief utilitarian moment produced a temporary alliance with Indian reformers and led to the legalization of

---

[29] Tanika Sarkar, *Hindu Wife, Hindu Nation: Community, Religion, Cultural Nationalism* (Delhi, 2001); Padma Anagol, 'The Age of Consent Act Reconsidered', *South Asia Research*, 12 (1992), 110–18.

[30] Mrinalini Sinha (ed.), *Selections from Mother India* (Delhi, 1998).

widow remarriage. In Eastern Punjab, on the other hand, the regional state was entirely committed to the status quo vis-à-vis the custom of levirate practised by Hindu, Muslim, and Sikh Jats.[31] The primary motive was to preserve family holdings to ensure agriculture and revenues in a resource-poor state. Widows were condemned, often against their will, to remarriage with brothers-in-law, so as to preserve family fortunes, and to ensure the reproduction of army recruits who often came from Jat families. Widows' pleas for marriages outside the family or for continued widowhood with some property entitlements were firmly refused.[32]

Official conservatism is especially evident in the state's reluctance to provide assistance to women who converted to Christianity. In 1872, Huchi, a young Hindu girl, converted and resisted cohabitation with her Hindu husband. Courts and even missionaries allowed her husband to take her back by force, even though the conjugal family treated her as an outcaste. She was permitted to choose her faith, but not her husband.[33] A similar concession to patriarchal interests took place in Malabar when Nayar men began to oppose the traditional matrilineal residence and inheritance patterns. These rules had kept married women within natal households where property was transmitted from mother to daughter. In theory, this put Nayar women through an initial form of marriage with Brahman Namboothiri men and then allowed them serially monogamous relationships with Nayar men. In practice, the first marriage with Namboothiris could be merely notional. Under this regime, Nayar men—now educated and employed in the modern employment sector, and earning individual incomes—could not leave their self-earned property to their children. The Malabar Marriage Act of 1896 retained the system with few changes, but its procedures initiated a large debate on the validity of matriliny. In 1933, by a further act of legislation, Nayar men were allowed to bequeath their own incomes to their children. Their right to set up conjugal households was also recognized. It was the product of the new social order that valorized the break up of matrilineal, impartible households, the formation of smaller, patrilocal conjugal units, and the emergence of a new notion of educated,

---

[31] The custom of a brother or male next of kin marrying a man's widow to prevent land passing out of the family.

[32] Prem Chowdhry, 'Customs in A Peasant Economy: Women in Colonial Haryana', in Sangari and Vaid (eds), *Recasting Women.*

[33] Gauri Viswanathan, *Outside the Fold: Conversion, Modernity and Belief* (Delhi, 1998).

'modern', dominant caste Nayar masculinity. Nayar men demanded expanded tenancy rights for themselves and opportunities for individualistic masculine enterprise through a modification of domestic and property arrangements.[34]

Reform in property laws often brought forth new ideas of male status and subjectivity among the propertied classes. Rammohun Roy, in the early nineteenth century, engaged in a strenuous debate with Justice Mcnaughten about individual male rights within a co-parcenary joint family system. While Mcnaughten invoked the early medieval Dayabhaga treatises on inheritance and insisted on non-divisibility of co-parcenary holdings, Roy interpreted the texts more flexibly to create a space for individual property rights and obligations. He went further and claimed that in the absence of easier provisions for individual and absolute property rights, male enterprise and self-esteem were stifled. He similarly argued that widows should have more than mere usufruct rights to their husband's share of household property, if they were to live less vulnerable and dependent lives.[35]

There was more to the colonial sanction of orthodox custom and the infrequency of reformist legislation than the fear of political consequences. I have already mentioned the complicity between Western and Indian patriarchies, which belies the notion of a determinedly transformative colonial state, bent on creating a class of anglicized Indian collaborators, or aspiring towards cultural hegemony in which the brown woman was saved from the brown man. While the state was more willing to accept a liberal Brahmanical interpretation during the three decades between the 1820s and the 1850s, the shocks occasioned by the 1857 Rebellion led to a more cautious and conservative approach. The Utilitarian moment was both modest and transient but in its place came initiatives for change pressed by Indian liberal reformers. By the end of the nineteenth century, it was increasingly associations of Indian women who would seize the initiative for reform, in female education and health, and for suffrage.

---

[34] G. Arunima, *There Comes Papa: Colonialism and the Transformation of Matriliny in Kerala: Malabar, c 1850–1940*, (Delhi, 2002). K. N. Panikkar, *Culture, Ideology, Hegemony: Intellectuals and Social Consciousness in Colonial India* (Delhi, 1995).
[35] Sarkar, 'The Fire Eaters'.

Education, Family, and Caste

Old religious texts were supposedly the ground on which new selves, liberal as well as orthodox, were founded. Translations, compilations, commentaries, amplifications, and interpretations appeared in prose, a genre that was close to everyday speech and which was accessible even to the newly literate. Over the course of the nineteenth century, the Koran was translated into Persian and then into Urdu. Sacred books became delinked from the sacred language. Maulvis also pioneered the growth of Urdu religious tracts and newspapers. Their intention was to overcome the impasse that their faith confronted with the loss of Muslim state power, and with the possibility that the alien government might convert Muslims or force them to live under non-Islamic personal laws. Even though by the late nineteenth century such fears had largely been allayed, the sense of a crisis threatening faith and community remained overpowering. Faith increasingly came to be seen as lying in the hands of individual Muslims, men as well as women. There was a vigorous campaign to ensure that its true tenets should be disseminated to the entire community of the faithful or the *umma*. Modern religious seminaries competed among themselves to educate religious teachers and specialists and to standardize conduct and belief. Oral disquisitions and inter-faith as well as intra-faith debates penetrated remote villages and fatwas were printed in massive numbers, dealing with queries about everyday lives. Print culture expanded individual access to religion for both men and women and conferred greater responsibility for religious conduct on them.

Some Muslims in the nineteenth century tried to combine Islam with modernity, especially with Western education and Western science: Delhi College in the earlier half of the century and Aligarh University in the latter part.[36] More common were disputations within the orthodox tradition

---

[36] Christopher Shackle (ed.), *Urdu and Muslim South Asia: Studies in Honour of Ralph Russell*, (Delhi, 1991); Faisal Devji, 'Gender and the Politics of Space'; Barbara Metcalf (ed.), *Moral Conduct and Authority: The Place of Adab in South Asian Islam* (Berkeley, 1984); Robert Frykenberg (ed.), *Delhi through the Ages* (Delhi, 1986); Aziz Ahmad, *Islamic Modernism in India and Pakistan* (New York, 1967): David Lelyveld, *Aligarh's First Generation: Muslim Solidarity in British India* (Princeton, 1978); Francis Robinson, *The Ulama of Farangi Mahall and Islamic Culture in South Asia* (Delhi, 2001); Rafiuddin Ahmad, *The Bengal Muslims 1871–1906: A Quest for Identity* (Delhi, 1981).

about freedom of interpretation. Among the gentry in north India, older courtly values of hospitality, strict orthodoxy, and ostentatious investments in cultural products, were gradually overtaken by somewhat different conceptions of proper conduct and comportment. Education and seriousness, piety and self-reform, all contributed to the reconfiguration of the Muslim household such that it would become thrifty and self-contained, and in which familial emotional ties became more important. It also queried the traditional enclosed female world, secluded from the Muslim male domain. The male householder became far more obviously an active ruler within the household, educating children and wives with Urdu books, and ensuring true Muslim practice within homes. Authority within the community became partially delinked from patronage and property. It needed to be earned and not merely inherited through a conspicuous display of piety and education, and a stronger sense of exclusive community identity. Western as well as Hindu ways were excluded.

Anxieties about creating a more cohesive Muslim community focused attention on the interior of the household. Islamicization of Muslim women was a problem, as they were not exposed to preaching in the mosque or to teaching in seminaries, nor used to reading religious literature with comprehension, since the holy book was in Arabic, a language that some could read, parrot-like, but could not understand. The new attentiveness with which they were now regarded as mothers of future Muslim generations, and as Muslims in their own right, produced anxieties about the unreformed *zenana* where women spoke the *begumati zuban* or a Creole language filled with Hindu references, and where they practised rituals that were often syncretic in nature. Simultaneously, the new Muslim man sought a wife who would take on more middle-class roles. Hence, discussions emerged about how to create the new woman and in the process increasingly women too seized the initiative, especially from the early twentieth century.

Some of the reformers prohibited Urdu reading for women, since Urdu literature had a low life of its own, or contained dangerous erotic and romantic elements. Bi Ashrafunnissa later revealed how she taught herself to read Urdu in great secrecy. Begum Rokeya Hussain wrote in Bengali for Bengali Muslim girls. Other male authors, however, wrote novels in Urdu to combine entertainment with instruction. These were wildly popular among women, creating in them a new self-image and self-esteem as pious Muslim mothers and wives. Some of the novels—of Nazir Ahmad Dehlavi, for instance—were sensitive to the anguish of secluded domesticity. Some others, like Thanawi's, more determinedly reformist and pious, figured ideal Muslim womanhood as segregated from Hindu domestic influence. At the same time, the segregated and enclosed Muslim female identity was combined with notions of a female selfhood, not mired in familial identity or relationships, but free and equal in the presence of God.[37]

Some reformers, like Sayyad Ahmad Khan, encouraged the education of wives and mothers, but could not countenance the thought of schooling for girls and insisted that they be taught at home. Others, like Mumtaz Ali, would try and exploit scriptural resources to encourage the notion of gender equality as the distinctive hallmark of Islam. By the turn of the century, the decision no longer rested with them alone. The Begums of Bhopal set up primary schools for Muslim girls in the teeth of public opposition, and in the following decades, Begum Rokeya Sakhawat Hussein would follow suit in Patna and in Calcutta.[38] Reforms thus had no fixed trajectory that could be fully controlled or managed. Intentions did not always match consequences.

There was a similar fear of schooling among the Hindu orthodoxy as well, even by those who supported female education within the family. Schools were non-familial spaces, where girls acquired an individual identity beyond their family and community. Even when carefully secluded in special transport they still left their homes and travelled through public spaces. In Bengal, where Ishwarchandra Vidyasagar set up the first schools for girls in Calcutta, and even in villages, schoolgirls and their families were lampooned, intimidated, and ostracized. There was for much of the nineteenth century, a widespread reluctance to provide for home-based education, even limited literacy, since that was supposed to lead to widowhood. Rashsundari Debi, an upper caste, rural housewife, developed a yearning to read: she taught herself the letters in her kitchen while doing household chores. Later, she wrote the first full-length autobiography by a woman in the Bengali language.[39] The public actions of educated women justified some of the orthodox fears. When they wrote, they deeply criticized domestic

---

[37] Metcalf, *Moral Authority*; Gail Minault, *Secluded Scholars: Womens' Education and Muslim Social Reform in Colonial India* (Delhi, 1998); Sonia Nishat Amin, 'The Early Muslim Bhadramahila: The Growth of Learning and Creativity, 1876–1939', in Bharati Ray (ed.), *From the Seams of History*, 107–48.

[38] Minault, *Secluded Scholars*.

[39] Tanika Sarkar, *Words to Win: Amar Jiban, A Modern Autobiography* (Delhi, 1998).

conditions. Tarabai Shinde and Pandita Ramabai in western India and Kailashbashini Debi in Bengal sometimes produced sharper critiques of upper-caste Hindu households than did male reformers.[40] Pandita Ramabai eventually left the Hindu fold and converted to Christianity and Rokeya was suspected of Christian leanings.[41]

In any case, female education was a particularly fraught issue since it involved questions of masculinity. If companionate marriages with educated wives and enlightened motherhood could be projected as more fulfilling and supportive of masculine existence, complementary rather than competitive, they could also be regarded as emasculating. Colonialism left few spaces for masculine enterprise and control. If education, an important marker of male success and authority, was to be shared with women, it would dissolve a principal sign of gender difference. Men feared that they would lose authority over women if their wives acquired the resource that hitherto set men apart from women. There were similar fears about low caste instruction, since knowledge had traditionally been caste- and gender-determined. As I remarked earlier, educated women were caricatured in folk art and in farces as men in female garb, as home wreckers, and as biologically ill-disposed to bear and rear children. Their reformist friends and husbands were similarly portrayed as feminized, henpecked, and impotent.

If liberal reformers sought to rectify women's deprivation by conferring legal rights on women, religious reformers and revivalists later in the nineteenth century would also introduce changes that were similar in form but different in intent, and without directly addressing the question of legal rights. The Arya Samaj in late nineteenth-century Punjab and western Uttar Pradesh encouraged female education, schooling, and widow remarriage. The basis for their support was, however, quite different. They said little about universal natural justice or gender equality, and reform was not framed in terms of legal rights. Instead, the changes they proposed were justified on the grounds that they needed to expand and strengthen the Hindu community owing to increased competition with other communal groups. Widow remarriage would enhance the Hindu population, but this was tempered by requiring widows to only marry

---

[40] Rosalind O'Hanlon, *A Comparison between Women and Men: Tarabai Shinde and the Critique of Gender Relations in Colonial India* (Delhi, 1994).

[41] Geraldine Forbes, *Women in Modern India* (The New Cambridge History of India, iv/2; Cambridge, 1996).

widowers, and any such relationship would terminate following the birth of children.[42] These relationships were confined to procreation: the emotional and sexual needs of men and women therefore remained repressed even within remarriage. The emphasis on education and remarriage was grounded in the needs of the community, not the individual. Nonetheless, the Arya Samaj did extend and expand female education in societies where it had previously been absent or severely constrained. Educated women would in turn often become leading figures in womens' organizations. The Child Marriage Restraint (Sarda) Act was passed at the initiative of Harbilas Sarda, an Arya Samajist. Once again we find that the consequences of reformist efforts often broke free from their intent. A number of self-purificatory Sikh movements and sects also formulated schemes for marriage reform, female education, and domestic roles which diluted the prevailing martial ethos in favour of men assuming greater domestic responsibilities.[43]

Like liberal and upper-caste reformers, the lower castes threw up their own leaders from the mid-nineteenth century. Jotirao Phule came from a caste of cultivators whose claims to warrior status, he charged, had been denied by dominant Brahmanical castes and which consequently had led them to be placed amongst the lowest castes. He remythologized low castes as an ancient, indigenous nation of warlike, powerful, and egalitarian cultivators. This vision of non-Brahmin men was one that combined productivity and martiality. A similar warrior ethos was claimed and used by Mahars of western India who had made their way into the army, and had gained some educational and job privileges despite their untouchable status.[44]

In contrast, B. R. Ambedkar articulated a politically conscious untouchable masculinity that did not depend on a martial ethos or on peasant virtues. Instead, his construction of masculinity was self-consciously intellectual, rationalist, and reliant on a vocabulary of universal justice.[45] The right to education became a conspicuous feature of efforts to reconfigure lower-caste masculinity in the south as well, undermining the norms of

---

[42] Madhu Kishwar, 'The Daughters of Aryavarta', in J. Krishnamurty (ed.), *Women in Colonial India*, 78–113.

[43] Kenneth Jones, *Socio Religious Reform Movements in British India* (Cambridge, 1989).

[44] Rosalind O'Hanlon, *Caste, Conflict and Ideology: Mahatma Jotirao Phule and Low Caste Protest in Nineteenth Century Western India* (Cambridge, 1985).

[45] Christophe Jaffrelot, *Analysing and Fighting Caste: Dr Ambedkar and Untouchability* (Delhi 2004).

exclusion and ignorance that Brahmanical authorities had insisted upon. At the beginning of the nineteenth century, Christian missionaries had begun to provide primary education to the so-called 'slave castes' in southern India while also campaigning to abolish their slave-like status. Upper-caste and Syrian Christian landlords resisted this fiercely, fearing that conversions to Protestantism would result in the loss of a captive agrarian labour force and the erosion of their privileges.[46] In many instances of lower-caste reform, Brahmanical orthodoxy was repudiated along with its patriarchy. Dalits pursued different but equal gender relationships as a way of distinguishing themselves from the upper castes. E. V. Ramaswamy Naicker, or Periyar, as he was called, formulated a different form of marriage ceremony within his Self-Respect movement to signify the equality of women in Madras from the 1920s.[47]

However, unlike radical traditions of lower-caste protest, upwardly mobile low castes pursued Sanskritization and sought to move from polluted to cleaner occupations, and claimed improved ritual status. Very often, these efforts at Sanskritization would be signalled by their gender practices.[48] By the mid-nineteenth century, the prohibition of widow remarriage and the practice of infant marriage had become widespread among many low or untouchable castes. There are also indications that earlier in the century, the number of low-caste widows who immolated themselves along with their husbands had exceeded the number of upper-caste satis. Prosperous peasants tended to withdraw their women from agricultural operations. In Punjab, even when women continued to work on the fields, they would try and avoid being listed in censuses and surveys as anything except housewives. Domestication and seclusion became the norm wherever they were affordable. Later in the century, with the spread of liberal reforms among upper castes, however, Sanskritization could involve an alternative trajectory of female respectability. Some of the turn-of-century lower-caste associations began to urge female education and an older age of marriage. Significantly, women from low castes began to write and demand these rights.

---

[46] Koji Kawashima, *Missionaries and a Hindu State: Travancore 1858–1936* (Oxford, 1998).
[47] V. Geetha and S. V. Rajadurai, *Towards A Non Brahman Millenium: From Iyothee Thass to Periyar* (Calcutta, 1998).
[48] Saurabh Dube, *Untouchable Pasts: Religion, Identity and Power among a Central Indian Community, 1780–1950* (New York, 1998).

One of the most loaded semiotics of political insubordination and of the making of new low-caste rebel identities for men and women was the refusal of dress codes that defined caste hierarchies, often in gendered terms. The sect of Shri Narayana Guru, which encompassed low-caste Ezhavas, began to use umbrellas and shoes in public places to defy the physical signs of caste hierarchy.[49] Since only upper-caste women in parts of southern India were entitled to wear the breast cloth, lower-caste women were made to uncover their breasts in the presence of upper-class men to signal their low status. Christian missions in the south encouraged the low-caste Shanar female converts from the late eighteenth century to cover their breasts in public spaces. The breast cloth movement continued through the early decades of the nineteenth century and spread among unconverted Shanars as well.[50] In the early twentieth century, dominant caste Nayars tried to prevent untouchable Pulaya women from adopting a particular kind of necklace that had been reserved for Nayar female use.

Rural and Urban Identities in Transition

The impact of the transformation of the agrarian economy on the gendered subjectivities of rural people has not been adequately studied, as the dominant historiographical focus has been on rebellious peasants. However, studies of peasant insurgency and tribal unrest afford glimpses, albeit somewhat limited, into changing masculinities and gender relations. New forms of peasant leadership begin to appear during these rebellions that had masculine overtones such as among the Oraons. The growth of the cult of the Devi among tribals of Gujarat initiated drastic and somewhat puritanical changes in religious and cultural practices, including abstinence from alcohol. They, like so many others, looked outside their communities for political inspiration and models of conduct. In some cases, such as the Munda, Christian missionaries played an important role while others drew upon Hindu or Gandhian inspiration.[51] What most appear to have shared, however, was a male-centred notion of leadership and structures of authority. For instance,

---

[49] Uday Kumar, 'Self, Body and Inner Sense: Some Reflections on Sree Narayana Guru and Kumaran Asan', *Studies in History*, 13 (1997), 247–70.

[50] Robert Hardgrave, *The Nadars of Tamil Nadu: The Political Culture of A Community in Change* (Bombay, 1969).

[51] K. S. Singh, *The Dust Storm and the Hanging Mist: A Study of Birsa Munda and His Movement in Chhotanagpur* (Calcutta, 1966); Sangeeta Dasgupta, 'Reordering a World: The Tana

the Santal insurrections of the mid-nineteenth century involved the identification and the elimination of female witches from within the community as a purificatory rite before they rebelled. Among the tribes of the northeast, in contrast, where female economic initiatives, property ownership, and decision-making processes were more common, political resistance to colonial economic policies and administrative changes involved much more female leadership. For example, women were very active in the anti-colonial Manipur uprisings of 1904 and 1939 and women from families of tribal chiefs, like Rani Guidalu in the 1930s, were prominent in the Civil Disobedience movement.[52]

In historical studies of the rural economy under colonial rule, a reordering of gender relations with a negative impact on women is often assumed. For instance it is believed that women ceased to contribute to household incomes as domestic production, such as spinning, declined due to imported yarn, or that women were withdrawn from the labour force by Sanskritizing castes. This, however, now appears to be a partial picture. If women of peasant castes were withdrawn from the rural labour force, their ranks were partially replenished by untouchable and tribal women. Also, upwardly mobile peasant communities, in an attempt to prove their high status, may have concealed a range of female occupations from the queries of census enumerators. In addition, Mukul Mukherji has challenged the picture of a generalized collapse of female rural work due to mechanization.[53]

In emerging rural labour regimes like plantations, there was a steady demand for female labour from the mid-nineteenth century. Women workers were doubly in demand as producers and as reproducers. Tea picking was considered best done by women and the tea plantations deliberately feminized large parts of their labour force.[54] Moreover, they wanted to ensure a labour force that would reproduce itself, given the harshness of the plantation work. Samita Sen has shown how deliberate female recruitment—often by fraud and by coercion—was resisted by

---

Bhagat Movement, 1914–1919', *Studies in History*, 15 (1999), 1–14; David Hardiman, *The Coming of Devi: Adivasi Assertion in Western India* (Delhi, 1987).

[52] Radha Kumar, *A History of Doing* (Delhi, 1993).

[53] Mukul Mukherji, 'Impact of Modernisation on Womens' Occupations: A Case Study of the Rice-Husking Industry of Bengal', in Krishnamurty (ed.), *Women in Colonial India*, 180–98.

[54] Piya Chatterjee, *A Time for Tea: Women, Labour and Postcolonial Politics on An Indian Plantation* (Durham, NC, 2001).

middle-class reformers, exposing, especially, the sexual oppression of labouring women by European managers and the breakdown of family structures. The reformer's agenda was to terminate female recruitment in the name of female purity and family values. While women were easily exploited by European managers, ironically, the economic needs of a constant resupply of labour induced the authorities to invest in maternal health.[55] Dagmar Engels found the health statistics of women workers there to be above all-Bengal averages.[56]

The self-perception of men and women working in mines changed in profound but often contradictory ways. Coal mines reduced labour costs by employing women who enjoyed a self-confidence and sense of equality with men even within a highly exploitative labour situation. Yet in the Kolar gold mines in the princely state of Mysore, women workers were completely excluded from mine work thereby creating a masculine, macho, and brash environment. But even here men were confronted with female sex workers whose independent and 'modern' ways they feared and admired. This male labour force, engaged in particularly arduous and ill-paid labour, nonetheless, experienced a sense of freedom from upper-caste domination in the villages and derived pleasure, howsoever limited, from the promise of urban consumption.[57]

Urban work and life similarly transformed the subjectivity of men and women in a variety of ways. Nandini Gooptu has observed that lower-caste municipal workers saw caste-based sanitary work as desirable, for these were perceived as government jobs which also released them from direct upper-caste domination experienced in the rural context.[58] Large-scale urban factories recruited few women, although during strikes and when additional labour was needed, destitute urban women were utilized as a cheap, reserve army of labour.[59] Early factory legislation reduced womens' working hours

---

[55] Samita Sen, 'Questions of Consent: Womens Recruitment for Assam Tea Gardens, 1859–1900', *Studies in History*, 18 (2002), 231–60.

[56] Dagmar Engels, *Beyond Purdah? Women in Bengal, 1890–1939* (Delhi, 1996).

[57] Janaki Nair, *Miners and Millhands: Work, Culture and Politics in Princely Mysore* (Delhi, 1998).

[58] Nandini Gooptu, *The Politics of the Urban Poor in Twentieth Century India* (Cambridge, 2001).

[59] Radha Kumar, 'Family and Factory: Women in the Bombay Cotton Textile Industry, 1919–1939', in J. Krishnamurty (ed.), *Women in Colonial India*, 133–62; Samita Sen, *Women and Labour in Late Colonial India: The Bengal Jute Industry* (Cambridge, 1999).

and excluded them from certain categories of particularly risky work, making it less economical to employ female labour. Moreover, the logic of industrial activity was built around limiting employer's responsibilities for welfare, thereby encouraging men to leave their wives and families in rural areas. Aged or infirm workers thus returned to their rural homes. Migrant male workers therefore did not enjoy home lives and eked out a precarious and laborious existence. Yet, the city, with its multitude of cheap pleasures, was something of a release from the drabness of rural poverty. Moreover, those who worked with heavy machinery or experienced the solidarities of collective labour and union politics enjoyed a sense of pride, skill, and political agency. Chitra Joshi's work shows how, in the present moment of deindustrialization, past times of organized work and politics are recalled, now bathed in the melancholy glow of a lost value.[60]

Urban modernity provided opportunities for the assertion of marginal and alternative sexualities, even as laws were tightened up to regulate their activities. Homoerotic, lesbian, and transgender experiences and lifestyles were familiar to mystics, to marginal communities and in literary and theatrical performances. Novels and autobiographies often expressed such desires in unnamed but vivid ways and these became recurring subjects of public discourse. Growing urbanization expanded red light areas in cities and towns. Prostitutes came to enjoy a larger clientele even as their growing numbers stirred middle-class anxieties and pleas for stricter spatial segregation.[61] Prostitutes resisted humiliating lock-ups in military hospitals when a mid-nineteenth-century law tried to protect European soldiers from the threat of venereal diseases by obtrusive medical check-ups and forced confinement of sex workers.[62] The law was finally withdrawn. If they suffered from more explicit social stigma, some sought self-esteem through new, highly paid professions in the public theatre and in the early cinema. Although the state legislated against homosexuality, the practice was not definitively named outside the statutes, and remained a grey zone in popular consciousness, its indeterminacy providing it with protective cover. Section 377 of the Indian Penal Code of 1860 which proscribed homosexual intercourse, defined it as the act of sexual penetration, 'against the order of

---

[60] Chitra Joshi, *Lost Worlds: Indian Labour and Its Forgotten Histories* (Delhi, 2003).
[61] Veena Oldenberg, *The Making of Colonial Lucknow* (Princeton, 1984).
[62] Kenneth Ballhatchett, *Race, Sex and Class under the Raj: Imperial Attitudes and Policies and Their Critics* (London, 1980).

Nature'. It has not yet been explored how often this section was actually applied against offenders: certainly, there were no sensational court cases to try homosexuals as was the case with the trial of Oscar Wilde in England in the 1890s. The legal emphasis on penetration left the area of lesbian lovemaking outside the parameters of legal control.[63]

Identities in Flux

Literature and cultural performance like music, theatre, and cinema expressed imaginings and desires that were socially transgressive but culturally relevant or, at least, found to be profoundly interesting: extra- and premarital love, love for widows, love for the prostitute.[64] There was a greater urge to the composition and articulation of individual selves through cultural texts. Such selves, in order to capture an interested market, needed to declare some distance between themselves and the social identity they inhabited, to demonstrate points of rupture and a sense of a unique interiority. That interiority had been earlier a sign of mystics, great poets, men of privilege and importance. Now, even ordinary people and quotidian lives would be heard, seen, and read, if they could portray a distinctive individuality successfully. A new appetite grew for consuming lives of ordinary men and women, of housewives and prostitutes, of autodidacts and low-caste savants.[65] At the same time, experiences of collective life, especially of the self-chosen ones, were valued in cultural representations. Nationalist literature and theatre, and from the 1940s, Left writings and drama, depicted political solidarities and movements to urban and rural mass audiences and readers. New political identities sometimes meshed with older, given ones. Individual and collective identities of class, gender,

---

[63] Arvind Narayan and Gautam Bhan (eds), *Because I Have A Voice: Queer Politics in India* (Delhi, 2005); A Compilation of Voices, *Rights for All: Against Queer Desire under Section 377* (Delhi, 2005).

[64] On women singers in the new regime of gramophone companies, see Amlan Das Gupta, 'Women and Music: The Case of North India', in Bharati Ray (ed.), *Women of India*.

[65] Ghulam Murshid, *Reluctant Debutante: Response of Bengali Women to Modernization*, (Rajshahi, 1983); Malavika Karlekar, *Voices from Within: Early Personal Narratives of Bengali Women* (Delhi, 1991); Charu Gupta, *Sexuality, Obscenity, Community: Women, Muslims and the Hindu Public in Colonial India* (Delhi, 2001); Francesca Orsini, *The Hindu Public Sphere: 1920–1940* (Delhi, 2002); Antoinette Burton, *Dwelling in the Archive: Home and History in Late Colonial Bengal* (Delhi, 2003); Susie Tharu and K. Lalitha, *Women Writing in India* (New York, 1993).

and community, were created and recreated as much through literature, performance, and speeches as they were through experiences of particular forms of life and labour.

Select Bibliography

ELIZABETH BUETTNER, *Empire Families: Britons and Late Imperial India* (Oxford, 2004).

ANTOINETTE BURTON, *Burdens of History: British Feminists, Indian Women, and Imperial Culture, 1865–1915* (Chapel Hill, NC, 1994).

URVASHI BUTALIA, *The Other Side of Silence: Voices from the Partition of India* (Delhi, 1998).

INDRANI CHATTERJEE, *Gender, Slavery and the Law in Colonial India* (Delhi, 1999).

E. M. COLLINGHAM, *Imperial Bodies: The Physical Experience of the Raj, c.1800–1947* (Cambridge, 2001).

GERALDINE H. FORBES, *Women in Modern India* (The New Cambridge History of India, iv/2; Cambridge, 1996).

DURBA GHOSH, *Sex and the Family in Colonial India: The Making of Empire* (Cambridge, 2006).

KUMARI JAYAWARDENA, *The White Woman's Other Burden: Western Women and South Asia During British Rule* (London, 1995).

J. KRISHNAMURTY (ed.), *Women in Colonial India: Essays on Survival, Work and the State* (Delhi, 1989).

PHILIPPA LEVINE, *Prostitution, Race and Politics: Policing Venereal Disease in the British Empire* (London, 2003).

——(ed.), *Gender and Empire: Oxford History of the British Empire Companion Series* (Oxford, 2004).

LATA MANI, *Contentious Traditions: The Debate on Sati in Colonial India* (Berkeley, 1998).

CLARE MIDGLEY (ed.), *Gender and Imperialism* (Manchester, 1995).

GAIL MINAULT (ed.), *The Extended Family: Women and Political Participation in India and Pakistan* (Bombay, 1981).

——*Secluded Scholars: Women's Education and Muslim Social Reform in Colonial India* (Delhi, 1998).

NANCY L. PAXTON, *Writing under the Raj: Gender, Race, and Rape in the British Colonial Imagination, 1830–1947* (New Brunswick, NJ, 1998).

PANDITA RAMABAI, *Pandita Ramabai's American Encounter: The Peoples of the United States (1889)*, trans. Meera Kosambi (Bloomington, Ind., 2003).

BHARATI RAY (ed.), *From the Seams of History: Essays on Indian Women* (Delhi, 1995).
——*Women of India: Colonial and Post-Colonial Periods* (Delhi, 2005).

KUMKUM SANGARI (ed.), *Recasting Women: Essays in Indian Colonial History* (New Jersey, 1990).

TANIKA SARKAR, *Hindu Wife, Hindu Nation: Community, Religion and Cultural Nationalism* (New Delhi, 2001).

——*Rebels, Wives, Saints: Designing Selves and Nations in Colonial Times* (New Delhi, 2009).

MRINALINI SINHA, *Colonial Masculinity: The 'Englishman' and the 'Effeminate Bengali' in the Late Nineteenth-Century* (Manchester, 1995).

——*Specters of Mother India: The Global Restructuring of an Empire* (Durham, NC, 2006).

13

The Desi *Diaspora: Politics, Protest, and Nationalism*

Vijay Prashad

Diaspora is migration during the era of nationalism. It refers to the scattering of peoples certainly, but only when this dispersion is accompanied by a political and emotional gathering in far-off lands under the sign of the nation. Diaspora is an idea that only makes sense when set alongside the concept of nationalism.

Prior to nationalism's birth in the nineteenth century, people moved routinely. They travelled from their local places of birth and social sustenance to territories so far that they lost touch with their early homes. Long land routes over mountains and sea routes across treacherous waters made the transit both expensive and often singular—only those who made their lives as traders across water and hills went back and forth. They settled in the islands of today's Indonesia and Malaysia, in East Africa; they travelled to Persia, Egypt, and beyond, perhaps as far off as Spain to become part of what would later be called the Gypsy population. South Asia had a longstanding relationship with South East Asia and with East Africa, with the interchange of peoples, goods, and ideas. This perhaps goes back to the ancient world, spurred on by the trade between the Roman empire and the various monarchies of south Asia. The most dramatic period of the interaction between Africa and Asia around the Indian Ocean (or the Afrasian Sea) begins after 400CE, when the peoples, animals, vegetation, and ideas moved back and forth to cast their influence on the entire region. The people who migrated in these times took with them social practices, habits, and materials from their homelands, moved to far-off locales and set to work in the construction of a new ethos, one that was defined in conversation with the materials and ideas that they found in those parts.

The ancient and early modern migrations of people from the Indian subcontinent are a prelude to the diaspora of the late nineteenth century and after, but they are not a part of it. What defines the diaspora of the late nineteenth and twentieth centuries, in the era of nationalism, is that as people left a homeland that was already seen as a 'nation', they continued to bear fond memories of that homeland and saw themselves as somewhat patriotic to it. The modern diaspora, the only diaspora really, fashioned itself as linked to a homeland to which it either wanted to return (after a period of formal indenture or other forms of overseas employment) or else to which they wanted to travel for visits as frequently as possible. Even among the indentured population, who had both the least mobility and the least disposable income, the desire to maintain 'family ties' with the homeland had an enormous impact on the social and political imagination.

Even though the word 'diaspora' comes to us from the Greek for scattering (which implies any migration) and even though it is classically used to refer to the Jewish diaspora after the destruction of the Jerusalem Temple in 79CE, the concept in modern times refers specifically to the idea of a departure from a national homeland and a nostalgia for that homeland. The *desis*, or those who hail from the *desh*, homeland, form a diaspora when they leave the subcontinent in a time when nationalist ideas have already become vibrant in their various localities, either through concrete struggles or else through the cultural materials (songs, stories) that have become commonplace in their region. The four regions within the Indian subcontinent that sent the largest number of migrants across the globe are Punjab, Gujarat, Tamil Nadu and Bihar—all areas that had begun to experience peasant struggles against imperial rule, often, but not always configured as a people's demand to rule themselves and their surplus. The struggles of the Santals and Mundas (Bihar), of the Naikda (Gujarat), of the Konda Dora and Koya (Tamil Nadu) are an indication of the high level of anti-colonialism among the 'tribals' of these regions. The No-Revenue movements in the several districts of Gujarat and Punjab attest to the general demand on the surplus. Two historical perquisites produce the conditions for the age of diaspora: the birth of the idea of nationalism, and the technological ability to maintain contact with the homeland (either via the post, telegraph, telephone, ship, aeroplane, or more recently the Internet).

Plantation Indenture

Massive rebellions of enslaved peoples in the Americas (Haiti, 1792; Barbados, 1816; Guyana, 1823; Jamaica, 1831–2), a decline in the market share of the slave plantation profits, as well as a rise in anti-slavery agitation in the metropole, brought a gradual end to chattel slavery in the nineteenth century. Despite the end of chattel slavery, the immense manual labour-driven production system erected by the British (and other Europeans) still required a sustained supply of workers. The slave system had never produced an adequate means to reproduce labour, and after emancipation many of the newly freed workers did not want to come back to work on the plantations. In Australia the planters turned to convict labour; in South Africa to 'apprentices' (captive children) and 'Prize Negroes' (freed slaves), and in the Caribbean they tried first to hire free Africans from other islands (so that, for example, freed slaves from St Kitts came to work in Trinidad), then free African Americans en route to Africa, West African emigrants, European labour on indenture contracts, and then Portuguese speakers from Madeira, Cape Verde, and the Azores. But finally Australia, South Africa, and the Caribbean (as well as South America) turned to the labour markets of British India and China from where thousands of emigrants left to do 'coolie work' (formerly 'nigger work') on the plantations of early capitalism.[1]

'Free' labour was not to replace slave labour, because the planters refused to hire Africans in the Caribbean on negotiable terms and the Africans refused to work in slave conditions. The imperial plantocracy fell upon the idea of indentured labour first in Mauritius, then elsewhere: indentured labour was hired for a term of five years (with the option of an additional five) and then sent back to their places of origin.[2] Recruiters (*arkatis*) worked in the Gangetic plain and on the Coromandel Coast. Between 1834 and 1916, 30.2 million people left India, 23.9 million returned, leaving behind 6.3 million in the plantation colonies.[3] *Arkatis* exaggerated the

---

[1] David Eltis (ed.), *Coerced and Free Migration: Global Perspectives* (Palo Alto, 2002) and in Kay Saunders (ed.), *Indentured Labour in the British Empire, 1834–1920* (London, 1984).

[2] Marina Carter, *Voices of Indenture: Experiences of Indian Migrants in the British Empire* (Leicester, 1996) and Walton Look-Lai, *Indentured Labour, Caribbean Sugar: Chinese and Indian Migrants to the British West-Indies, 1838–1918* (Baltimore,1993).

[3] K. Davis, *The Population of India and Pakistan* (Princeton, 1951), 102.

wages, told the peasantry of the region that the Caribbean, Africa, and Fiji were not far from Calcutta, and generally underplayed the conditions of work. Wracked by the high revenue demands by the colonial state in India, many among the peasants had been primed to believe in the words of the *arkatis*.[4] The exaggerations made the betrayal even stronger. 'I no go no way again, I have to wuk, I have to slave Trinidad,' sang Moolian of the travails of his indentured life.[5]

The colonial state called these workers 'coolies', although the word bore within it the mark of utter disrespect. There is no established etymology of it, for some attribute it to the Tamil for 'hire' (*kuli*), others find it in use in sixteenth-century Portugal after the name of a Gujarati community (*Koli*), still others notice that it sounds like the Chinese for 'bitter labour' (*ku-li*), or, like the Fijian term for dog (*kuli*). One way or the other to be called a 'coolie' is to be denigrated, and to be considered at best as a labourer with no other social markers or desires. The word 'coolie' operates, then, like the nineteenth-century English word for factory worker, 'hands' (where the entire ensemble of human flesh and consciousness is reduced to the one thing that is needed to run the mills of industrial capitalism). But 'coolie' is not quite the same as 'hand', because the former word applies more to those vilified by white supremacy as lesser beings, while the latter word is generally used for white labour. In 1914 a member of the Ghadar [Revolt] Party of mainly Punjabi agricultural workers in California offered his comrades the following poem to underscore the special import of the word 'coolie':

> We are faced with innumerable miseries.
> We are called coolies and thieves.
> Wherever we go, we are treated like dogs.
> Why is no person kind to us?[6]

The word 'coolie' enters the European lexicon in the context of imperialism to index a person of inferior status who simply labours for hire. Whereas the European labourer, by the nineteenth century, was seen as a juridical citizen who could formally bargain for his (sometimes, her) rights as a seller of labour power, the 'coolie' was seen as racially suited for various forms

---

[4] Brij V. Lal, *Girmitiyas: the Origins of the Fiji Indians* (Canberra, 1983).
[5] *The Still Cry: Personal Accounts of East Indians in Trinidad and Tobago during Indentureship, 1845–1917*, complied by Noor Kumar Mahabir (Tacarigua,1985).
[6] *Ghadar di Goonj*, 1 (1914); Harish Puri, *Ghadar Movement* (Amritsar, 1993).

of hard labour particularly in tropical conditions. Colonial anthropologists and planters argued that the constitution of the coolie allowed them to handle the heat, humidity, and hard labour better. While the Europeans, we are told, had a sense of judgement, the coolie was easily inflamed by the passions of the sunshine and of unreason. Europeans who moved from the trades and the fields to the factories had to sell their labour as a commodity, where each hour of work time earned them a set (sometimes negotiated) wage. The labour of Asians, like Africans and Amerindians, however, was not commodified in an identical fashion. Instead it was 'animalized', and the productive efforts of the workers were treated by white supremacy as the rote part of their ill-fated primitive existence.[7]

Alongside the indentured labour, merchants and *dukawallas* (Swahili for shopkeeper) travelled to South and East Africa using their extensive contacts and experience in the Indian Ocean trade to insert themselves into the interstices of the colonial economy.[8] Areas abandoned by the colonial state and by imperial capital, such as tending shops in the interior, trading in petty commodities, and processing cotton for export, became the preserve of the Indian merchant.[9] It was these merchants who hired M. K. Gandhi in 1894, and his time in South Africa earned him a place in the history of the *desi* diaspora.

The overseas Indians did not immediately see themselves as a discrete community. The planters and the colonial state saw them from the inception of indenture as a community of labourers. Across the plantation colonies, the indentured labourers began to fashion cultural worlds of their own in the small spaces of leisure afforded them by the harsh work regimen. In the Caribbean, for instance, the indentured workers celebrated Muharram, which became a festival of all people under the name Hosay (from Hussain). Muslims, Hindus, Christians, Animists, and others joined in one day in the year to take their carnival of *tadjahs* (or *taziyas*, replicas of Hussein's tomb) from one plantation to another in a contest of design and imagination. In 1884, as the historian Prabhu Prasad Mohapatra shows us,

---

[7] Jan Breman, 'Introduction', *Imperial Monkey Business: Racial Supremacy in Social Darwinist Theory and Colonial Practice* (Amsterdam, 1990).

[8] Claude Markovits, *The Global World of Indian Merchants, 1750–1947: Traders of Sind from Bukhara to Panama* (Cambridge, 2000) and Vishnu Padaychee and Rob Morrell, 'Indian Merchants and Dukawallahs in the Natal Economy, c. 1875–1914', *Journal of Southern African Studies*, 17 (1991), 71–102.

[9] Mahmood Mamdani, *Politics and Class Formation in Uganda* (New York, 1976).

the Hosay festival coincided with major labour unrest.[10] As a consequence of the demonstrations, the colonial state restructured Hosay with the intention that each confessional community must conduct its own festivals and it must have its own religious leaders. The officials bemoaned the complexity of cultural productions such as Hosay and the 'loss of culture' of the indentured workers. Since the coolies and ex-slaves had 'forgotten' their 'original' cultures, the colonial state advocated the development of dogmatic religious and cultural boundaries between peoples.

Encouraged by colonial authorities, representatives of Brahmanical orthodoxy, both the Sanathan Dharma Sabha and the Arya Samaj, came to the Caribbean to put a stop, in effect, to polycultural practices like Hosay.[11] Clerics of Islam also travelled to the far-flung colonies in an attempt to 'reclaim the lost brethren' to the Islam of the homeland.[12] The 'India' being taught by the religious proselytizers had a very sharply communal colour. It was not the India of struggle, but that of Shuddhi and Tabligh (proselytizing movements). The missionaries, whether Hindu or Muslim, did provide an invaluable service in that they taught Indian languages and customs, but these did not have the flexibility of the traditions within the subcontinent. These proselytizers claimed to fight against the state-supported Christian missionaries when in fact, apart from the Canadian Mission (Presbyterian Church), the colonial regime cleared the terrain for the Swamis and Mullahs (Hindu and Muslim religious leaders) to create cultural fissures across the landscape of the working class. Each of

---

[10] Prabhu Prasad Mohapatra, 'The Hosay Massacre of 1884: Class and Community among Indians in Trinidad', in Arvind Das and Marcel Van Der Linden (eds), *Work and Social Change in South Asia: Essays in Honor of Jan Breman* (New Delhi, 2002). Also Kelvin Singh, *Bloodstained Tombs: The Mohurrum Massacre, 1884* (London, 1988).

[11] Steven Vertovec, '"Official" and "Popular" Hinduism in Diaspora: Historical and Contemporary Trends in Surinam, Trinidad and Guyana', *Contributions to Indian Sociology*, 28 (1994), 123–47. Much the same was encouraged in South Africa, where, during the decisive 1912–13 struggle, Swami Shankeranand visited Natal (where he felt he 'never had occasion to realize that he was in a land which is hostile to Asiatics') to generate enthusiasm for Hinduism over class antagonism. 'The Swami', *Natal Advertiser* (31 Dec. 1912); 'Young Men's Vedic Society: Inaugural Ceremony', *Natal Advertiser* (30 Nov. 1912); 'Dipavali Festival', *Natal Advertiser* (20 Oct. 1912); Vijay Prasad, *Everybody was Kung Fu Fighting: Afro–Asian Connections and the Myth of Cultural Purity* (Boston, 2001).

[12] In the 1950s, Muhammed Rafeeq felt that Muslims in Trinidad 'maintained the cardinal doctrines with unadulterated purity'. This illusion was only partly true due to the influx of clerics in the late 19th century. Muhammed Rafeeq, 'History of Islam and Muslims in Trinidad', *Islamic Review* (Sept. 1954), and Mary Arnett, 'Trinidad Muslim League', *Muslim World*, 48 (Jan. 1958).

these groups, for example, tried to rally East Indians from the standpoint of an *Indian* religion and culture rather than engage them in the polycultural practices of their new homeland. What these proselytizers did was to re-centre 'India' in the consciousness of the East Indians, who sought a language, culture, and religion for their children and themselves almost as a comfort zone in a harsh social environment.[13] Hosay was thus curtailed, while an orthodox kind of spirituality and domesticity that did not at all resemble everyday interactions or actual life experiences was promoted amongst the East Indians.

The actual lives of the *desis* included the brutality of indenture, the monotony of work life on a plantation, the attempt to find solace in religious and spiritual traditions, the problem of negotiating the divisions between the Africans and the Asians, the difficulty of forming family and other social networks in the midst of the plantation, and the effort to make the landscape both familiar and sacred. These elements formed the basis of the everyday life of the people, but the orthodox leadership ignored them. The colonial state and the planters (whose combined operation can be termed the plantocracy) gave the orthodox priests the authority to speak for 'Indian culture', and these priests made the most of it to reduce the richness of local traditions (the cultures of solidarity, of struggle, of peasant customs, of folk values). The everyday experiences and the ideology, which developed from those daily struggles, crafted the categories for a series of events in the diaspora that took place in 1913–14. The various movements led by indentured labourers in different colonies during that period offer us some indication of the labourers' self-consciousness of their common condition. Bharath, an indentured labourer, sang of the plantocracy taking labour from the ships, the *jahaj*: 'take out four hundred, five hundred, some pick out de jamaica, some pick out de b.g.[Guyana]/natal ooutari [takes], jamaica ooutari, guyana ooutari.'

The events of 1913–14 made it clear that the Indian labourers around the world, from Fiji to British Guiana to Canada, shared a common predicament: their labour was needed, but not their lives. Labourers struggled to make sense of their existence in racially charged areas, given the British finesse in dividing the local populations: in Fiji, between *desis* and Fijians and in the Caribbean, between *desis* and Africans. Four events dominate this

---

[13] Clem Seecharan, *India and the Shaping of the Indo-Guyanese Imagination, 1890s–1920s* (Leeds, 1993).

period: Kunti's Fiji letter, the foundation and activities of the Ghadar Party, the strikes in Natal, and finally, in 1914, the trials of the Komagata Maru.

Kunti's Cry

The plight of Indians in Fiji was dramatically brought home when Kunti's story appeared in the newspaper *Bharat Mitra* on 8 May 1913. Kunti, an indentured labourer, wrote that she had been sent to work in an isolated part of the plantation by her overseer. The overseer followed her and tried to rape her, but she freed herself, jumped into a nearby river, and was luckily freed by a young Indian. When she tried to report the incident to the white plantation owner he said, 'Go away, I don't want to hear about field things.'[14]

'Field things' were a common occurrence in most plantations, and Kunti's letter dramatized the immorality of the brutal plantation system. The indentured labourers worked in gangs under an overseer who treated them as chattel. 'No trick of sophistry or twist of logic', wrote a nineteenth-century Creole writer, 'can ever avail to defend the system of semi-slavery paraded under the guise of indentured immigration.'[15] Low wages, poor living conditions, terrible oppression by the overseers, disdain from managers, no avenues of redress, combined with unhappy futures, made the plantation lines a very bleak place. Revolt against cooliedom was frequent. The colonial legal apparatus in Fiji, however, worked on the side of the planters, prosecuting indentured labour on criminal grounds for labour protests.

Within the barbarity of indenture, gender relations familiar in British India came under stress. Women earned a wage like men, and stripped of the suffocation of local traditions, many women used this control over wages to exert some social power. Threatened by these social changes, men acted violently or disrespectfully towards women, who then would leave their husbands. As the historian of Fiji Brij Lal puts it,

Powerless and vulnerable, [indentured women] had little choice in the matter of morality. Their world was turned upside down, and they were caught in

---

[14] Brij V. Lal, 'Kunti's Cry: Indentured Women on Fiji Plantations', *Indian Economic and Social History Review*, 22 (1985), 55–71 and Totaram Sanadhya, *My Twenty One Years in the Fiji Islands, and, The Story of the Haunted Line* (Suva, 1991).

[15] Walter Rodney, *A History of the Guyanese Working People, 1881–1905* (Baltimore, 1981).

confusion about roles and obligations. The new experience and new opportunities widened their horizons. They wanted greater respect and recognition within the parameters of recognized cultural and social institutions, not outside or in breach of them. They, too, wanted the security and the comforting cushion of culture – minus its excessive patriarchal prerogatives.[16]

Although the British immediately doubted her veracity, Kunti's letter shocked Indian nationalists. Totaram Sanadhya's narrative of Fijian life and of Kunti's plight struck a chord in British India, although the response had more do to with masculine protection of women as much as outrage at the abuse of Indian workers overseas. The letter and the outcry over it spread to the plantation colonies whose East Indian inhabitants identified with the issue of violence against women (such as rape, murder, and suicide). Under pressure from the nationalist movement in India, spurred on by such protests as Kunti's letter, the Viceroy and his Council leaned on the imperial authorities on behalf of the indentured labourers. Such fissures provided space for the voice of one field labourer to make an international impact.

Ghadar Party (October 1913)

Peasants and intellectuals from the Punjab, who came to the US in the wake of the 1907 political agitation in that region of India, founded the Ghadar Party in San Francisco in October 1913. These peasants, rebels, and army men settled along the Pacific seaboard where they came into contact with other people of colour who shared common stories of oppression. Some of the intellectuals, like the exiled Indian nationalist, Hardayal, also met with anarchists and socialists, notably with the Industrial Workers of the World. Their political party, Ghadar, became a vehicle for the gathering of the *desi* diaspora on issues that affected those scattered in distant lands and its periodicals were a mechanism for the transit of the common indenture story.[17]

---

[16] Brij V. Lal, *Bittersweet: An Indo-Fijian Experience* (Canberra, 2004) and 'Veil of Dishonour: Sexual Jealousy and Suicide on Fiji Plantations', *Journal of Pacific History*, 20 (1985), 135–55.
[17] Emily Brown, *Har Dayal: Hindu Revolutionary and Rationalist* (Tucson, 1975); Sohan Singh Josh, *Hindustan Ghadar Party: A Short History* (New Delhi, 1978); Harish Puri, *The Ghadar Movement* (Amritsar, 1993); Maia Ramnath, *Haj to Utopia: How the Ghadhar Movement Chartered Global Radicalism and Attempted to Overthrow the British Empire* (Berkeley, 2011).

To educate Indians of their situation, the Party launched the multilingual paper *Ghadar* on 1 November 1913. *Ghadar* did not just work for the freedom of India, but also for Indians overseas who bore the marks of the 'new system of slavery'. With branch offices in many of the plantation colonies, *Ghadar* was indeed the voice of the overseas Indian calling for an end to slavery by the British both in India and in the empire at large. 'The world derisively accosts us: O Coolie, O Coolie,' the Ghadar-di Gunj sang, 'We have no fluttering flag of our own. Our home is on fire. Why don't we rise up and extinguish it?' The centre of the agitation was the 'homeland', but the Ghadar activists also dramatized the unequal treatment of Indians in the empire. *Ghadar*, along with Gandhi's Natal paper, *Indian Mirror*, and other pamphlets and publications, took the tale of injustice around the empire and their political education was given a symbol and a manifestation in the Natal strikes of late 1913. In their goals set out at their August 1913 meeting, the founders called upon the organization 'to liberate India with the force of arms from British servitude and to establish a free and independent India with equal rights for all,' and it noted, 'Every member was duty bound to participate in the liberation struggle of the country in which they were resident.'

In one of their many poems/songs that spread their message, the Ghadar Party railed against the quietism of the Indian National Congress.

> Freedom will not come through supplication,
> Political power will not come by appeal.
> Don't offer cowardly petitions.
> Lift up the sword, they will not remain.
> What have your petitions wrought?
> Brutal foreigners have plundered our homeland.

The Ghadar Party developed a cadre of dedicated freedom fighters, many of whom returned to India in *jathas* (religious squads) to seed a nationwide rebellion against the British Raj. They had no desire for 'home rule' or for 'dyarchy': they wanted Purna Swaraj (complete freedom) long before Gandhi moved the Congress to adopt that resolution on 31 December 1929. In the Party's newspaper, *Ghadar*, Hardayal wrote, 'Tribe after tribe are ready to mutiny. Your voice has reached China, Japan, Manila, Sumatra, Fiji, Java, Singapore, Egypt, Paris, South Africa, South America, East Africa and Panama' (14 July 1914). The energy of Ghadar swept the Indian diaspora and it produced a generation of radicals within India, such as Bhagat Singh, who moved the Freedom Movement from cooperation to non-cooperation: one of the Ghadar Party's famous early slogans was, 'Complete Independence or Non-Cooperation'.

Natal Strikes (October–November 1913)

As the peasants and intellectuals of California created an organized form for the struggle, in South Africa, the miners and sugar cane workers met a lawyer who learnt the arts of mass non-violent resistance from them.[18] The Indian workers on the plantations extracted coal in the interior of Natal and tended sugar cane near the coast. They were an integral part of the economy, even being the main builders of the region's railways.[19] In a bid to further control the workers, the state demanded a £3 poll tax. Initially, M. K. Gandhi and the merchant-dominated Natal Indian Congress (NIC) did not champion the cause of labour whose main short-term demand was the repeal of the tax. In mid-October 1913, as Gandhi called upon the NIC to assist the workers, he felt the earth move under his feet. The NIC needed to broaden its support base to take on the government, but it also could not entirely abandon the mass movement organized by such people as Thambi Naidoo of the Johannesburg Tamil Benefit Society. Against the poor work conditions, the poll tax, and the legislative denial of non-Christian marriages, several thousand Indian miners put down their tools by 17 October 1913. The colonial state was unwilling to negotiate, and the mining companies were in no hurry to retrieve the coal. Gandhi and the miners tried to force a confrontation when four thousand of them marched illegally into the neighbouring state of Transvaal. The South African Prime Minister Jan Smuts did not arrest them, and hoped that economic necessity would drive the strikers back into the mines. 'Mr Gandhi appeared to be in a position of much difficulty,' said Smuts. 'Like Frankenstein, he found his monster an uncomfortable creation and he would be glad to be relieved of further responsibility for its support.'

From the south of Natal, another 'monster' made its appearance, without the assistance of the NIC. Fifteen thousand sugar-cane workers joined their

---

[18] Maureen Swan, *Gandhi: The South African Experience* (Johannesburg, 1985); Uma Dhupelia, *From Cane Fields to Freedom: A Chronicle of Indian South African Life* (Cape Town, 2000).

[19] D. H. Heydenrych, 'Indian Railway Labour in Natal, 1876–1895: The Biggest Indian Work Force in the Colony', *Historia*, 31 (1986), 11–20.

coal worker brethren, as did domestic servants and workers in the city's produce markets. Sugar, unlike coal, can rot in the fields, and if the workers became enraged they would burn them ('cane fires') in protest. The strikes on these plantations near the major metropolis of Durban scared the planters and the state.[20] When the recently subdued Zulu peoples began to make overtures to join the movement, they sent an additional shiver through colonial officialdom.[21] The colonial state exerted its muscles and sent in the police to crush the workers. Smuts released Gandhi from jail and negotiated a deal. Gandhi, then, not only learnt the power of mass movements, but he also understood the value of a deal. By November, the government routed the strike, but news of it had not only travelled to other places but had also entered the lore of the anti-imperial struggle. Gandhi returned to India to lead the movement against the British Raj, and he became a national hero, whereas the unknown miners, Gandhi's teachers, are largely forgotten.

Komagata Maru (April–September 1914)

A minimum postulate of the British empire was that its subjects could settle anywhere in the empire. However, the 'settler colonies' (Australia and Canada) were reticent to allow people of colour to taint their shores:

> For white man's land we fight
> To Oriental grasp and greed
> We'll surrender, no, never
> Our watchword be 'God save the King'
> White Canada forever.[22]

Asiatic Exclusion Leagues across the Americas fought against Asians even as lumber, railway, and mining capitalists needed their labour power. The British empire and the USA came to a 'gentlemen's agreement' against the Asian workers. Theodore Roosevelt told Canadian Members of Parliament, 'Gentlemen, we have got to protect our workingmen. We have got to build

---

[20] Bill Freund, *Insiders and Outsiders: The Indian Working Class of Durban, 1910–1990* (Portsmouth, 1995).

[21] Shula Marks, *Reluctant Rebellion: The 1906–1908 Disturbance in Natal* (Oxford, 1970).

[22] Joan Jensen, *Passage from India: Asian Indian Immigration to North America* (New Haven, 1988).

up our western country with our white civilization, and we must retain the power to say who shall or shall not come to our country.'

Along the Pacific seaboard, in numerous Gurdwaras and Khalsa Diwans, Punjabi peasants, rebels, and army men discussed the exclusions and racism. One enterprising Sikh, Gurdit Singh, gathered support for a scheme to challenge the exclusions by transporting Asians to Canada. He hired a ship, the *Komagata Maru*, that its passengers renamed the Guru Nanak Jahaj.[23] As news of the ship reached Canada, the press warned of a 'Hindu Invasion of Canada'. When the ship reached Vancouver, it was not permitted to land, and after a scuffle at the docks and two months in abeyance, the 'ship of fools' was forced to return to India.

As the ship came within sight of Bengal, a colonial gunboat approached it and took it under guard to Budge Budge. There the colonial state tried to isolate the returnees and rush them to Punjab. In the midst of a scuffle with the police, one of them attacked Gurdit Singh, which provoked an all-out melee. The police opened fire on the passengers, killing nineteen of them. The story of *Komagata Maru* entered into the lore of the overseas population, highlighting the contradiction that white supremacists wanted the labour of Asians, but not their lives. The returning Punjabis from the western coast of North America formed the backbone of the revolts against British rule in Punjab during 1915.

Two consequences follow from the incidents of 1913–14: first, an understanding among Asians in the plantation colonies of their common socio-economic destinies, however these are differently inflected; and second, an intensified call from Indian nationalists for an end to indenture, articulated as an end to the abuse of the labour power of males and of the morality of females. The campaign against indenture, indeed, hastened the transformation of the Indian nationalist party (the Congress) into a mass movement.

Nationalism at Home and Abroad

Drawing on this far-flung campaign, Madan Mohan Malaviya of the Congress moved a resolution to ban indenture in the Imperial Legislative Council in March 1916. The Viceroy of India, Lord Hardinge, announced that he had 'obtained from His Majesty's Government the promise of the

---

[23] Hugh Johnston, *The Voyage of the Komagata Maru: The Sikh Challenge to Canada's Colour Bar* (Delhi, 1979).

abolition in due course'. For Hardinge, 'due course' meant 'within such reasonable time as will allow of alternative arrangements introduced'. Gandhi, who understood the frustrations of the indentured and ex-indentured Indians, found this intolerable, even as many established nationalists would have otherwise taken this assurance on its face. He pushed Malaviya in February 1917 to ask for immediate abolition, but the British refused to entertain the request (likely due to the exigencies of the war years). Gandhi had the tacit support of the Congress elders, but he knew that his campaign within India had to derive the same sort of energy as his campaign in South Africa. He needed to go to the people. Gandhi's initiative drew a passionate response from local Congress workers. Indeed, some of them had a long-term investment in anti-indenture politics. In the late 1880s, Dwarkanath Ganguli of the Indian Association visited the indentured workers in the Assam tea plantations, but his attempt to bring their plight to national attention received no sympathy from the newly established Congress. The experience of Ganguli foreshadowed that of many local Congress workers whose attempts to raise the question of labour rights withered before the 'moderate' Congress leadership.[24] They now flocked to Gandhi, who raised the issue of labour in a domain (the diaspora) that did not immediately impinge on the class interests of the Congress elites (as did the situation in Assam). The diaspora struggles helped to open the Pandora's box of populism and class agitation that overtook the decade of the 1920s within India.

The abolition of indenture in 1920 did not dull the organized political force of the diaspora. From Africa to America, the *desi* diaspora persisted in the fight for greater rights for themselves in their new homelands as well as complete freedom for India. The most commonplace organization created in the aftermath of the indenture campaign and with the growth of Gandhian mass anti-colonialism was an affiliate of the Congress Party. From the Congress Committee of Suva, Fiji to Nairobi's Eastern Africa Indian National Congress to the Indian National Congress of 16, Coffee Street, San Fernando, Trinidad, Gandhian anti-colonialism spread its message. By the late 1920s, every country with even a handful of Indians had a Congress group. Generally merchants or people of relative means among the Indians overseas gathered together and wrote to the Indian National Congress for

---

[24] Ganguli was not alone. Alongside him was the remarkable Ramkumar Vidyaratna who, in 1888, wrote *Kulikahini* (*Sketches from a Cooly Life*), a vivid portrait of the exploitation of indentured workers that foreshadowed the texts of 1913–14.

the right to affiliate to it. They had to provide an undertaking not to violate the broad views of the Congress and pledged to work amongst the Indian community. Some of these organizations numbered in the thousands (such as the Natal Indian Congress), while others had only about thirty members (the Bharat Welfare Society in Maryville, California).

The India Home Rule League of America (IHRL) provides a useful example of many of these organizations. Formed in 1917 by Lajpat Rai, Dr K. D. Shastri, and Dr N. S. Hardiker in Chicago, the IHRL sought to 'disseminate knowledge about India to the people of America' and 'to counteract propaganda that, at the time, was very virulent'. Headquartered in New York City, the IHRL published a journal (*Young India*) and sent out its members to lecture 'among labour, social and educational bodies'. Apart from being a news service, the IHRL attempted to 'aid Indian labourers in New York City' (it ran a night school) and it disseminated its propaganda materials in Canada, South America, British West Indies, Panama, Africa, Japan, China, Philippines, Fiji, and New Zealand.[25]

If these organizations encouraged cross-class unity, it was because most classes in the diaspora shared a common strategy for Indian freedom: the British had to be ousted from India. Disagreements on class lines, however, emerged in terms of the work the organization did in the adopted countries. In South Africa, for instance, the Natal Indian Congress faced a serious challenge when radical Indians affiliated to the South African Communist Party posed the problem of Indians and South African liberation before the mainly mercantile leadership of the Congress.[26] One of the issues before the militants was that the merchants used the Congress as an instrument to further their own business interests. The Congress in India had already identified this development, so that in 1929, Sarojini Naidu indicated that the New York leadership is 'exploiting the Indian National Congress for personal ends'.[27] Despite these issues, many of the *desi* organizations never-

---

[25] All-India Congress Committee (AICC) Papers, File no. 17, 1920, Nehru Memorial Museum and Library (NMML), New Delhi; Vivek Bald, *Bengali Harlem and the host Histories of South Asian America* (Cambridge, 2012).

[26] Bill Freund, *Insiders and Outsiders: The Indian Working Class in Durban, 1910–1990* (Pietermaritzburg, 1995), ch. 4.

[27] Virendranath Chattopadhyaya to Jawaharlal Nehru, 19 June 1929, AICC Papers, no. 0–4, 1928, NMML. In 1939, another Indian based in New York reported, 'Another group of Indians, mostly businessmen, who are in better economic position, have been trying to get some sort of trade-treaty arranged between Delhi and Washington. These people are not doing anything for

theless fought for the widest rights of their constituencies whether in the plantation colonies or else in the advanced industrial states. As members of the sugar worker's union in Guyana, *desis* fought against British colonialism as much as against the sugar capitalists, while the India Welfare League and the India League of America campaigned both for Indian freedom and for the right of Indians to the franchise and to property.[28]

Indians in Britain, obviously, were in their own league. The earliest Indians to make their lives in Britain came from the working class. Lascars (sailors), servants, and slaves arrived from the seventeenth century as part of a small labour migration that foreshadowed later developments. Enslaved workers like 'Catherine the Bengali' or weavers like 'John the Indian' played a prominent role in the landscape of English society. Some rebelled in their own way, such as 'John of Madras' who became a Christian under the eye of his mistress, who made him dance and sing 'Indian style' for her guests. John stole 20 guineas from her, burnt down her house, and was hanged at Tyburn in 1724.[29]

Being the heart of the empire, England attracted additional migrants from amongst the aristocratic and landed bureaucratic elites who either settled in England or who maintained a second home there, or whose children travelled to England to earn their degrees (and so advancement in the imperial system). While the political views of the aristocrats remained fairly uniformly loyal, that of the emergent elites might have surprised the English. Frustrated by the lack of advancement and by racism, many of them become vehement critics of empire. For this reason, of the three most prominent Indians who entered the British parliament, only one was a Conservative (Sir Mancherjee Bhownaggree) while the other two took very strong positions against imperialism (one as a Liberal, Dadabhai Naoroji, the other as a Communist, Shapurji Saklatvala). The demographic heft of the Indian community in Britain came not from the students and the

---

the working-class or poorer Indians. They are catering their activities to their own group.' AICC Papers, File no. FD-2, 1939, NMML.

[28] For the India Welfare League (founded by Mubarak Ali Khan) and the India League of America (founded by J. J. Singh) see Jensen, *Passage from India*, 277, and J. J. Singh, 'Zero Hour in India', *Magazine Digest*, (1946).

[29] Michael H. Fisher, *Counterflows to Colonialism: Indian Travelers and Settlers in Britain 1600–1857* (New Delhi, 2004), 44–6; Rozina Visram, *Ayahs, Lascars and Princes: Indians in Britain, 1700–1947* (London, 1984); and Shompa Lahiri, 'Contested Relations: The East India Company and Lascars in London', in H. V. Bowen, Margarette Lincoln, and Nigel Rigby (eds), *The Worlds of the East India Company* (Suffolk, 2002).

princes, but from the soldiers and the sailors. They formed the bulk of the Indians and unlike their more educated and well-off kin, these lascars and subedars faced the insecurity of life in a hostile society. Under the guidance of Kaka Joseph Baptista and others, they gathered in the Home Rule League to push for India's freedom. The League agitated for India's freedom during the First World War among the growing English working-class organizations and among the Indian students who came from prosperous backgrounds. Many notable Indian nationalists (such as Krishna Menon) cut their teeth in the League, which was eclipsed by the Indian National Congress once it made its call for mass agitation against British rule.

These organizations across the diaspora provided a unique service not only to the communities that lived there (by educating them about imperialism), but they offered shelter to exiled Indian revolutionaries. When these fighters came and lived amongst Indians elsewhere, they met people with different ideas and from different political movements. The Indian revolutionaries met with Marxists and Socialists, with Irish Republicans and with pan-Africanists, with anarcho-syndicalist unionists and civil libertarians. These discussions and this interchange of views did much to introduce a generation or more of Indian nationalists to a cosmopolitan world view.

Diaspora and the Independent Indian Nation

When India won its independence, the diaspora celebrated. Events from Suva to Stockton drew Indians together, and despite Partition, communal amity remained the order of the day. A decade later, India's new Prime Minister, Nehru, made it clear that the diaspora would have to make its home elsewhere. He pledged his support for those who faced oppression overseas, but he noted that Indians overseas 'should always give primary consideration to the interests of the people of those countries; they should never allow themselves to be placed in a position of exploiting the people of those countries, co-operate with them and help them, while maintaining their own dignity and self-respect'.[30] Even as the Indian

---

[30] Nehru was consistently of this view. In 1928, he wrote to U. K. Oza of the *Democrat*, in Jinja, Uganda, 'Indians who go to foreign countries go there not to exploit the inhabitants of those countries but to live in cooperation with them for the mutual advantage of both. We go on these terms abroad and we expect others to come on these same terms to India. If necessary the Indians ought to be prepared to take a back place as the natives of the country are concerned' (6 Dec. 1928). AICC Papers, File no. O-4, 1928, NMML.

government cherished those who claimed India as their 'homeland', Nehru recognized that they had to make their lives where they lay their heads.

The Indian state adopted a national ideology whose main concept was sovereignty: the state had to be sovereign from external control and it must remain accountable in a formal way to its citizens, who are juridically sovereign over it. For that democratic reason, non-citizens, even if they had filial and emotional ties to India, could not have any statutory rights. Furthermore, many of the regions in Africa and the Caribbean that had populations with ties to India were also in the process of state construction on the principle of sovereignty. They would not countenance any external interference in their formally democratic institutions. This was the reason for the Indian state's advice to its diaspora, and in most cases the citizens of other lands with links to India had already begun to follow it.

Migration of Indians continued despite the freedom of India. After the Second World War, the British economy experienced a shortage of labour. The arrival of Caribbean and Asian (mostly Indian) labour into the transport and textiles trades expanded the labour supply and enabled British capital to stabilize wages. The Indians and Pakistanis who travelled to Britain in this period came from regions already in turmoil as a result of Partition, although, coincidentally, these regions had previously sent migrants to England. Punjabi soldiers who had been demobilized after each world war had settled in Britain, and they now welcomed their displaced relatives from both sides of the new border. Merchant marine seamen, lascars, had come in large numbers from Kashmir (mainly what would become the Pakistani side, the town of Mirpur) and from Bengal (mainly as ship's cooks from the district of Sylhet, which would after 1971 be part of Bangladesh). These people acted as the bridgeheads for relatives and friends who flocked to their towns (Mirpuris to Bradford) and into their occupations (Sylhettis into the Indian restaurant trade). They would also find work in the transportation and factory trades.[31] Racism in society translated in the late 1950s into racism in state policy, as immigration law made it harder for migrants of colour to enter Britain. Those who remained in Britain, and their children born there, fought exclusionary policies and social injustice as *British* citizens, whether in civil rights battles, labour struggles, or else in the

---

[31] Rashmi Desai, *Indian Immigrants in Britain* (London, 1963); Ron Ramadin, *The Making of the Black Working Class in Britain* (Aldershot, 1987); and Winston James and Clive Harris (eds), *Inside Babylon: The Caribbean Diaspora in Britain* (London, 1993).

transformation of family and social codes within and without the Asian community.[32]

Where migration to Britain slowed down (partly due to immigration restriction that began in 1962), that to the US picked up. With the 1957 launching of Sputnik by the USSR, an alarmed US government moved to secure additional technical labour to expand its own space and armament industries; with the passage of Medicare, the US also needed to rapidly expand its medical personnel. In 1924 the US had effectively ended migration from Asia. Its 1965 Immigration and Nationality Act revised this and allowed highly skilled migrants into the country so those who migrated to the US came from new social classes quite different than those who went to Britain in the 1950s.

Until the 1970s, the Indian government gave its blessings to the diaspora but did little to 'gather' it. From the late 1970s, the economic dislocations of the Indian economy, the Congress's abandonment of economic nationalism, and the growth of religious and cultural nationalism in its place led to a reassessment of the role of the diaspora. In 1976, the Emergency government announced 'steps to encourage investment by non-resident Indians'. The newly minted Non-Resident Indian (NRI) had a new responsibility: no longer was this highly skilled sector to be denigrated as a Brain Drain, but it was now to be encouraged as a Cash Cow to help the Indian state increase its foreign exchange reserves. In 1982, Manmohan Singh of the Indian Planning Commission and future prime minister said, 'Indian communities abroad are noted for their hard work, initiative, and enterprise. As a result, they have accumulated large resources of investible funds.' The Indian government needed this money to cover its newly expanded military and technical imports. But the NRIs failed the government: in the crucial period of liberalization from 1991 to 1994, only 8 per cent of foreign direct investment into India came from the NRIs, and after this initial burst of enthusiasm the numbers have decreased. The NRI, nevertheless, is now part of the economic plans of the liberalized state.

The concept of the NRI obscures the pre-independence diaspora whose history is separate from more recent middle-class migrants, particularly those that have gone to the United States. In 1999, therefore, the Bharatiya Janata Party (BJP) pushed the People of Indian Origin card, for those who

---

[32] A. Sivanandan, *A Different Hunger* (London, 1983) and Amrit Wilson, *Finding a Voice: Asian Women in Britain* (London, 1978).

could gain special economic privileges in India for a fee (about $300). Most analysts believe that the high fees encouraged only five thousand people to secure these cards. Four years later, the BJP-led cabinet and then the parliament allowed NRIs from strategic parts of the world to hold dual citizenship: the United States, Canada, the United Kingdom, parts of the European Union, New Zealand, Australia, Israel, and Singapore. The children and grandchildren of the indentured labourers are given lip-service by the Prime Minister, but no access to dual citizenship: Trinidadians, Guyanese, and South African Indians do not have the kind of capital that the BJP government wants to see enter the Indian economy.

The post-indenture plantation colonies went in two directions, but both decidedly racialist. One set of social formations adopted a fraught pluralist ethic and therefore acknowledged the presence of various peoples even if it did not offer a strategy to redress inequalities between groups who had been held apart by colonialism (Trinidad and Guyana are good examples). Another set of societies, led by Uganda and Fiji, sought to expel or to racially oppress their Indian populations. Equally marginalized was the economic migration of South Asians to the Gulf states, a labour transit that functions as the indenture system of our times. These migrants became central to the balance of payments but the indignity that they suffered rarely became a matter of national interest.

The growth of an exclusionary economic identity of the NRI came alongside the emergence of a cultural definition of nationalism.[33] Whereas the earlier history of the diaspora operated with a theory of nationalism as a secular platform to help raise the well-being of people of Indian origin, the post-1970s form of nationalism concentrated on race and religiosity as the foundation of national identity. Now the migrants would be part of the cultural unity of India regardless of their territorial location. Such a convenient feint provided fodder for the religious obscurantist of various denominations. The Vishwa Hindu Parishad (World Hindu Council), founded in 1964, would expand throughout the diaspora in the 1970s. The total income of NRIs in the US, Canada, and the European Union is now in excess of $160 billion, almost half of India's Gross Domestic Product. Only a fraction of this finds its way into India for productive investment, but money did enter the country for the use of Far Right political organizations.

'Diaspora' is not a trans-historical category. Our understanding of it is linked to the concept of nationalism, and as the definition of the latter

---

[33] Vijay Prashad, *Uncle Swami: Being South Asian in America* (New York, 2012).

changes, so does that of the former. Not only does the category 'diaspora' require that of 'nationalism', but that the story of Indian nationalism before and after independence is incomplete without consideration of the processes and personalities of the diaspora. Gandhi makes little sense without his South African crucible; Indian revolutionary developments make little sense without the Ghadar movement. These are fundamental to the elaboration of Indian anti-colonial nationalism, just as the more recent migrations to North America are integral to the growth of Hindutva nationalism.

Select Bibliography

CLARE ANDERSON, *Convicts in the Indian Ocean: Transportation from South Asia to Mauritius, 1815–1853* (New York, 2000).

TONY BALLANTYNE, *Between Colonialism and Diaspora: Sikh Cultural Formations in an Imperial World* (Durham, NC, 2006).

CRISPIN BATES (ed.), *Community, Empire and Migration: South Asians in Diaspora* (London, 2000).

JUDITH M. BROWN, *Global South Asians: Introducing the Modern Diaspora* (Cambridge, 2006).

MARINA CARTER, *Voices of Indenture: Experiences of Indian Migrants in the British Empire* (Leicester, 1996).

MICHAEL FISHER, *Counterflows to Colonialism: Indian Travellers and Settlers in Britain, 1600–1857* (New Delhi, 2004).

BILL FREUND, *Insiders and Outsiders: The Indian Working Class of Durban, 1910–1990* (Portsmouth, 1995).

BRIJ LAL, *Girmitiyas: The Origins of the Fiji Indians* (Canberra, 1983).

CLAUDE MARKOVITS, 'Indian Merchant Networks Outside India in the Nineteenth and Twentieth Centuries: A Preliminary Survey', *Modern Asian Studies*, 33 (1999), 883–912.

——JACQUES POUCHEPADASS, and SANJAY SUBRAHMANYAM (eds), *Society and Circulation: Mobile People and Itinerant Cultures in South Asia, 1750–1950* (London, 2003).

DAVID NORTHRUP, 'Migration from Africa, Asia, and the South Pacific', in Andrew Porter (ed.), *The Oxford History of the British Empire: The Nineteenth Century* (Oxford, 1999).

VIJAY PRASHAD, *Karma of Brown Folk* (Minneapolis, 2000).

Report of the High Level Committee on the Indian Diaspora (New Delhi, 2001).

SANDYA SHUKLA, *India Abroad: Diasporic Cultures of Postwar America and England* (Princeton, 2000).

IAN TALBOT and SHINDER THANDI, *People on the Move: Punjabi Colonial and Post-Colonial Migration* (New Delhi, 2004).

PETER VAN DER VEER (ed.), *Nation and Migration: The Politics of Space in the South Asian Diaspora* (Philadelphia, 1995).

ROZINA VISRAM, *Asians in Britain: 400 Years of History* (London, 2002).

14

The Political Legacy of Colonialism in South Asia

Nandini Gooptu

Burgeoning interest in democratization and governance in the post-cold war world has produced a rich crop of studies on democratic politics in the Indian subcontinent. This body of work, along with research on the politics of the early years after independence, has enhanced our knowledge of the political continuities and ruptures from the colonial period. Postcolonial studies have also deepened our understanding of the colonial political legacy, by engaging in a reappraisal of the nature of colonial rule itself and pointing to the significance of culture, knowledge, and discourse as a major, if not the primary, site of exercise of colonial power. Recent research has analysed the 'postcolonial predicament' of politics in the Indian subcontinent, and drawn attention to the seemingly inescapable nature of the colonial discursive legacy.[1] Postcolonial theorist Robert Young has, however, emphasized that the 'postcolonial does not privilege the colonial', and that postcolonial studies are 'concerned with colonial history to the extent that that history has determined the configurations and power structures of the present'.[2] This chapter explores ways of interpreting the political legacy of colonialism in South Asia, primarily with a focus on the state and democratic politics. While discussing a variety of manifestations of the colonial political legacy, the chapter seeks to illuminate how the colonial inheritance has been understood from different analytical perspectives. An exhaustive account of, or explanation for, all aspects of politics is not intended here, nor an equal coverage of all South Asian countries. The chapter covers the

---

[1] e.g. Carol A. Breckenridge and Peter van der Veer (eds), *Orientalism and the Postcolonial Predicament* (Delhi, 1994).

[2] Robert Young, *Postcolonialism: An Historical Introduction* (Oxford, 2001), 4.

following broad areas. An initial identification of colonial political institutions and practices that persisted in the postcolonial context is followed by an enquiry into the reasons for their perpetuation. The causes are sought in the political dynamics of independent nations and the agency of their political actors, rather than viewing the colonial legacy as a direct and uncomplicated transfer from the Raj without the possibility of alternative outcomes. The role of elites and their political motivations and strategies are juxtaposed against the significance of subaltern politics and pressures from below in determining the nature of continuity and change. The chapter interrogates the constitutive role of colonialism in shaping the nature of postcolonial politics and proposes a contextualized historical analysis of the legacy of colonialism in its many and varied manifestations and appropriations by South Asian political actors, both elite and subaltern.

Democracy and Authoritarianism

One of the most significant political issues in postcolonial South Asian politics is the problem of democratic consolidation and authoritarianism. The latter is somewhat less relevant to India than to Pakistan, whose postcolonial history has been dominated by authoritarian military regimes with only a few civilian interludes. The difference between India and Pakistan, as Jalal has pointed out, is, however, one of degree than of kind.[3] It hardly needs emphasis that the Indian state has demonstrated pronounced authoritarian tendencies, and the ethic of development has gradually yielded to an underlying culture of national security. Democracy has been effective in India largely in its procedural and institutional aspects, as Atul Kohli in his celebration of India's democratic 'success' has acknowledged,[4] and not in any substantive sense.[5] How far was this state of affairs bequeathed to the subcontinent by colonial rule?

I take as my point of departure the Indian Constitution, which was fashioned as the most important political statement of freedom and liberty in newly independent India and self-consciously projected as a break with

---

[3] Ayesha Jalal, *Democracy and Authoritarianism in South Asia: A Comparative and Historical Perspective* (Cambridge, 1995).
[4] Atul Kohli (ed.), *The Success of India's Democracy* (Cambridge, 2001), 3.
[5] Niraja Gopal Jayal, *Democracy and the State: Welfare, Secularism and Development in Contemporary India* (Delhi, 1999), 25–7, and *passim*.

the colonial past.[6] In some interpretations, the Constitution and independent India's political system represented the incremental gains and maturity of liberal and representative political ideas and institutions, and the rule of law in India, as it developed through the colonial experience, though not necessarily as a direct bequest of the Raj in all respects.[7] For nationalists who framed the Constitution, however, its spirit proclaimed a radical departure from colonial politics. This was most clearly demonstrated in the enshrinement of the principles of fundamental rights, citizenship, universal franchise, and popular democracy, as well as in the inclusion of what Granville Austen has described as 'humanitarian socialist precepts' in the Directive Principles of State Policy, namely the acceptance of the responsibility of the government for the welfare of the masses and the duty of the state to promote social, economic, and political justice, and to secure adequate livelihood and education for its citizens.[8] While some of these ideas were no doubt of Western intellectual and philosophical provenance, they could scarcely be considered the benign inheritance of colonialism. Indeed, some of these ideas had been little rehearsed in colonial India. The idea of democracy, for instance, 'stood in a lonely corner', Khilnani notes,[9] and both he and Washbrook have elaborated that notions of the democratic rights of citizens, as distinct from arrangements for political representation, were largely absent in the discourse of colonial politics.[10] Similarly, the idea of a 'civilizing mission' or social reform did not rest on any conception of the obligation of the state towards its subjects' welfare, and, in any case, considerations of security, stability, and parsimony usually gained precedence over reform. As the foundational document of postcolonial Indian politics, then, the Constitution would stand testimony to the repudiation of a colonial political inheritance, at least in spirit.

---

[6] Granville Austen, *The Indian Constitution: Cornerstone of a Nation* (Delhi, 1999); Rajiv Bhargava (ed.), *Politics and Ethics of the Indian Constitution* (Delhi, 2009). For a discussion on the Constitution, see also Stuart Corbridge and John Harriss, *Reinventing India: Liberalization, Hindu Nationalism and Popular Democracy* (Delhi, 2001), ch. 2.

[7] e.g. Percival Spear, *The Oxford History of Modern India, 1740–1975* (Delhi, 2nd edn 1978), 390, and *passim*.

[8] Ibid. 75–83.

[9] Sunil Khilnani, *The Idea of India* (London, 1997), 28.

[10] David Washbrook, 'The Rhetoric of Democracy and Development in Late Colonial India', in Sugata Bose and Ayesha Jalal (eds), *Nationalism, Democracy and Development: State and Politics in India* (Delhi, 1998), 37–40.

The reality of politics has been rather different, not only in India with its liberal constitutional framework, but also in Pakistan, where no immediate attempt was made to mark a symbolic break with the past and its first constitution was not promulgated until 1956. It is widely acknowledged that the Indian Constitution harboured a number of conservative and anti-democratic elements from colonial polity. Moreover, the liberal and democratic prescriptions of the Constitution were compromised by political practices and institutional arrangements inherited from the Raj and from the milieu of colonial politics. It is well known that the framers of the Constitution borrowed extensively from the 1935 Government of India Act and 'thus drew quintessentially "colonial" forms of political relationship into the core of the[ir] emergent national democratic state'.[11] While being based on a Westminster-style parliamentary democracy, the Constitution erected a highly centralized state structure dominated by the executive, reminiscent of colonial political centralism, which predisposed Indian politics towards authoritarianism. Federal principles, although different in many respects from the provisions of the 1935 Act,[12] were nonetheless severely attenuated, following colonial political arrangements that had skewed the political balance of power in favour of the central state vis-à-vis the provincial units of the Indian union. The colonial state had construed democratization as controlled devolution and the limited transfer of power to regional units, while the central executive maintained firm control over the most significant aspects of government.[13] The Indian Constitution not only replicated this relationship, but the central state also retained the draconian power to dismiss democratically elected regional governments. The Gandhian model of a decentralized polity with village panchayats as its fundamental units and a very weak state at its apex had been discussed in the Constituent Assembly, but these proposals ultimately found little support.[14]

While there were then obvious colonial continuities, can these be interpreted as the structurally inevitable outcome of colonialism, or an inescapable colonial heritage? Several options were available to, and considered by, the framers of the Constitution, in addition to the British colonial

---

[11] Ibid. 43.
[12] Sumit Sarkar, 'Indian Democracy: The Historical Inheritance', in Atul Kohli (ed.), *The Success of India's Democracy* (Cambridge, 2001), 30–1.
[13] Washbrook, 'Rhetoric of Democracy', 42–3.
[14] Austen, *Indian Constitution*, 26–45.

framework. These included the Euro-American liberal tradition, the Gandhian model based on supposedly indigenous institutions, the so-called pre-colonial 'durbar' tradition of benevolent despots as envisaged by those inclined towards Hindu nationalism, or even the European totalitarian and Soviet systems.[15] Out of this range of available alternatives, Indian political elites of the Constituent assembly[16] elected to opt for a centralized state and a limited federal polity. It was the product of a highly contested process of deliberation and ultimately of a conscious choice or strategy on the part of ruling elites, or at least a dominant section of them. In Pakistan too, governing elites at the centre, in the early years after independence, continued to operate under the 1935 Government of India Act. Despite Jinnah's arguments in favour of federalism during deliberations over independence and partition, the independent Pakistani state ironically hastened to restrain the federal principle and embarked resolutely on the path of centralized bureaucratic authoritarianism, with a prominent position for the military. The promulgation of the constitution was held in abeyance until 1956, only to be almost immediately overturned by a military coup.

In addition to a highly centralized political system, the independent states of South Asia inherited the colonial apparatus of the armed forces as well as an armed constabulary police for civil law and order. These fitted well into the continued security preoccupations of the successor states of the Raj and served to buttress bureaucratic authoritarianism with coercive force. Pakistan was more overtly concerned with security issues, with its perceived sense of threat from India, which led it to join US-led regional security alliances and allowed the military a prominent place in the polity. The dominance of the military, and what has been termed the 'political economy of defence' in Pakistan,[17] very substantially perpetuated the tradition of the British Indian garrison state. The state continued to extract resources from the population for defence and military expenditure, in what might be seen as a postcolonial variant of military fiscalism. In India, the national security orientation of the state had been less explicit in the early years, at

---

[15] Austen, *Indian Constitution*, 27–8.

[16] The Constituent Assembly was a representative body of a limited nature, elected under restricted franchise and dominated by members of the Congress or individuals brought in by the Congress, including representatives of the so-called 'depressed classes' or minority communities, but excluding non-Congress Muslims, socialists, and Hindu Mahasabhaites. Ibid. 8–25.

[17] Ayesha Jalal, *The State of Martial Rule: The Origins of Pakistan's Political Economy of Defence* (Cambridge, 1990).

least in its external dimensions, and hence the role of defence and the defence forces was much less emphasized. Even here, though, the issues of internal security and political stability, viewed through the prism of national unity and integration as well as communal conflict, were extremely significant. Indeed, the army was deployed for political integration in a number of erstwhile princely states. Indian and Pakistani ruling elites embraced colonial administrative and institutional practices in other respects too, such as the judiciary, the basic structure of civil and criminal law, and above all, the so-called 'steel frame' of the bureaucracy.[18] The colonial bureaucracy was smoothly pressed into action in independent India and Pakistan in the interest of economic development and political control. In Pakistan, the ruling elite chose to hold the legislative process at bay for several years without promulgating a constitution, and ruled through bureaucratic fiat from the centre. This ensured the long-term pre-eminence of this unelected institution in Pakistani polity, second only to the dominance of the military. In both India and Pakistan, the bureaucracy emerged as the instrument of the centralized state to exercise political control right down to the locality. Jalal, among others, has emphasized that 'bureaucratic authoritarianism inherent in the colonial state structure remained largely intact'.[19]

Similarly, colonial patterns of collaboration and political mediation between the state and its subjects were maintained by the independent states in many respects. Following the colonial tradition, successive governments in independent India and Pakistan have relied for regime stability on alliance with various dominant classes, especially in the countryside.[20] This includes upwardly mobile and politically mobilized sections, such as those who benefited from state-sponsored commercialization of agriculture and agrarian capitalism after independence.[21] Patronage of, and collaboration with, powerful landed classes, to whom it gave all manner of privileges, was the strategy of political control of the Raj in its heyday. The gradual failure

---

[18] David C. Potter, *India's Political Administrators, 1919–1983: From ICS to IAS* (Oxford, 1996).
[19] Jalal, *Democracy and Authoritarianism*, 18.
[20] Corbridge and Harriss, *Reinventing India*, 11–12; Dietmar Rothermund, *An Economic History of India: From Pre-Colonial Times to 1986* (London, 1988), 130–3; Washbrook, 'Rhetoric of Democracy', 47–8; Akbar Zaidi, *Issues In Pakistan's Economy* (Karachi, 2nd edn, 2005), chs. 2, 3.
[21] Lloyd I. Rudolph and Susanne Hoeber Rudolph, *In Pursuit of Lakshmi: The Political Economy of the Indian State* (Chicago and London, 1987); Francine Frankel, *India's Political Economy, 1947–2004: The Gradual Revolution* (Delhi, 2nd updated edn, 2005).

or erosion of this strategy had eventually sealed the fate of the Raj in the subcontinent, while political parties in both independent Pakistan and India adopted this as their fundamental mode of political operation. This form of machine politics of patronage curtailed the possibility of popular political participation in the institutional structures of democracy, as a class of political mediators and power brokers placed themselves between the state and its citizens. Thus, in India, while citizens were granted universal franchise, yet for a majority of the population, this right did not lead to their effective participation in democratic governance and political institutions. Patronage politics not only undermined democratic political practice, it also had major implications for economic development. Political regimes in independent India and Pakistan, due to their reliance on the political support of landed interests, found it difficult to tax the countryside and ran into serious problems of mobilization of resources for development purposes, precipitating a crisis of development. The sources of the subcontinent's development failures, thus, derived in no small measure from the persistence of the practices of colonial politics. Moreover, having to rely on powerful rural allies, independent governments found it difficult to implement redistributive policies or any structural transformation of the agrarian economy that might have undermined dominant interests, thus perpetuating and even worsening the problems of livelihood and poverty.

It is evident, then, that South Asian ruling elites chose to embrace the legacy of the Raj in many respects. The question arises why they did so. The first and obvious set of explanations suggests that the need of the hour was almost unanimously perceived in ruling circles to be economic development, national unity, security, and political stability, albeit with different emphases in Pakistan and India. Late colonial experience or political wisdom had suggested that these goals could be best achieved by a strong, centralized state. As Chatterjee has noted, the 'grounds of justification' for continuing the institutional heritage were 'largely instrumental and pragmatic'.[22] Thus, for instance, in India, Gandhian ideas of a decentralized and virtually state-less polity were swept aside and a powerful colonial legacy was embraced. Equally, the bureaucracy was allowed free rein, driven by the need to bring about economic development and to manage the

---

[22] Partha Chatterjee, 'Introduction', in Chatterjee (ed.), *Wages of Freedom: Fifty Years of the Indian Nation-State* (Delhi, 1998), 7.

potentially disruptive consequences of development policies and capitalist modernization, not to mention the urgency to mitigate problems of law and order, unity, and political stability. In a different vein, Chatterjee and Kaviraj,[23] with somewhat different emphases, have argued that the multi-class alliance forged for the anti-colonial struggle, as well as the specific conditions of colonial politics and civil society, as distinct from developments in the West, had prevented a bourgeois revolution and thwarted the bourgeoisie from assuming hegemonic powers to engineer social transformation. The Indian bourgeoisie and ruling elites, therefore, chose to depend on the coercive powers of a bureaucratic state of colonial provenance and took recourse to 'passive revolution', whereby they relied on an alliance with dominant classes, with a selective appropriation of subaltern politics.[24] In Pakistan, the Punjabi-dominated ruling elite at the centre feared political challenges from regional elites. Their need for self-preservation, as well as security concerns, led them to disregard the federal principle and perpetuate centralized bureaucratic authoritarianism and a 'political economy of defence'. While military dominance helped to maintain the vested institutional interests of the army within Pakistan's polity, this was made possible by the fact that the Pakistani army, manned at the top mostly by personnel from the Punjab (the main military recruitment base of the British Indian army), shared the same social and ethnic origin as the powerful landed interests of that province, who now dominated Pakistan's polity.

The explanations of the colonial aftermath, discussed so far, focus on elite strategies and practices—their self-interest, internal competition, ideological preferences, political compulsions, and pragmatism. The analytical emphasis is placed on state structures and the formal domain of institutional politics. Turning to the wider non-institutional arena of late colonial and early postcolonial politics in South Asia, we see mass political mobilization, left-wing insurgency, and extensive sectarian violence. In this context, political elites came to attach utmost importance to political stability, the maintenance of order, and the prevention of a major social or political upheaval. The sources of authoritarianism can be located in these elite

---

[23] Sudipta Kaviraj, 'On State, Society and Discourse in India', in James Manor (ed.), *Rethinking Third World Politics* (London, 1992), 72–99; Partha Chatterjee, *The Nation and Its Fragments: Colonial and Postcolonial Histories* (Delhi, 1997), ch. 10.

[24] Chatterjee, *Nation and Its Fragments*, 211–14; Partha Chatterjee, *Nationalist Thought and the Colonial World: A Derivative Discourse* 1986; London, 1993), 30.

responses to mass politics. Indeed, the colonial legacy of authoritarianism, within and outside state structures, became more and more pronounced with time, in almost direct proportion to the expansion of subaltern political movements and democratic political participation in the postcolonial era. One of its recent political expressions is right-wing, conservative Hindu nationalism as a form of 'elite revolt'[25] against democratization and a 'plebianization of the political field'.[26] However, interestingly and paradoxically, not only did the context of mass politics ensure the perpetuation of anti-democratic tendencies, but, as Sarkar has demonstrated,[27] this also helps to explain the introduction of democratic measures, such as universal franchise in India, which marked the sharpest break with the past. Democratic arrangements were not magnanimous gifts of elites, presented in a fit of 'absentmindedness'[28] to the masses, nor did they emanate in any consensual way from the ideological conviction of elites. Members of the Constituent Assembly, elected under restricted franchise, based on education and property ownership, hardly constituted a progressive force and were unlikely to have a natural affinity for mass democracy. Rather, their democratic turn represented the attempts of political elites to contain and control mass mobilization by legitimate institutional means, instead of through force and coercion alone. The expansion of popular politics in the late colonial period signalled a growing democratic urge in Indian politics, and at times also involved a leftward turn towards socialism and communism. Sarkar argues that these developments persuaded the ruling elites and policy makers to embark on a democratic path, incorporate democratic principles in the Constitution, and rein in authoritarian tendencies to some extent.[29] This was intended to ensure the legitimacy and stability of the newly emerging political structure, by directing mass political energies into the straitjacket of electoral mobilization.

The role of subaltern politics is also relevant in explaining the perpetuation of the colonial mode of politics of patronage and local collaboration,

---

[25] Corbridge and Harriss, *Reinventing India*, chs. 6, 8.
[26] Thomas Blom Hansen, *The Saffron Wave: Democracy and Hindu Nationalism in Modern India* (Princeton, 1999), 8 and *passim*.
[27] Sarkar, 'Indian Democracy', *passim*.
[28] Khilnani, *Idea of India*, 34.
[29] Sarkar, 'Indian Democracy', 28–30.

mentioned above. It would be wrong to suggest that the Indian political system was somehow trapped in this mode of colonial politics, out of which it was impossible to escape. In the context of late colonial politics and mass mobilization, India's democracy and development policies might have been based on popular support instead of on patronage politics and elite consensus. The early stability of India's democracy, and the nature of its development regime, have been explained in terms of an accommodation of three 'dominant proprietor classes', viz. landed interests, business, and capital, and the upper echelons of the bureaucracy and the political elite.[30] To secure a wider source of support for democratic politics and development beyond these classes might not have been impossible, given extensive mass political action and left-wing popular political mobilization in the late colonial and early postcolonial periods. However, this would have required extensive redistributive policies, thus imperilling the interests of ruling classes and elites themselves. Substantive redistributive policies had been in the framework of discussion in the Constituent Assembly, for instance, but these were ultimately relegated to the Directive Principles of the Constitution and rendered non-justiciable. Instead, continuing the colonial practice of collaboration between ruling elites within state structures, on the one hand, and dominant classes of various kinds, on the other, was the logical option pursued by the inheritors of the Raj. Not surprisingly, in this respect too, colonialism provided the template for political practice in postcolonial India.

The discussion here thus far has shown that while colonial rule, and its political ideas, institutions, and practices, clearly left a significant mark on independent India and Pakistan as can be expected, the specific effects were largely mediated through the agency of South Asian political actors and the outcome was shaped by political contingencies. Elites selected elements from colonial politics, and from Western liberal political traditions more broadly, to respond to the political situation of subaltern challenges and power struggles in the early postcolonial years.

Colonial Modernity and the State

A rather different framework for explaining authoritarian politics is based on the historical experience of 'colonial modernity', with the 'modern state'

---

[30] Pranab K. Bardhan, *The Political Economy of Development in India* (Delhi, 1998).

argued to be its most important expression.[31] This state was not distinctive for its extractive, security, or military functions, which it shared with some pre-modern and pre-colonial ones. The modern state was a radical departure from the past in the Indian colonial context because of its claims to sovereignty and the right to reorder society, as well as in its discourse of scientific rationality and its impulse to classify, systematize, and taxonomize all aspects of society.[32] As Kaviraj notes: 'The British colonial state represented the great conquering discourse of enlightenment rationalism', and it sought to restructure, although not with complete success or without resistance, 'the productive system, the political regimes, the moral and cognitive orders'.[33] While the colonial state may have been ineffectual in some respects in the actual exercise of power, this did not detract from the *idea* of the all-powerful, modern state. The nationalist elite inherited not only the structure of that state but also the idea. Despite their rhetoric of liberty and freedom in anti-colonial struggles, the structure, function, and fundamental nature of the state remained more or less intact under post-colonial nationalist dispensation. Chatterjee comments, 'ideas of republican citizenship often accompanied the politics of national liberation. But without exception...they were overtaken by the developmental state' that 'deployed the latest governmental technologies to promote the well-being of their populations'.[34]

The reason for this, it has been argued, has to do with the entanglement of nationalist elites with 'colonial modernity' and 'the desire of the elite to replicate in its own society the forms as well as the substance of western modernity'.[35] The nationalist elite, led by Nehru, in seeking to legitimize its hegemony in independent India and as the successor to an alien Raj, espoused economic development and modernization as its key goals, which helped to distinguish it from the colonial regime. However, elite conceptions of development were inspired by Western models of industrial

---

[31] Kaviraj, 'On State, Society and Discourse in India'; Chatterjee, *Nation and Its Fragments*, ch. 10.

[32] Bernard Cohn, *Colonialism and Its Forms of Knowledge: The British in India* (Princeton, 2006); Kaviraj, 'On State, Society and Discourse in India'.

[33] Kaviraj, 'On State, Society and Discourse in India', 78.

[34] Partha Chatterjee, *The Politics of the Governed: Reflections on Popular Politics in Most of the World* (New York, 2004), 37.

[35] Partha Chatterjee, 'Introduction', in Chatterjee (ed.), *Wages of Freedom*, 12.

capitalism, focusing on science and technology.[36] Thus, the Gandhian alternative of decentralized, rural development, hostile to science and technology, and based on a minimalist state, failed to capture the imagination of all but a tiny minority of elites, although arguably the Gandhian imagination of quintessential village republics as the arena of national regeneration was hardly 'indigenous', for it drew upon 'orientalist' ideas of India's antique rural essence. Drawing upon the notion of alternative or multiple modernities,[37] Gyan Prakash has argued that the nationalist elites' espousal of science and reason did not, however, amount to an uncritical embrace of 'Western' modernity, but led to what he describes as a 'modern articulation [which was]...irreducibly different from its colonial expression';[38] or 'a modernity of one's own, one that differed from western modernity'.[39] Notwithstanding such caveat about the distinctive character of India's elite modernity, it had limited support beyond the elites, and the realization of the elite vision of thoroughgoing modern transformation required intervention at all levels of society and in the realms of education and culture.[40] The strategy to translate this vision into practice placed the modern bureaucratic state at the heart of the elite project of transformation in postcolonial India, even if its impact was supposedly softened by Indian 'principles of ethical conduct for common good', as Prakash has argued,[41] or held in partial restraint by a liberal democratic polity. Being in the discursive thrall of the 'modern state' and modernization, Indian elites found it impossible to imagine any other form of state. 'Here lies the root of our postcolonial misery', laments Chatterjee, 'in our surrender to the old forms of the modern state'.[42] Moreover, Indian elites deployed the argument of science and rationality to remove discussions about economic policy from the domain of public debate and deliberation. 'Experts' asserted control over development policies, 'created a sort of elite confidentiality',[43] and

---

[36] Chatterjee, *Nation and Its Fragments*, ch. 10.
[37] e.g. Sudipta Kaviraj, 'Modernity and Politics in India', *Daedalus* 129/1 (Winter 2000), 137–62.
[38] Gyan Prakash, *Another Reason: Science and the Imagination of Modern India* (Delhi, 2000), 199.
[39] Ibid. 201.
[40] Partha Chatterjee, 'Introduction', in Chatterjee (ed.), *Wages of Freedom*, 16.
[41] Prakash, *Another Reason*, 212.
[42] Chatterjee, *Nation and Its Fragments*, 11.
[43] Kaviraj, 'On State, Society and Discourse in India', 90.

sought to insulate themselves from being buffeted by the turbulent cross-currents of politics and democratic accountability. All this, not surprisingly, predisposed the Indian postcolonial state to authoritarian, coercive and interventionist government and plagued the consolidation of democracy. At the same time, economic and development policies came to rely heavily on science and large-scale, capital-intensive technology.

The above line of interpretation has revealed an important dimension to the problems of democracy and development in postcolonial South Asia as a colonial legacy. However, it has to be borne in mind that the Nehruvian vision of the modern state was not the only one prevalent at the time of independence. At the very least, a radically different Gandhian model was also available, as mentioned above. The Nehruvian state became the dominant one only after an ideological and political struggle.[44] This is, of course, recognized by those who have argued about the importance of the 'modern' state as a colonial outgrowth. However, by failing to draw out the significance of this highly contested process, and by focusing on the final triumphant form, it is possible to privilege one form of the state as the quintessential manifestation of the modernity-driven mindset of the postcolonial elite, rather than as the product of a deliberate, and deliberated, political choice. This emphasis on 'modernity' as the main category to analyse the state, can lead to a devaluation of the fact that colonial and postcolonial states have been driven by other preoccupations, such as with security and political stability, which played a very significant role in shaping their authoritarian character. Moreover, the role of mass politics, political dissent, or resistance, might be underplayed in this line of argument. As discussed above, the responses of elites, in state structures, to mass politics was critical in shaping the form and functions of the state. By downplaying these factors in our analysis and by assuming that nationalist elites perpetuated the modern state mainly due to a lack of an alternative imagination, we stand the risk of absolving these elites of any direct responsibility or agency for political authoritarianism, other than indirectly, for their inability to transcend 'modernity'. To argue, in effect, that the elites perpetuated the most coercive form of the state because, as postcolonial subjects, they could not think of anything better, would suggest that they did not consciously will this state into existence for their own power. In other

---

[44] Sarkar, 'Indian Democracy', *passim*; Khilnanai, *Idea of India*, 29.

words, the postcolonial 'modern' state in South Asia generally, and the Nehruvian state in particular, was not simply shaped by colonialism and its forms of knowledge, but also by the compulsions of power and politics. Undeniably though, the ground for the consolidation of the modern state in independent India was prepared, both discursively and practically, by the legacy of the colonial state, with its institutions such as the civil service and the army; its coercive laws; its attempted creation of a regime of order, reason, and science; its projects of classification, enumeration, technological modernization, and disease control, even if flawed and limited.

Elite and Subaltern Politics: Towards Democracy

Kaviraj has extended the discussion of colonial political modernity to explain how the colonial legacy contributed to democratic deficit in India.[45] He has argued that the Indian constitutional and institutional political system was set up and conceived by an elite, who used the language and idiom of Western modernity in their political practice. This elite had been schooled in the lessons of modern politics within colonial political institutions and in the broader public sphere constituted by colonial politics. Although they departed in many ways from the political principles and practices of the Raj, the political *discourse* (as distinct from ideology) framing their politics continued to refer to Western values, forms of political conduct, and institutional norms and practices. Of course, there were people of many different *ideological* hues among the political classes—Hindu nationalists, conservatives, socialists, democrats, and so on. However, they all partook of the same *discourse*, language, and forms of politics, which being Western, was at the same time, far removed from the subaltern political universe, even when this elite undertook policies to benefit the masses. This, Kaviraj explains, solidified a 'hostile unfamiliarity between elite and subaltern political semiotics', and accentuated an 'ironical divergence between populist government policies and popular consciousness'.[46] Ultimately this bred mutual incomprehension or unintelligibility between the 'modernity' of elite politics and the 'vernacular' domain of subaltern politics. This caused a fundamental disjunction and disarticulation between the state and political institutions and the public sphere constituted

---

[45] Kaviraj, 'On State, Society and Discourse in India'.
[46] Ibid. 90.

by it, on the one hand, and popular politics and ideology, on the other, leading to a highly imperfect democratic polity, despite its democratic institutional trappings.

Kaviraj's arguments draw attention to the continued significance of colonial idioms of politics for elites. However, his analytical perspective needs to be expanded to admit that the 'modern' language of politics straddles elite and subaltern domains. For instance, in his study of postcolonial rural north India (western Uttar Pradesh), Akhil Gupta marvels at the ability of farmers to 'switch codes' effortlessly between indigenous practices and the language of 'modern' development, and at the intermingling of 'contradictory logics and incommensurable discourses' in what Gupta calls the 'border zone of hybridity and impurity'.[47] In contrast to Gupta's perspective, Kaviraj appears to have overestimated the depth and insurmountability of the chasm between elite and subaltern political languages, as Corbridge and Harriss have maintained.[48] Yet, it is precisely the espousal of some of the 'modern' notions of rights and justice by subaltern groups that have shaped recent developments in Indian politics in the later twentieth century, particularly the expansion of mass democratic participation, leading to the deepening and resilience of India's democracy, as an unusual case among postcolonial countries.[49] The colonial legacy, in this case, does not emanate from the institutions, practices, and discourses of the colonial regime. Instead, it is the multiple histories of adaptation, negotiation, opposition, and other forms of engagement with colonial rule and modernity that continue to shape Indian politics and contribute to India's democratic political culture. Norms drawn from the so-called 'modern' realm of politics have increasingly shaped popular expectations about the conduct of politics, government duties, and democratic accountability. This is shown, for instance, in Jonathan Parry's research on industrial workers in central India, who have developed a heightened awareness of the 'crisis of corruption' in public life. Parry attributes this to workers' entrenched belief in certain norms about the public conduct of politics and administration, derived from the modern, constitutional language of politics. Violation of, or deviation from, such norms is condemned as

---

[47] Akhil Gupta, *Postcolonial Developments: Agriculture in the Making of Modern India* (Durham, NC and London, 1998), 5–6.

[48] Corbridge and Harriss, *Reinventing India*, 39, and parts II and III *passim*.

[49] Kohli (ed.), *Success of India's Democracy*.

'corruption' by workers, argues Parry.[50] Similarly, the liberal nationalist language of citizenship has provided a powerful political vocabulary to deprived groups. The recent 'democratic upsurge' of lower castes and their entry into the domain of institutional politics through what Jaffrelot calls the 'silent revolution' in India[51] have been marked by their usage of the terms of 'modern' political discourse, albeit with vernacular inflections, as we shall see below. The emphasis on social justice and equality in the Constitution has animated the language of emancipatory politics of lower caste communities in recent decades, as demonstrated, among others, by Jaffrelot, Michelutti, Bajpai, and Gorringe.[52]

Studies of the kind mentioned above demonstrate subaltern capacity to appropriate and reinterpret elements of so-called 'modern' colonial political discourse within the framework of their own political ideas. This reveals an important dimension of the colonial legacy as it affects subaltern classes. It shows that 'modern' forms of politics and the discourse of 'colonial modernity' did not constitute a closed elite political idiom, alien to the masses. Moreover, elitist colonial modernity cannot be held solely responsible for the inability of the postcolonial state to gain legitimacy and strike deep roots in Indian society. Admittedly, democracy eluded the masses for long, and the state became an oppositional entity, and even a symbol of oppression in many cases. However, this was not simply because of a discursive or semiotic political hiatus between elites and subalterns, but because of political practices and institutional arrangements that ensured the political exclusion of the masses,[53] not to mention the failure of the state to address economic and social inequalities that prevented access to democratic institutions and substantive participation.[54] Kaviraj's analysis has been useful in drawing attention to the significance of the 'modern'

---

[50] Jonathan P. Parry, 'The "Crisis of Corruption" and "the Idea of India"', in Italo Pardo (ed.), *Morals of Legitimacy: Between Agency and System* (New York and Oxford, 2000), 27–55.

[51] Christophe Jaffrelot, *India's Silent Revolution: The Rise of the Low Castes in North Indian Politics* (Delhi, 2003).

[52] Rochana Bajpai, *Debating Difference: Minority Rights and Liberal Democracy in India* (Delhi, 2011); Lucia Michelutti, *The Vernacularisation of Democracy: Politics, Caste, and Religion in India* (Delhi, 2008); Hugo Gorringe, *Untouchable Citizens: Dalit Movements and Democratization in Tamil Nadu* (London, 2005).

[53] Corbridge and Harriss, *Reinventing India*, ch. 9.

[54] Niraja Gopal Jayal, *Democracy and the State: Welfare, Secularism and Development in Contemporary India* (Delhi, 1999), 25–7, and *passim*.

discourse of politics inherited from colonialism. However, the full implications of this in Indian political practice have to be understood with reference to the ways in which this 'modern' language can have many different appropriations, creative reinterpretation, and hybrid reformulation, both among elites and subalterns, and can be pressed into action for both reactionary and emancipatory politics, and for inclusion or exclusion. A genealogical and hermeneutic approach to political ideologies and ideas enables us, not only to excavate the colonial origins of 'modern' political concepts, but also, and more importantly, allows us to trace their gradual mutations and reinterpretations, in order to serve new political purposes in postcolonial contexts. Examples from the history of caste politics in India best illustrate this process.

Identity Politics and Caste

Caste, communal, ethnic, and sectarian politics have, of course, dominated South Asia's colonial and postcolonial history. Undeniably, the colonial history of caste and communal representation, and community-based laws and policies, bred contradictions at the heart of the Indian constitution and institutional practice. The conception of fundamental rights in the Constitution was based on individual rights-bearing citizens. Yet, the colonial history of group or community representation and political contests over the rights of cultural minorities or 'deprived' or 'backward' groups, including lower castes, rendered it difficult to avoid the recognition of the rights of communities. This led to the continuation of community-based preferential policies and affirmative action or 'reservations' for 'backwards classes', notably 'historically deprived' lower castes and 'backward' tribes. Although this was designed to achieve social justice and equality, the continuance of this particular policy after independence in modified form also sowed the seeds of intractable theoretical and philosophical problems at the heart of the Constitution and in public policy between individual and collective rights, which have led to debates and even violent conflicts over group rights.[55]

In this context, the notion of a 'postcolonial predicament' has been most powerfully invoked in the discussion on caste and community-based

---

[55] Bajpai, *Debating Difference*.

politics in independent India.⁵⁶ For Breckenridge and van der Veer, the discursive formation of orientalism 'has become internalised in the practices of the postcolonial state, the theories of the postcolonial intelligentsia, and the political action of postcolonial mobs', and has been 'transposed now into the very sinews of public life and group politics'.⁵⁷ Orientalist discourse, translated into practice through the colonial 'administrative *imaginaire*', it is argued, created new identities and subjectivities.⁵⁸ Indians utilized and reconstituted them for their own purposes, and found it impossible to transcend the terms of this discourse. Inevitably, Indian society and politics still continue to be organized along these community cleavages and divisions. These arguments have been developed further, notably by Dirks, to argue the particular salience of caste identity in postcolonial Indian politics. Caste, Dirks argues, has come to stay through its colonial reification as India's religious essence and as the fundamental category of social identity and organization. As a consequence, caste now manifests itself in many political forms, including mobilization in debates over affirmative action and social welfare, in progressive movements, in opposition to official nationalism, and in articulating claims about 'privilege, participation and exclusion'.⁵⁹ 'Further, caste has become the ghost hovering over many contemporary discussions about nationhood, citizenship and modernity.'⁶⁰ In these multiple manifestations, caste continues to play out the terms of colonial discourse.

These interpretations have indeed gone a long way in illuminating the persistence of identity-based politics in India. However, Frederick Cooper's cautionary comments on African history are worth recalling here. Writing about the colonial inheritance in African political history, Cooper has argued that colonial legacies do not shape the postcolonial future in any inevitable or unavoidable way, but are conditioned by ongoing events, practices, debates, and struggles.⁶¹ He warns against certain analytical pitfalls that might occlude our understanding of postcolonial history, notably

---

⁵⁶ Nicholas Dirks, *Castes of Mind: Colonialism and the Making of Modern India* (Delhi, 2002), 294; Breckenridge and van der Veer, *Orientalism*.

⁵⁷ Breckenridge and van der Veer, *Orientalism*, 11.

⁵⁸ Ibid. 6–7.

⁵⁹ Dirks, *Castes of Mind*, 5–6, 17.

⁶⁰ Ibid. 276.

⁶¹ Frederick Cooper, *Colonialism in Question: Theory, Knowledge, History* (Berkeley and London, 2005), 21.

'leapfrogging legacies', which he describes as the claim that 'something in time A caused something in time C, without considering time B, which lies in between'.[62] An example of such 'leapfrogging legacies' would, for instance, entail directly linking colonial discourses and debates on caste with backward caste political mobilization for the extension of reservations in India in the 1980s, without reference to the intervening history of the development of a language of constitutional rights and social justice for lower castes in the several decades after independence. An avoidance of 'leapfrogging legacies' of this kind helps to guard against privileging the 'colonial' analytically in our understanding of the postcolonial period, and serves to problematize the apparently ubiquitous constitutive role of colonial discourse. Instead, a genealogical approach to trace links with the past is useful, without implying inevitable continuity or discursive determinism, unmediated by the intervention of Indian agency. From this perspective, discourses that emerged during colonialism, to do with social identities, can be analytically seen as resources that lent themselves to numerous appropriations. In this process, the terms of colonial or orientalist discourse are also often breached by the penetration of other discourses. An enquiry into such hybrid formations, and, importantly, how they articulate with forms and structures of power in the postcolonial context, yields illuminating insights into the multiple manifestations of the colonial legacy. A particularly interesting case is that of the Other Backward Classes (OBCs), specifically various intermediate low Shudra castes, located between upper touchable castes and the lower untouchable castes.

William Pinch, in his study of the Shudra castes of *yadavs, kurmis, kushbahas*, in the Gangetic plains of north India in the colonial period, shows how a new *Kshatriya* warrior identity developed in the course of caste reform movements.[63] These groups drew upon colonial constructions of their culture, tradition, and myths of origin to assert a history of martial exploits. In the postcolonial period, many of these rural Shudra castes in north India, especially *yadavs*, experienced a degree of upward economic mobility and they began to challenge the social and political dominance of the upper castes.[64] Caste continued to dominate the language of Shudra politics, but in new ways and for very different reasons. They campaigned

---

[62] Cooper, *Colonialism in Question*, 17.
[63] William Pinch, *Peasants and Monks in British India* (Berkeley and London 1996)
[64] Jaffrelot, *India's Silent Revolution*.

for an extension of reservation policies to OBCs, by referring to their historical deprivation and backwardness, for these arguments became increasingly relevant to India's competitive democratic politics and to affirmative action for 'backward classes'. At the same time, they resurrected their martial identity, now intermingled with more recently acquired ideas of socialism, egalitarianism, and democratic rights. As Michelutti shows, Shudra caste politics now effortlessly straddles mythic and democratic imaginaries.[65] Michelutti's ethnographic study of the recent politics of *yadavs* in north India reveals that their political rhetoric is replete with references to what might be seen in some interpretations as a 'modern' discourse of democracy, representation, and social justice, although the *yadavs* themselves trace the roots of these to the ancient heritage from their putative, mythological martial ancestor Lord Krishna, who is said to be the original Indian democrat, republican, and socialist. To elucidate the 'socialist martial' ideas of *yadavs*, Michelutti cites the following, among others, as an example of this enmeshing and interpenetration of a so-called 'modern' political lexicon and a 'vernacular' imagination:

> Lord Krishna was a great man and the Yadav community should be proud of the path that he left to them. Lord Krishna gave them three principles: democracy, social justice and commitment to equality. These are the bases of our future. He was a democratic leader. He used to respect the views of his citizens. He used to believe that the person who is elected by the citizens has the right to rule. He was the first person to begin a 'democratic way of governance': but others say that France gave birth to democracy.[66]

The history of *yadav* politics demonstrates the discursive inheritance of the Raj, and the colonial roots of caste politics today. At the same time, it drives home the potency of a language of democratic rights in postcolonial India, without which the colonial legacy of caste identity among *yadavs* would have taken quite different forms. Caste gained political salience here, not because of its colonially derived discursive power alone, but because of postcolonial developments in political ideology and practice.

---

[65] Michelutti, *Vernacularisation of Democracy*, ch. 6 and *passim*.

[66] R. M. S. Yadav, 'Indian Politics and Yadavs', *Yadav Kul Dipika*, special Jubilee number 69–70 (1999); cited in Michelutti, *Vernacularisation of Democracy*, 175.

Conclusion

The *yadav* case illustrates the point that to appreciate and evaluate the significance of the colonial political legacy, it is necessary to engage with postcolonial political and social history to tease out which elements of the colonial legacy have continued to be important, why, how, and in which form. The colonial legacy cannot be understood as a fixed entity, that somehow reproduces itself or that is mechanically reproduced by Indian actors. The colonial legacy of political institutions, practices, and discourses is undoubtedly extensive and far-reaching. However, its significance and specificity lie not in the proposition that it is inescapable or that it has created an insurmountable political impasse, but because it provides a range of powerful resources that have been used in a variety of ways by South Asian political actors, both elite and subaltern. The importance of the colonial past lies in its immense potential for political appropriation in the present. The political institutions, practices, and ideas that colonialism left in its wake derive their power and relevance largely because South Asian people have chosen to deploy them, with modification and reinterpretations that are relevant to the context of postcolonial politics. An interpretation of the political impact or consequences of colonialism then requires analyses of South Asian political agency as well as the dynamics of postcolonial power and politics and their interplay with colonial forms. This exercise calls for a multilayered and synthetic approach to conceptualize the political legacy of colonialism, rather than attributing singular causality or primacy to any one set of factors. An engagement with the discursive domain of power, as suggested by perspectives on the 'postcolonial predicament', is necessary, but with an emphasis on the complex articulation and interplay of discourse with specific forms of power in the postcolonial setting.

Select Bibliography

GRANVILLE AUSTEN, *The Indian Constitution: Cornerstone of a Nation* (Delhi, 1999).
RAJEEV BHARGAVA (ed.), *Secularism and Its Critics* (Delhi, 1998).
CAROL A. BRECKENRIDGE and PETER VAN DER VEER (eds), *Orientalism and the Postcolonial Predicament* (Delhi, 1994).
DIPESH CHAKRABARTY, ROCHANA MAJUMDAR, and ANDREW SARTORI (eds), *From the Colonial to the Postcolonial: India and Pakistan in Transition* (Delhi, 2007).

NEERA CHANDHOKE, *Beyond Secularism: The Rights of Religious Minorities* (Delhi, 1999).
PARTHA CHATTERJEE, *The Nation and Its Fragments: Colonial and Postcolonial Histories* (Delhi, 1997).
——(ed.), Wages *of Freedom: Fifty Years of the Indian Nation-State* (Delhi, 1998).
STUART CORBRIDGE and JOHN HARRISS, *Reinventing India: Liberalization, Hindu Nationalism and Popular Democracy* (Delhi, 2001).
NICHOLAS DIRKS, Castes *of Mind: Colonialism and the Making of Modern India* (Delhi, 2002).
ZOYA HASAN, E. SRIDHARAN, and R. SUDARSHAN (eds), *India's Living Constitution: Ideas, Practices, Controversies* (Delhi, 2002).
CHRISTOPHE JAFFRELOT, *India's Silent Revolution: The Rise of the Low Castes in North Indian Politics* (Delhi, 2003).
AYESHA JALAL, *Democracy and Authoritarianism in South Asia: A Comparative and Historical Perspective* (Cambridge, 1995).
NIRAJA GOPAL JAYAL (ed.), *Democracy in India* (Delhi, 2001).
SUDIPTA KAVIRAJ, 'On State, Society and Discourse in India', in James Manor (ed.), *Rethinking Third World Politics* (London, 1992), 72–99.
SUNIL KHILNANI, *The Idea of India* (London, 1997).
ATUL KOHLI (ed.), *The Success of India's Democracy* (Cambridge, 2001).
SURMIT SARKAR, 'Indian Democracy: The Historical Inheritance', in Kohli (ed.), *Success of India's Democracy*, 23–46.
DAVID WASHBROOK, 'The Rhetoric of Democracy and Development in Late Colonial India', in Sugata Bose and Ayesha Jalal (eds), *Nationalism, Democracy and Development: State and Politics in India* (Delhi, 1998), 36–49.

INDEX

adivasi 220–1
Age of Consent Act 296–7
Age of Reform 25
agrarian society 113
agriculture 46–7, 59–60
Ahuja, Ravi 67
Alavi, Seema 111
Ali, Haidar 35
Ali, Mumtaz 302
Ali, Salim 228
Aligarh University 300
Ambedkar, B. R. 148, 154, 155, 164, 227, 304–5
Andhra Pradesh 133
Anglo-Russian Rivalry 26
Appadurai, Arjun 82, 92–3, 231
Archer, Mildred 236
Archer, W. G. 248
architecture in colonial India
　differences between presidencies 242–3
　Indo-Saracenic 244–5
　influence of Greek and Roman styles 243
　Saracenic 243–4
Arcot 236
Arnold, David 218
Arya Samaj 123, 303–4, 318
Asiatic Society of Bengal 196, 197, 254
Assam 216
Austen, Granville 336
Awadh 219

Bachchan, Harivamsray 275
Bagchi, Amiya 57
Baker, C. J. 140

Baker, Herbert 245
Balachandran, G. 50
Ballantyne, James 94–5
Bandyopadhyay, Hemchandra 267–8
Banerjea, Rakhaldas 246
Banerjea, Surendranath 162
banjaras 69, 70, 108, 110, 215
Bankimchandra 270, 276
Banks, Joseph 192, 194, 204, 209
Bangladesh 20, 330
Basalla, George 192
Basu, Buddhadeb 275
Bayly, C. A. 8, 35, 60, 88–9, 106, 114, 124–5, 128–9, 140, 162
Bayly, Susan 102, 125
Beddoes, Thomas 203–4
Bengal 21, 51, 69, 108–9, 121, 145, 169, 182, 217, 221, 236, 302
　and nationalism 154–5
Bentham, Jeremy 177–8
Bentinck, William 31, 178
Bernier, Francois 198
Bhabha, Homi 285
bhadralok 121
Bharati, Subrahmanya 266
Bharatiya JanataParty 331–2
Bhatkhande, Narayan 234, 257
Bhatt, Balkrsna 268
Bhownaggree, Mancherjee 328
Bihar 219, 314
Bikaner 235
Birdwood, George 248
Black Act 183
Blake, William 258–9

INDEX

Bombay 121–2, 126, 169
  Presidency of 109
Bose, Subhas Chandra 289
Bremen, Jan 145
Burma 221

Calcutta 121, 239
  Government House 243 fig.3
Cambridge School 3, 4, 6, 11
Canada
  opposition to Indian migration 324–5
Caribbean 315
cash crops 47
caste 92–5
  and historicity 102–3
  and non-Brahman
    movements 114–15
  and sedentarization 113–15
  and untouchability 114
  see also colonial knowledge
Chakrabarti, Pratik 193
Chakrabarty, Dipesh 144–5, 152
Chand, Mihr 237–8
Chatterjee, Joya 132
Chatterjee, Kum Kum 106
Chatterjee, Partha 142, 156–7, 285, 340, 341, 344, 345
Chaturvedi, M. D. 228
China, trade with 52
Chiplunkar, Vishnu Shastri 250
Civil Disobedience (1930–34) 138, 288, 307
Clerk, George 17
Clive, Robert 29
Cohn, Bernard 5, 91–2, 231–2
Cole, Henry 248
College of Fort William 172
Collins, Wilkie 272
colonial knowledge
  and caste 91–2
  and census 91–3

  incorporation of indigenous
    knowledge 87–8
  precolonial foundations of 93–4
  role of local informants 77, 85–94
colonial modernity 343–6
colonial science
  connections with Edinburgh and
    London 201–2
  and dissemination 207–8
  and East India Company 209–10
  importance of informal networks 194–5
  influence of the Lunar Society of
    Birmingham 202–3
  relationship with radicals and
    dissenters 205–6
  theory of diffusion 192–3
colonial state
  anxiety and hybridity 31
  authoritarianism as legacy 335–41
  and bureaucracy 118–19
  and colonial modernity 343–6
  conservative inclinations 25
  and contradictions 20–1, 101
  debates over its transformative
    power 104–5
  and debt financing 38–9
  differences between Presidency
    Governments 21–2
  economic imperatives 51–5
  hybrid nature 31–2
  influence of racial attitudes 24–5
  influence upon successor states 339–40
  legal characteristics of 169–70
  and minority rights 130
  paradoxes of 16–7
  revenue base 36–7
  role of the military 20–4
communalism 160–1
Communist Party
  and gender 290–1

coolie
　etymology 316–17
Cooper, Frederick 351–2
Corbett, Jim 225
Cornwallis, Charles, First Marquess 54, 241
criminal conspiracy act (1913) 187
criminal tribes 111
criminal tribes act (1871) 186–7
criminality
　and racialization 186–7
Curzon, George, First Marquess 30–1

Dalhousie, Marquess of
　　(James Broun-Ramsay) 25, 28
dalit 154, 155, 164
Dalmia, Vasudha 23, 274
Daniell, Thomas 239
Das Gupta, Ashin 67
Datta, Rajat 37
Datta, Satyendranath 275
Debi, Kailashbashini 303
Debi, Rashsundari 302
Dehlavi, Nazir Ahmad 301–2
De-industrialization 46–7, 61–2
Delhi
　design of new capital 245–6
de Man, Paul 264
Deoband 148
Depression of 1920s and 1930s 64–5
Dey, Bisnu 275
diaspora 13
　definition of 313, 314
Dirks, Nicholas 231
Dodson, Michael 94–5
Dow, Alexander 44
'drain' theory 44, 49–50
Dravidian language 88
Drayton, Richard 195
Dufferin, Marquess of (Frederick
　　Hamilton-Temple-Blackwood) 26

Dumont, Louis 101
Dutt, Gurusaday 249–50
Dutt, Michael Madhusudan 267
Dyer, General Reginald 27

East India Company 18, 40, 51, 53–4, 55,
　　59, 61, 102, 108, 111, 122, 182, 293
　charter renewal 53
　and educational policies 124, 129
　and European rivals 78
　expenditures of 32
　exports to India 53
　and opposition to conquest 23–4
　and opposition to settlement 24–5, 52
　and sedentarization 72
　sponsorship of science 191–2, 194
　trade monopolies 52
Easton, Natasha 236–7, 242
economic development
　contradictions in 55–9
　effects of military expenditure 39–40
economic growth 45–9
economic policies
　and idea of village communities 51
economy
　and British capital 58
　and British exports 57–8
　and consumer demand 62–3
　and exchange relations 69–70
　and global economy 58–9
　in 1750 59–60
　influence of maritime trade 60
　legal structures 168–9
　and logic of development 71–2
　and population mobility 70
　regional economies 61–2, 65–6
　and risk sharing 70
　taxation system 55
　and theories of development 66–9
　transportation developments 57

economy (*cont.*)
  within an imperial framework 66–7
education 292–3, 302–4
  art schools 247–50
  see also East India Company
environment 12
  and forestry 214
  impact of railways 219
  precolonial setting 214–16

Faiz, Faiz Ahmed 264–5
famines 48, 67–8, 73
Ferguson, Niall 45
Fergusson, James 251–4
Fiji 316, 319
  scandals over treatments of Indians 320–1
forests 218–22
  and sedentarization 110–11
Foucault, Michel 5, 76, 80, 146–7, 232
Francis, Philip 26, 45
free trade 57
Frere, Bartle 23

Gadgil, Madhav 218
Gandhi, M. K. 101, 125, 138, 158–9, 188, 225, 226, 233, 333
  and decentralized model of governance 337–8, 340–1
  and gender identities 288, 289
  and Hinduism 161, 164–5
  and Indian diaspora 326
  influence of John Ruskin and Lockwood Kipling upon 234
  influence of William Morris and Ananda K. Coomaraswamy upon 259–60
  and masculinity 287
  and panchayats 182

and science and technology 345–6
and South Africa 317, 322, 323–4
and untouchability 155
and women in politics 156
garrison state 20–4, 30–1, 36–7
Gascoigne, John 195
Geertz, Clifford 232
Gender
  complicity between western and Indian patriarchies 299
  and education 292–3, 302–4
  and labour 307–9
  and the law 293–5
  and religious texts 300–1
  and social reform 291–3
  and urbanization 309–10
  see also nationalism
Ghadar Party 316, 321–3
Ghazal 264–5, 280
Giri, V. V. 226
Gosvami, Kisori Lal 269
Gould, William 131
Gramsci, Antonio 5
Grove, Richard 87
Guha, Ramachandra 218
Guha, Ranaji 85, 141
Gujarat 141, 314
Gupta, Akhil 348
Guru, Shri Narayana 306

Habermas, Jurgen 264
Habib, Irfan 71
Haileybury College 172
Hardiman, David 141
Hardinge, Charles First Baron 325–6
Hastings, Warren 169, 237, 239
Hastings, Francis Rawdon Marquess 42
Havell, E. B. 248
Haynes, Douglas 158–9

Hind Swaraj 164, 166
Hindi 119, 127–8
Hindu Mahasabha 161
Hinduism
    and militant nationalism 121, 122–3
Hindutva 162, 163, 166
historiography 3–6
    and area studies 3
    characterized by binary relationships 6–14
    and global forces 13
    Marxist 4, 152
    and modernity 4–11
    and nationalism 8–11
    nationalist 4, 11–12
    and regionalism 11–13
    and visual and material culture 232–3
    see also Cambridge School; Subaltern Studies
Hobson, J. H. 53
Hodges, William 238–40, 243, 258
Home Rule League 329
Hunter, Alexander 247
Hyderabad 159–60

imperial ideologies
    and security imperatives 16–17
    liberalism and its paradoxes 16–17
    racialization of 24
Ilbert Bill 24, 184
    precursors to 183
Inden, Ronald 81–2, 231, 285
indentured labour 315–16
    see also Indian diaspora
Indian Army
    financial demands 32–4
    see also martial races; military fiscalism
India
    authoritarian tendencies in independent India 341–2
    British views of 81–3
    and democratic deficit in independent India 344–8
    democratic upsurge in independent India 349–50
    frontier expansion 34
    and orientalist discourse in independent India 351
    place within imperial economy 54–5
    precolonial migrations 313–14
    security concerns in independent India 338–9
    and shudra caste politics 352–3
Indian Budgets
    and military spending 18–19
Indian capital 56
Indian Constitution 165–6, 335–8
    centralizing tendencies 338
    and federalism 337
    and Government of India Act (1935) 337
    individual versus community rights 350–1
Indian diaspora
    in Britain 328–31
    and Government of India after independence 330–1
    harshness of daily life 319
    and hybrid cultures and orthodox responses 317–18
    and plantation economies 315–16
    political struggles and impact on India 326–8
    politicization of 319–20
    principal regions for emigrants 314
    and racism in Britain 330–1
    and the United States 331–2
Indian Home Rule League of America 327
Indian Mutiny 56, 109
    see also Rebellion of 1857

Indian National Congress 125, 131, 133, 137–8, 149–50, 155, 161, 162, 290
  critiqued by Ghadar Party 322
  and extremists 162
  and forest laws 225–6
Indian Penal Code 187
Indian Princes 25
  and subsidiary alliances 39
Indian Society
  and class 103
  and communal tensions 122–3
  emergence of scribal and commercial elites 118–23
  and Hindustani ecumene 123–4
  relationship between caste and class 106
  religious communities 103–4
  sedentarization and demilitarization 107–8, 111
  and urbanization 120, 122–3
  vernacular communications 123–8
  and vernacular print cultures 119
  see also caste
indigo rebellion 25
  and visual culture 253
industrial revolution 61, 62
Iqbal, Muhammad 265–6, 274–5, 276
  diverse influences upon 277–9
irrigation 73, 216, 217–18, 222–3
Irschick, Eugene 90–1, 110

Jaffrelot, Christophe 349
Jalal, Ayesha 132, 335
Jallianwalla Bagh 27, 188
Java 50
Jinnah, Muhammad Ali 148, 338
Jones, William 171, 196–7, 205
Joshi, Chitra 309
jute 56

Kalidasa 275
kalighat 248–50

Kalsi, Amrik 271
Kashmir 153
Kaviraj, Sudipta 341, 344, 347–8
Kaye, John William 40
Kerala 154–5, 157–8
Kettle, Tilly 237, 258
Khan, Sayyid Ahmad Khan 128, 131, 302
khilifat 288
Khilnani, Sunil 336
King, Christopher 263
Kirtikar, Vasudeva J. 276–7, 278
Kitchener, Herbert First Earl 30–1
Kohli, Atul 335
Komagata Maru 324–5
Krishnamurti, R. 270
Kumar, Dharma 68
Kumarappa, J. C. 277

Lal, Brij 320–1
Lancashire textile lobby 57
Latour, Bruno 234
law
  codification of laws and customs 177–80
  differentiation into Hindu and Muslim legal identities 173–4
  Hindu law schools 184
  links to Persian literary traditions 266
  mechanism to check challenges to state authority 185–90
  premium on ancient textual authorities 172–3
  and press controls 187–8
  problem of framing it in terms of modernity 263–4
  relationship to precolonial traditions 170–1
  reliance on local intermediaries 173, 181–4
  and social reform 175–6
  support of patriarchy 297–9

and utilitarianism 176–7
widow remarriage 295–6
and the 'women's question' 158
Lawrence, Henry 33
Lawrence, John, First Baron 28, 30
Lever Brothers 58
Levine, George 272
Liberalism 25
and its paradoxes 17–18
Lind, James 202–3
literature
and realism 272–3
and the novel 268–70
Bengali 262
Bengali poetry 267–8
cosmopolitan eclecticism 274–6
dangers of reading it against western traditions 270–1
Hindi 262
hybridity of the Indian novel 271–2
rupture between premodern and modern poetics 263–4
Sindi poetry 275
Tamil 262, 266–70
Tamil novel 279–80
Low, D. A. 141
Lucknow 21, 236
Lutyens, Edwin 245–6
Lytton, Edward Bulwer-, First Baron 25, 37, 187–8

Macaulay, Thomas Babington 31, 178, 180, 183
and minute on Indian education 82
McKendrick, Neil 68
Maclean, Charles 205–7
Macleod, Roy 210
Madani, Husain Ahmad 148
Madras 51, 73, 80–1, 90, 169
Banqueting Hall 239–41

Presidency of 109
Mahabharata 267, 268
Maharashtra 125, 162 *see also* Marathas
Mahars 126
Maine, Henry S. 17, 171
Malabar Marriage Act (1896) 298–9
Malcolm, John 20, 23, 182
Mangles, R. D. 18, 40
Manipur Women's Wars (1904, 1939) 160
Marathas 110, 116–17, 127, 154, 237
Marshall, Peter 37, 112, 210
martial races 21–2, 29, 112, 222, 287, 304
Marx, Karl 45, 46, 68
Mauritius 315
Mawdudi, Maulana 148
Mayo College 244–5
medicine 198–9
global influences on colonial medicine 200
use of local remedies 199–200
use of mercury in India 200–1
Mehta, Uday Singh 17
Menon, Chandu 268
Menon, Krishna 329
Metcalf, Thomas 243, 246–7
Mewar 235–6
military expenditures 56
military fiscalism 18–19, 39–40, 54, 60–1, 65, 338
impact on Indian economy 40–1
and importance of loans 38–40
and the Punjab 40–1
Mill, John Stuart 45
missionaries 155, 208–9, 305, 306
and Indian diaspora 318–19
Mitra, Rajendralal 251–4
Mitter, Partha 247
modernity 264
and colonialism 284–5
and postcolonial historiography 284–5

monsoon agriculture 68
Montgomery, Robert 30
Morriss, Morris David 45
Mughal Empire 34–5, 60, 65, 68,
    78, 79, 100, 107, 169, 196, 214
  estimate of its population 71
  visual culture 235–6
Mukherjee, Meenakshi 268, 269, 273, 276
Mukherji, Mukul 307
Munro, Thomas 45, 182
museums
  and colonial taxonomy 241–2
music
  classical tradition and
    transculturation 257–8
  and early recordings 256–7
Muslims 126, 129, 131
Muslim League 161, 290, 291
Mysore 35, 78, 227, 308
  and Tipu Sultan 69
  and Wodeyar state 35

Naicker, E. V. Ramaswamy 148, 305
Naidu, Sarojini 327
Nandy, Ashis 85, 90
Naoroji, Dadabhai 328
Natal 323–4, 327
nationalism
  binary relationship with
    colonialism 135–6
  and brahmanical domination 148
  and Cambridge School 138–41
  and caste 153–5
  and the environment 225–28
  and feminist historians 143
  and gender 149, 155–60, 287–8
  and Hinduism 130–1, 144, 147–8
  and Hindutva 158
  and labour 145–6
  legacies in successor states 165–6
  and low caste movements 144

  and Marxist historiography 139–40
  and mass culture 151
  and modernity 145
  Muslim political mobilization 135–6,
    148
  and orientalism 136
  and postcolonial theory 146–7
  and print culture 151
  and regional vernaculars 124–8
  and religion 160–5
  and Subaltern Studies 139–44
Nehru, Jawaharlal 161, 163, 166, 227,
    233, 344–7
  and Indian diaspora 329–30
  on women and politics 289
Noakhali 289
Non-Cooperation Khilifat
    (1919–22) 138, 161
non-resident Indians 331

oriental despotism 28–9, 79, 80
orientalism
  contradictions within 81–2
  open-ended nature 86
  see also colonial knowledge
Orsini, Francesca 262, 263

Pakistan 35, 135–6, 148, 335
  and bureaucratic
    authoritarianism 338
  impact of Punjabi-dominated
    elite 341
  role of the military 19, 338–9
Paluskar, Vishnu Digambar 257
Pant, Rashmi 92
Parthasarathi, Prasannan 67, 69
partition 227
partition of Bengal 288
peasantisation 63–4
penal colonies 189–90
per capita income 48

Permanent Settlement (1793) 37, 51, 60, 109, 112
Perry, Jonathan 348–9
Persian 123, 127–8, 275
Phalke, D. G. 251–2
Phule, Jotirao 127, 148, 154, 304
Pinch, William 115–16, 352–3
plantations 216–17
Pomeranz, Ken 67
population growth 48–9
Prakash, Gyan 193, 242, 345
Pratap, Ajay 220
Pratt, Mary Louise 234
prevention of seditious meetings act (1911) 187
prices
 agricultural 63–4
Pritchett, Frances 280
Punjab 19–20, 35, 56, 109, 162, 222, 305, 314, 321–3, 325
 key recruiting area for army 40–1

Quit India (1942) 27, 138, 159, 188–9, 288

Rai, Mridu 153
railways 219
Rajputs 83–4
Ramabai, Pandita 303
Ramamirthan, L. S. 275
Ramayana 267, 268, 275, 279
Ramaswamy, Sumathi 127
Rashtriya Swayamsevak Sangh 158, 161, 163, 164, 291
Rebellion of 1857 16, 23–4, 25, 26, 31–2, 40, 100, 111, 112, 137, 189, 228, 243
Religion
 role of the colonial state 129–30
revenue settlements 109
Reynolds, Joshua 258
Richman, Paula 279

Ripon, George Robinson, First Marquessof 182
Rostow, W. W. 67
Rowlatt Act (1919) 188
Roxburgh, William 209
Roy, Rammohun 179, 292–3, 299
Roy, Tirthankar 45
Rumi 266
Russell, Patrick 197
ryotwari 53

Said, Edward 5, 80, 101, 146–7, 231–2, 233
Saklatvala, Shapurji 328
Sanskrit 88, 95, 123, 267, 268, 269, 279
Sanskritization 153, 305, 307
 and nationalism 148
Santal insurrection 307
Sarshar, Ratan Nath 270
Sarvadhikari, Rajkumar 184
Sastri, Natesa 275
sati 292, 295–6, 297
satyagraha 189, 226
Saumarez, Richard Smith 92
Savarkar. V. D. 163, 164, 189
Scott, Helenus 204–5
Shinde 237
Shinde, Tarabai 303
Shivaji 116, 125, 129, 162
Shuja ud-Daula 237–8
Siddiqa, Ayesha 19
Singer, Wendy 159
Singh, Bhagat 233
Singh, Ganga 227
Singh, Manmohan 331
Singh, Ranjit 8, 35
Skaria, Ajay 220
Sleeman, William 185
Smith, Adam 44, 46, 53
Smuts, Jan 323–4

Society for the Promotion of
    Industrial Arts 247
Solomon, W. E. Gladstone 248
South Africa 317
Srinivas, M. N. 148
Stephen, James Fitzjames 24, 25, 31,
    41, 180, 185
Stern, Philip 18
Subaltern Studies 1, 3, 4–6, 84–5,
    101, 105, 150, 152, 153, 156,
    164, 285
Subrahmanyam, Sanjay 78
subsidiary alliances 39
    see also Indian princes
swadeshi 140, 256, 288
swaraj 188
Sylhet 330–1

Tagore, Abanindranath 234, 250, 251
Tagore, Rabindranath 158, 166,
    268, 287
Talbot, Cynthia 123
Tamil 127, 132
Tamil Nadu 154, 314
Telengana movement 290
Temple, Richard 247
thagi 185–6, 224
tigers 223–5
    symbol of Tipu Sultan 215–16
Tilak, B. G. 158, 162, 187, 250–1
Tipu Sultan 241–2
    see also Mysore; tigers
Tobin, Beth Fowkes 241
Tod, James 83–4
transportation changes 73
tribal peoples 215
Trautmann, Thomas 87–8

Tulsidas 279
Tyabji, Badruddin 184

Urdu 119, 127–8, 301–2

Varma, Ravi 251
Vedanta 276–7
Vellala communities 116
Venugopal, T. S. 266
Vidyasagar, Ishwarchandra 302
Vishwa Hindu Parsihad 332
visual and material culture and
    autonomy 234
    'Company Painting' 236
    film 251–3
    Indian aesthetics and European
        Romanticism 258–9
    photography and lithography
        250–1, 254–6
    and purification 234
    and transculturation 234
Viswanathan, Gauri 80–1

Wellesley, Arthur, Duke of
    Wellington 24
Wellesley, Richard 206, 243
widow remarriage 303–4
Wood, Charles 24
World War One 49, 101, 188
World War Two 27, 48, 188, 227

Yadav politics 353–4
Young, Robert 334

Zbativel, Dusan 262
Zoffany, Johan 237, 241
Zvelebil, Kamil 262